D0269669

To b

OR

# WENTWORTH PAPERS

## 1597–1628

# WENTWORTH PAPERS
## 1597–1628

edited for the Royal Historical Society

by

## J. P. COOPER

M.A., F.R.Hist.S.

CAMDEN FOURTH SERIES
VOLUME 12

LONDON
OFFICES OF THE ROYAL HISTORICAL SOCIETY
UNIVERSITY COLLEGE LONDON, GOWER ST., W.C.1
1973

© Royal Historical Society

ISBN 0 901050 20 2

Printed in Great Britain by Butler & Tanner Ltd,
Frome and London

# CONTENTS

# ABBREVIATIONS

Bodley        Bodleian Library, Oxford
*C.J.*        *Journals of the House of Commons*
Hunter        J. Hunter, *South Yorkshire. The History and Topography of the Deanery of Doncaster* (London, 1831)
Knowler       *The Earl of Strafforde's Letters and Dispatches*, ed. W. Knowler (London, 1739)
Notestein     *Commons Debates 1621*, ed. W. Notestein, F. H. Relf and H. Simpson (New Haven, 1935)
P.R.O.        Public Record Office, London
*SC*          Wentworth Woodhouse Muniments, Strafford Correspondence, deposited in the Central Library, Sheffield (unless otherwise stated, the documents are cited by their numbers; thus *SC*, xx/21, is volume xx, item no. 21)

# PREFACE

I gratefully acknowledge permission to print the Wentworth Papers given by their owners, Earl FitzWilliam and the Trustees of the FitzWilliam Settled Estates, and their custodians, Mr. J. Bebbington, the City Librarian of Sheffield, and his predecessor, Mr. J. Lamb. I also thank the Bodleian Library for permission to print the extracts from the Johnston manuscripts. All users of the Wentworth Papers owe a very special debt to Miss R. Meredith, the Archivist of the Central Library, Sheffield, and her staff for long and successful work in caring for the Wentworth Woodhouse Muniments and making their contents more easily known and accessible. I am also indebted to Mr. C. L. F. Thompson of Hertford College, Oxford, who transcribed most of the letter book *SC*, ii. Especial thanks are due to Mr. K. V. Thomas for devoting so much time and labour to this volume. All errors are entirely my responsibility.

J. P. C.

# NOTE ON EDITING

Editing has been based on the general rules in 'Report on Editing Historical Documents', *Bulletin of the Institute of Historical Research*, i (1923), pp. 7–14.

Generally extension has been used without any special indication whenever there is no reasonable doubt as to meaning, even though the spelling may be open to query. Thus *exa–ed* has been rendered by examined, *Ma$^{ty}$* by Maiesty, *y$^w$* by yow, *y$^r$* by your, *gent* by gentleman, *S$^r$* by Sir and so on, though an attempt has been made to follow what appears to be the normal spelling of the writer concerned. Abbreviated names have usually been extended, except in signatures.

Editorial insertions and emendations have been placed in square brackets. Dashes have been used to indicate lacunae in the text for which no plausible interpolation can be made. Punctuation and capitalization have been modernized.

The addresses of letters have been omitted, except when they are considered to have features of special interest. The new style year has been used in the descriptive headings of the documents, thus 20 March 1621/2 is given as *20 March 1622*.

TABLE I—WENTWORTH'S CONNECTIONS

Thomas Wentworth = Margaret, da. and heir of William Gascoigne of Gawthorpe
d. 1588                     d. 1593

John, Lord Darcy d. 1602 = Agnes

Sir William Wentworth d. 1614 = Anne, da. of Robert Atkinson d. 1611 (see Table II)

Elizabeth = Thomas Danby
d. 1629        d. 1581

Catherine = Thomas Gargrave
d. c. 1631      executed 1595

Jaspar (2) = Margaret = (1) Michael Darcy d. 1588
Blitheman

John, Lord Darcy of Aston d. 1635

Christopher = Frances, da. of Edward, Lord Morley
d. 18 July 1624        d. 1654

Prudence = Dr. Richard Barrie of Hodroyd

Sir Thomas Danby = Katharine, da. of Christopher Wandesford
b. 1610
d. 1660

SIR THOMAS WENTWORTH = (1) Margaret, da. of Francis, earl of Cumberland d. 1622
= (2) Arbella, da. of John, earl of Clare d. 1631

Margaret = (1626) Sir Richard Hutton, son of Sir Richard Hutton

Elizabeth

Sir George Savile of Thornhill d. 12 Nov. 1622 = (1) Mary, da. of George, earl of Shrewsbury d. before 1600
= (2) Elizabeth, da. of Edward Ayscough d. 1626

Sir George Savile d. 1614 = Anne d. 1633

Sir George d. 19 Dec. 1626        Sir William d. 1644

# TABLE II—WENTWORTH'S MOTHER'S CONNECTIONS

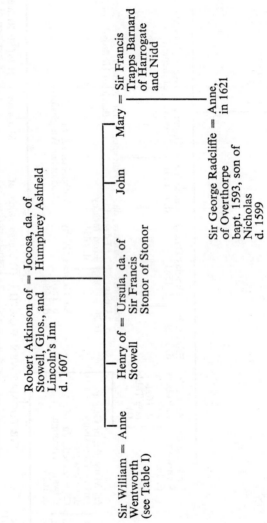

Robert Atkinson of = Jocosa, da. of
Stowell, Glos., and    Humphrey Ashfield
Lincoln's Inn
d. 1607

Sir William = Anne
Wentworth
(see Table I)

Henry of = Ursula, da. of
Stowell      Sir Francis
             Stonor of Stonor

John

Mary = Sir Francis
       Trapps Barnard
       of Harrogate
       and Nidd

Sir George Radcliffe = Anne,
of Overthorpe         in 1621
bapt. 1593, son of
Nicholas
d. 1599

# INTRODUCTION

First it must be emphasized that this is a selection from the papers
from Wentworth Woodhouse now deposited in the Sheffield Central
Library. The papers printed by Knowler have been listed with a
brief note of their contents so that their relationship to the rest of
the material may be seen. Where Knowler misdated letters or
omitted postscripts, corrections and omissions have been given, but
only two of the letters have been reprinted (nos. 30, 269). Virtually
all the surviving papers of Sir William Wentworth, Strafford's
father, have been included.[1] The main omissions from Wentworth's
own papers are those concerning the wardship of his nephews George
and William Savile.[2] These need to be placed in the context of pro-
longed litigation in the Court of Wards and in Star Chamber.[3] Most
of Wentworth's correspondence with his steward Richard Marris,
Charles Greenwood, rector of Thornhill, and his servant and solici-
tor Peter Man[4] about the details of the management of his estate
and household has been omitted,[5] as has Wentworth's long account
of his first wife's last illness and death.[6] A few other letters have been
omitted because they seemed trivial in content; otherwise most of
Wentworth's correspondence and all his speeches until the end of
1628 have been included. A very few letters from those of 1629 have
been included because they throw some light on parliamentary
affairs or complement earlier ones. The only other papers of later
date are the fragments of Sir George Radcliffe's life of Wentworth,
which were probably written after the Civil War. These seemed worth
printing as an appendix, since they do give further information about
Wentworth's career and his relationship with Radcliffe, as well as a
vivid and attractive account of Wentworth's second wife, Arbella
Holles, which bears out Gervase Holles's statement that her father,
the earl of Clare, gave his children 'education equall to the best and

[1] *SC*, xx, 198 and 205 (from his son William), 192 (from privy council), 196
(from Dr. W. Goodwin), 206 (from Peter Man); xxi, 5 (unsigned, undated,
copy); xxii, i (from Thomas Wentworth of Elmsall) are omitted.

[2] These are mainly *SC*, xx, 86–99.

[3] See below, Appendix, pp. 320–22. The main documents are P.R.O., St.
Ch. 8/261/9; Wards 9/94, fo. 677; 9/95, fos. 53, 657 and 9/536–38 and 563.

[4] Man described himself in 1619 as 'having bene servante and sollicitor many
yeres' to Sir William and to Wentworth, P.R.O., St. Ch. 8/261/9, no. 27.

[5] The letters from Wentworth are in *SC*, xxi and those to him mostly in *SC*,
xx (a); they became much more numerous after 1628.

[6] *SC*, xxi, 16.

beyond most of the nobility. . . .'[1] Radcliffe also provides facts and views about education which thus supplement an interesting feature of the main collection, illustrated in Sir William Wentworth's papers and to a lesser extent in Wentworth's correspondence with his younger brothers.[2]

A few pages concerning the Parliament of 1614, which were probably removed from Wentworth Woodhouse by the antiquary Nathaniel Johnston and are now in the Bodleian, have been included (nos. 23, 24, 26, 27). They provide some insight into Wentworth's early political attitudes and add a little to our knowledge of that ill-reported Parliament's proceedings, though rather more comes from Wentworth's letters to his father (nos. 22, 25).

An unusual feature of the collection is the considerable number of letters from Wentworth. While this is mainly due to the survival of one letter-book of his letters for the years 1617–25 (*SC*, ii),[3] he also kept copies or draughts of some of his letters before and after these dates. His letters to Marris were probably recovered by his servants after Marris's sudden death by misadventure in 1635[4] and those to Sir Edward Stanhope may have been collected by his son, the second earl. Another distinctive feature is the existence of a number of Wentworth's speeches. The most interesting are the two delivered in the country, in 1614 (no. 29) and at the collection of the subsidy in 1621 (no. 152). The autograph versions of Wentworth's own speeches in the Commons raise a number of questions as to their relationship to what was actually said. One was definitely sent to Radcliffe as a report of what Wentworth had said (no. 352), but were any of the others prepared beforehand, or were they a record produced afterwards with a view to possible circulation as separates? The very heavy corrections to the speech of 1 May 1628 (no. 350) might be interpreted as a process of polishing for public circulation. The speech for which most separates seem to survive is that of 22 March 1628, but unfortunately no version of it exists among Wentworth's own papers.

[1] *Memorials of the Holles Family 1493–1656*, ed. A. C. Wood (Camden Ser., 3rd series, lv, 1937), p. 109.
[2] Sir William's views should be compared not only with Radcliffe's (below, p. 325–26), but also with Christopher Wandesford's *A Book of Instructions . . .*, ed. T. Comber (Cambridge, 1777), pp. 9–10, 18, 70, '. . . in the Generall to exercise yourself in those Studies which tend rather to the Improvement of your Manners than the Advancement of your Knowledge . . . to know not only what virtue is, but how to practise it. Without learning he will not be able to assist in government or to behave according to his degree.'
[3] Copies of a number of the letters in the letter-book are also in *SC*, xxi; *e.g.* nos. 21–32, 35.     [4] Knowler, ii, pp. 486 and 483.

Dame Veronica Wedgwood has written that Sir William's papers 'suggest an ambitious, weak and credulous man'.[1] He was certainly ambitious for his family and heir, but he explicitly denied that he ever sought authority or honour for himself 'having many children, a weak bodie' (p. 12). If he was cautious and long suffering in his dealings with Gilbert, earl of Shrewsbury, he was ultimately determined to defend his right in what was in material terms an exceedingly small matter (p. 44). In this he was following his own precepts, which are singularly tough-minded in their assessment of men's selfishness and the need to guard against anything which might damage a man's standing and reputation. His advice has its Polonius-like passages, but they are fewer than is usual in writings of this genre. Perhaps it was because he himself had been relatively passive rather than active in public life that he cherished prophecies and providences of future greatness for his family, and was influenced by guidance coming in a dream to purchase Harewood and was so ambitious for his son. If his verses show a conventional, if poignant, awareness of the transitoriness of power, his advice shows a fascination with the means of obtaining it. He conveys with considerable force the mechanics of local rivalries and the way traditional means of influencing judges and juries and of seeking the favour of the powerful, or of avoiding their displeasure, remained part of the assumptions underlying public life and individual behaviour. Sir William's view of mankind is almost Hobbesian in its insistence that men are ruled by fear and reverence strength in others, not virtue.[2] Their papers show that both Sir William and his son obeyed

[1] C. V. Wedgwood, *Thomas Wentworth, first earl of Strafford* (London, 1961), p. 20.

[2] Wandesford in 1636 adopted a much more moralistic stance and advised against undertaking 'any suit upon confidence of the favour of the judge, interest in juries, or the like circumstantiall by-helps . . . the victory obtained by such false and degenerate helps brings neither honour in present, nor peace and satisfaction to your own Mind. And thus are you disappointed and your Adversary provoked to work under you by the like mines and art to blow you up.' Both Wandesford and his patron, Sir William's son, stress the need for good relations and reputation with neighbouring families by avoiding offence and faction, as the foundation of acceptance and authority in local affairs. Where Sir William had stressed the need to court the judges of Assize and the Lord President, Wandesford only mentions the latter point, while emphasizing the need to court the Lord Chancellor in order either to be included in commissions or left out of them. Wandesford also thought dependence 'upon some Person of Honour and Power' at Court would be needful to give countenance in the country, while Wentworth advised his nephew Sir William Savile not to go to Court before he was thirty; *A Book of Instructions* . . . (Cambridge, 1777), pp. 60–62, 70–72, 82; Wentworth to Savile, December 1633; Knowler, i, pp. 168–70.

his precepts in keeping copies of messages and letters in their dealings with others about matters which were, or might become, the subject of contention. Both his father-in-law and the earl of Cumberland apparently valued Sir William's integrity and judgement (nos. 14, 15). His wife has been seen as evidently 'the stronger character', apparently partly on the basis of her epitaph; as Sir William wrote this epitaph, such a view might be taken as a further tribute to his powers of expression.[1]

Such considerations do not necessarily invalidate Dame Veronica's assessment of Sir William, but it is scarcely possible to agree with her that 'his instructions to his son . . . indicate a deep, if conventional, Puritan piety . . .'[2] The piety is there, but his attitude to Catholics seems un-Puritan in wanting to avoid controversy with them and accepting that 'They hold the same fundamentall points that wee doe . . .' (p. 18). Such an attitude was perhaps the more becoming in one who had chosen his wife from a family where her brother and sister had both married recusants (see Table II). Sir William's father had married his daughter to Thomas Danby, the son of a recusant father, in that father's lifetime. The eldest son of their marriage married the daughter of another recusant.[3] Nevertheless Sir William brought up his own son to be a staunch and Calvinistically inclined Protestant, who as a member of the Commons showed consistent hostility to recusants in the parliaments of the 1620's.

This was also a feature of the parliamentary career of Wentworth's great political rival, Sir John Savile of Howley.[4] Yet both were ready to try to secure recusant support in parliamentary elections, notably in that of 1628, when Wandesford anticipated that the recusants would hold the balance. Knowler's selection of letters about elections was a good one so that the new documents add little for the election of 1620, or to our general knowledge of the methods of seeking support. But they do show how uncertain of success Wentworth was in 1628, how the prospects for a Parliament were already being canvassed in 1627 and that his resistance to the loan was not seen as having guaranteed him victory (nos. 311, 326, 337). They also offer a new, if tantalizing, glimpse of the by-election of Feb-

[1] Wedgwood, *Wentworth*, p. 21; see below, p. 35.

[2] *Ibid.*, p. 20.

[3] See Table I. Sir Thomas Danby's presentment as a recusant is recorded for 1570–73 by Dom Hugh Aveling, 'The Catholic Recusants of the West Riding of Yorkshire', *Leeds Philosophical and Literary Society, Literary and Historical Section*, x, pt. vi (1963), p. 303.

[4] These statements are based on an examination of the main unpublished accounts of the Commons' debates, as well as those in print.

ruary 1629.[1] More generally the documents do illustrate how mutable and transitory distinctions between Court and Country attitudes and behaviour were in the course of both protagonists' careers. Savile was the nominee of the Crown and the Lord President in the Yorkshire elections of 1604 and 1628, as Wentworth was in 1620 and as both may have been when they were both elected in 1614.

Both were also victims of the Crown's displeasure for their conduct in the Commons. Both aspired to Buckingham's patronage, yet both appealed to the country for support, and both saw themselves as mediators, explaining the actions of Crown and Parliament to those whom they represented, and both justified themselves as the procurers of special benefits to the country. This last is an explicit theme of Wentworth's speech at Rotherham in 1621 (no. 152); it is implicit in the publicity Sir John secured for himself in getting the Yorkshire quota to the loan on privy seals of 1626 reduced. If Wentworth had had connections at Court from the first through the marriage arranged by his father, Savile's beginnings are not so clear. But under James I he claimed that for thirty years 'last past he had been imployed in sundrye servics of verye greate ymportance and weighte . . . concerninge the affaires' of the Crown 'and the commonwealthe of this realme' and for the most part of that time had been *custos rotulorum*.[2]

Court and Country were interdependent factors in their careers; standing and influence in the country supported their claims for preferment and influence at Court, on which in turn their prestige in the country could be nourished. In 1627 and 1628 each in succession overdrew his credit with the country. Savile had identified himself too closely with Buckingham and with policies involving extraordinary exactions on the country and comparative leniency in fining recusants. As the new Lord President Wentworth could not procure the election of the man whom he wished to succeed him as knight of the shire, though he may not have given him official endorsement. Yet the man elected, Sir Henry Savile of Methley, had been an active collector of the forced loan and, though formerly a strong opponent of Sir John Savile, was now overwhelmingly supported by the clothiers in and around Leeds.[3]

Most of what is known about the voters in the contests between

[1] No. 217 shows that he did not, as has sometimes been assumed, contest the shire in the 1624 election.
[2] P.R.O. St. Ch. 8/258/5, undated, *c.* 1612.
[3] Nos. 374, 376. Sir Henry says that Wentworth had not publicly given his official support as Lord President to his rival, whose identity is unfortunately unknown to me. It might perhaps have been Sir Edward Osborne or Sir Francis Wortley.

Sir John Savile and Wentworth comes from Wentworth's supporters, who wrote as if all the gentry were on their side and as if Savile's supporters were all plebeians in revolt against their natural superiors. While Wentworth had support from most of the best families in the West Riding, Savile had gentry support even in 1621 and much more before 1621 and in 1625 and 1626. To see their contests as a clearcut economic conflict of the landed interest against trading and clothing interests is certainly to oversimplify. Savile dominated the clothing districts, but Wentworth had support even in Leeds and still more round Halifax. Savile's procuring of the incorporation of Leeds in 1626 made him as many, perhaps more, enemies than friends among the clothiers. As knight of the shire in 1621 Wentworth was much concerned with the depression of trade and the need to promote the cloth industry, though he seems to have devoted relatively less time to speaking on such questions than Sir John did in 1624.[1] Wentworth's last recorded speech in the Commons was a defence of the right of Hull and others to fishing at Greenland, despite the patent to the Muscovy Company.[2]

Sir William Wentworth had lived and died, Sir John Savile had made his career[3] and Wentworth had begun his in the shadow of the greatest territorial lords in the West Riding and probably the richest peers in late Elizabethan England, the Talbot earls of Shrewsbury. But when Wentworth and Savile were fighting out their rivalry the Talbot inheritance had passed to three co-heiresses, none of whose husbands established strong roots in Hallamshire before 1642.[4] Wentworth was able to pursue his ambitions, free from that constant need to consider his relationships with a powerful neighbour which had so preoccupied his father.[5] However, Wentworth was much involved in attempts to reach agreement between the heirs general and the heir male, their uncle, Edward, the eighth earl. For if Edward destroyed or changed the settlements made by his father and grand-

[1] In 1624 Wentworth was more hostile to the Merchant Adventurers than Savile; P.R.O., SP 14/166, fo. 191, Sir Edward Nicholas' diary.

[2] Warwickshire County Record Office, Newdegate Diary, iii, p. 56; 25 June 1628, in the debate on the report by Radcliffe from the committee which had considered and condemned the company's patent.

[3] He was born in 1556.

[4] Gilbert, the seventh earl, succeeded in 1590 and died in 1616; his brother and heir male died in 1618. On his death Hallamshire and most of the other lands went to Gilbert's three daughters as heirs general; see below, pp. 97–99.

[5] W. T. MacCaffrey, 'Talbot and Stanhope, an episode in Elizabethan politics', *Bulletin of the Institute of Historical Research*, xxxiii (1960), pp. 74–85, gives some idea of the lengths to which earl Gilbert was prepared to go in pursuit of a quarrel with a neighbour with much more powerful connections at Court than Sir William Wentworth.

father, this was likely to endanger the title of Wentworth's Savile nephews to Rufford which had been settled on them through their Talbot grandmother (see Table I). When Edward died in 1618 this danger went, but Wentworth was still involved as supervisor of Edward's will and in complicated transactions with his widow, from whom he bought some land.[1] While he certainly devoted much time and effort to defending his sister's and nephews' interests, there are also signs of a predilection for complicated financial schemes, which involved elements of risk, almost of gambling, with in one, case the plan for marrying his brother to Lady Craven's daughter, an element of duplicity (pp. 323–24), and which were all means justified by the end of advancing the interests and fortunes of his family. He was to find greater scope for such propensities as Lord Deputy.

Wentworth from 1614 had cast himself as a moderate, mediator between Court and Country, a restorer of supposedly archetypal harmonies. His views on how to attain such a restoration implicitly resemble Bacon's in emphasizing what Bacon called 'commonwealth matters', legal, administrative and economic reforms. His correspondence shows that he was reasonably well informed about foreign affairs, yet the record of his speeches in the Commons shows him taking little interest in questions of foreign policy. In 1624 there was ostensible harmony between Commons and Court on a foreign policy towards which Wentworth was disapproving or lukewarm; the result seems to have been that he played a relatively minor part, even though a good start was made in executing a programme of constructive legislation of which he had approved in 1621.[2] He preferred to look forward to a second session 'to build up the political walls and repair the ruinous breaches of the commonwealth'.

Wentworth's parliamentary career should be viewed, like those of other leaders of the Commons, in a context in which contacts with the Court, not isolation from it, were the rule. Wentworth's contacts may have been closer and more direct at times than those of some other leaders, but their effectiveness varied at different times; they were particularly good in 1621 and much less so in 1624. The correspondence brings out the importance of Ingram as a go-between long after Cranfield's fall. He was Wentworth's principal contact with the

---

[1] Wentworth bought the manor, rectory and glebe lands of Kirkby Malhamdale from the countess and by February 1620 was engaged in disputes with the tenants about leases, boundaries and timber; P.R.O., C2, Jas. I, W27/76; C3/327/14. He then sold off the tithe to his sister and some land to tenants; some of the money raised went to the countess, or to pay her debts while he kept some of the land; below, nos. 145, 161; *Econ. History Review*, 2nd Ser., xi (1958), p. 229, n. 2.

[2] He had missed the beginning of the session owing to illness (no. 222).

Court during his confinement in 1627. There are hints that councillors and courtiers were also anxious to keep communications open. This was the sort of communication that became increasingly rare after 1629, as the years without parliament went on.

Wentworth's political actions were consistent with his political rhetoric. His speech at his first sitting as Lord President echoes much of that at Rotherham in 1621 and it should not be read as a manifesto for prerogative rule. For it was delivered when Weston and Wentworth still hoped for a fruitful second session to the Parliament of 1628. Wentworth's appetites for power, for profit and for revenge on those who thwarted him, had always been strong. Opportunities for their gratification moved him inexorably away from the mediating position prescribed by his political rhetoric. But that rhetoric which he shared with most of the spokesmen of the Commons was sufficiently vague and ambiguous in its assumptions of harmony between royal prerogative and parliamentary privilege and between the rights and duties of subjects to exculpate him from any charge of changing his political principles. Where the change is undeniable is in his churchmanship. He had been on good terms with Abbott and still more closely associated with the circle round bishop Williams of Lincoln; in 1624 he had joined in the attack on the bishop of Norwich in the Commons for inhibiting preaching ministers and allowing papistical images.[1] There are no signs of any change before the end of 1628 and his friendship with Laud only began in 1630. But it was the change in his churchmanship which signals his turning away from the middle ground towards absorption in the politics of the Court, though, unlike Charles and Laud, he remained unafraid of parliaments.[2]

[1] *C.J.*, i, p. 784; Bodley, MS. Tanner, 392, fo. 81ʳ.

[2] It should be noted that only documents deposited at Sheffield have been used. Recently other papers, including three letters from Sir Henry Savile of Methley and five memoranda about Pontefract, all dated 1621, have been found at Wentworth Woodhouse; see A. J. Fletcher, 'Sir Thomas Wentworth and the restoration of Pontefract as a parliamentary borough', *Northern History*, vi (1971, published 1972). It should also be noted that no. 134 was printed by Sir Charles Firth from a transcript by Knowler, *Pages relating to Thomas Wentworth, first earl of Strafford* (*Camden Miscellany*, X (Camden Society, 1895), p. 2).

# I. SIR WILLIAM WENTWORTH'S VOLUME

**1.** *Sir William Wentworth's advice to his son* (*SC*, xl/1, *fo. 1ʳ*)
*Anno domini* 1604 & 2 of Kinge James.

William Wentworth of Wentworth Woodhus esquyer (Baptized 3 of
July 4 of Elizabeth 1562)[1] being neare the age of 45 yeares his advice
and councell to Thomas Wentworth his sonne and heire (Baptized
13 April 34 of Elizabeth 1592. 22 yeares old 1604)[1] touching the
managing of his priuate estate and affaires; all written with his owne
hande.

(*fo. 2ʳ*) Touching the good gouernment of your person and affaires,
albeitt I verelie hope that your own discreccon guyded from aboue,
by the grace and power of a most mercifull heavenlie father, will
give unto yow the twoe inestimable benefitts of a prosperous lyfe
and a happie ending. Yett, for that it pleseth God manie tymes to
make the wise advice of some aged faithfull frend the meanes of
these blessinges, by working in yong men a sounder iudgment then
their smale experience could otherwayes easelie attaine unto, I, your
naturall father, whose intentts admitt no guyle and whose experience
hath nott bene the least among others, have thought good, according
to my smale measure of witt, to deliuer to yow my best opinion and
councells touching the well ordring of your self and your private estate.

GOD. First then feare God, loue him and trust in him. Euery night
befor yow slepe and euery morning befor yow ryse, saie prayers;
and if yow lye waking in the night, first think of God and euery
morning, after yow are readie, in some private place upon your knees
praie unto and praise our good God, whose blessings haue bene
diuers hundreth years plenteouslie poured upon your house. Att
other tymes whensoeuer yow are alone, first thinke of him and his
goodnes befor yow thinke of anie other thinge. Beare a good conscyence, be just, humble, charitable and mercifull; be moderate in
all thinges and frugale in expenses, for wasters and proude men be
verie fooles. Be wyse to avoide such plotts as undoubtedlie envye
and hope of gaine will laie for such men as yow are, into the which
who so (*fo. 2ᵛ*) faleth, lett him look for smale fauor. Be verie carefull
to governe your tongue and neuer speake in open places all yow
thinke; nether ever talke openlie[2] yll of anye, for whatsoeuer
yow speak that waie even in your own house most commonlie is

---

[1] In the margin, probably in the hand of Sir George Radcliffe.
[2] 'all yow thinke' has been struck through.

discouered and will certainlie at some tyme do yow harme. Butt to
your wyfe, if she can kepe councell (as fewe wemen can), or to a
private faithful frende, or some old servant that hath all his lyvinge
and creditt under yowe, yow maie be more open, yett euer talke thereof butt to one. If untrewe, or evill speches, be reported of yow, manie
tymes the wysest course is not to seme to heare of them; for they will
sone dye withoutt your discreditt, wheare the ripping into them maie
brede mischefe, bludshede and manie tymes undoing of wyfe and
children. In anie case labour to be patientt and rather walke awaie
then fale to yll wordes and choller with anie body. Take hede in
the name of God yow neuer command anye to stryke another; for
if death ensewe within a yeare yow knowe the danger.[1] Neuer take
a quarrell at the first rebounde; rather walke awaie when itt is beginninge and preventt itt by avoyding dangerous companie and sometimes by seeming not to heare those words; for plotts wilbe laid to
gett a praie and blessed is he that God giues grace to disapoint them.

PROUIDENCE. In anie case liue according or within your
allowance, though itt be nott greate; and whosoeuer perswadeth
yow to the contrarie is either unwise or falsharted to yow. ( *fo. 3*ʳ)
When my father dyed I ought nott one penny which made me
beare other payments charged upon my lands more easelie. In
anie case take hede of the usurer, of commodityes and of the mer-
chantes bookes. Hould him a bondslave that casteth himself into
nedeles debt and dare not show his face in euery place and a foole
thatt consumes him self and his for want of iudgment and foreseeing
the end of such things. Vaine hopes bring begery, butt provydent
fearing the worst in things present and to come, by God's goodnes
brings welth and comfortt. And a prosperous estate makes and
kepes frends which otherwise will fale awaye and makes enemyes
either be reconcyled or att least greeved and not too prone to dis-
pight. If anie cunning merchantt will giue yow 100ˡⁱ or twoe to paie
him duble at the death of your father or some frende, blesse yow
from his companie, for those men gett riche praies by such bargaines
with manie, though some seldom times they lose. When yow buye,
take no daie but redy monye, otherwise the price and stuf wilbe
according. Tye not yourself euer to buye in one place, unlesse yow
fynde thatt faithfull dealing that I could neuer amongst merchantts.
Take hede yow neuer cast your self behinde hande, for when yow
thinke to free yourself in a yeare, itt wilbe three befor yow cann
effect itt, so manie difficultyes will fale unlooked for, and be sure
that in that case nothing but care and wise endevor can redeme yow
in that tyme from debt and danger. In anie case avoide the companie

---

[1] [*Margin*] wilfull murther.

off all butt those that be honest and will not beg of yow or some ways putt yow to charge.

(*fo. 3ᵛ*) Touching the KING our Soueraigne lord, praie for him and obey his lawes; for in his safety consisteth the weale and prosperity of his subiects and the common welth is the ship we saile in. His greatest MAIESTRATE in the cuntry as president, or lieutenantt, be yow well known to them and deserue their favors[1] by your discrecion, humilitie and remembring your duety with presentes in dewe tyme; yet euer take heede that no man lyvinge ouerreache yow for greate sommes of mony, nether ever lende to greater men then yourself more then yow meane to lose. If one of the Judgs of Assyse dwell in your cuntrie forgett not to present him yearly in discrete sortt, also sometymes go to his house to see him and make sure in his companie rather to be humble and forbearing then bould, for they are used to be flattered and forborne. If euer the Judges do sitt in anie towne whear yow are chefe lord (as once they did for the Anncienty [Ainsty] anno 1604 at Thorpe arche)[2] do yow not forgett to goe or sende some discrete servant to remember your duety and giue them some wyne and sugar etc for otherwise it wilbe yll taken and remembred. Also yow maie if yow haue anie tryall or anie frend to speake for mete them coming to York by the waie, for they loue to be waited on. If anie great man be to make an arbitrament betwixt yow and your adversarie wherin yow mean to haue fauor, yow must first, after good sound advice and councell, resolue what end maie seme resonable and yet be in the end for your creditt and proffit.[3] Then deale with some favorite of that great mans and enstruct him secrettlie and promise him a certaine reward, if your desyre be effected, but giue litle or nothing befor hand; speak sone as may be for fear of preventing.

(*fo. 4ʳ*) For NOBLE MEN in generall itt is dangerouse to be familier with them, or to depend upon them, or to deale with or trust them too muche.[4] For their thoughts are bestowed upon their owne waightie causes and their estates and actions are governed by pollicy. Againe albeitt they be most courtlie in wordes, yet they could be contented that riche gentlmen weare less able to liue without depending on them, even as the gentlman lookes with a discontented eye upon the stoute riche yeoman. In anie case neuer

---

[1] [*Margin*] som use in a great matter for fauor to offer to lend Cˡⁱ or Cᵐᵏ etc upon bond because they would not offer itt as a gifte though they look not for repaiment.          [2] [*Margin*] when the plague was at Yorke.

[3] [*Margin*] In no case be confident in your case, because it is good, but fear the worst.

[4] [*Margin*] if a great man fale his riche favorits are in great danger.

engage your self for your superiors by bonds &c nor lende them more then yow can be willing to giue them. As itt is no wisedome and manie tymes danger to fawne and depend upon noblemen, so in anie case be carefull nott to make them hate yow. For their revenge by reason of the greatnes of their mynde and power att one tyme or other will doe yow displesure; and against their displesures yow can nott defende yourself without greate witt, much cost and peradventure danger of your lyfe, therfor be providentt and iudiciall that waie. If the Sheriffe or anie Maiestrate or Commissioner send yow a letter from anie grete person directed to them and yow for anie thing concerning yow, which letter they will haue returned after yow haue had notice of it, doe yow neuer faile butt with all spede take a true copie of that letter[1] before yow send itt backe and, not resolving hastely, consult at leisure rypely what provident and discrete course to take therin. For your doings and words herin are lyke ynough to com to a reckoning. Litle said sone amended; well forsene seldom repented. If anie nobleman desyre to haue anie plesure done which gladlie yow (*fo. 4ᵛ*) would not afforde him, yet be so provydentt that for a smale matter yow provoke him not to a hatefull or hard opinion, for those smale matters for certaine wilbe remembered.

The Companie of your EQUALLES, whose estate is nott declyninge and in whom ther is a good conscyence and a well governed tongue, is very fitt for yow; and for want of suche, the companie of your inferiors that be of good welth, humble and discrete in their deedes and wordes. As yow growe elder so lyke of the companie of those that be rather elder than your self and avoide the more youthfull companie whose frailties and error do commonlie brede inconvenyence.

(*fo. 5ʳ*) If yow desyre AUTHORITIE or degree of HONOR, yow must make meanes for itt, otherwaies itt will not be laide upon yow ther be so manie that make suite for it. For myne own perticuler humor I was euer well contented to be withoutt them, having many children, a weak bodie &c. Yett he that wilbe honoured and feared in his cuntrie must beare countenance and authority: for people are servyle, nott generous and do reverence men for feare, not for loue of their vertues which they apprehend nott.

SHERIF. By the sheriffik of Yorkshir ther comes great losse and danger, therfor to avoide itt yow must with giftes &c deale with both the judges of your circuit, or one of them that dost most, to leaue yow out of the ly[s]te. It is verie nedefull that some yeares before yow

---

[1] [*Margin*] Good to take coppyes of anie thing of importance that maie after be called in question.

doubt to be in the licte (*fo. 5ʳ*) yow premeditate how to manage the office. For some times by means of a gret person one that is not in the licte may be prict sherife. Therfor by the advice of 2 experienced councillors at the lawe haue readie a draught beforhand for your under sheriffe to seale with fitt covenants. Take heade of a folishe or knavishe undersherif[1]; itt is good to bethink yow whear such an undersheriffe and officers are to be had. If yow haue anie servantt or frend that is wise and carefull, he maie stand as undersheriffe with the advice of some that hath bene undersheriffe and is honest, having recompense, who maie be for the whole yeare about your said servant; then all the monie levyed will com to your own hands. For apparell and housekeeping be moderate, not respecting foolishe rumor; onelie decencie is ynough, for within fiue years after yow will so iudge of itt. The surest waie is to haue no undersherif, butt a servant or faithfull frend, as is said, and so to receiue all the mony your self. Of late iii or iiii undersherifs haue bene in the Flete at once and haue made the bonds worth lytle or nothing.

To your PARENTES be humble, dutyfull and patyent. Followe their example in the good and refuse what is amisse in them. Be nott ryotouse beyond your allowance, nether in your mariadge conclude, naie attempt nothing, withoutt their privitye.

(*fo. 6ʳ*) Your BRETHREN and sisters yow must loue and assist in their honest causes with countenance and good councell. Allwaies charge them to kepe creditt, to liue within their compas, to avoide dishonest and beggarly companie, to haue care how they marrie and befor they attempte itt, to take the councell of their faithfull aged frends. Lett them forbeare to gett any thing with an yll conscyence and to bargaine, or haue anie dealinge, butt with knowne honest men. And if they haue anie cause in controversie wherin conscyence is against them, let them make means to compound it; and though their cause be good, yet let them by mylde and wise means avoide suits all they maye. For the charge therof is grevous and the eventt uncertaine; howsoeuer the lawiers shall perswade them the contrarie for their own gaine. Lett them avoyde stryving with mightier men then them selues.

(*fo. 6ᵛ*) OF KINSFOLKES esteme the companie of them most thatt be riche, honest and discrete and use them in your causes befor others. If they be porer and yett of a good conscyence and humble regard them well. Yett if anie of all these haue lands or goods ioyning with yow in no case trust them too much, for such occasions brede suits and future enmityes. Ever feare the worst, which discrete

[1] [*Margin*] q[uery] for the worth of the office if yow sell itt and for good suertys &c.

suspectt is the surest meanes under God of your defence. Let none of them that come to your house haue anie greate good countenance but those that be honest and vertuouse.

(*fo. 7ʳ*) Lett your HOUSEKEPINGE be frugale and so proportioned that at least the one half of your yearlie rents and profitts be yearlie laid up towards uses of charity, profitt and advancement of your house. Lett there be good orders and peace in all your house and lett the dores att night be surelie shutt up by some trustie auncyentt servantt and your men so lodged as they maie defende your house. Most of your seruants would be of the more aged sortt but especially the officers of your house. And if yow spend but a third parte of your revenewe in your house yow shall doe the wyser and better.

(*fo. 7ᵛ*) Take hede of superfluitye in BUILDING, for that is a monument of a gentlman that wanted discrecion and iudgment. Let your house be too litle for a daie or twoe, rather then too greate for a yeare; and for the furniture of your house, lett it be decentt, not costlie, as also your apparell which otherwise wise men will hould vanitye.

(*fo. 8ʳ*) Amongest your NEIGHBOURES deserue to be counted a man of a syncere conscyence and lett your worde be as good as an obligation. Therfore be not hastie to promisse, lest yowe repentt itt after; nether euer iudge before partyes haue said to yow what they can. In matters of greate importance trust none, but ether those that of longe tyme haue reioyced in the prosperity of your house, or of whom your father or your self haue had a longe and greate experience. And if it be a matter of secresie, talke therof euer to one alone. Whosoeuer comes to speak with yow, comes premeditate for his advantage. Therfore presume nott of your own witt (if the matter be worth anie thinge) to make a sodaine answer, but take a newe daie and after consultation giue a constant and premeditate answer. Or if the answer do necessarilie requyre haste, then walk by and debate therof with some wise servant or frend, or for want therof, debate the matter privatelie with your self before such answer. In anie case be suspitiouse of the conscyence of anie that seme more santlyke then others and smoth lyke oyle, having many tymes God and Conscience in their mowthes, when their harts are far from him; for I haue sene diuers deceiued by these subtyle hypocrytes. Therefore neuer perswade your self that anie man is honest, nether beleue comon reportte, unlesse your self, or some of your wyse faithfull frends, haue long tyme had experience of the partyes lyfe and actions.

(*fo. 8ᵛ*) Touching FRENDES make choice especiallie of 3 or 4 or 5 knights or esquyres that were faithfull to your father, for those are lykest to be faithfull to yow. These men would not be such as ar fallen into decaie, nor unconsionable, nor such as haue lands lying within yow or ioyning with yow, for then future discencion is to be feared. Haue a verie greate care euer to deserue ther good opinion, with all faith and observance for they are youre strengthe and comfortt under God. If your frende be ambitiouse, he is the worse, for hope of prefermentt and worldlie glorye will danger to ouerwaighe the respectt of his private frend, yet itt being known to yow thatt faulte maie the better be tollerated.

Take heede how yow lend MONY to your superior; butt sometimes to helpe a frend that is able to repaie, also iust in his payments, is verie convenientt. Otherwise lend none, if yow be wise. (*fo. 9ʳ*) For monie to anie Maiestrate turne five leaues backward.

For SERUANTES be verie carefull to kepe only those that be borne of good and honest frends and be well willing, humble, diligentt and honest.[1] Yett in anye case trust them not more then yow nedes must in matters that maie greatlie concerne your danger. For allmost all trecheries haue bene wrought by seruants and the finale end of their service is gaine and advancementt, which, offred by anie to them that wants itt and longes for itt, bringes a dangerouse temptation. Onelie some auncyentt honest seruants of your fathers whose welth and creditt depend most upon your hous and are seated on your ground are lyke to be fast and trew to yow then other hyrelings &c. Yett build no iudgmentt upon thinges they speak, though they be honest; for ordinarilie such men do mistake and misreport matters for wantt of lerning and sounder iudgmentt, though they be honest and meane truth. For your BAILIFES of your manors ever give care to that that anie can laie to their charge and try out the truth. Lett your bailifes be men of a stayd witt, thoughe they be no fyne seruing men; if they once dominyer their diligence and humilitye will faile. If your menyall servantt be wise, humble and dilygentt aboue others, giue him with discrecion some monie att tymes beyond his wages to encoradg him. (*fo. 9ᵛ*) So if he haue faults tell him frendlie and secretlye of them. If your servant flatter yow, he is not honest. If he speke for prefermentt too spedely or shortlie after yow enter to your lyvinge, take hede of him, for if he meane truthe, he will not be too hastie that waies. If he be ydle, he is not much worth: kepe few of them and those such as being of good frends, do maintaine themselues withoutt wages. If your servant be proud, he will be your

----

[1] [*Margin*] Take hede what yow speake befor them, if yow be wyse, especially tuching anie great person. If ii of your seruants will marrie withoutt consent of frends and providence how to liue, parte them. Not good to kepe those that will marie longe, for they wilbe confederate &c.

enemy. For anie PREFERMENT to them after good deserts and long service, I would advice yow to be moderate, lest yow repent too late. After ANNUYTYES granted men are verie seldom found diligentt and thankfull, for hope is att an end by possession of the thing desyred and mans nature is most corrupt that waye. Therfore your servantt shall become and contynewe more dutyfull by maryng some wydow of your ground (wherin neuer compell woeman) or having a tenement as tenantt att will havinge no lease (if yow be wyse) before another and something cheaper[1] then by having anie annuitye, as is said.

The Steward of your house would be of some rype yeares, att least aboue 40 yeares and rather a plaine man then of a subtill witt. For your Sollicytor be carefull in your election of him, he would be unmaryed, secrett, not geven to drinke, no beggarlie fellowe, of a iudiciall witt and one that will not kepe suits afote or raise them for his own advantage. And if he performe any prosperouse end of a suite, giue him something att every such tyme; many of these Sollicitors wilbe corrupted. Deliuer your evydence to your (*fo. 10ᵣ*) sollicitor by a note indented; and lett euer twoe men goe together into your evydence studye. In anie case neuer sett your hande or seale to wrytinge of anie importance befor yow be dyrected therin by councell lerned and also before yowe haue att good leisure and verie consider-atelye red ouer the same your self. For I haue sene great inconveyence of such an error and do assure yow thatt he thatt thinkes he sees all at first is not wyse. Kepe safelie a true copie of euery bond, covenant, or promise that yow passe by wrytinge to anie man.

Lett all your evydence once in a quarter of a year or oftner, if nede, requyre be looked for dust or ratts &c. And for your grandmother's perpetuity[2] (though in truth itt is worth litle for want of a fyne, the land being before entayled) lett itt be safely kept for sometyme itt may fortune in some courtt to be showed for your advantage, as once it was for me; the counterpaine in truth I burned when I was yong and of smale experyence. Therfor lett anie evidence thatt maketh either for yow or against yow or anie old thing that semes lytle worth be keptt; for att some unlooked for occasion they maie do some good.

Lett your sollicitor haue speciall charge neuer to giue creditt to anie atturney in matters of waight as error upon iudgment against yow or such lyke, for they be unlerned and careles and make a gaine howsoeuer yow lose, but rather build upon the considerate iudgment of a good councellor.

If yow haue a man in your chamber to serue yow, lett him be

[1] [*Margin*] So haue yow him in feare and at commandment.
[2] [*Margin*] Entayle of Gascoigne of Record in Chancery.

aboutt or aboue fiftye years old and secrett of his tongue, els yow
weare better wantt him. Take hede how yow entertaine anie servant
that is anie thing like to giue intelligence of thinges to anie that be
not your frends.

(*fo. 10ᵛ*) SUITES by all wise means avoyde, as the lawiers them
selues doe, yett must yow defend your inheritaunce, so far your
conscyence will warrant yow. Neuer countenaunce a bad cause, for
thatt is to work against God, butt compound itt. Manie tymes the
lawiers tell yow what is lawe, butt they tell yow not what courtes of
Equity your cause maie be brought into and ouerruled, litle to your
creditt and gaine. Therfor loke into the ende in your own care and
provydence, ouer and besides the lawiers councell, who liue by the
suits and contention of others; and thoughe he beare a good conscyence, yet he can nether councell soundlie, if lerning or good instruction faile him, or your adversary manage his cause by all extraordinarye meanes; nether itt is possible for him to haue thatt care
and feare of yll successe therin that yow must haue; therfor do nott
repose an undoubted confydence and assurance in all he shall saie.
Now as yow ought to haue an inwarde hartie desyre to liue without
suits, so must yow make show upon some occasions to be prone to
them when yow are wronged which show of contention appearing in
2 or 3 examples will make men fearefull to do yow wrong. For no
man will willinglie haue suite with a powrefull man thatt is taken to
be contentiouse or apte to enter into suits. Though your cause be
neuer so iuste, if itt be of anie importance, yett must yow labor the
iudge for laufull fauor and expedition and procure his good opinion
by discretion and giftes.[1] (*fo. 11ʳ*) Then the undersherif must in
tyme haue a brace of angells to returne an indifferent iurie and for a
tales of honest men. The same iurie must be labored also and, after
they haue given a verdict with yow, yow must giue them more then
usuall and either get them to your chamber and giue them wyne and
suger and manie thanks, or if they will not com, let your servant do
itt for yow in some other place to ther lykinge. If your adversarie
be expert and rich, take hede yow be not prevented by your del[ay]e.
For the proportion and manner of your gifts, take advice of some
wise aged frend that knowes the parties conditions and customes. In
anie case take hede your gifte be not putt into the hands of anie that
maie treacherouslie kepe itt bak. For I haue known the lyke and the
iudge made hatefull, being thus deluded as he thought contrarie
promise, did ouerthrow the parties iust cause at the hearinge. Haue
euer one aboutt the undersherif to giue yow warning what writts
of seizures are against yow &c. and then without delay, if nede be,

[1] [*Margin*] A nage, a sattin dublett, before and betyme.

take lerned advice &c. Itt is a very wise point to retaine a councillore
even in the begining that is sonne, or sonne in lawe, or great favorite
to one of the iudgs, who maie at the hearing haue caused the said
iudge to move order if yow fear the end.

Be dyrected in your STUDIES by some lerned iudiciall man of
the university, me thinke[s] lodgik, philosophie, cosmographie and
especially historyes yeild excellent matter of instruction and iudgmentt. Also be resolved what houres yow will ordinarily kepe for
them. In anie case haue some insight in the lawes, for it wilbe a great
contentment, comfortt and creditt and quyet for yow.

(*fo. 11ᵛ*) LETTRES. Comande your chefe servants that receaue
your lettres of secrett instructions euer to tak presentte notes of them
and to send safelie or bring yow your said lettres with all convenyentt
spede. For your servantt to daie maie be your hatefull enemy to
morowe. Touching letters to enemyes loke 5 leaues forward under
the tytle of enemye, also for plesures by frends.

LETTERS to frends and strangers wryte as few as yow can and
let these be penned with so good discretion as yow nede nott care
though they weare proclaymed in anye tyme to come.[1] For itt is a
common custome of men to kepe letters safelie and sometymes many
yeares after to produce them for evydence against the author of
them, either in open courtt or otherwise. Also if inferior persons
write to yow so as itt be fitt to returne them answer, either do it by
word of mouth, or cause one of your servants to write to him
your answear, unles some other cause requyr your own hand.

For points of RELIGION rather be in conversation religiouse
then speake earnestlie against the Catholiques, for they be very
lerned and wyse men and can saie much for their cause. They hold
the same fundamentall points that we doe; onelie ambition, pryde
and covetousnes and want of charitie do cause this hatefull contention.

Use no violentt EXERCYSES as foteball, piching heavy barrs,
leapinge, running leape, dauncing aboue grond highe, vauting, or
anie such lyke, as shoting in a bow to strong for yow &c that maie
straine yow in anie parte of your body. For though yow fele nothing
presentlie, yet being old they will paine yow.

(*fo. 12ʳ*) YOUR TENANTES use charitablie, yett with discretion,
and be not to greate a looser or too much ouerraught with them. For
notwithstanding all their fawninge and flatterye, they seldome loue
their landslorde in their hartes. Lett no tenant whosoeuer haue a
lease, unles yow be contented to make him your maister, or can allowe
him to ioyne with your enemyes. For I haue had good and sound

---

[1] [*Margin*] Your frend to daie your enemy to morowe.

experience of such grevouse effects. Againe your tenants having leases maie suie yow, or anie your frends, in an action of trespasse, if yow or they do butt com upon the ground to them letten. I haue knowne diuers leases made, upon payment, or tender of a certain some of monie, to be voide: and for covenants whatt to plowe and whatt maynure to putt in to the grounde and when &c;[1] but I lyke much better to haue men tenants att will. For their houses and groundes, lett them be yearlye vewed by 2 trustie servants together with the bailife of the manor touching ther reparation. If yow be a man of iudgmentt, your well deserving tenantt will neuer be affraide to be cruelly removed. In choice of your tenant ever prefer him thatt is of a staid witt and hath welth and is lyke to encrease itt. Whatt yow want in fore gifts yow haue in yerely rent which is better. If anie bring yow Presentes receiue them not till yow knowe of them that they haue no matter to move yow in; for otherwise to take itt is against your creditt and profitt.

Officers, Bailifes: if anie of your tenants or officers have grounds or farmes &c. of anie greate man or anie (*fo. 12*) or [? of] their frends depend of those greate men, take hede how yow trust them too muche with anie secrett &c. For if displesure happen your said tenants or officers must for feare be against yow or not with yow.

BUY LANDE, nor bargaine with none but those men that haue a good conscyence and be able to warrant itt and nott beggerlye. And if necessity, or opportunity that maie not be lost, constraine yow to deale with dangerous persons, do itt not onelie by advice of lerned councell, but also sound advice of frends.[2] In anie case take hede yow parte nott with the birde in hande for the birde in the wod. Take hede of large offers and fayre promisses of gaine, for those are the snares and euer haue bene to entrap plaine people.[3] A cosyning companion will seldom or neuer conclude unless he haue the present profitt and he that offers more then reson will verie seldome (*fo. 13*) or neuer performe reason. For security of lands to be bought I refer me to your lerned counsell, butt if yow sell lande and doubt of the true paiment for the same, lett your land be lyable to a reentree till the last pennie be paide and if yow can haue statutes, or recognissancs, for covenants or paiments, they are the best; if not, then bonde with ii or three good sureties, yf they can be had. In anie case before yow enter into anie spech for buying land cast your accompt verie carefullie what yow are to spend that yeare every waie.

[1] [*Margin*] towards the end of theyre yeares.
[2] [*Margin*] *CAVEAT EMPTOR.*
[3] [*Margin*] I could neuer fynde man so honest herin but he would speake cunninglie to gaine in the bargaine.

For manie times att the first sight we seme able and are not. Yett must yow euer haue twoe or three hundreth pounds in gold lying by yow besides the silver that God sends yow; for warres or other service of your prince, or anie private necessitye, maie come very sodainlie and unlooked for.

Touchinge REPORTES whatsoeuer youe heare, unles yow knowe the reporter to be wise and verie honest, be not light to beleue itt. Nether giue creditt to mens words or othes unles yow be assured of their good conscyence. For in matters that concerne mens' private respects and their profitt they are not much to be trusted. Againe even honest men will mistake and so consequentlie misreportt things wonderfully.

(*fo. 13ᵛ*) For your WYFE lett hir be well borne and brought up but not too highlie,[1] of a helthfull bodye, of a good complexion, humble and vertuouse, some few years younger then your self and nott of a simple witt. A good portion makes hir the better and manie tymes not the prouder. Take advice of your wise auncyentt frendes befor yow attempt anie thing touching that matter. For hir frends woll laie plotts and worke upon yow and corrupt your seruants and frends all they can to procure such a riche matche for their daughter or kinswoman. In the covenants of mariadge be adviced both by lerned councell and your discrete frends. For hir ioyncture lett itt nott be too large, lest your heyre fele the smarte and a second husband the swete of that grosse ouersight. After mariadge and thatt she haue borne yow some children yow may, if yow think she deserue and nede itt, enlarge her ioynture, yett in anie case for no longer tyme then she shall remaine wydowe.[2] Euer remembring that after your death, yea though she be wyse and well given, she is most lyke to be the wyfe of a stranger and peradventur no frend to your house. Therfor if yow be wise, make your son your executor and deale with hir as liberally as yow thinke good by legacie, wherin consult with some aged faithful frend. In most of your conveyancs leaue clauses of revocation (*fo. 14ʳ*) by advice of lerned councell, for thoughts maie alter. Lett hir ioincture be seperated from your heires landes, if itt maie be, so as occasion of contention be cutt of. Giue hir good councell how to governe hir tongue and to avoyd not only base but bad companie and guyde hir therin. Yow must presentlie after mariadge advice and charge your wyfe to abstaine from hearing anie tenants' suits touching their tenements &c, as your mother euer refrained, otherwise itt wilbe nether to your profitt nor creditt. For

---

[1] [*Margin*] Maryinge a superior bringes euer charg and often danger.
[2] [*Margin*] We see daily old wydowes fonder then yong both for choice of husbandes, servants and frends.

flatteringe tenants will sone seduce a woman, who neither is lyke to
haue a true intelligence of the matter, nor so sound a iudgmentt as
the wyser sortt of men haue.

(*fo. 14ᵛ*) For your CHILDREN teache them every morninge and
eveninge to saie their prayers devoutlye and to feare God. Giue them
lerninge and good education; in your owne experience yow maie
knowe how to make choice of a scolemaister for them, but in anie
case let him be a known sober, godlie man and aboue 40 yeares old,
if itt maie be. For I do utterlie dislyke of a yonge scolemaister, what
faire semblant soeuer be in him.

Lett your eldest son's servantt be no begger and of age aboue or
aboutt 40 yeares, nott simple, but of a sad witt, both able to giue
him advice and good example.

Your younger sonnes, if they haue no lande, must haue annuities
and, if outt of your landes yow grantt to euery of their first wiues to
such of your sonnes as haue no lande a certaine rent charge in lieu
of her ioyntur, maie itt advance them in mariadge; if they will follow
good advice some of them would be kept to the study of the lawes
and if there be many of them, lett one be prentise to a marchantt.

(*fo. 15ʳ*) All your SONNES would goe to the uniuersity at xiiii
yeares old and staie thear two or three yeares, then to the ynnes of
courtt, before xvii years of age and be well kept to ther studye of the
lawes and encoradged therto and kept from ryotouse companie. Your
sonne and heire especially yow must often in pryvate councell and
command to feare God, to be advised in all thinges, not rashe, to be
frugale, not miserable, provident, patientt, well gouerned of his
tongue, to make choice of good companie and avoyd yll company.
Acquaint him with your estate, suits, frends, yllwillers &c. If your
sone haue anie great thinges letten to him by lease, or anie such leases
as executor to yow, yow maie advice him, as I haue advised yow for
the defence of them.

For your DAUGHTERS I leaue the manor of their education to
the advice of some aged discrete Matron's direction.

(*fo. 15ᵛ*) If yow wish that God maie blesse your POSTERITY, be
yow iust and gett nothing with a bad conscyence. Avoide usury and
selling anie thing to pore men to a long daie for a great pryce. Blesse
your self from all kynde of bryberye and corruption, Neuer take a
cruell advantage upon a mortgage, bonds &c of pore men. Be pitty-
full, yet with true discrecion; lett your children followe these steps
also and then undoubtedly God will blesse them.,

The SALE I made of your grandmother's lande is lawfull very
much for the quyett and profitt of your house. My mother's perpetuity
to me had never fyne acknowledged of itt and therfor the land being

entailed by hir uncle Fr. Gasc[oigne] was by my fines &c lawfully sould and the purchasers haue paid me iustlie. Therfor I charge yow neuer harbroughe one thought to cale in question anie of those lands, for in law and conscyence yow can not.

Lett not your passions be too much caryed awaie with an excessiue desyre of a woman's BEWTY, for manie the fayrest withoutt are fowlest within. And their nature is so fraile and variable and temptations so ryfe as nether for anie worde nor othes will a wise man trust them for constancy.[1] And thinke not butt this spoken from longe and sounde experience. Therfor flee wanton companie and quarrelors; iudge all thinges of the world nothing.

REUENGE not euery harme and see in true discrecion whatt wronges be tollerable and what not. Some must be requyted, butt in anie case without offence or danger of lawe, even to worke a man's quyett. And sometyme a man must sue yll fellowes and after that either pardon them upon submission &c or punishe them more sevearly. Some must be winked att. Itt is very fitt for men to make showe of (*fo. 16ʳ*) a revengefull mynd and something enclyning to contention, whear the contrary inwardlye must be sought for. For nothing butt feare of revenge or suits can hould backe men from doing wronge and he thatt can nott mixe seuerity and showes of crueltye and revenge with lenitye and gentlnes shalbe contemned.

Use all the wise means yow maie to haue PEACE with all men and no grevouse contentions. For a pore man that hateth yow maie sometyme fynde oportunitye to displesure yow greatlie and of the contrary a mouse maie eate asunder the nett in which the lyon lyes entangled. Yett sometymes in honest pollicie, yow must seme something contentiouse and readie to sue men that doe yow wrong, of purpose to curbe their beastlie and base natures which otherwise will nott care for yow. Affect nott popularitee, nor care what fooles speake of yow; do thatt that standeth with true discrecion and a good conscyence and lett yll men and adversaryes say what they can, for no man can be well spoken of of all.

(*fo. 16ᵛ*) If yow haue an ENEMYE or aduersarie of accomptt thatt sends twoe men to yow to deliuer a message, unles they will nedes resolutely publishe itt, do yow talk privatelie butt with one of them, lest the other be wittnes against yow also; and receiue you the message and take daie to send an answeare by 2 men, butt nott in wrytinge, unlesse he write such a letter as in true discrecion you ought to answer and then (all choller sett asyde)[2] be verie careffull to

---

[1] [*Margin*] Loue, anger and ambition, the 3 most pourefull passions.
[2] [*Margin*] In anie case write not till your anger be quyte gone, vizt. not befor one night be passed.

ponder every word therin. In anie case lett itt be calme and myld without all bytternes, whatsoeuer yow meane to doe. Kepe a coppie therof, lett itt nott haue manie words in anie case and be so written, as his frendes maie see your discrecion which your enemy more feareth than unwise great words. Butt indede I would rather advice yow to answer his letter onelie by message, sending 2 men with itt, for their safety and witnesse &c. If after the recept of the message abouesaid in private, itt be such as yow would haue published for your advantage, yow maie will the messenger to publishe it befor your servants who must all this while stand not far of for your defence (for no enemy is to be trusted), otherwaies yow maie affirme that yow take no knowledg of his message. Use the messenger curteouslie, if he behaue himself decently and so sone as he is gone, sett doun in a note his wordes *verbatim* if yow can, the daie and the witnesses and kepe itt surelie till a perfect reconciliation. The 2 men yow doe send, as abouesaid, would be patient and forbearing, nott crossing, or contentiouse, butt such (*fo. 17*<sup>r</sup>) as hould itt the partt of honest men to make the better betwixt yow and your adversarie. Whensoeuer a RECONCILEMENT shall happen betwixt yow and your enemye, be nott so unwise as afterwards to trust him. For secrett poison is lyke to lye invisible in his hartte, what protestations or showes soeuer to the contrarie; and commonly those men that haue most witt and can speake best for themselues ar least to be trusted. Yett in true discrecion use him with verye wary curtesie and with all charitee, butt if yow be wise, use not his companie too much.

If yow would haue your frend in secrett to doe yow plesure against an adversary, either speake to him your self, or send some secret discrete person to him with your letter, wherin only write that yow are to make a request or thatt the bearer hath a suite unto him,[1] referring all to his relation, and if the gentleman be your famylier fast frend, then write not, butt sende by some known token. For your frend afterwards may becom your enemy, a thing very common in these daies. In anie case when yow mete with your adversarie argue not with him, rather departt, for such passionate debating is the mother of mischefe.

(*fo. 17*<sup>v</sup>) GAMINGE in anie case avoyd, unles the companie be undoubtedlie very honest and no common gamsters and such as plaie smale game onely for recreation and good companie. For itt is most certaine that a gentleman of worth shall seldom or neuer plaie great game att anie kynde of game among great gamsters, butt either

---

[1] [*Margin*] a secrete discrete frend better then anie servantt, unles some one long proued servant whose house and lyving is under yow and lyke so to remaine.

he shal be cosyned or ouerraight, or els fale to quarrell, or both of them. For the sleights and villanouse confedracyes and deceipts att game are infinite. Therfor he that can not forbeare att all tymes gaming for great somes of money, if he be a man of anye reckoninge thatt will nott use shifts in his game, showes him self a man of smale iudgment. And itt is a verie base and beastlie parte to be so palpably made a foole and a disartt as he shalbe, if he plaie as afforesaid. Againe be not ignorant that noble men and knights and esquyers of great lyving that use to plaie great game, knowe all or most of the secrett deceipts and advantages in gaming and will take helpes of them oftner then shallowe fellowes perceiue. Therfor if yow be wise neuer plaie more then yow ar contented to loose without any grudging or repentance.

(*fo. 18*) Most humbly I besech God, or most mercyfull and gratiouse father, to giue grace to you and yours to feare him and walke in his waies and then undoubtedlie he will guyde, protect and blesse yow in this worlde and after deathe crowne yow with glorie in his euerlasting kyngdom and with those unspeakable ioyes that nether mortale eye hath sene or eare hath herd, to whom be all honor dewe thanks and reverence, now and for euer, so be itt.

Psalm 31: *O how plentyfull is thy goodness which thow hast layd up for them that feare the; and that thow hast prepared for them that putt ther trust in the, euen before the sonnes of men.*     by me Wm. Wentworthe

Psalm 62: *O trust not in wrong and robery, giue not your selues to vanitye; if riches encrease, sett no your hartes upon them.*     Wm. Wentworthe

**2.** *Verses possibly by Sir William Wentworth.*

(*fo. 19*)     *Ante obitum beatus nemo*

Who sekes to fynde in this fals flattring world
a depe contenment that maie longe endure,
wants iudging skill and sownd experience
which laie examples still before our eyes
that heare on earth is no assurance found,
nor settled ioye of longe contynuance.

The covetous man that makes his heven of gold
is hungry still and neuer satisfyed:
tormented, lyke to staruing Tantalus,
that dyes for thirst amid the watery waues,
or the grosse asse with dainty viands laden
that feeds on thistlls in the open fields;

what vyler error maie possess the mynde
of Man whose witt should manage all the world?
and whose bright soule is ymage of that God
eternally that rules both earth and heauen
and therfor should nott so be overwhelmed
in the foule gulfe of this base sinfull world.

The ambitiouse man that fryes in honor's fyre
and hath his thoughts lyft up aboue the clouds,
they vanishe thear as smoke in open ayre,
whilst burning hopes do reach at soueraign sway.
For either death doth ende the tragedy,
(*fo. 19ᵛ*) or if he do survyue some victoryes,
he fyndes no periode of his highe desyres
that restles move as doth the rowling stone,
oft kept by fortune for a deadly fale
amid his smyles and his triumphant ioyes,
as whilom noble Bellisarius was
after fair showes of fals felicitye.

**3.** *Sir William's Account of the Providences vouchsafed his family*
(*SC*, xl, 1, *fo. 22ʳ*).

*Anno domini* 1607, 5 of Kinge James

When I consider in generall that man was created by the Almightie
for no other end then to sett furth to the uttermost of his pouer the
glorie of his Creator, to serve him, to praie unto him and to praise
his holie name and in perticuler casting bake myne eyes doe regarde
the infinite blessings which my pore house hath receiued by a long
tract of tyme even until this presentt of his most mercyfull bountee
and goodnes; and lykewise the most fatherlie and louing corrections
together with verie manie comforts, the which itt hath plesed his
dyvine Maiestie, for his meare mercys sake, to bestowe upon me, a
most wreched sinner. Even then and I deplie touched with feare
and trembling to be thankfull and for euer to praise, honor and
magnyfye his holie name, saying with the prophett Dauid, what
reward shall I giue unto the Lord for all the benefitts that he hath done
unto me? I will receiue the cup of salvation and cale upon the name
of the Lord. O Lord, I besech the deliuer my soule; O, take not away
the comfortt of thie grace from me, butt establishe me with thie
holy spiritt. And seing that diuers of these blessinges haue bene
(*fo. 22ʳ*) miraculouse, yett not made known to manie, I thought my
self not onely bound to impartt the same to some of my discreter

frends, the which I haue done, lest I might seme carelesse in setting
furth the glorie of God, but also to leave in wrytinge for yow and
yours, if it so please God, so much therof as I can beare in remembrance, as a speciall means by his grace to bring furth in yow
and them the fruicts of Religion, Conscyence and thankfullnes to
the dyvine prouidence that hath in this extraordinary manner
contynued and blessed your house. My meaning is not to discourse
of things of greate antiquyty touching the same, leauing that to your
petygrees &c. Onelie this I haue herde thatt our name and progenie
hath for a long tyme before the Conquest bene of worship and
reputation and that thear are att this daie in the Lowe Cuntries
records thereof in some towne, butt I can nott as yett lerne the
certaine place.

And my father (whose many vertues, conscyence and truth deserved to be reverenced) I haue herd him saie thatt he could neuer
heare before, nor in his tyme, thatt anie of our name haue bene
advanced either by being priests, merchants, or lawiers, being the
three ordinarie ( *fo. 23*r) ladders to preferment, butt either by
mariadge or service of the prince &c; and among diuers hundreths
of them, not anie haue dyed for conspyring of anie treason against
the kings or queens of this realme. To speak then of those things
that haue bene done within the memory of man; first I thinke itt not
amisse to laie before your eyes the present estate and weaknes of
many greate and auncyent houses round about yow which following
the ordinarie course of worldly thinges are att this daie weakned
with age and much declyninge. Albeitt your house, all praise, honour
and glorie be to God therfor, doth still augment and prosper and for
three or four of the last discents therof hath by the goodnes of God
had such owners as haue, I trust in godly and conscionable manner,
much encreased and advanced the same. Yow must thinke thatt the
almightie searcher of the harts of men loveth truth, conscyence and
charitie and hateth the contrarie. Therfore he thatt hopes for his
grace and fauor must nott savor too much of worldly wykednes.
Mie father whose hart was religiouse and full of truth, hath manie
tymes seriouslie willed me to serue God and ( *fo. 23*v) be thankfull
&c, saying to me that he before his birth was by God's especiall
fauor foreshowed and marked to advancment; lykewise thatt itt
was myraculoslie revealed to him befor I was borne thatt he should
haue one sone. First, said he, old Sir William Gascoigne's lands in
H[enry] 7 his tyme were rated by year aboutt eighte hundreth pounds
and fyftye at least, and therfore verie unlike it was in man's eyes then
thatt euer he, my father, being of so smale lyvinge, should so sone
after mary the onelie daughter and heire of that so greate a house

and the rather because one of the Gascoignes, as my father had crediblie herd, had before tyme slaine verie foule one of the Wentworthes and had great truble for the same; and therfore itt might seme that that house had lesse goodwill to those of our name and blud. Old Sir William Gascoigne, having liued till he was neare a hundreth years old and much of his tyme having kept the countenance of a great Erle rather then a knight, did neuertheles leaue this goodlie inheritance entiere to his sonne, called yong Sir William Gascoin, (*fo. 24*<sup>r</sup>) who most ryotouselie brought that goodly lyvinge to a low ebb in respect of thatt, thatt was left to him. This Sir William Gascoigne the yonger coming to hunt the bucke in the Park att Wentworth Wodhus before my said father was born (as he told me) the buck at last was taken in the ponde neare the house by the hounds. Wherfore my father's mother, being then greate with childe of him, came with hir mother in lawe to bid him wellcom &c. Wherupon he, beinge of a wyld willfull disposition, looked in my grandmother's face (for in truth I haue herd discrete men saie that he had a strange gyfte to coniecture beforhand manie things thatt weare to com) and swore a great othe that she was with child with a boie and earnestlie swore he would with the tip of his finger onely, dipt in the buck's blud, marke that boy for his owne upon his mother's cheke; saying he was assured thatt itt would be a boie and havinge a bearde the red spott would not be sene, when he was a man. She refusing, he (*fo. 24*<sup>v</sup>) threatened to laie all his whole bluddie hande upon hir face, unles &c. Therupon my grandmother, seinge noe remedye, suffred him to touche hir cheke with the tip of his finger dipt in blud, which marke, said my father to me, I heare showe unto the and opening the hears of his beard, I ther sawe itt plainelie, charging me to serue God &c.

After the death of yong Sir William Gascoigne, his sonne William Gascoigne Esquyer had diuers sonnes borne, butt all dyed in ther minority and my mother came to be the sole daughter and heire to him of suche lands, as weare left and not entaild to the heire males. For those lands Francis Gascoigne, brother to William and uncle to my mother, enioyed. This Francis had two wiues and onely a sonne by the latter which liued butt aboutt 3 years and so, for want of issue of Francis, his lands also came to my mother after his death. Nowe to returne to my father, being a single man he coming to Bowlint whear my mother, (*fo. 25*<sup>r</sup>) being a yong woman, remained with the old ladie, hir grandmother, who might do most touching hir mariadge. Itt pleased God thatt the said old ladie att the first sight of my father lyked verie well of him and perswaded hir self that she perceiued truth in his face &c and so by God's goodnes and hir furtherance the mariadge was consummate.

My father, having lyued with my mother aboutt xi yeares and having then issue onelie four daughters, itt pleased God to vysytt him with a burninge fever wherof he languished so thatt both my mother and his mother weare almost in dispaire of his recouerye. He lying thus verie weake in that chamber which now is used for the dyninge chamber, he told me that my mother and his mother leaving him alone aboutt noone to his rest, as they thought, went down into the kiching. Att which tyme, as he hath most confidentlie to me affirmed, he was not aslepe, but onelie laie with closed eyes, as syck men being verie weake use to doe, and when (*fo. 25ᵛ*) he opened his eyes, he saw stand by his bedsyde a wellfauored gentlwoman of a mydle age in apparell and countenance decentt and verie demure; and thinking the sight verie strange, he said to hir, 'Gentlwoman, from whence com yow?' She answered, 'Wentworth, I come from God'. He said, 'what is your name?' She said hir name was God's pitty and that God had sent hir to signifye unto him thatt he had compassion of him and that he should haue no more fitts of that fever. She told him he should liue manie more years and haue a sonne borne and therupon she took outt of hir pockett a box of oyntment and dipped some of hir fingers therin and offered to putt hir hand into the bed aboutt the myddest therof. Butt he, bashfullie holding the clothes down, semed to restraine hir hande, but she said, 'I must touche the'. Wherupon he suffring hir, she putt hir hand into the bed and touched his privities and presentlie toke hir hand awaie and then said, 'when thow art well, go to the (*fo. 26ʳ*) well att St. Anne of Buxtons and thear washe thy self and thanke God for thie deliuery.' He had, as he affyrmed, much conference with hir, greatlie to his contenttment. She tould him, as he said, of manie thinges to come and some thinges, as he said, which he would nott revaile. What those thinges weare, I knowe nott, butt I coniecture itt was some prediction of some perticuler prosperitees of his house and posterity. God, for his mercie sake, blesse us with grace and thankfull harts for the same.

As he was thus conferring with this heavenlie spiritt, he tould me that mye mother and his mother came up the staires, wherupon presentlie the vision vanished away. His mother comming to his bedsyde, said to him, 'sonne how do youe?' He answered, 'O mother, yow haue done me that displesure in coming to me that yow can neuer recompense.' Wherupon she, knowing his good nature and duty towards hir, said to my mother, 'Alas daughter, he raves'. 'No mother', said he, 'I rave nott, butt can deliuer to yow by God's grace matter of comfortt, touching my health (*fo. 26ᵛ*) and well doinge', and so related the most of this matter to them both, charging them to thanke God, butt to make no words therof. My mother hath also seuerally avowed the same to me. According [to] that prediction he recouered his health, wentt to the well att Buxtons, washed himself and most humblie thanked God &c. Afterwards itt pleased God that I was borne, being the last child he had. My father liued till I was aboutt 27 years old, I being then unmaryed, though I much desyred not to haue lost so much time, because I had neuer a brother.

During my father's lyfe from the death of Francis Gascoigne, my mother, having then in possession hir whole inheritance, could neuer be brought to asure hir land unto me after hir death, being a woman of a great witt and stomacke. After the decease of my father mye estate was butt smale, for my mother's inheritance being about as much as myne, she held as tenant in taile; also hir ioyncture outt of my (*fo. 27ʳ*) father's lands was more then the third part of the same. She was made sole executor to my father and, knowing the same, had befor his death removed much mony, as was verelie beleued, and all the best goods to Gauthorp. And I had only the goods and utensells at Wentworth Wodhus, being verie old, both quick and dead goods by legasye and my lands charged by my father's will with a thousand pounds *de claro* at lest for debts and my house verie ruynous. I do verelie beleue and so manie haue said that my father left monie to discharge me of all this dept; butt he, having formallie in his last will charged his lands with the same, I was forced to paie all substanciallie. Wherupon the first yeare after he dyed I liued verie priuatelie and sparinglie and repaired my hous and bestowed some cost of my grounds, gardens, orchards &c. Then I went to London, whear itt pleased God to send me your mother for my wyfe, being a woman endewed with manie vertues and brought twoe (*fo. 27ᵛ*) thousand pounds well paid. After which time it pleased God of his most mercyfull goodnes for the space of fiue years, or thereaboutt, to blesse me wth all kynde of wordlie comforts thatt my hart could desire: namelie contentment of mynde, youth, helth, strengthe, children even as I would, plentie of all things I could wishe for, frends manie and known enemies, or open adversaries, nott anie; I sued no man nor no man me. Butt afterwards itt pleased God that manie suits and displesures weare raised against me and therupon in diuers years one waie and other I spentt about four thousand pounds and much care bestowed and some perills of my lyfe, by the mercyfull goodnes of God avoided. The parties with whom I had dealing weare for the most partt gentlmen of the better sortt, pollitque and subtill, yett by the assistance of God they gott nothing, butt losse and no creditt att my hands. Allwais I had a care nott busilie to innovate, or claime anie (*fo. 28ʳ*) thinge, butt onelie

# 30 SIR WILLIAM WENTWORTH'S VOLUME

to defend and kepe my living in such sortt as my father left itt; and if I could perceiue, as in the case of the claime by the feoffees of the scole of Leedes that conscyence was against me I euer laboured and sought composition, as not having any intent by synister means to worke against God and truth.

During my time I thanke God without anie desire of dishonest gaine, I had a care to leaue some decent staie of lyving for my manie children and therfor purchased some things in plaine and honest manner for which I paid for the most part deare. Then it plesed God to giue me an oportunitee to buy Harwod, which by the speciall fauor of God I compassed, far beyond the expectation of of manie of the wyser sort. The house of Harwod Castle, being for manie years devyded betwixt the Redmans and Rythers was at last by James Ryther's pollicies and purchase unyted in him self. Butt his proud ouerweening condition, albeitt he had especiall good giftes of nature, brought him to dye[1] in the Flete for debt and his sonne Robert Rither to sell all his inheritance. These Rithers and Redmans being men of greate (*fo. 28ᵛ*) worship and coradge, albeitt they had some tymes maryed with the house of Gauthorp, could neuer remaine in firme frendship with itt. For they claimed to be lords of Harwod, as indede itt semes they weare and the Gascoignes they held for freholders, who claimed to haue a manor in Gauthorp or Lofthus &c. Butt the Gascoignes being euer to mightie for them bore them verie hard, both with suits, quarells and countenance. Diuers greatt men, knights and erles, made awards betwixt them and Richard, Duke of Glocester, then protector, made one awarde betwixt them, butt the settled rancor of ther harts and remembrance of old displesures would neuer suffer longe agrement.

Att last it plesed the mercifull goodnes of God thatt after the death of my mother I came to be the inheritor of the house of Gauthorp. Att which tyme Mr Robert Ryther, being a yong man, greatlie indepted for his father and something for him self, resolved to sell Harwod, using therin the especiall councell and confidence of the Countesse of Cumberland and Sir Robert (*fo. 29ʳ*) Staplton, both of them persons much experienced and verie pollitique and remayning for the most partt at London, itt was offred to diuers

---

[1] The Redmaynes were a family with Cumberland origins who intermarried with the Gascoignes, so that Whitaker assumed that their half of the manor of Harwood had passed to the Gascoignes by inheritance. James Ryther was denounced by Archbishop Sandys as a church papist who protected Catholics and depended on Sir Thomas Fairfax. He died 4 September 1596. J. T. Cliffe, *The Yorkshire Gentry* (London, 1969), p. 241; T. D. Whitaker, *Loides and Elmete* (Leeds, 1816), pp. 166–67.

great persons, butt the price was beyond measure and the encombrances dangerouse and allmost without number, as will appeare by my euidence. Wherfore men had no greate stomak to it, butt God's mercy and fauor, that led my father by the hand to his mariadge, guyded me in lyke manner to unite and ioyne in one thes two houses. Wherin as all the daies of my lyfe I am bound to think of itt most seriously and with all humilitie and reverence to giue thankes to the Almightie for the same, so in perticuler knowe ye thus much thatt withoutt the selling of lands to the vallewe of 400[li] at lest per annum, it was not possible for me to raise mony to purchase Harwod.

My mother had in hir wydowheade assured hir lands by perpetuitie unto me, butt that perpetuitye was of no force against me, by reason no fine was passed by hir; those lands being before entayled by Francis Gascoigne with a fine by him and exemplified so was I at my (fo. 29[v]) remitter. Otherwise if my mother had acknowledged a fine upon the perpetuitie, I could hardly haue sold anie of those lands to haue bought Harwod. My mother, being aged and giuinge too much care to those that flattered hir for their own gaine, did in hir wydowhead by fine make a lease of the manor of Arthrop in Linconshir to my sister Darcie and hir husband for threscore yeares, if my said sister so long lyved. Sone after my brother Darcie dyed and diuers years after thatt, the same night that my mother dyed, upon intelligence itt plesed God to putt me in mynde to ryde with all spede in the cold winter night to Awthorp. Wher aboutt or befor 6 a clok in the morning I entred the house that my father built, albeitt ther was some order given to kepe me outt, butt my sodaine coming, as God would, caused me to finde the dores open &c. My brother Darcie and my sister had in that matter delt unfaithfullie and ungratefullie with me and against ther promise and word given unto me. Shortlie after (fo. 30[r]) Jespar Blithman, hir second husband, well percyving the conveyance of Arthorp to Mr Darcie and my sister &c in law not to be good for a great part (for the tenants had neuer atturned &c) compounded with me to haue during his wife's lyfe a Rent charge of 60[li] per annum and so yeilded the land to me. Without this land I could not convenyentlie haue compassed Harwod, wherin yow must note the especiall prouidence and most mercyfull kyndnes of the Almightie towards your hous.

Againe my mother in the wydowhed of my sister Darcie had drawn wrytinges ready to the sealing, vizt. a lease for xii yeares of the Manor of Burton Lenerd to my sister and also one other lease of the house and demaines of Gauthorp for one year to hir also, next after the death of my said mother, notwithstanding that my said sister had all hir goods &c. Butt it plesed God, as I haue herd verie crediblie by the means of that unfortunate Thomas Gargraue, who maried one of my sisters and was much aboutt my mother and greatlie in hir fauor thatt he much grudging att the excessiue preferment of ( *fo. 30ᵛ*) my sister Darcie (as the onelie hinderance of his profitt) as I haue herd, did fullie satisfie my mother thatt my sister Darcy was undoubtedlie resolved after hir death to mary Jespar Blithman, a pore gentleman and younger brother and sometime servant to my father and after hir husband; albeitt she boldlie denyed the same. Wherupon my mother neuer sealed those 2 leases, which if she had done, I could not well haue compassed Harwod. For I might not withoutt greate inconvenyence haue sold other lands then those I did.

Also I haue herd verye crediblie thatt by the speciall provocation of Thomas Gargraue my mother in hir wydowhead (after much suite made by me unto hir in vaine) did assure all hir lands unto me, after hir decease, as is said. For she did itt upon my deliuery of bonds &c into hir hands for his use, of which I made no haste till it plesed hir to promise such assurance, being the foresaid perpetuitie. So this gentleman Thomas Gargraue whose good gifts of nature I was verie sorie to see blemished with want of the fear of God; yett I trust he dyed in a better mynde, being executed att York upon an enditement for poisoning one Gardiner, his man, and also for breach of prison, being committed for fellonie. Att ( *fo. 31ʳ*) thatt tyme the Erle of Huntingdon was presidentt of the Councell at Yorke and lyeutenant of the shire, who hated Gargraue mortallye. I haue herd thatt att the gallowes he protested himself cleare for Gardiner's death, butt his breach of prison, being committed for fellony, was in extremitee fellonie.[1] True it is thatt I durst neuer kepe him companie, though he remained manie daies att my father's hous, and he bearing no goodwill to me, yet God gaue him both will and pouer to do me the 2 foresaid important plesures, which no frend I had could doe, of purpose to serue his private ends. The causes whie I might nether trust him, nor kepe companie with him, weare the experience I had of his most dangerous nature and subtiltie in his imagined plotts, though by protestations and letters he laboured excedingly to insynuate himself into my good opinion and company. If I had dyed without issue, he had bene, in right of my sister, possessed of the third parte of myne inheritance and then our name had ended in our house.

Itt was well known thatt once he bought poison and tryed itt upon

---

[1] This was in 1595, Hunter, ii, p. 213. Hunter quotes from an account by Gargrave's daughter Prudence, who denied that Gardiner was poisoned, but he does not mention Huntingdon's enmity.

a dog; againe itt is well known that he distilled poisons and kept them in glasses. His father, Sir Cotton Gargraue being a man very wyse, beleued (*fo. 31ᵛ*) even to his last gasp that he was by him most impyouslie empoysoned, as apperes also in his last will of record att York. His 2 innocentt daughters,[1] being aboutt iii and iiii years old, dyed upon verie few daies syknes and both on one daie, or within xxiiii houres together, both having ulcers alyke in ther heads. Sir Cotton had a hole in the brest under the pap wherof he dyed. This man's most strang courses with his wyfe I omit, being wearie to cale to mynd too manie of these thinges, butt thatt I maie show good reason whie I refused his companie. For I lyke not to iudge anie man, nether to speake yll of the dead, but I praie God haue mercie of his soule and ours too, amen.

Now how unlyke itt was that I should be able to buye Harwod and enioye itt peaciblie, butt that God of his mercifull goodnes had so ordained, itt will appeare. Yow should understand that I had a thousand pounds in my purse, the price of Harwod being set at a leaven thousand pounds, being too deare by 4000ˡⁱ at least, of which after some hundreths were abated. Now to sell land before I was assured to conclude for itt, I thought nott good. Notwithstanding I delt with my tenants of Burton Lenard and agreed for what somme of monie euery man should buye his farme &c, if I bought Harwod, otherwise not to sell anie. (*fo. 32ʳ*) Also I knew certainlie wheare to haue monie for other lands, hauing had the lyke conference for the sale of them &c. Having made this preparation, I called to me your mother and i or ii discrete persons thatt I durst well trust and sytting privatelie in councell, we drew to consideration the dangers of my entryng into so waightie a bargaine. First, the pryce being more by 4000ˡⁱ then the land was worth in true vallewe; secondlie, the very manie and great encombrancs thatt dailie came to light; thirdlie the paiment of so great sommes all att London; fourthly, the parties want of monie, butt not of pollicy, with whom I was to deale and statutes for the monie, which, if I forfaited, I loked for smale fauor; fyftlie the uncertainty of all payments to me by them that I should sell land unto; sixtlie the first paiment of 4000ˡⁱ and at London, hard to be raised and thear paid in tyme, unles I should absolutelie sell land and take monie befor I was sure of Harwod and if so itt weare, yet might I faile to have itt iustlie returnd att London at my daie, nether had I time (*fo. 32ᵛ*) suffycientt for these things &c. Of all others I maie not forgett how my tenants of Burton Lenerd delt with me most lovinglie and faithfullie. For I being of necessitie to goe to London to haue conference with the foresaid Countesse and Sir

---

[1] [*Margin*] suspected to be poisoned.

Robert Staplton touching this matter, I talked with my said tenants of Burton, who, albeitt I had no tyme to draw their conveyancs being verie manie, they notwithstanding, having conditionallie agreed with me, as is said, and having no bond or anie wryting from me, said to me, 'Sir, we knew the true iust dealing of your father and we do hope thatt yow meane nothing butt truth towards us. We will putt into your hands three thousand pounds toward your first paiment and we will take your conveiancs att leisure; for we doubt not, butt God will prosper your procedinges.' This was the especiall fauor of God and a thing seldom hard of, for so manie cuntry people to agree all in one to make such an adventure. The which, I thank God, they repented nott and God hath blessed them to liue honestlie and well of the same. Seaventhly, if I should happen to die before these paiments (*fo. 33ʳ*) made, my sonne being then an infant and warde to the Queene that then was, my statutt would be in danger to be forfaited and diuers my lands extended, also the doubt of clearing the encombrancs and many such perilles.

After a long and carefull consideration of my abilityes &c we rose, nott being able to see for that tyme that for feare of a great yll neighbor, I should danger to make shipwracke of myne own estate. Diuers tymes these matters were by us seriouslie and providentlie debated, butt lytle lyked of. Att last we determyned to bestow one other daie, or a great part therof, in councell touching this matter and then resolutly to pursew itt, or reiect itt. And after we had laid before us whatsoeuer att all tymes we cold bethinke our selues of, we all late at night rose up. My self together with their advyce most constantlie (as I thought) resolued neuer more to speake a worde in thatt matter, as a thing in our understanding of most assured danger and yll successe. Butt God, who holdeth the harte of man in his hande, showed his most tender mercie to your house in altering my resolution, which in humane reason I thought (*fo. 33ᵛ*) to be most settled and surelie grounded.

So going to bed and on my first slepe, I dreamed and thought that my father appered unto me, saying these words to my very remembrance, 'Sonne, what do youe for Harwod?' Me thought I answered, 'By my troth, Sir, nothing, for the price is so excessiue and the incombrancs so manie thatt in reason, I maie nott adventure upon itt'. Me thought he said to me, 'It makes no matter, go forward with it in the name of God.' I answered, 'Sir, I have considered of itt verie advisedlie and I can not deale with itt, butt in trewe reason I shall danger the ouerthrowe of my estate.' Me thought he saide againe, 'It makes no matter, go forwards with itt in the name of God.' Wherupon I presentlie awaked and tould your mother whatt I had

dreamed and did fele in my self (contrarie to the constant courses
I euer used upon the lyke sound deliberations) a desyre to adventure for ytt, verelie believing that this motion proceded from the
speciall fauor and blessing of God. In which opinion I was still confirmed, for some of the clothiers, thatt returned my monie trulie,
brok ther creditt with others presentlie after.

And thus having surmounted all difficulties in the course (*fo.
34ʳ*) of thatt matter, being guyded by the pouerfull and mercyfull hand
of the Almightie, I haue established the inheritance of Harwod upon
yow,[1] whom in the name of God I charge euer to beare a good
conscience, which is to a man an exceding comfortt. Also to be piti-
full to the pore and bountifull to them, faithfull to your frends in
their honest causes, yett verie carefull how yow trust anie to much,
for deare frends to daie are manie tymes mortale enemies to morowe.
Never be unthankfull for a good turne; governe your tongue with all
circumspection and moderation. Be patientt, be wyse and feare
God and then no doubt God will establishe yow and your sede after
yow, if they serue him in lyke manner; to which Almightie God and
our most mercifull father, be all praise, honor and glorie, both now
and for euer: so be it.     Wm. Wentworth: 1607.

**4.** *Next in the volume comes Sir William's epitaph on his wife, who
died 22 July 1611 (printed in Hunter, ii, p. 83, note 1). This is
followed by some collective and even more laborious verse to her
memory by 'hir dutifull Children', then (fo. 38ʳ).*

To the memorye of his worthy and most vertuous mother, the Ladye
Anne Wentworthe, late of Wentworthe Woodhus, Thomas Wentworthe, hir eldest sonne that did soe muche love and honour hir,
dothe consecrate these:

> Gone is the mirror of the female kinde,
> Glorye of vertue and hir clearest lyght,
> Whoe whilum shone in bewties of the mynd
> Fairer then Phoebe in the frosttye night,
>   Oh she the greater sorte exceled as farre,
>   As heaven's fair lampe exceeds the twinckling starr.

---

[1] Wentworth on 16 February 1616 petitioned in Chancery stating that Sir
William had paid £11,000 for Harewood and claiming that Robert Mawde's
father had wrongfully enclosed waste and wrongfully acquired evidences both
belonging to James Rither; P.R.O., C2, Jas. I, 19/25. James Ryther in an undated project, probably around 1590, says that the Gascoignes had bought up
many freeholders in Harewood and added their lands to the demesnes of Gawthorpe. He estimated there were 8000 acres of common and more waste than
enclosed ground; British Museum, Lansdowne MS. 108, fo. 50ᵛ.

Constant she was, to goodness wholly bent,
Hir thoughtes most chast, for pittie neare to seeke,
Devout in praiers, in whiche muche tyme she spent,
Compleat in graces, secret, silent, meak;
   She clothed the naked and releved the poore,
   Both in hir plentye and hir smaller store.

(*fo. 38ᵛ*) Hir workes were mercye, ioyned withe wisdome still
She comforted full many a sorie wight,
Employed hir power God's word for to fullfill.
And as the gratfulle sleepe doth seaze the wearye sprite,
   Soe did she die and without fear or paine
   Gaue upp hir blessed soule to God againe.

Lyke Danae's daughters in this mournfull verse
In vaine I stryve hir vertues to unfolde,
Syth all my powers of witt cannot rehearse
Hir manie gracs rightlye to be tould;
   In silence therfore, thus constrained, I rest
   And in my soule I safely may protest

That tyme, truthe's mother, shall discover still
Newe losse and griefs for which tears shall abound,
From husband, widowes and poore orphans will
And neighbour townes, their sorowe shall resound,
   All these shall think the heavens themselues to frowne,
(*fo. 40ʳ*)   Thoughe God above hir blessed soule doth crowne.

Thear rest in ioyes that eie hath never sene,
Late saint on earthe, nowe glorious saint above,
Thy life a paterne and thy deathe a meane
To drawe men's thoughts to God's both feare and love.
Thy life a sourse from which much grace did flowe,
   Thy deathe, the tree where heavenlye fruits doe growe.

## II. SIR WILLIAM WENTWORTH AND THE EARL OF SHREWSBURY

**5.** *Sir William Wentworth and the earl of Shrewsbury 1597–1612 (SC, xx/82).*

A note of some of Sir William Wentworth's duetifull respects and actions touching the Earle of Shrewsbury for 17 or 18 yeres.

1. First the said Sir William during that time suffred the said Earle's kepers and seruants wholie to comaund his grounds and woods wherein time owte of mynde his ancestors haue norished and bred deere. [*Margin*] loke my lord's letter 1597.

2 *Itm* where one of the Earle's gentlemen has furyouslie torne her late maiestie's proces and stroken one of the servants of the said Sir William, being a spetiall balif to arest a friend of his, and reviled the said Sir William, the said Sir William notwithstanding did forbeare all redres for the Earle's sake. [*Margin*] his lordship's 2 letters Jan. 1596.

3 *Itm* at his lordship's earnest request the said Sir William went to York with all the freholders he could possiblie procure for the chusing of Sir John Sauill one of the knigts of Yorkshire.[1] [*Margin*] his lordship's 2 letters Sept 1597.

4 *Itm* A° 1599 Sir William hauing purchased lands within the Earle for about 1100$^{li}$, at the Earle's request lett him haue those lands for the same money he paid.

5 *Itm* 300$^{li}$ or therabout parte of the said 1100$^{li}$ due to him was unpaied by the Earle untill his maiestie came to receiue his Crowne here, being 3 yeres after the same daie.

6 *Itm* in A° 1599 a forreine invasion beinge pretended and the Earle being comaunded to prouide a greater nomber of horses for seruice then he had redie, the said Sir William at his owne chardges sent him owte of Yorkshire 2 seruiceable men and horses. [*Margin*] his lordship's 2 letters Aug 1599.

7 *Itm* at the request of the said Earle Sir William made Wormall his undersherife, 44 Eliz., which Wormall, as is beleued upon premeditacon, hath euer since procured the extreme troble and losse of the said Sir William. [*Margin*] his lordship's letter at London.

8 *Itm* Sir William being so sherife of Yorkshire at the speciall request of the Earle suffred Sir Anthony Ashley to take the profitts

[1] For this election, see J. E. Neale, *The Elizabethan House of Commons* (London, 1949), pp. 88–92.

of the Counetie Court, worth by estimacon 250$^{li}$ per annum, hauing
only a gratuity of 10$^{li}$ per annum at the most. [*Margin*] his lordship's
letter 1601.

9 *Itm* Sir William being seized of the lands of one Mr Wilson
upon an Elegit, found to be worth 40$^{li}$ per annum, but indeed much
better, did at the request of the said Earle suffer Wilson to occupie
thos lands taking onlie 40$^{li}$ per annum accordinglie. [*Margin*] his
lordship's letter 1608.

10 *Itm* Sir William hath sometime lent the Earle money. [*Margin*]
His lordship's letter March 1599.

11 *Itm* the said Sir William during the said time of 17 or 18 yeres
hath euer forborne to deale in anie matter which might seme to be
against the said Earle.

12 *Itm* where the said Earle 4 yeres sence inclosed into his new
parke 8 acres of a comon where Sir William was immedyat cheife
lord and the Earle his freholder. The said Sir William at the Earle's
mocon suffred the learned counsel of the Earle to take notes of Sir
William his euidenc and after a yeare that no euidence for the Earle
wold be shewed to Sir William, the said Sir William brought an
action of trespass, yett making suit for composycion, but the Erle
refusinge,[1] Sir William gott a verdict.

13 *Itm* againe after the judgment the said Sir William moued the
said Earle that a lawyer and gentleman of eyther syde might compound that matter, meaninge his lordshipp should haue yt very
cheape, but the Earle refused, wishing he mighte haue a new tryall
and in August last 1612 he sent a message to the said Sir William
wishing him to pull down the paile &c.

**6.** *Gilbert, earl of Shrewsbury's letters to William Wentworth.*

(*a*) (*SC*, xx/73) Mr Wentworth, I have receaued your letter and am
sorry to understand the rashe abuse that was lately offered unto you
by one that is towards me, who shall understande my mynde therin
playnly when I nexte [see] him which I thynke wil be within thes x
dayes, for that uppon occasion I purpose (God willinge) to be then in
Nott: shyre (though I returne up hither forthwith). I will not fayle to
send for him purposely aboute this matter and then you shall here
further from me. In the meane tyme I thynke myself much beholden

---

[1] Lambeth Palace Library, MS. 702, fo. 55$^r$; the countess of Shrewsbury to
Henry Butler, 4 March (no year, but probably about 1609) '. . . and tell Jhon
both from my lord and me that if he sopres the evedence he can geue touching
the quelit betwex my lord and mr wentworth his aliance will not be sofecient
to protect him . . .'

to you for your respectfull procedynge towards me and I pray you forbeare to deale any further therin untill you here agayne from me and so I very hartelly take my leaue. At my house in Brodstrete this 8 of Ja. 1596[7] Your very louynge frend and neyghbore Gilb. Shreusbury. To my very good frend Mr William Wentworthe Esq att his house. [*Endorsed*] my lo. Shreusb touching Ra. Re[re]s[by].

(*b*) (*SC*, xx/74) Mr Wenteworth, your man who carryed you my lettere can tell you how nere he mett Mr Th. Reres[b]ye to this house with whome after I had conference at large of the matter did persuade his brother and so he will be contented (upon my direction) to acknowledge that the words that he used to your man of you were rashe and collaryck and herafter will give you no cause of offense, receuing none from you; and herewith I pray you be satisfyed and I shall thynk my selfe beholden unto you. And I pray you returne the lettere agayne by this bearer that I sente you this morning and so in extreme haste I tak my leave this 22th of Ja. 1596[7], your assured frend Gilb. Shreusbury. To my v. gd. frend Mr W^m Wentworth esq. [*Endorsed*] My lo. Shreus. touching Ra: Resby.

(*c*) (*SC*, xx/75) Mr Wentworth, I haue receaued your letter and doe giue you my best thanks for your most frendly dealynge with your neyghbores for theyr voyces, which I take in very kinde and thankfull parte and am right glad of your purpose to goe to Yorke, wher I shall wish you all good success. I haue sent you by this bearer a doe, beynge sorry I knew it no soner that I might haue sent you a brace; you are too sparynge of my venison, I mean to bestow none on you, but such as your selfe shall command, hauing giuen direction to all my keepers of Sheffeld, Kymerworth and Tankersley to provyde you whensoeuer you shall send to them for. And for Cox his well serving your turne when your father in law was with you, I haue tould him he wanted as much to his name as will make him a coxecome for his labore, who hereafter, if he make you not amends when you commande, I will another in his roume of more discretion and honesty. I will troble you no longer for this tyme, but with my ryght harty comendacons, comitt you to the Allmighty from Worksop in hast this last of Sept: at nyght 1597. Your assured louinge frend Gilb: Shreusbury. To my very good frend Mr Willm Wentworthe esq at his house at Wentworth Woodhouse, with spede.

(*d*) (*SC*, xx/76) After my verie hartie comendacons, whereas I haue receaued letters from the lords of the priuie counsaile by the Queenes Maistie's express comandment that I shall provide all the horse and geldings serviceable that I can make on a soddaine and with them to

WP—D

attend her Maiestie's person, now at this tyme when it is advised that the Spaniards do intend an invasion into this kingdome. And forasmuch as of my selfe I am no wayes hable in this short tyme to prouide and furnish my selfe with any suche number as her Maiestie and her counsaile doth expect in that behalfe, I am boulde therby to intreate the furtherance of my good frends, amongst which number esteeminge you for one, I will make boulde to intreate you to send me such hable horses fitte either for harnes or for lighte horses, as you can procure for me, with such men and furniture for them as shall be fitte for service, to be with me in London by the xxth of this August. And I will returne you the same againe after their service, if theare be anie, unlesse they shall happen to miscarie in the feild. And as at this time this occasion (as it is generallie conceaued) is as important as is possible to be imagined, so shall your frendlie dealinge with me hearin be with all thankfulnes receaued and acknowledged and so I comitte you to the protection of the Almightie. From the Court at Nonsuch, this viith of August 1599, your very lovinge Gilb. Shreusbury. To my verie louinge frend Mr Willm Wentworth esq. at Woodhouse with speede.

(*e*) (*SC*, xx/77) After my verie hartie comendacons, whereas I was latelie boulde to wryte unto you amongst others of my good frends to supplie my want with sutch horses and geldinges as convenientlie you could and that you haue accordinglie very kyndlie sent twoe geldinges, which (as I understand) ar fitt for service. Theis ar to signifie my most hartie thanckes unto you for the same and forasmutch as yt is conceyved by the enemies detractinge of tyme that he hath changed his determination and so there wilbe no present proceedinge in this service. I haue returned them againe unto you, being verie sorie that your sending upp hath bene so chargeable and troblesome to you. But yf hereafter occation shall happen in this kynde (which I trust God of his goodness will prevent) I doe then assuredlie hope to geve you sutch certayne Notice thereof as their travaile shalbe no more in vaine. And so resting verie readie wherein I may requite your kinde goodwill, I comytt you to the protection of thallmightie. From the court at Nonesuche this xxiiith of August 1599, your verie assured lovinge frend, Gilb. Shreusbury. To my verie assured good frend Mr Wm Wentworthe Esq at Woodhouse dd.

(*f*) (*SC*, xx/78) After my verie hartie comendacons &c, these are to give you hartie thanks for your consent by your letter of the 28th of Febr: laste to lette me have Maddowe hall at such rate as yt standes you in and withall to certefie you that I doe willinglie accepte thereof. My earnest desyre ys that the conveyance thereof maye be made presentlie unto me in such sorte as my servant Kydman shall have directions; I am content that they to whome you haue lett yt may continewe the same under me accordinge to your bargayne with them untill Candlemas next and though your said letter requyre payment of the whole some to be payde for yt before I shall haue anye commoditie by yt, yet I make noe doubte but you will give such reasonable dayes for payment therof, as yourself had of the partye whoe solde yt you. Your servant Jackson hath satisfied the request which I made to yow for which I very hartely thanke you and will not fayle to keepe my daye with you. And for my tenement at the Stead in Caster his occupacon, yf at my coming into the countrye (upon inquyrye made) I shall fynde my estate therein such as I may parte with it and other circumstances concerning in reasonable manner, I shal be verie willinge to lett you have it. And soe I comitt you to the proteccon of the Almightie from my house in London the xxiith of March 1599 [1600], your very lovynge frend, Gilb. Shreusbury. To my verie lovinge frend Mr Willm Wentworth Esqr at Woodhouse.

(g) (SC, xx/79) After my verie hartie comendacons, wheare I understand that you are pricked for sheriffe of Yorkshire and that Mr John Wormhall is desirous to serve as your undersheriffe, although I do not doubt but his sufficiencie and honestie be verie well knowne unto yourselfe. Yet shall I pray you receaue my testimonie thereof also, the which I may giue him both out of my former owne knowledg of the good report which he hath for the same and especiallie for that uppon record he hath latelie leaft his sufficient justification therof against such his enemies as in the Starrechamber sought vehementlie to haue impeached his credit and good name; wherof notwithstanding he hath leaft so good witnes in that honorable court as better could not haue been wished. Wherefore I will make bould to straine my uttermost credit with you that for my sake the rather you will be contented to yeeld unto this his suite. He will I doubt not giue such securitie therin as shall to yourselfe seeme reasonable and I shall take in verie kind part what favor you shall show him at this my earnest request. And so I comend you to the proteccon of the Almightie. From Bedford house, this 25 of November 1601.

[Shrewsbury's hand] Yf I were not very well assured of this gentleman his suffitiency euery way and that his honesty is equall to any man's that I know, I wolde not be thus earnest with you to bestowe him in this place as I am, but upon this grounde and for some partyculer respects besyds, which conserne myselfe (which I will imparte unto you whensoeuer we meete next) I will intreate you as euer you will satisfy my desyre in any thyng that you will not refuse me in this and I shall take it as thankfully as you can imagyne and euer remayne your assured louyng frend Gilb. Shreusbury.

Mr Wentworth, when I remember how much I am beholding to you for your pacience in forbering sume muneys dew to you, I shold rather find out how to requit your cortese then to make any new request, but so will I wish to this berer that I can not refeucs to comend him to you, as a man every way so well comended by the best that I know not how you can beter that your self. Want of paper makes me end abrobtly but with comendacons to Mrs Wentworth.

(h) (SC, xx/80) After my very harty comendacons, whereas the Queene's Maiestie by letters patents under the great seale of England bearynge date in the fortith yeare of hir raigne (as I am informed) did graunte the office of clark of the county cowrts of Yorkshyre in the name of Sir Anthony Ashley and Mr Lake, who hathe for many yeares enjoyed the same, by vertue of lyke letters Patents formerly graunted to others; I am now geven to understand that you goe aboute to impeache this graunte and to preiudis the sayd patentees, by grauntynge the sayd office to some other by vertue of your sheriff-wike as belonginge therunto. Wherfore I thynke good to let you understand that (of my knowledge) if you be obstinate therin, it will breede you muche troble and inconuenience, for not only by law but otherwise they will be hable infinitely to troble you. The lyke course hath ben attempted by others your predicessors and, as I thynke, by my cosen Clyfford the last yeare, but he was glad to gyve it ouer and (as I have hearde) wyshed he had never meddled at all therin. I pray you therfore consider throughly therof, before you proceede too far and if you will follow my advise (which is the same that I wolde doe myselfe, if I were in your case) you sholde not stande in it. I must confess they bothe are my very good frends and for theyr owne saks I wyshe they may inioye hir Maiestie's graunte withoute any interruption, but therwithall the respect and good affection that I beare to you maks me hartely to desyre you sholde not styr or interpose your selfe in a matter wherin I am confident you can not prevayle. And so, leavynge it to your wysdome, I will take my leave and with my most harty well wyshynge, comitt you to the protection of Allmighty God. From the Courte at Whytehall, this xxiiith of Ja. 1601[2], your very asured frend, Gilb. Shreusbury. If you thynke good to let it apeare to theis 2 gentlemen that you doe for my sake the more respect them I shall take it very thankfully. To my very good frend Mr Wentworth esq, heigh sherif of the Cunty of Yorke. [Endorsed] answered Feb 1601.

(i) (SC, xx/81) Mr Wentworth, I am intreated by my very good frend Mr Peter Evers to desyre you to doe him a curtesy for my sake the matter beyng this; he havynge bene bounde for Sir Thomas Rearsby for the payment of a MC[11] Sir Thomas hathe geven him leave to pay bothe the pryncipall and interest, or else to have laine by the heeles for his labor. But he hath payde and is now blowynge a seeke for his remedy. He hath a recognisance of Sir Thomas for security and therupon hath a iudgement and a wrytt of *elegit*. Now his desyre is to be ryghtly informed the trewe state of his lands and goods, as nere as may be, which he is perswaded no man in the parts can better doe then your selfe (if you be so disposed) to thend that therby he may the better execute his wrytts so as they shall not be fruteles. My earnest intreaty therfore to you is that you will privately acquaynt him with your knowledge in that behalfe and also you will direct him to some suche a one who may be assistant unto him for the performance of thes thyngyes and I will assure you that he will use it with suche discretion and secresy as neyther your selfe shall be seene in it, nor that any thynge is done by any advise of yours in any sorte, which I wolde not doe, if I were not very well assured of this gentellman's discretion and performance of his worde to me in any thynge, as in this he hathe faythfully promised me. And so with my most harty comendacons, I comytt you to the Allmighty. At my house in London, this 26 of Feb: 1602[3], your assured louyng frend, Gilb. Shreusbury. To my very good frend Mr Wentworth esq at his house at Woodhouse. [*endorsed*] My lord Shrewsb. touching Sir Peter Euers.[1]

**7.** *Sir William Wentworth's disputes with the earl of Shrewsbury 1608–12* (*SC*, xx/84).[2]

If any shall suggest that Sir William Wentworthe did rashely or contemptuouslie serue procees of two of my Lord of Shrewsburye's

---

[1] The background to this letter is a violent quarrel between Sir Thomas Reresby and William Wentworth which had developed shortly after the trouble with Ralph Reresby (above, nos. 6(*a*) and 6(*b*)). It arose about land in Wentworth's manor of Hooton Roberts and led to Sir Thomas challenging Wentworth, who refused to meet him. Sir Thomas then assaulted Wentworth on the bench at Rotherham Quarter Sessions and was fined £1000 in Star Chamber, *c*. 1602; *Memoirs of Sir John Reresby*, ed. A. Browning (Glasgow, 1936), pp. xxxii–xxxv. An undated draft agreement before June 1596 shows that the dispute was about division of commons in Hooton and that Wentworth also claimed that the Reresby manor of Thribergh was held of the manor of Hooton Roberts so that Reresby owed suit of court and a freehold rent. Disputes about the relationship to the manor of Hooton Roberts were still going on in 1678; Sheffield Central Library, Wentworth Woodhouse Muniments, C. 6/199.

[2] A draught of part of this is to be found among the manorial documents deposited in the Central Library (WWM, C7–75).

people, it is to be ansuered that yt was not done sodenlie or undueti-
fullie.

For in August 1608 the Earle of Shrewsbery making a new parke
did inclose about eight acres of a comon called Orgraue moore,
where Sir William Wentworthe is immediate cheife lord and the Earle
but onlie a freholder and paies cheife rent viii$^s$ per annum to Sir
William Wentworthe for his freholde landes in Orgraue. Sir William
coming to the workmen at the pale wold not dischardge them, but
ment onelie to take some small rent of my lord for the same and a
wrytyng endented for posteritie. Sir William Wentworthe attending
his lordship dyuers times at last by my lord's appointment shewed to
Mr Fletcher, being of my lord's learned counsell, parte of his
euidence, vizt. a verie ancient charter and dyuers ancient rentalls
and court roolles together with Mr Sargeant Hutton and Mr Carvill's
opinions under their hands tuchinge his right and Mr Fletcher was
suffred to take notes of thos euidences. And Sir William Wentworthe,
being often promised an ansur and yett delayed more than a yeare,
my lord's officers neuer being willinge to showe anie euidences to the
said Sir William Wentworthe nor his learned counsell, at last willed
that Sir William Wentworthe wold showe his euidences to Mr
Fletcher the second time. Whereupon Sir William Wentworthe,
not hoping of any indefferent dealing did serve proces onlie of two of
my Lorde's people for tryall of the trespas, meaninge notwithstandinge to moue my Lord that anie indeferent men might order the
matter, or els that a freindlie tryall might be had without delayes.
For Sir William Wentworth hath bene redy for eightene yeres together before this tyme to doo my Lord anie service he could and
suffred my Lords people to comaund his grounds &c.

And after suite comensed Sir William Wentworthe procured Mr
Rookeby, a Justice of peace and *quorum*, in his name humblie to
desire my Lord to put the matter to order &c which motion was not
accepted; my Lord affirming that the said Sir William Wentworthe
had done him wronge and that he had proces to serue upon two of
Sir William Wentworthe's men and in truth he had proces for them
pretending that they had infrindged his libertie of Hallamshire which
is no libertye, neither came Sir William Wentworthe's men within
Hallamshire to serue anie proces.

And further after the verdict obtayned Sir William Wentworth
willed my Lorde's officers to signifie his desire that his lordshipp
would be pleased to lett one lawyer and a gentleman on either syde
determyn the matter &c. But Sir William cold haue none answer.

And lastlie in Michaelmas term $A^o$ *dni* 1610 Sir William procured
a gentleman at London to make the same offer to his lordshipp, but

his lordshipp then affirmed that Sir William Wentworthe had with great labor gotten a verdict and said he wold watche an opportunitye to haue a new tryall &c and so kepeth the ground still inclosed.

*Item* the said Sir William having purchased lands lying within the Earl's, for about 1100[li] did at the Earle's request sell the same to him for no more money than he paid, the last paiment whereof, being 300[li] or thereabouts, the said Sir William wanted about 3 years after it was due untill his Maiestie was redie to come from Scotland to take his Croune here, besydes diuers other expenses and paines which he hath taken at his lordship's request as the said Sir William can prove.

### The xxvi August 1612

This day came into the hall at Wentworthe Woodhus Mr Lee, the Balife of Sheffeild and fowre others of my Lord of Shrewsbury's men with him, weaponed with swords and daggars. The Balife affirmed to Sir William Wentworthe that he had a messaige to deliuer unto him from my lord, wherupon Sir William desired him to walke with him alone into the court before the hall doore and he wold receive the messaige, desyringe the rest to stay in the hall; but they, following with their weapons by their sydes, came verye nere unto Sir William in the said court, Sir William hauinge nether sword nor daggar about him. Whereupon Sir William walked owte of the court gates, willing Mr Lee onlie to come to him, but the rest wold nedes still followe after. Then Mr Lee did reed to Sir William a longe wrytinge, written as he said with my lord's owne hand, wherein my Lord by dyuers reportes seminge to beleue that Sir William had killed great numbers of my lordes deare in the groundes of the said Sir William and some in my lord's grounds and killed some of his houndes &c. Whereupon he affirmed he wold right himselfe and be his neighbour, whereunto Sir William answered Mr Lee yf that he wold eyther giue him that wrytinge or a true copie of yt, he hoped he should geue my lord in euerie particuler an answer to his better satisfacon. Mr Lee refusinge, Sir William answered thus farre, that these reportes and informacons were untrue and made by some ungracious persons to bread contensyon and that therefore he hoped my lord in his wisdom wold not beleue them. And then one of there companie affirmed that my lord wished the sooner the better that a new tryall might be had, touching the ground inclosed into my lord's park at Orgraue and willed Sir William if he wold to send the next day to pull downe the paile; who answered that he wold doo that which shold be thought fytt by him selfe and his learned counsell when he shold see his best tyme.

The wytnesses hereunto subscribed are privie unto and hard and see all thes things in this last note expressed bearing date 26 Augusti 1612, sauing to the reding of my lord's note and the contentes thereof, which was red privately by the balife to Sir William Wentworth, and the demand of a copie thereof and then he wold geue an answer thereto.

Tho. Wentworth   Nich. Dey   Thomas   Fletcher   + Th. Ashton's mark + Roger Goodison's marke.

# III. SIR WILLIAM WENTWORTH'S OTHER PAPERS

**8.** *Thomas Lord Burghley to Sir William Wentworth* (*SC*, xx/188).

After my verie hartie commendacons, whereas it hath pleased her Maiestie to constitute you high sherife for the Countye of Yorke and that the Clarkship of the Attachmentts in that Cowrte wherof I am President hath bin usuallie conferred upon some such person as the Lord President should recommend to that place; I, not dowbtinge but you will use the same manner of gratificacon toward mee as my predecessors haue receiued and myself obtained from such as haue bin Sheriffes before you, do hartelie praye you to bestowe that office upon my seruant Peter Chapman, whom I haue thought good to name unto you for the execucon of the same under you which I shall both take as an argument of your loue and good affeccon to mee and wilbe readie to requite it as occasion shalbe offered. And so I committ you to God's safe proteccon fom Newarke this 27th of Nouember 1601 your very louyng frend, Tho: Burghley. To my verie lovinge freind Willm Wentworth esquire, high Sheriffe for the countie of Yorke.

**9.** *Lord Sheffield, Lord President of the Council of the North, to Sir William Wentworth* (*SC*, xx/189).

After my hartie comendacons, whereas the king's maiestie is pleased to hold a parliament shortlie as by the letters from the Lords of his highnes counsell is signified unto me, I (being supreame magistrate under his highnes in these partes) have thought it my part to admonish yow that in the eleccon of the knightes of this shire yow have that dutifull regard which apparteyneth to the obedience of his maiesties proclamacon; that is not to elect anie such person as is in religioun either busyheaded or popishly affected. And therefore consideringe that two gentlemen of speciall note and worth, namely Francis Clifford esquire and Sir John Savile of Howley, knight, both persons against whome no exceptions can be made, neither are themselves there wives or frends, anie way affected to popery or heady courses in religion, have moved me for my favor and good allowance of them to stand for knightes of the Shire at this next eleccon. I do earnestlie desire yow that (all particuler respects sett asyde) yow will give your voyces of your selves and your tenants and such other frends as yow can procure with these two gentlemen onelie and to take paines to be with them at the day of the elecconn; which I do expect and desire at your handes that thereby yow may show your dutifull regard to his highnes comaund, as also that I may haue iust good occasion to thinke my selfe beholden to yow, the which in anie thinge within my power I will be ready to requite. Hereof I pray yow send me your present aunswere in writing under your hand to thend that if yow satisfie my request herein, I maie make it knowne unto his maiestie your tractable disposiconn unto his maiestie's comaundment, but if otherwise, yet that my self may be cleared of any neglecte of dutie in my place and so I bid yow hartelie farewell. At Yorke the xixth of February 1603[/4]. Your very loving frend, H. Sheffield.[1] To my verye lovinge frend Willm Wentworth esqr at Wentworth Woodhouse.

**10.** *William Lord Cavendish to Sir William Wentworth* (*SC*, xx/190).

Sir, I thank you for signifying your knowledg of Mr John Newby of Wakefeld and Mr Kay of London, jentelmen that I haue not herd of before now. That litle mony I haue hertofor retorned by Wakefeld men, I had always iiii or more of the best of them bownd for payment of yt; which course I am desirus still to hold, when I shall haue any such like occasion of payments in London. And so yf yt please Mr Nuby to ioyne with his neyghbours I am very desirus he shold haue part with them, but I know not of a present occasion. And so with my best wyshes to you I cease and will euer rest, your assured louing frend, W. Cauendyshe. From Hardwyck 20th May 1608. To my honorable good frend Mr Wm Wentworth at Wentworth Woodhowse.

**11.** *Wentworth to his father* (*SC*, xxi/1).

After my humble duty remembred, desireing your blessinge &c. Sir, I intend (God willing) to set forward on my iorney to-morrow, all

---

[1] Lambeth Palace Library, MS. 708, fo. 131; Robert Somerscales, John Bouth, Edward Morehouse to Gilbert, earl of Shrewsbury, from York, 12 March 1603/4. According to the earl's letters, '. . . we have laboured so many free-holders as possibly we could in our shorte warninge procure to geve their first voyces to Mr Clifforde' and their second voices according to the lord president's further nomination. The vice-president told them this was Sir John Savile and they were present at 'his conference with the counsell touchyng the eleccon before his going to the castell'. He was 'well contented' that Clifford should be first 'howsoeuer the freholders should be affected towards him and the number of his [Savile's] syde being much the greater . . . and upon the eleccon, beyng caryed upon the freholders' shoulders cryed himselfe "A Clifforde" . . .'

thinges being now in readines. I haue taken leaue of my Lord Treasurer, humbly thankinge his lordship &c. His Honor used me with very good respect and asking the reason why my name was Thomas and I telling his lordship the cause thearof, then, replied my Lord, your sone's name when God sends him shall be William and his Godfather must be William Cranborne. His lordship writt to my Lord Embassador in my behalfe and in like manner to my lord Clifford. I was allsoe this morninge to doe my duty to my lord of Northampton, who used me with much curtesy, saying that he would doe me any fauor he could and that the Wentworths of his lordship's knowledge wear gentlemen very anciently and honorably descended and protested he must needs loue me because he must loue my name and was right glade I had mached into such an honorable howse. All which he spoke very frankely and after a very curteous manner, so that I thinke itt not amiss and (still referring itt to your riper iudgement) if att your next cumming to London, you goe to see his Lordship. Mr Tailor was very forward in the dispaching of all my affaires and deserueth great thankes thearfore and thus, Sir, with my bownded thankes for your fatherly care and great loue, with my harty prayers for yo<sup>r</sup> long life and happines, humbly taking leaue, I rest, Yo<sup>r</sup> most louing and obedient sone, Th. Wentworth. London this x of December 1611. To the Right wor[ll] my approued louing father Sir William Wentworth, Barronett, thes I pray you deliver.

**12.** *Sir Peter Freschevile to Sir William Wentworth 8 January 1611/2 (Knowler, i, p. 1; SC, xx/191), about the education of Sir William's younger sons, William and John.*

**13.** *Wentworth's letters to his father from France, 1612–3 (SC, xxi/ 2–4).*

(*a*) After my humble duty remembred desiring yo<sup>r</sup> blessing, Sir, hauing this whished opportunity, I did iudge itt my duty to tender my humble obedience and loue being (God be praised) past 48 dayes iurney in parfaite health with all my company from thenc forward to day to Nimes and when I shall enconter the like occasion you shall by God's grace further understande our proceedings. In the interim euer praying for your long life with the health of you and yours, I humbly take my leaue and in haste rests, Your most louing and obedient son Tho. Wentworth. Montpeiller this 15 of September 1612. To the right worshipfull my good and louing father Sir William Wentworth Barronnet, giue thes.

(*b*) After my humble duty remembred, desiring your blessing, Sir,

by reason of the indisposition of my body one way weared with
a long iorney and the approche of winter an other way, which by
reason of cold and stormes would haue made the passage down the
Reine both trublesome and dangerouse, itt was thought fitting to
altere that our purpose. Whearfore att Lions we iudged itt the most
conuenientt to turne downe the riuer of Loire to Orleans, whear
I am safly arriued, God's name be prased. To haue gone thourow
Burgundy and so directly to Paris, besids a long and ill way, we
should haue arriued ther before the end of Nouember and by that
means haue been unprouided of money. We haue now thearfore
thus disposed of ourselfs to stay hear till the end of December by
this means to auoid debte, whear as if we should goe directly to
Paris before Cristmas, itt requiring thrice as great a charge, besids
newyears gifts, we should of necessity be driuen upon the sands;
neither shall I much hinder my exercises, for by God's goodnes I shall
learne a nufe to serue my occasions. Thus, Sir, planly doe I set you
doune my reasons, that thearin I may either haue your approbation,
or direction to some other course which by God's grace I will euer
dutifully obey; and thus euer praying for the long life with the increase
of all happines to you and yours, I humbly take my leaue and rest,
your most louing and obedient son Th. Wentworth. Orleans, this 5 of
Nouember *st. no.* 1612. To the Right worshipfull my approued good
and louing father Sir William Wentworth Barronet giue thes.

(c) After my humble duty remembred, desiring your fatherly bene-
diction for my Newyear's gift, that hauing obtained (that which I
thanke God you neuer yeat denied me) your fatherly blessing I may
striue this year following and all the rest of my life to deserue this
fauor with the rest of your infinit cares and benefits. Sir, hauing
receaued your letter (as I doubt not but you haue myn) dated the
20 of October last and thearin perceauing your advise, I haue resolued to change in some part our first determined course, mentioned in my letter which is, that about a weake hence I will by
God's grace goe to Paris, whear I stay 3 or 4 weakes, from thence
passe thourowe the Lowe Cuntrys, spending thear 2 mounths and soe
home, which by God's grace will be by the ending of Aprill next. Sir,
I am very sory for your siknes, but doe thanke God for that itt hath
pleased him of his great goodnes to restore you to your wonted
health which I desire may euer be continued. From all your ennemys
I doubt not but the same God which hetherto hath defended us
will still be our asseured and stronge protector. For S[ir] G[?eorge]
S[?avile] I doubt he is to neare ambitious S[ir] I[?ohn] who will not
faile to take all advantages, if the former be not very well auised;

the great belly I thinke will bringe us a Hercules that France may haue noe aduantage ouer England, bragging soe much of his Hercules Gallicus. Thus Sir, praying for the watched effects of all your undertakings with the health and longe life of you and yours, I humbly take my leaue, allwayes remaining, Your most obedient and louing son, Th. Wentworth. Orleans this i of January *st. no.* 1613. To the right worshipfull my approued good and louing father Sir William Wentworth Barronett giue thes.

**14.** *John Atkinson to Sir William Wentworth* (*SC*, xx/193).

Good Sir, mie best loue and seruice remembred unto you. I was latelie at Sir Francis Stonors,[1] whear I was moued first by him to ioyne in a letter with my brother to you that you wold declare that clause by which my brother is to forfeyt his estate, if hee not obserue it, to bee but a matter in trust pretending (bicause thay knewe thay had giuen cause to mee to thinke all motions that came from them to bee but cunning practises upon mee) that it was meerlie in this reguard, that it first beeing in my sister, your wife, shee diiing, it comes to you and you diinge it might come to an executor and he might deale as pleased him. Nowe if likewise my brother Bouuerie shold die, I wear in like danger, upon which ground they thought thayer request wold seeme reasonable. I since haue understood that my brother hath made ouer all his estate, as well lands as goods, to Sir Francis Stonor in what kind or with what limitation I knowe not, nor I thinke my brother himself well; so soone as I can learne, you shall bee made acquaynted. This made mee s[t]ir, when next the knight moued the first busines to mee, to stop his mouth with a request like his; which was that if hee wold declare those writings which my brother had signed to him to bee but matters in trust that then I wold ioyne in a letter with my brother to the end hee desiered. At this hee stormed exceedinglie and wondered that I wold seeme to meddle in matters betwixt a man and his wife and how it could concearne mee or anie that a man gaue this or that to his wife and then the worthines of his daughter that was had up and urged and followed with this and that fiddle faddle circumstonce as prouocations for mee to lay up my stomake at. But I gaue waye and consented with him in eauerie thing in outeward apparance, saueing to the first busines gaynst which I was irrecouerablie bent. Since which, as I feere, thay haue decreed to send my brother in embassie to you about thayer state affayres and to treate with you aboute this trust. All which circumstances make mee thinke that thear is some thing in the

---

[1] See Table II above, p. x.

conuayances my brother hath made ouer to Sir Francis preiudiced by
the conuayance made bi my father which is all the cause wherefore
thay are thus hot. But if my brother doe come aboute it, I knowe I
neede not tell you what to say to him. In the meane time I beseech
you soe to dischardge the trust my dead father put in my sister and
your self[1] that both his children and his children's children may haue
cause to prayse his wisdome and your honestie and soe my hartiest
loue remembred both to your self and all yours, I rest your loueing
brother, John Atkinson. To the right worshipfull mie verie loueing
brother Sir Wm. Wentworth kt barronet at his house called Woodhouse nere Rotherham giue these. (*endorsed*) Jo. Atk 1612.

**15.** *Earl of Cumberland to Sir William Wentworth (SC, xx/195).*

Good Brother Wentworth, these your often and kynde remembrances doe make us more and more indebted unto yow, beinge
such as are accompted verie rare and daintie in these parts. We must
still be thankfull for the same, not having here anie thinge estimable
or of worth to send unto yow. For your busines with Sir John
Crompton I perswade my self, if yow deale therein, yow wilbe well
aduysed and assured that his securitee be sufficient; I should be verie
glad (upon good condicons) to haue it concluded. My sonne Harrie
came downe hither with his Lady about x daies agoe, verie well, and
he purposeth (God willinge) about some busines of importance to
sett forward towards London againe uppon Tewsday or Wednesday
next. My wyfe and I doe greatly desyre to see yow here, if your health
and occasions will permitt yow; both which are and must be sufficient excuses, but howsoeuer none should be to us nor yow to none
more welcome. Your daughter Margarett will wryte unto yow soe
that I leave to her owne letter to answere what yow writt concerninge
her. And soe with my owne and my wyfe's hartiest comendacons
ever to your self whome we much esteeme, I leaue yow to God's
proteccon and rest, Your ever assured loving frend and brother,
Fr. Cumberland. Londsbrough this first of November 1612. To my
verie loving Brother Sir Wm. Wentworth Baronett.

**16.** *Cumberland to Sir William Wentworth (SC, xx/194).*

Good Brother Wentworth, your letters be ever exceedinge wellcome
to us, for we doe much desyre to heare often from yow how yow doe.

---

[1] Lambeth Palace Library, MS. 708, fo. 63, William Wentworth to Gilbert,
earl of Shrewsbury, 12 October 1607, 'I was sentt for in all haste into Glocestre-
shire by the sones of my father in lawe upon his death who trusted me with the
disposing of all he had . . .'

If yow lyk the condicons that Sir John Crompton will yeeld yow, then shall yow have noe cause to give over or break the Bargaine for anie feare or want of my monie, which, God willing, shalbe readie at my daie (if your payments then soe requyer) or at anie tyme after, how shortly soeuer it be, that forth with your owne payments and occasions, soe that, God willinge, I meane it shalbe readie to serve your turne withall without faile.

We doe all nowe desyre lykwyse to see your sonne and myne safely retourned. I shall hope he may be at London at the mariage which wilbe on Shrove Sondaie. I received letters verie lately by pacquett from my Lord Chamberlen, the copie whereof I send yow here-inclosed; he wrytes that my Lord of Dorsett expecteth my comminge and my sonne Cliffords alsoe at the begininge of the Terme to end all differencs between theim and me and that either of us should appoynt a knight that is noe lawyer to arbitrate for us; and that there is alsoe a maske apoynted to be at the mariage: viii noblemen and viii ladies, of which number my sonne is first of the 4 barons. I am hartily sorie, chiefly for your owne sake and secondly for myne that yow are not presently able to travell. For I protest were yow but able, without danger to your health to travaile to London this terme, I would before all the frends I have (as nowe wee stand) onely make choyce and relye upon your Iudgment to be the knight that should treate and mediate for me to ioyne with whomsoeuer they should apoynte, I should excepte none. Althoe it is the waightiest cause that ever I can haue in hand. I could perhaps (sith it seemes yow are not able to ryde) fynde out some other frends fitt to match with them, but none in whome I durst soe well conferr the weight of my whole estate as upon your self. My wyfe, my self, my sonne and daughters doe all respectively remember our loves unto yow and your daughter her dewtie and soe I leaue yow as myself to God's blessed proteccon and rest, Your euer assured lovinge Frend and Brother, Fr. Cumberland. Londesbrough this 13th of January 1612[/3]. To my verie loving Brother Sir Wm. Wentworth Baronett.

**17.** *Wentworth to Sir William Wentworth* (*SC*, xxi/6).

After my humble duty remembered desiring your blessing. Sir, as soone as I was cume to Yorke, I inquired out Doctor Deane[1] his loging and finding him within tolde him the cause of my cumming, desiring him that I might be beholden to him to take the paines

---

[1] This is presumably Edmund Dean, M.D., of Oxford, 1572–1640; J. H. Raach, *A Directory of English Country Physicians 1603–1643* (London, 1962), p. 120.

to goe and see you; which after some deniall, he att last consented
unto, which was as I did imagin to make the bargen better and soe
gett more money, soe that I thinke he will looke for 3$^{li}$, allbeitt he
can but stay with you one night and for any longer stay I could not
get him to assent unto. I receaued Th. Wilton's letter and hauing
conferred with the Doctor before, he was of the same opinion that
you are now of, which was that thear was noe stone, but only an
excoriation by reason of the sharpe medecins you had taken. I sent
the letter unto him that he might furnishe himself accordingly; you
may, Sir, bespeake for him after the assises if you soe please which I
iudge not amisse to haue him, allbeitt (as I esteeme) that naither his
learning, nor scill is great, you must, Sir, if please you beare with
him, for he is not infinitely wise. Thus praying from my harte that itt
would please God of his goodnes to restore you your accustumed
health with a longe and comfortable life, I humbly take leaue and
rest, your most louing and obedient sonne, Th. Wentworth. Yorke
this 22 of March as I take itt 1612[13].

**18.** *Sir William Wentworth's instructions for his younger children's
education (SC, xxi/8).*

Sir Thomas desires to know what course of life his father would haue
euerie of his brethren trained upp in.

First for Mr William to continewe his studye at law and Sir
Thomas to see that he wante not maintenaunce, but yf he be warde
and so loose the profitts of his lands for three yeares, then to make
up his other 40$^{li}$ for the first yeare 80$^{li}$, the second yeare 90$^{li}$ and
the thirde yeare 100$^{li}$ and yf further he need 10$^{li}$, to furnish him
therof.

Mr John after convenient tyme at Cambridge to be remoued to
London and yf he lyke to contynew his study in the law, he may.
Otherwyse he may lyve in the contry and be your frend and companion. When he marrieth, place him, yf he desire it on some of your
housses neer yow. Loue him both for his own worth and because he
beareth the imaige of your father that so much loued yow and let
him haue the same allowance that is before mentioned for Mr
William. [*Margin*] Yf he haue a desyre to trauaile and can find good
companie, he may spend some tyme therin.

Mr Robert to be brought up at Cambridge and so to the Inns of
courte; yf his disposition serve for a lawyeare, he may followe it,
yf not, then to take such other profession as he more affecteth and is
by yow allowed.

Mr Michael to be kept at school tyll 15 yeares that he may under-

stand lattin and wryt well, then one year to learne to do those things
that belong to a marchant's profession, then bound prentis and in the
meane tyme he to haue a plentifull maintenance during his mynorety.[1]

Mr Mathew ⎫
Mr Phillipp ⎬ for these 3 gentlemen to be brought up at Schoule,
Mr George ⎭
Cambridge and Inns of Courte and then to take such profession
upon them as yow shall aduise them, considering their naturall
desposition and their owne desire.[2]

Mtris Margaret ⎫ for the gentlewomen it is thoughte most fitt that
Mrs Elizabeth  ⎭
they shall lyue and be brought up with you and your ladye till they
marye.

My sister Elizabeth remoued when a sutor offers himself to my
sister Margaret.[3]

Wm. Wentworth   Aprill 1613.

**19.** *Wentworth to his father (SC, xxi/9).*

After my humble duty remembred, desiring your blessing &c, Sir,
I haue receaued two letteres from you for which I giue you humble
thankes. This likewise is the fourth that I now write. For Sir Jhon
Jackson, I myself with Mr Caruell was att his chamber; wee said
being in possession reason required that we should be first satesfied
and thearfore insisted upon tow points; first that he should shew that
Staniforth held of his mannor by knight seruice; secondly that soe
holding he held of his said mannor by priority. To the first he said
that he had att this time wards which held of his mannor of Boulton
by knight seruice, as also he had court roles to shew &c. To the
second he could not directly answeare more then from the reports of
his neighbours, and that, that was to be decided by Staniforth his
owne euidence. Soe wee found him in that as ignorant as oure selfes,
finally then with passages of good respect &c itt was agreed that
matters should rest till Cristmas, att which time Staniforth euidence
to be perused by your counsell and himself and soe with all kinde
frendshipe and respect sett a periode to this busines.

---

[1] He does not seem to have followed this career; in 1623 he was gaining military experience abroad; Knowler, i, p. 18.
[2] In the event they all went to University College, Oxford. For further information about the provision for Sir William's younger children, see *Econ. History
Review*, new series, xi (1958), pp. 228–29; and below pp. 129, 161, 171, 234–36.
[3] This was inserted in a different hand, probably that of Sir Thomas Wentworth.

WP—E

Now, Sir, he doth sufficiently proue that he holds of him in knight seruice, if he proue that he hold of his manner of Boulton which he holds offer of the king as a foresaide. For it is to be presupposed that he hath the same tenure and holds them of his lord in the like manner, as he holds of the lord paramonte, shewing noe deed to the contrary. Alsoe if Staniforth hold of his mannore by priority, then he is to haue the wardship of his body, excepte the father did by deed indented pase the hole estate to the son and to his heires males and for wante of such heires of him the said son, then to the right heires of him the son. For in this case the son cumming to itt as by purchase the wardship of the body belongs to the first occupant. But if itt be conueyed as abouesaid with the remaindure for want of heires of the son, to the right heires of the father soe that the father passe not away intirly from himself the fee simple, then the son cumming to it by discent and not by purchase, priority carieth itt. Seing then, Sir, that all relies upon the shewing of his euidence, I thinke itt not amisse (if itt soe please you) that Mr Caruell att his being in the cuntry showld first alone haue the perusall of the writings &c.

For my brother Jhons letter I did indeed help him to indite itt thearby to shewe him howe to doe an other time, rather then otherwise, for in truth I then saide you had (if I may be soe bold) a good nose and would soon find itt was none of his owne.

My lord of Rochester was yesterday created Baron of Raby and Earle of Summersett. He hath likewise as is said bought of the kinge Raby castell, Barney castell and other things anciently the Earls of Westmerlands rated to 1000[11] rent of assise, paying to the king 36,000[11]. Itt is credebly reported my lord Cooke to be made owne of the priuy counsell. My lord of Cumberlands cause was cald this day and the jury was likewise summoned, whearof only 3 made thear appearance. Then was itt motioned by my lord of Dorset's counsell that since the cause was of such weight and that itt would be hard to gett a Yorkshire iury appeare, that itt would please the court that a tales should be returned of such as liued about London, yeat had freehold in Yorkshire; which being denied them, for want of appearance of the iury, the cause was dismist till Easter terme. In the interim the sherif was to returne a iury of Yorkshire gentlemen, till which time the matter rests in the same termes itt did before, but the lawers on both sides well feed &c. Thus Sir, reioycing to hear of your good amendment, with my prayers for your perfect recouery, with the happnes of you and yours, I humbly take leaue to stile my self, your most louing and obedient son, Th. Wentworth. London this 6 of Nouemb: 1613.

Sir, my brother William hath his humble duty remembred with desire of your blessing and defers his writing att this instant by reason of my cumming downe into the cuntry, which by God's grace will now be shortly.

**20.** *William Wentworth to his father* (*SC*, xx/199).

Sir, after my humble duety wyth the desyre of your most herty prayers and continual blessings &c. May it please you I haue receiued your 2 letters, the one dated 23 of Nouember the other the 29; there was a third which was *verbatim* wyth that bearinge date the 23. I haue taken order by Mr Kay to haue it payed at Cambridge by a customer of Mr Kay['s] acquaintance dwelling at Cambridg, the rest of the money which is due to mee I expect at the day praefixed; for the letter bearinge date the 29 of Nouember, I shall accordingly proceed in the desyringe of Mr Threasorer his advice touchinge the chamber. I haue in my letter to my brother John willed him to sett downe with himselfe somme sett time for his comminge to London. The marriadge of my lord of Sommerset wyth the Lady Frances Howard, as it is thought, will be quickly. It was motion'd to the Innes of Court to praesent a maske at this mariadge, but it was deny'd. There is nothinge else that I cann set downe before your eyes no more then the desyre of your blessinge and my duety which induceth mee to pray for your speedy recouery and in my words and actions to declare my selfe Your dutifull and most louinge sonne, W. Wentworth. Lon[don]: Decem[ber, 1613][1]

**21.** *William Wentworth to Sir William Wentworth* (*SC*, xx/200).

Sir, after my most humble duety wyth the desyre of your blessinge &c. May it please you, I heard Sir Stephen Procter's[2] case which lasted 3 dayes. I will briefly set downe the substance of the depositions

---

[1] The marriage took place on 26 December. This letter presumably belongs to early December.

[2] The fullest account of Proctor's career is in *Memorials of the Abbey of St. Mary of Fountains*, ed. J. R. Walran, ii, pt. i (Surtees Society, lxvii (1878)), pp. 345–54. Further details of his feuds with his recusant neighbours, including Sir William Ingleby of Ripley and Sir John Mallory of Studley, are given in J. T. Cliffe, *The Yorkshire Gentry* (London, 1969), pp. 136, 209, 275–76. C. Roberts, *The Growth of Responsible Government in Stuart England* (Cambridge, 1966), pp. 11–14, gives a full account of the parliamentary proceedings against him in 1610 for abuse of his patent as Collector and Receiver of fines on penal statutes which led to his exclusion from the general pardon. The bill for his punishment is printed in *Proceedings in Parliament 1610*, ed. E. R. Foster (New Haven, 1966), ii, pp. 412–14.

both for him and against him (as I heard them) which is no other then the relacion of the matter. Mr Birkin, seruant to Sir Timothy Whittingham, comminge to Wentbrigge met at his inn wyth Boulin, one of the king's scullery, one that was euery way unknowne to him, where hee heard of him that hee was called into my lorde Wotton lodginge, there beeinge present my lorde Wotton, my lady and Sir W. Ingleby, whoe willed him not to speake any thinge at all against Sir W. Ingleby touchinge the gunpowder treason for that hee was their friend (and in somme examinations Boulin sayde absolutely and in somme noe) that there was one in blacke, whome hee tooke to bee my lorde of Northampton, whoe sayde the like and offered him an horse; yet had hee no horse of him, but of my lorde Wotton hee had one; in others he sayde that Birkin did aske him if it were not my lorde of Northampton, addinge it coulde bee no other, but the truth of this could not appeare. Birkin comminge to Yorcke acquainted Sir Henry Tancred wyth it in generall tearmes, whoe desyres him to comme to him after dinner, when heehad ioyned Sir George Chaworth wyth him. Hee casually at Yorcke mett wyth Sir Stephen Procter wyth whome hee dined and told this matter to him. After dinner Sir Stephen did accompanie him to these 2 counsellors and told them that Birkin was an honest man and that they might belieue him. Then Birkin told it in the manner, as I haue before related, and accused Boulin whoe was apprehended (as Boulin seyde hee herde by one whome he remembered not) by the helpe of Sir Stephen whoe pointed the officer to him. Boulin confessed the substance of that which hee was accused; Sir Stephen beinge at Fontaines called to him old Robert Boulin and enquired of him what sonns hee had. The olde man sayde he had 2, one dwelled in London, the other liued in the countrey, then sayde Sir Stephen hee that dwelled in London for him for hee knew much and yonge Boulin before he was examined desyred often to speake with Sir Stephen Procter in priuatt which could not bee granted.

One time Sir Stephen, beeinge at Westminster in one Mr Stucklys howse, sayde that were it not for my lorde of Northampton the gunpowder treason would comme owt more freely. One Handford brought a letter from my lorde Burley wherein it was shewed that Handford had heard some wordes spoken against my lord's honor, before this letter was deliuered, came to Floyd and brought to him a certaine note wherein were specified the speeches used by Sir Stephen to which hee would haue him depose. This note he brought to him (as hee sayde to helpe his memory); this Floyde, beeinge brought before my lorde of Northampton, did stifly denie it at the first, but when Handford did affront him after somme difficulty, by reason Sir

Stephen owed him 60[1] besydes the interest, hee did freely confesse wythowt any feare of any thretninges and menaces, as my Lorde of Northampton, my lorde W[illiam] Howard and Mr Griffin did depose. After all this this Floyde fell sicke and in his greatest extremity did uppon the sacrament disavow whatsoeuer hee had formerly sworne, as drawne from him by the wicked practizes of Handford and by threateninge to make him a party wyth Sir Stephen in the bill and thatt Sir Stephen was undone by this meanes and that hee was guillesse for any thinge hee knew; to this 2 or 3 deposed. Sir Stephen's counsel sayde that these were nothing but the suggestions of his enemyes who labored to make him infamous, because hee had done many seruices against the gunpowder treason, recitinge wythall what priestes hee had attached.

Boulin had no counsel. Birkin's counsel desyred the matter might bee deferred because they might haue time to bringe in their proofes; for Mr Attorney had moued such matters as they were neuer informed of, which was granted. Mr Attorney told them that their proofes would bee like reedes whereof some doe bend and double under the hand of him that thinketh to uphold himselfe by it, the other scratceth and woundeth the hand; the application is plaine. The next day the defendants' counsel came to answeare; first Birkin's counsel laboured to proue Berkin not soe greate an offendor as Boulin (for it was yeilded that these scandalls were untrue so that none indeuored to maintaine them) for, sayde they, if Boulin hath contraried him selfe and Birkin hath euer constantly deposed the same thinges in effect, though hee hath beene examined very often; therefore sayde they Birkin is the rayther to bee beeleeued and soe Boulin is no sufficient accuser of Birkin; an other reason, Boulin when seekinge to gett owt of prison, breake his legge, sayde the diuel was in him, whoe is the author of lies, whoe then will credit Boulin, when the diuell in a manner speakes in him; the relatinge of it to Sir Stephen was but to aske counsell.

Mr Attorney did the first day blaze Sir Stephen sayinge that hee had told the kinge that hee was in danger of his life and named one that should conspire against him, which after was proued to be deuised of him owt of malice, besides hee shewed how hee was excepted owt of the general pardon and added for a farewell that hee was the most seditious and aspiringe witt in the kingdome. To these Mr Hodgson answered that if hee were of such a witt, it was not likely that hee would associatt wyth him a boy and such an one as a wiseman would not admitt into his family, much lesse into his secretts. For the former hee sayde the kinge was satisfied and somme of the honorable Lordes there present knew it. His maiesty willing to doe right to euery one did except him owt of his gracious generall pardon,

because his enemys then accusinge of him might haue liberty to produce their proofes, of all which imputations hee hath acquitted him
selfe. The 3 day the king's sollicitor Mr Yeluerton thought to haue
prooued Floyde's sicknesse counterfeite, but not beeinge able by the
reason of the weake praesumptions which were for him.

So the court gaue their censure. Sir Julius Caesar spoake first that
many praesumptions combined together were in the ciuill law a most
stronge proofe, so that in this case all the praesumptions couched
together were able to perswade him as a priuate man that Sir
Stephen was guilty, but not as hee was a iudge. Boulin was fined
2000[l] and imprisonment during the king's pleasure and that hee
should stand uppon the pillory at Wes(t)minster and Yorcke and
there to be whipped; Birkin as much saue onely hee should not be
whipped, because hee was a man of some fashion. Baron Autum
[Altham] did concurr, but as for Sir Stephen hee fined 3000[l] as
guilty of the conspiracyes uppon those praesumptions before sett
downe by mee in the beginning; hee desyred that hee might confesse
his fault at Yorcke. So the chiefe baron and the chiefe justice, but
that they did not speake of the last clawse. My lord chiefe justice of
England sayde that a scandal against a peare was a scandal to the
king for that they were by him made his fellows and partners in
gouernment and thereuppon they are called *comites. Pares* were
onely them of the upper house of Parliament, as earles and barons,
all under this degree were of the lower whoe onely in respect of [one]
an other are *pares*, but now by the common speech called commons
and those of the upper were only called *pares* or peeres. For my
lorde of Northampton hee could witnesse that, beeinge put in
commission for the discouery of gunpowder treason, there was none
more diligent then hee; hee meruayled that this gunpowder treason
had not conuerted more papists then hee hath, seeinge that the like
harme intended to them as to us. The reason which moued him was
this; in the invasion of 88 there were 2 of Irish byshoppes admitted
into the king of Spaine's counsell whoe persuaded to prouide for
horses and such necesaries and not to rely uppon the English
catholuques; for the policy of Englande is such that praesently
uppon the bruite of an invasion off goe their heades. A mad fellow
standing by fell a laughing, sayinge '*Hoc facit pro nobis*, God shall
haue theire soules, the earth their bodyes and wee their goods'. So
wyth them all is fish that comes to the net. Boulin was fined as before,
as for Birkin's relating to Sir Stephen, it was a greate offence. For
now hauinge declared it to an other hee was now no more maister
of it, whereuppon might haue sprunge a double inconvenience if Sir
Stephen had spoken of it, first a murmuringe amongst the weaker

sort, secondly a warninge to the authors to impeach the remedy which the counsell might haue applied (for after hee had accused Boulin to the counsel hee spoake of it afterwards). As for Hand-ford['s] note hee brought to Floyd it was not good, because a wit-nesse ought to depose of himselfe and that onely which is in his mind at the time of his examination hee did concurr. For the fine of Sir Stephen hee did concurr and added that hee showld bee put owt of all commissions of peace or for any manner of gouernment in his country, because hee would haue the law followed by none but by good men. My lordes the Judges al agreed that all these praesump-tions layde togeither did prooue Sir Stephen guilty, though no one by itselfe was able, it beeinge impossible that so many could concur in one that was guiltlesse. My lorde byshoppe of London did concurr in all, saue onely Sir Stephen who was a man unknown to him, yet hee could not see how hee should bee guilty in the conspiracy when his consent by writing, speech, or any other meanes, much lesse his procuringe of them could appeare; as for his scandalous wordes against my lord they could not appear, hee deninge of them hauinge but Handforde against him, seeing that Floyde upon the sacrament doth recantt his former depositions. Then spake my lorde of Northampton 'I will satisfie for a thinge done of late', which was the retayninge of Tichborne for his attorney in this suite, beeinge a con-vict papist, some thereby reportinge that my lorde ment to haue shrowdid from the punishment that the law doth prouide against such. To which my lorde sayde that hee knew him not to bee of that re-ligion, but onely hee retayned [him] because hee was commended to him by seriant Hutton and others for a painefull [m]an diligent in his office, but if hee had knowne of his religion yet had the retayninge of him beene no harme. For my lorde Burly, lord Threasorer, did retaine Mr Plowden as one of his counsell, though hee and euery one knew him to bee a papist, hee retayned him as a lawer and not as a profes-sor of any religion, and at last hee sayde that if it were donne otherwise then hee had spoken, hee was guilty in all the scandalles.

My lorde Archbyshoppe sayde that uppon complainte, search beeinge made in his howse, there were found many forbidden bookes, namely one which did defend the gunpowder treason which called the traitors the unfortunate gentlemen and hee must confesse that when hee saw this fellow stand pierchinge [? preaching] in the court hee was something moued (and as hee was speaking my lorde Chan-cellor spake something, but I could not heare him). Then my lorde Archbysshoppe left that matter and spoake to this effect that for the sclaunder no man there was that thought it true. For the punish-ment of Boulin hee added this that hee should loose his eares; his reason was this, a certain young man for picking owt the eyes of birdes, least when he came to bee a man hee should picke owt the eyes of men, so hee thought of Boulin when hee would prooue to bee of riper yeares, hee could not bee retayned, therefor now hee were seuerely punished. As for Birkin's reuealinge of it to Sir Stephen was but to aske counsell of which hee could not dislike, he sayde it was (wyth due respect to the law hee spake) an hard law, if one could not bringe his author that hee should bee principall; for so if an upright man should accuse one for treacherous wordes, if the other would bee so obstinate as to denie it uppon his oathe, the good subiect might bee brought in danger and if hee had not accused the speaker, hee had beene guilty of hie treason in concalinge of it. Therefore hee thought it should haue beene hard to censure Birkin, seeinge hee hath beene so long in prison and hath already beene at such charges as hee hath. For Sir Stephen it was not likely hee would conspire wyth a boy and a clearcke against my lorde of Northampton of whome hee had receaued testimonys of fauor and did so acknowledge. My lorde chancellor sayde hee was of the same mind and had so delivered his mind wheyther my lorde Archbyshopp had so sayde. What shall becomme of Sir Stephen is not knowne by reason the court is equally deuided. The last day in the terme Talbot of Ireland his case was herde for ther late stirres in Ireland; hee was fined 10,000[1] but I did not heare it; thus prayinge God to keepe you and helpe you, I rest, your most dutiful and louinge sonne, W. Wentworth. London, Febru: [1614].[1]

[1] The date must be about 17 February, *The Letters of John Chamberlain*, ed. N. E. McClure (Philadelphia, 1939), i, pp. 508-9. Chamberlain says that Proctor was sued 'for false accusation and conspiracie against two knights in Yorkeshire and for seeking to bring them within compasse of the powder treason' as well as for casting aspersions upon Northampton and Wotton. Neither Chamberlain nor the authorities cited above, p. 57, n. 1, reveal the final result of the case.

# IV. PAPERS RELATING TO THE
# PARLIAMENT OF 1614

**22.** *The opening of Parliament 1614; Wentworth to his father* (*SC,*
xxi/7).

After my humble duty remembred, desiring your blessing &c, Sir,
this day was the first of the Parlament, whear after the oath of
supremecy and allegeance administred to the lower house, wee went
to hear the king's maiesty's speach which was diuided into three
parts: *bona animae, bona corporis, bona fortunae.* In the first part he
spoke sumthings touching the increase of Papists, his maiesties care
and watchfullnes to preuent ther increase, but rather by the clearing
of sum points as yeat obsqure and the exeqution of that which hath
allready been inacted then by more stricter order, bycause that seuerity
is soe far from altering men's consciences that itt doth rather confirme
them in thear opinions, with the particulars whearof he would lett
the house haue notice att more leisure. Under the head of *bona
corporis* he spoke of his royall issue and among the rest, of the prince
Palitine his many vertues and the reasons whie his maiesty affected
that mache before any other, to witt in regard of his religion; lastly
that the electore Palatine and his issue might be made free dinozens.
     Under *bona fortunae* he first spoke of his many occasions of
expense without any releef from the commons and thear did desire
to haue a contribution from them, as he would be willing in requitall
to grant them a restribution and maintaine them in their liberties.
For wheras sum said he went about to take the power of the Parlament from them by reason of the Proclimations which wear obserued
as laws inacted, his maiestie answeared they wear but only to remedy
present inconveniences till they wear ordered by the Parliament,
among which that touching combats was named for an example.
Then did follow a protestation that he had neuer harbored so unworthy thoughts to labor any particulars for this parlament and
thearby to hinder a free election, but did rather rely upon the bare
rock of thear affections then upon the sandy foundations of a packed
party and that he would haue an other sessions att Michelmas; and
wishing thearfore that for this present thos things which wear of
more importance (meaning as I thinke the contribution) should be
dispached and the rest deferred till then; that he would haue the
parlament hearafter called more often, when his owne particular
should not be interested any ways, not any thing more to be spoked
then my lords, my masters, how may the common wealth be best

gouearned? Then made he mention of sum that did ill offices the last parlament, whom he praid God to forgiue, intimating a great little man, as I conceaued, desiring that this might be begun and ended with loue and satisfaction on all parts.

The king's speach being thus ended, my lord Chanceler signified to the gentelmen that they wear to retire in to the lower house and chuse there speaker, whear being accordingly assemblyd Sir Ralf Winnwood (latly made principall secretary and owne of the priuy counsell) commended unto the house with a speche for thear Speaker Mr Randall Crews (who excusing himself from that honorable charge, by reason of his insufficiency) and commended for his modesty by Sir Julius Caesar, still mouing that he might be chosen, he was by the voyces of the house nominated and chosen, Sir Ralf Winwod and Sir Julius Caesar conducting him to his chare.

Thus, Sir, haue you all that passed this first day of Parlament, which by reason of my extraordinary hast needs be confused and ill written, but I hope at my next returne into the cuntry to present you with this and all other accidents which shall happen this Parlament in better method and in the meantime leauing itt to your discretion to the dispose of this ill fashioned letters, humbly crauing your fauorable censure and euer praying for the increas of your health and number of your happy days long amonge us, I end with this full asseurance of being. Your most obedient and louing son, Th. Wentworth. London late att night this 5th of Aprill 1613.

**23.** *The debate on the Attorney-General's seat in the Commons, 8 and 11 April 1614 (Bodley, MS. Eng. Hist. c. 286).*[1]

(*fo. 48*ᵛ) ... The next day being Saterday[2] and the howse seat; thear was a question moued wheather euer any atturney generall euer was or this now atturney Sir Frances Bacon wear to be admitted. Itt was said that by little and little *s[e]nsim sine sensu* our liberties wear taken from us, that anciently none so much as wore the king's

---

[1] This is a volume of the papers of Nathaniel Johnston which includes notes of proceedings in this Parliament in Wentworth's hand. Johnston certainly had access to Wentworth Woodhouse and may have removed these papers from there. Fos. 46ᵛ–48ᵛ give an account of the opening of Parliament, the election of the Speaker and the king's first two speeches, which do not add anything significant to what can be found in the *Commons' Journal*; *Cobbett's Parliamentary History of England*, i (London, 1806), pp. 1149–58; *Historical Manuscripts Commission*, lxxviii, *MSS. of R. R. Hastings*, iv (1947), pp. 230–41.

[2] This appears to be a mistake for Friday, 8 April; the account also covers the proceedings on Monday, 11 April, *C.J.*, i, pp. 456, 459; for a full account, see T. L. Moir, *The Addled Parliament of 1614* (Oxford, 1958), pp. 85–87.

liuery, or had any pension from the king, could haue been admitted the howse, nay that owne was put out in king Edward 3 time bycause he was the queen seruant. For allbeitt the king be the head and we the body, yeat itt faired not as with the naturall head and body, for the politik head and body are now distinke things separated own from another. But now the priuie counsell, king's sargant and sollictor wear admitted the latter times to be of the howse, which allbeitt they could not in truth, yeat hauing president they wear only hear-after not to be admitted, as being hear out of ther proper place, as soe ouerbore all whear otherwaies they might serue as good members ( *fo. 49ʳ*) like the water that when he was in his owne course in his owne bed, itt was a pleasant and usefull eliment, but the ouerflow thearof by being out of his place was the cause of great harme and losse; that Sir Thomas More being asked the question whie the bishop's faction was more powerful in parlament then the king's, answeared that was not to be questioned since that the bishops had many of their dependants on the howse whear none of the king's liuery or that [none] his seruants could be admitted to be of the howse, how much the lesse then the atturney generall now, thear hauing neuer been any before, this man being an inseperable instrument of the royallty and thearfore neuer of this howse. For the cristiline humor of the eie admitts noe culler, nor the purity of this howse any that wear incorporated in that stoke or any ways cullered with that still, that thearfore he was to be sent for into the higher howse as hearto-fore he hath been and allbeitt he wear not a star of the first magni-tude, yeat might he be of the second, thou not a member yeat an assistant in that upper speare. Whearupon itt had like to haue been put to the question, till itt was motioned that the should not [take] soe violent a course, but rather appoint a comm[ittee] that should haue power to searche presidents and accordingly to informe the howse which thea— might proceed to a finall resolution which was g— assented unto. The committe was accordingly assembled, after sea[r]che the returned what the had found in the recor[ds] to the howse which was only this that the had fownd records for sum that had been spekers and attur[neys] ( *fo. 49ᵛ*) but could not find suffi-cient proofe to haue att owne and the same time been both speaker and atturney, or of the howse and atturney soe that for anything they could gather ther was noe certaine proofe that euer thear had been king's atturney of the howse. For thos men of which they made mention might very well haue afterwards been mad atturneys and att the very instant not to haue had that place. Hubbard was indeed of the last parlament, but was not atturney when the writts went out and being made atturney during the sitting of the same parlament was only retaine[d] of a necessity in regard of diuers informations to be giuen to the howse, best knowne to himself.

Then stept up Mr Secretary, giueing the howse to understand that itt was the king['s] desire that the howse would be pleased to admitte this attorney upon condition thear should be none euer hearafter and that otherwise he could not but confesse his owne error whoe had committed the Irishe lords bycause they would not admitt Davies for their speaker, being the king['s] atturney, if we in England sould iudge itt that by law the king's Atturney could not be of the commons howse of Parlament. Upon thes tow reasons of intreaty and touching the Irish Lord[s] the Parlament was content to receaue him, but then was itt moued wheather for this i sessions only or for the hole parlament, which thowe itt was concluded with the latter, yeat the former had many voyces. But he was admitted with a spetiall order that none should euer thearafter be admitted. The first bill that past the howse was a bill touching the naturalising of the Conte Palatin being sent unto us from the Lords, the which bill being amended in sum points and brought into the howse, itt ther passed and soe returned to the lords thear againe to receaue his passe.

**24.** *Debate on the bill on impositions, 18 April 1614 (Bodley MS. Eng. Hist. c. 286).*[1]

(*fo. 41ʳ*) Thear was put up into the howse a bill touching abolition and taking away of impositions, to which Sir Morris Barckley, saying that this flood of impositions brooke into this commonwealth, principally by reason of an iudgment in the Exchecere which gaue power to the king att his pleasure to haue the auctority to raise them, which allbeitt they brought a great treasure into his Maiesty's coffers, yeatt itt lost him a double treasure. The first in the loue of his subiects, the second making them unwilling to releeue him which they might doe otherwise more plentifully and certainly willingly, if they wear taken away; thearfore concluded the bill was good and desired that itt might be committed.

To which Sir George Moor spoke, saying that itt was aganst the orders of the court to commit a bill before thear was sumthing alleged aganst itt and thearfore seeing that the auctority of thes impositions was grownded upon that iudgment in the Exchecer that therfore itt should be arg[ued] in the howse before committment wheather itt was lawf[ull] or no.

---

[1] This was the second reading of the bill 'concerning Taxes and Impositions upon Merchants', *C.J.*, i. pp. 466–67, which is the only other record of this debate.

The replication of Mr Fuller was that itt was [ar]gued ten days togaither the last parlament and declared that the kinge could not lay a newe imposition upon any commodity without the auctority of Parla[ment].

Sir Harbert Crofts said he iudged itt fitt to be committed, sumthings corrected amisse in the bill. Mr B[r]ooke was [of] the same opinion for committment, but not to be delt with (*fo. 41*) till after Easter that in the interim thos that argued the case the last parlament should make collections of thear notes and how itt was left of then. His opinion was that allbeitt they should not obtaine this bill to passe in the higher howse, yeat nottwithstanding to lay thear continuall clame to itt to haue them utterly abolished. For allbeitt ther could not be gotten a lawfull possession, yeat ther was right to a lawfull entry which, otherwise letting itt goe unspoken of owne decent,[1] itt would be then clamed of right; that the king if he haue power to impose thes new impositions, itt must be either by his lawfull power or absolute power. Touching his lawfull power, itt was neuer soe iudged by the common law before this iudgment in the exchecer. Thearfore not the opinion of antiquity, for absolute power the king had none to make any law touching the preiudice of his subiect aither for life, liberty, or goods, but either by laws inacted or to be inacted. For England obays to noe laws but such as themselfs make.

Mr Whitlock[2] continued this debate, saying the first imposition that euer was laide upon any commodity without consent was by Queen Marie upon cloth, being an imposition to haue a marke laid upon that commodity, whear she had lost 2[li] upon wool, which neuer the lesse was complained upon i[mo] Eliz. as a thing aganst law, which is not reported by the iudges and thearfor to be presumed to be ordered as aganst law, else certainly would itt haue been reported, the iudges hauing euer been carefull to report anything beneficiall to the king. That wheras in the last Queen's time thear was imposition laid upon wine and sum other marchandise, that now thear was imposition upon 1100 seuerall commodities, thearfore that thear should be (*fo. 42*) a declaration of the law in this case.

The next[3] that spoke was Sir Robert Owen, affermed that allbeitt our king's prerogatiue was as large as any other monarke what soeuer, as the king of France or Spaine could not lay impositions without consent of parlaments, or *les estats* as they call; that the like case was not of the Lowe Cuntry men, for thear they impose

---

[1] *I.e.* for one descent.
[2] *C.J.* gives Brooke as the next speaker.
[3] *C.J.* gives Middleton and does not name Owen as speaking.

upon themself bie a democratical gouernment. His motion then was that for the satesfaction of such as had not been of the last parlament that itt might againe be argued or att the least good notes taken of the last conference.

Mr Midelton continued to moue that right might be declared, saying that hear was great wronge dune both to the king and subiect, to the latter they wear matters of extraordinary greeuance, to the former of extraordinary deceit. For, sathe he, I dare undertake, if the dealers for his Maiesty had truly paid all the money into the excheccer that they haue receiued from the subiect, his Maiesty need not to haue greeued his subiects with any supplie as nowe he dothe; thearfore willed itt might be committed and againe argued *causa qua supra.*

Sir Dudley Diggs continued in speaking against thes impositions and aganst that erroneous iudgment in the Excheker, f[or] soe he termed itt, that in Edward the Confessor's time thear was an imposition of this kingdum called Danguilt, sett upe for the same reasons as itt is likely as thes are, which being in his time practised his collectors sh[ewed] him a great masse of this money soe leuied whearupon [it] seemed to the king a saw a diuel sitting, whearupon he utterly tooke away that same taxation to the subiect. (*fo. 42ᵛ*) That in the like case he did not dowbt but if the king should looke weel upon this yearly reuenew he should see sum little diuel or other setting upon the heap that would moue him to take away them which won the Confessor soe much loue of his subiects and glory with posterity, but that he would haue delt in with all tendernes and respect to his maiesty that could be. Lett the bill be thearfore committed, the reasons declared upon which the last parlament grownded thear resoluti[ons], but not againe att large argued as to great a losse of time which nowe was soe preciouse.

To which Mr Hacwell replied that in respect that thear was 300 gentelmen of this which wear not of the last parlament thearfore the matter to be againe debated att a committe to be of the hole howse.

Mr Hawkins[1] then spoke, saying that the right of this busines was noe ways questionable, thearfore he would leaue itt, but he would shew that under the culler of extreme profitt thes impositions wear very preiudiciall to his maiesty and that for 3 reasons. The first, that by reason of thes excessiue impositions the marchant could not make after 10 in the 100 of his money, which was the reason that they chuse rather without hazard to put thear money to use after 10 in the 100 then to continue thear trade, by which means the cuntry

[1] Hoskyns, *C.J.*

was eat up, noe commodities brought in to the kingdume. Sum thi[nk] that in time thear would be noe custume howse for want of custum, but itt would be change[d] into a contraction howse. (*fo. 43ʳ*) The 2 reason was that the contractors bought the crowne land [at] under rates and allbeitt the got a 100, nay 200, att a hundreth, yeat they pay noe imposition. The 3 [reason] that they sold thes lands to the subiects att excessiue rates which afterwards wear brought in question to thear utter undoings; finally then, seing that the ceasing of trade and pouerty of the subiect being the effects of thes imposition[s], the must needs be very preiuditiall to the king's profitt. Thearfore concluded that, thoe itt seemed a matter of present profit, yeat would itt turne to a future yeat asseured and notable losse to the king and kingdume.

Mr Whitsun followed, applying that story of our sauior touching Martha and Mary, in that the former minded many things, but Marie the chefe, soe that wee minded many thi[ng]s as the king's bills of grace, but that this was the chefe thing to be regarded that they wear unlawfull, not heartofore used in this kingdum. The first imposition that euer reade of was an imposition upon wools transported in Ed[ward] the 3 time, which, allbeitt thear was then wars with France and other great occasions of export, was complained of. Whearupon the [king] praid that they be contented only till Penticost which next insued and then itt should be redressed, which answear argued a guilt and wrong; that thearfore a supplication might be drawn to his maiesty that he would be pleased out of his fauor utterly to take away all impositions and since matter of reuerence [to] the king was only the lett to the proceeding hearof, that thearfore the committe should thinke of sum course whea[rby] to make good the king reuenew in lew of the impositions. (*fo. 43ᵛ*) For his part he had rather pay monthly a subsedy then that the subiect should be so trauaild by the customes and the king soe infinitly deceaued by the collectors.

Sargant Montaigue[1] said itt was now a needfull and seasonable motion that itt should be committed and by the committe order taken how to proceed in this weighty busines.

Sir William Strownde then moued that the day appointed might be before the terme and the lawers commaunded to attend the committe, else when the terme was bygune they would all be wanting, as alsoe that then the howse should be cald; the last part of the motion being only denied, ther was a committe of the hole howse, the day twesday fortnight after being the 5 of Aprill,[2] the place the howse.

[1] Sir Henry Montague, *C.J.*      [2] This is wrong; the date should be 3 May.

**25.** *Wentworth to Sir William Wentworth* (*SC*, xxxiv/16). *Proceedings about the French Company.*

After my humble duty remembered desiring your blessing; Sire you haue been acquainted with sum proceedings of this parlament, yeat theare is part remaining. Thear was a bill exhibited against certaine marchants, that under a culler of trading into France had gotten by patent a Monopoly, that none should trade thether, but such as weare meare marchants, would be of theare company and subiect to thear orders; they had authority alsoe by the same patent to take an oath of there fellows that they should be true to the said company, had power to imprison any that weare delinquents and to breake open howses to searche if theare weare anything contrary to the said patent.[1] This being made knowen to the howse by the burgesses of Cornwall and othere the western cuntry, the mattere was lefte too a committe of the hole howse, the time and place appointed. The patenties consell alleged, that this company was formed in the yeare 1611 by reason of the ill cloths that weare heartofore transported into France, to restraine that loose kind of trafficke into a well settled cowrse, and for many othere benifits which the commonwealth should reap thearby. The first was theare being forfaited att Rouen *anno* 1606 50,000$^{li}$ worthe of clothe, and seised on by the king of France his officers, in regard itt was not according to an edict in that purpose inacted; a conference being held at Blois, betwixt the Frenche and Englishe, how to redresse this lose, by theare espetiall mediation, the clothe was restored, the formere edict nullefied, and a new one made, that Englishe clothe should be noe more confiscate, but if they weare not good to be returned backe only.[2] The 2 was, that by the laws of France noe strangere dying in the kingdum can make his will, but all his goods cums unto the king as executore: but yeat by thear means the Englishe are inabled to dispose of ther goods according to ther affections. 3. that gentlemen trauiling thos parts haue ther moneys more safely, more speedily returned then in former time, by reason of thear factors in all the parts of those cuntryes. 4. that for 3$^{li}$ and ode money, any might be of ther company, if they weare meare merchants whear other companies take 50$^{li}$ for euery seuerall admittance. 5. that non by thear orders being suffered to buy any wines before Decembere, nore bring itt abord till itt had stood 15 days in caske, the best wines wear brought into

---

[1] The patent is printed in *Select Charters of Trading Companies, 1530–1708*, ed. C. T. Carr (Selden Society, xxviii, 1913), pp. 62–78; *cf.* pp. xxiv–xxvi.

[2] See B. Reynolds, 'Elizabethan Traders in Normandy', *Journal of Modern History*, ix (1937), pp. 301–3.

Burdeaux before there ships wear laded and if thear wear any corrupt and bad wine it was easily descerned before the imbarkment, standing 15 days &c. soe that now the wines wear much better than heartofore. 6. that now going all togaither to Burdeaux in winter laded with clothe, being a season whearin such commoditys weare desired, the vent of clothe is now muche more then euer itt was. 7. to showe plainly that this was a company set up, for the publike and not for any priuate good, itt was not granted upon theare seeking, but imposed upon them by the lords of the priuie counsell. Lastly that they weare redy if itt should be soe thought fitt to deliuer up the patent into the howse. Whearupon the marchants absented themselfs, leauing the committye priuately to argue the matter and to consider of thes reasons.

Whear on the contrary side itt was alleged: First that this patent was an undoing to the west cuntry: for hauing been heartofore a cuntry of great traffike, thear was nowe noe ships almost but a few fishermen, to the great weakening of that part of England which heartofore furnished the hole kingdum wth marriners. 2. that thear chef profitt lay in thear often and speedy returnes which benifit they wear nowe depriued of by staying for the Londoner, whearas in times past they made 3 returns for thear owne, by cause the Londener must haue 3 winds, whear owne carryes them into France. 3. that in thos parts, gentlemen, masters of ships, and mariners bare parts with the marchant, all nowe excluded by this worde, mear Marchant, which would turne to thear undoing, for the mariners grow carelesse, hauing no part in the fraiths, and others unwilling to learne that art seing thear greatest benifitt taken from them. 4. that the wines wear much dearer, noways bettered. 5. the vent of clothe much lesse as appeared by the custum bookes. 6. that whear they alledge that any mear merchant might for $3^{li}$ and ode be incorporate wth them; itt was true, but neuerthelesse thear exactions wear intollerable, for whear the king hade a $100^{li}$ custum they had besids for thear shares att the least $10^{li}$. 7. that the patent was against the common law, which allowes euery man freely to dispose of his own goods. 8. aganst magna carta, which giues to euery borne subiect freedum of trade. 9. contrary to a statute the last parlament inacted, by which the company of Spanishe marchants being of the same nature wear dissolued, the patent canceled, and inacted that freedum of trade into Spaine and France should be granted to all men.[1] 10. that the patent was void in the very grant for two reasons: the first, a *non obstante* in a statute affermatiue is of noe force, being only effectuall in a negatiue law; that this statute was affirmatiue

[1] 3 Jac. I *cap.* 6.

thearfore etc. The second reason; that all grants from the kinge to diuers persons must haue euery particular mans assent, or els to be void, that thear wear many names used in the patent, to be of the company, which neuer gaue theare consents, or euer willing thearunto. Lastly, by thes reasons itt plainly appeared, not to be imposed upon them, but earnestly affected to serve priuate ends, which must necessarily spring from the fontains of priuate gain and commodity, that thearfore they wear to be punished, for laying the beginnings upon the priuy counsell, in going about by that means to delude the howse, and for daring to attempt any thing contrary to the fundamentall laws of this kingdume and a statute to that purpose soe lately inacted. For thear patent to be canceled and freedume of trade againe opened.

Then was itt moued that thear patent might be deliuered according as they offered, for seeing they wear to be punished, aither lesse or more according to theare obstinatenes or otherwise, this would be one good argument in deliuering or denying the same, likewise that they shoulde giue sum better testimony to the howse, that this society was imposed upon them by the priuy counsell. The marchants being admitted the second time and the patent according to thear offer demanded, they desired that the might haue sume time giuen them to confer with the residue of the company: they being but xx, not daring to doe any thing wthout the others consent; for the second, which was to clear themselfs not to haue labored for this grant, they could not giue the howse any satisfaction, but that they weare confidently possessed that this pursuite tooke roote from themselfs and not wthout grownd, for as I haue confidently heard itt cost the marchants 10,000[li] before itt was effected.[1] Then weare the marchants commaunded to retire, and the committy to resolue what they thought fitt to be related to the howse; itt was thearfor thoughte a dishonor to the howse to waite thear leisure in hauing the patent, but resolued that it should be sent for by commaundment from the howse. But being the next day related[2] (which was the day the parlament broke up), itt was thear finally concluded, that in regard the court was not to sitt of a week after, they might see whether the patent would be deliuered in the interim; if not, then att the next sitting they should be commaunded to bring itt into the court and this is all the proceedings in this matter, but surely I thinke itt will goe aganst the marchants.

[1] When the patent was brought in on 3 May; 'It was alledged it was ymposed upon them and controverted wherfore was there a greate summ given unto some lord, and 300[l] to Secretaries . . .', Notestein, vii, p. 630.
[2] The report was made 20 April; C.J. i, pp. 469–70.

Since my last dispache towards you I haue receiued a letter from my uncle H. Attkinson which I hear send you that I may receaue your direction howe to frame him an answeare. Heare is likewise a letter from my brother Jhon unto you which I should haue heare sealed, but the superscription cums soe near the end I could not effect his desire, but I will write unto him to amend itt hearafter, his hand and inditing are in my opinion well bettered. The lord Sheffeild sum say would sell his presidentshipe, but of this no certainty. For my part I iudge itt very unlikely, sure I am alltogaither unusuall. I know not weather Mallorie will followe his petition or noe, bycause a matter of the same nature touching the knights of Cambridgeshire was heard in parlament,[1] whearin the complainants had noe remedy, a matter fowler in my conceit aganst the sherif (and the knights chosen) then this of ours. I haue hear sent you a copy of ther petition aganst us. For the vaine and diall the messinger will giue you satesfaction. A bill touching taking away of imposition is to be spoken too Twesday cum seauennight being the 5 of Aprill,[2] the subsedy propounded Thursday after, but more of thes by the first commodity of writing. I haue inquired out a good clarke which may serue you if itt be your pleasur in Conway's roome and me, as iustice of peace; you may informe your self more fully of this bearer, and accordingly lett me know your opinion, thus euer praying for your health and long life, I humblie take leaue and rest, yor most obedient and louing son, Th. Wentworth. London, 25 Aprill, 1614. If itt be your pleasure I could desire that this bearer might returne and dispatche your busines hear in Mr Man's roome bycause I haue likewise sum imployment for him.

**26.** *Report of the Commons' Committee on Impositions, 5 May 1614*[3] *(Bodley. MS. Eng. Hist. c. 286).*

(*fo. 40*ʳ) Sir Edwin Sands' Report touching impositions. 5 April 1614. Had obserued an old rule to himself that a man which was to aduise in counsell should speke without preface, without passion, the first for auoyding tediousnes, the second to eschew partiall[ity], but thus far he would use a preface to tell us what we might expect from him. In a iudge thear was required integrity, in a counseler

---

[1] *C.J.* i, p. 468, 19 April.

[2] This presumably should be Tuesday, 3 May; *C.J.*, i, p. 471.

[3] The date in the text is that of the opening of the parliament. Much briefer reports are in *C.J.*, i, p. 472; Notestein, vii, pp. 633–34, *cf.* p. 638, 12 May. The leaves have been bound into the volume in the wrong order; fo. 40 continues on fo. 45.

wisdum and in a reporter fidelity, in the last kind he would relate what was proposed att the committee. As the sick man turneth him self from owne side of the bed too another to find ease, but failes bycause the desease is within him, soe did we att the committee in the difference wheather to proceed by bill or petition or by both; but the greefe remained still with us, a great desire the subiect should be eased, great difficulty how, which was a great cause of irresolution. Then the king's prerogatiue was argued with reuer[ence] and fear, reuerence in regard of his maiesty, fear in respect of the subiect. Itt was said ther that the king could not lay impositions without a[ct] of Parlament, as was seen by all practise common la[w] and statute law in this kingdume, that if he has power (he might *Struck through*) by the same reason inact laws [with]out assent &c (*fo. 40ᵛ*) which was in the beginning of a manuscript conformed to haue beene read that the king could not impose, bycause he could not make laws and wheras it was restra[ined] that he might lay impositions of imported marchandize, thoo not of inbreed commodityes, by cause he that might restraine them might [per]mitt them upon thos terms that should best please him, but moderately, resonablie and conueniently. Itt was answeared that he might as weel and by the same reason impose upon inbreed commodities as well as upon imported; if he could then doo itt, itt must be either by legall power, or out of absolute auctority; if by the former, then aither as a matter of fact or law, itt was neuer dun w[ith]out assent, then noe matter of fact and being neuer dun then not lawfull. For itt is a good argument in law to plead that itt hath not been dun or thear is noe example. If out of absolute auctority then hath he noe law to gouerne him, which is a case very miserable and aganst the grownd of the common la[w]. Itt was farther said that the first statute aganst imposing was a negatiue law that noe impositions aboue such a rate which did preuent encrese, but argued a power of imposing. Itt was answeared that itt had b[een] attempted but allways complained on and that thos ac[ts] wear to preuent the king's prerogatiue that itt might [be] (*fo. 45ʳ*) definit which otherwise would proue *indiuiduum vagum* and that such custums wear giuen by assent of Parlament to that purpose; in the negatiue that none should offer to encrease them hearafter; that the custums of cloth wear giuen to Ed[ward] the 3 by act of parlament, not by prerogatiue, the rest called *mala toleta* laid upon the subiect all ended in Edward the 3 time, for they were no sooner pressed but repressed. But to the second point of the subiect's right, itt was said directly the subiec[t's] right in this point was ancient, yea as ancient as ther ha[th] been any peple, for the Saxons, Danes and Conqueror neuer lay *custudines*, as they wear termed, upon the subiect till Edward the 1 time, who by reason of his warrs rased custu[ms] upon wools and skins which being complained on was holely taken away in Edward the 2 time and raised againe by Edward the 3 by reason of his great wars, which afterwards being complained of, he desired time only till Penticost next after by reason of his expens and then he would take them of. By which it was inferd when the lion leaueth his power to goe to intreaty, his hope is little to preuaile by right, els would he not incline to the weak remedy. From which time till Queen Marie's time ther was noe impositions which wear then raised by strangers, the Spaniard and principally by the duke of Alua in a disorder[ed] gouernment and when the Spaniards had thought to haue made slaues of us. Which neuerthelesse was complained of in 1 Eliz., not reported by iudge Dier, therfore nothing concluded for the Royallty, else itt would haue been [repor]ted whear in they might haue drawen any thing to the [king]. But now the subiect had receaued a principall and greatest wound by the last — in the Exchecher a iudgment erroneous by which the gaue pow[er to] the king to impose, soe that now whear as before (*margin*: Sir Th. Smith in his polici of England that the king hath noe power to impose) (*fo. 45*ᵛ) impositions wear few and finit, they wear now 1330 and indefinite. Wheras heartofor neuer any king clamed impositions as of right belonging unto him, soe that itt now came to the point wheather we wear free or bound, had anything or nothing. Philosophie sath that he is bond which is not his own, law sath that he is bond that hath goods but noe propriety; in both thes cases we are bond, if the king may att his pleasure impose. For touching the first we are not our owne as long as itt is left in the king's prerogatiue to impose upon our personall goods, as well as upon imported; and we haue no propriety in our goods as long as the king's prerogatiue is unlimited to impose as much upon us as he pleaseth, againe no man knows how his goods are his owne and therfore noe proprieti.

Thearfor was itt determened to proceed both by bill and petition; first by bill to the Lords and for fear itt might be thear stopped, as itt was the last parlament, that therfore we should put up our petition to the king to, as desiring rather itt should dy att his maiestie's feet then in the hands of ill nurses. Lastly the question was moued how we cold giue any supplie till wee know what is our owne, for then it will be worthy thanks. Seing then *per media venitur ad fidem*, we should stay the king's supplie till this bill was passed and that we knew what was our owne and how then to releeue the kinge. Itt was farther said that ther was but owne way to be releeued from this desease which was by princly grace, as itt was said *hoc mihi quod nullis amor est medicabilis herbis*; sauing, sath owne, the herbe of grace this must not be obtained then by capitulation or extorting *voluntas non cogitur*; we must goe then with a supplication, accompanied with a present most needfull acceptable and worthy a king, that soe the king's wants being plentifully releeued and the subiect eased by the taking away impositions, *currat lex, fiat iustitia*, to the mutuall comforts of us all.

**27.** *Speeches by Wentworth for the 1614 Parliament (Bodley MS. Eng. Hist. c. 286).* [One edge of the sheets is damaged. There is no evidence that the speeches were spoken in the Commons.]

(*fo. 50ʳ*) Sir,[1] itt was a complainte in the declining liberty of Rome th[at] thear were many speakers, few valiant. Surely, Sir, we la[bour] of the same desease, fore in soe many discourses noe ma[n] hetherto hath been soe resolute as to nominate any par[ticu]lar undertakere. This conferms me in tow [th]ings th[at] theare is noe unsownde member in our body [and] itt had been the best course to haue ancred our[selves] upon his maiesties royall asseurance, yeat am I not [of] the gentelman's opinion that spoke last for th[ere are] many things require that action should [make] thear motion of which nature I iudge this. Wee are past [the] Riuer Rubicon, itt is too late to turne backe, [let] us then leaue the orators, becum doers. Ph[ysic] teacheth that ill humors being once stirred must of necessity be expelled. Truly, Sir, I thinke that to free ourselfes from this imputation which we haue laid upon our selfs, we must use the same good remedy by remonstrance to his Maiesty, seing as itt fairs with the state of the body, soe is itt with the body of the state. Thearfore my poore opinion is that we should sig[nify] to oure most iust king that in our selfs we are fully satesfied by his maiestie's gracious wor[ds] that thear is noe undertakers, only that we wo[uld] haue him likewise fully satesfied th[at] our libe[rties] and loues went hand in hand, our zeals to our — cuntry and king kissed each other and th[ey] wear not to be drawn one by the vaine hopes of a[ny] priuat men's preferments whosoeuer further then our — zeals and loyallties would willingly yeald unto. (*fo. 50ᵛ*) Lastly and chefly that the cuntries for which we serue might be as well satesfied from us by such a remonstrance to the King, as we from his maiesty that ther wear no such catchepoles among us. This is my humble motion which with the same humility I submitt unto your graue considerations.

A speache that I conceaued upon the question wheather Sir Robert

---

[1] This speech was presumably intended for the debate on the undertakers on 12 April.

Killegrey[1] was to be admitted to his place or to the barre for to make answear to that which was laid to his charge and to acknowledg his falt.

May itt please you, Mr Speakere, I cam hether resolued too a constant silence fore many reasons and many particular infirmities best knowen unto my self. Yeat had I rather nowe incurre the censure of youthfull arrogancy then spote the sincerity of my conscience and the zeale I bear to this howse with an obstinate and unseasonable taciturnity. Partiall I cannot be in my opinion by reason of any priuate ends to my selfe, in regard I am alltogaither unacquainted with the gentelman, neuer kn[ew] his name till euen now, neuere spoke to him in all my life. His frends are to me in as fare a distance, yeat [dare] I giue them thus farre credence that I am possessed of the gentelman's worthe and hopes and soe far sory for him that as Sir Robert Killegrey I should incline to a fauorable construction, if in the other balance I did not weighe him as an offendore aganst the freedume and dignity of this howse. Thearfore, Sir, you may be pleased to iudge thes words the thoughts of my harte, free from any priuate respects ore reference, for such in good faith they are. I cannot informe you, as sum graue and worthy gentelmen haue dun, concerning the ancient orders and (*fo. 51ʳ*) former presidents of this howse, I confesse age and inexperience disinable me in both, only I will put this howse in remembrance of owne weel knowen and fresh in all oure remembrances: we proceeded ag[ainst] Mr Chanceler of the Duchy for infringing our liberty in that he writt a menacing letter to Mr St Jo[hn] to desist &c.[2] We all know he desired to answ[er] for himselfe, was thear any place allowed him b[ut] the barre? Yea itt was iudged both for a mercifull an[d iust] censure. For me I protest I am of the same op[inion] yeat, Mr Speakere, theare weare many circumstances [to] haue mitigated that censure. First the pitty of aged a[nd] white haires seduced by a bad instrument, t[he] place that he held in the commonwealthe, seru[ice] formerly dune, a coulorable title from his predesess[ors] who had chalenged right in the nomination to t[he] places. Lastly that allbeitt a publike wronge, yeat — shewe but offered too a priuate gentelman in the c—. All the circumstances doe aggriuate itt agenst this gentelman, for thes be his words, 'you shall put noe more triks upon [us] I will see you out of the chare.' Nay Mr Speakere d[oes not] only menace but lies violent hands, upon whom? [Not] upon a cuntry gentelman

---

[1] Sir Robert Killigrew and Sir William Herbert tried to drag Sir Roger Owen from the chair of the committee on undertakers on 12 May; their punishment was debated on 13 May, *C.J.*, i, p. 483.

[2] Sir Thomas Parry was excluded on 11 May, *C.J.*, i, pp. 480–81.

but upon a very worthy sincer member of this howse, not upon a priuat gentelman, but upon a publike person repres[enting your] person, Mr Speaker, att a grand committy and [not] in a remote cuntry, but an affront dune in co[mmon] howse of Parlament in the very well spr[ing of] (*fo. 51ᵛ*) iustice.

Thes circumstances in my poore iudgment makes this offence as great as the former and shall we then extend our mercy more upon this green heade then upon thos gray and aged hairs, beare more respect to a yonge gentelman then too a graue conseler of estate, fauor this man's future hopes more then thothers acted seruices, spare this person in his fury more then thother, conceauing itt to be the right of his place and that by the false councell of a bad seruant? O Mr Speaker, this makes me tremble to imagin we should intertaine soe fearfull a president to the utter disaduantage of all our liberties. Lett us then proceed without respect of persons, for when iustice personateth itt leaues to be iustice, lett sum proportion be held in the punishment of thes delinquents, least we be taxd of partiallity. Let noe other place be allotted to this gentelman but the barre, lett itt be considered what you Mr Speaker shall then say unto him and after hearing what he can answeare for himself and be againe withdrawen, lett the howse proceed farther either in punishment or mercy, as shall seem best to ther wisdums. This is my humble motion which I submitt unto the graue consideration of this howse.

# V. SIR THOMAS WENTWORTH'S PAPERS[1]

**28.** *From Cumberland. 12 Feb. 1614 (SC, xx/201).*

Sonne Wentworth, your good respect to performe what I desired [in] sending your wife and daughter hither doth give me great content for which I hartely thanke yow and shall ever be ready in any occasion to deserve your love therein and kindnes. I much wished to have had your company with me this journey wherein I would have respected yow as my owne sonne Harry. But in that yow so earnestly alledge the inconveniency that might happen to yow in your absence, I will not further presse yow thereto, being as loath as your owne father to advise any thing that might preiudice yow. I shall long to heare of your father's amendement. I spoke with doctor Deane now as I came, he tells me there is no doubt but he shall shortly be recovered. I pray yow to comend me to him; I have not now more to wryte, but to tell yow that I take great comforte in yow and my daughter your wife as in any. And so I pray God ever to blesse — with my very harty comendacons I bid yow farewell, Your loving — Fr. Cumberland. Skipton castle this xiith of February 1613[4].

**27.** *Speech in Wentworth's hand for the collection of the free gift o, 1614 (SC, xxi/208, undated, but probably about October 1614[2]).*

An unskilfull painter presented in ostentation to skilfull Apelles a picture saying 'This I drew euen now'. 'Truly,' answered Apelles, 'hadst thou bin silent, yeat should I easily haue coniectured such workmanship to haue bin slighted through haste.' I foresee most assureudly the like censure fall heauy upon this undigested and new fashioned discours being to pass the file of those that are Apelleses in this art. Yeat so farre am I from glorying in mine owne imperfections that the unexpected refusall of thes gentlemen, much more able, had wrought in me the effects of a still and constant silence, weare it not that the richnes of the stuffe I am to handle (albeitt ill fashioned) will sparcle forth some of his beautie thorow the vaile of my ill ordered speache, whear if it were touched to the life *mirabiles excitaret amores sui.* I will then with your good leaves faithfully and breefely impart unto you my conceite upon soe short a prouision.

By this that hath been read unto you, you may know the warrant by which and understand the cause that occasioneth this our present

---

[1] Unless otherwise stated, all letters in this section are either to Wentworth or from him.    [2] *Acts of the Privy Council of England, 1613–1614,* pp. 557–59.

meeting. Now albeit I am powerfully perswaded that out of your own discretions you be ready to lay forth frankly and freely seeing the apparent aduantage you shall therby gaine unto yourselves by liuing under a riche Prince and reaping for use a well settled and certaine peace. Yeat with patience permitt me to offer unto your due considerations some reasons as sweetning and leading points to all the rest of our proceedings.

Comon fame, I doubt not, hath brought unto your hearings the rumor of great leauy of arms which stirre now in the low Germany, couertly ayming at things not certainly knowen, whear the cloude breaks noe man foreseeing. His Maiesty's cautionary townes ther, his Navy hear, by these uncertainties, much indangered, yea this his kingdome and our deare countrie subiect to an unexpected and perilouse inuasion. The necessity of treasure to divert this storme, how nearly our owne safety inuites us thereunto and what weight these carry to moue a speedy supply, I leaue them to your riper iudgements to conceaue and fall upon things better knowen to myselfe.

The mouers for this present beneuolence are exceeding many, but because I may iustly feare my owne weakenesse in relating them and rely upon your former and iuditious collections before you presented yourselfes in this assembly, I will applie and fixe myselfe to 4: 1, the passages of the last Parlament 2, auncient and late precedents; 3, the obligation binding us therunto now more then ever; 4, and last, our owne future benefitt and comfort.

My service employed by this countrie in the last Parlament inables me more then every priuate man, to speake to this first motiue which albeit att the prime itt carrie with itt a contrary shew, yeat upon better aduice itt will beare another countenance: *desinet in mulierem formosam superne piscis.* For itt may be sayd the Parlament, not administring to his Maiesty's wants did itt upon sound grounds, soe their proceedings our rule. The allegation I confesse ingenuous, but be pleased better to informe yourselfs. That famous and wise counsell in generall stood more upon the forme then the substance of the gift; againe all were soe sensible of the king's wants that noe man but in his particular iudged itt soe needfull that he would have ransacked his owne priuate estate, but the members of that howse being ther as you know, publick persons wear, it might be, unwilling to undertake that for others, which for themselves they would have readily performed. Soe you see the obstacles wear new circumstances of giuing and the condition of the giuers.[1] Thes are your

---

[1] The debate of 7 June 1614 shows several members ready to vote supply to avoid a dissolution; *Proceedings in Parliament 1610*, ed. E. R. Foster (New Haven, 1966), ii, pp. 415–21.

perswasions, for can ther be a more honorable' manner of bestowing then a free gift and a gift recorded with the name of the giver? *hoc habui quodcunque dedi.* Wherin I beseech you observe the graciousnes of his Maiesty, for by this meanes he will know the meanest of his affectionat subiects that he may have them in his gratefull remembrance. Or can you shew yourselfes better followers of the Parlament then to doe as they would, had they bin, as we all now are, priuate persons and subiects? Sure then you may not and I hope you will not omitt soe fayre an opportunity.

I will proceede then to the 2 motiue which you shall finde ranged under auncient and late precedents. The best touche of truth, the powerfullest perswasions are the number of years and multitude of beleevers. Bothe thes are yours, for first in the speache of the Duke of Buccingham written by Sir Thomas Moore there is mention made of a beneuolence to king Edward the 4th granted out of the tender respect the subiect had of his wants. Secondly the hole frame of this kingdume hath now yeilded hearunto, insoemuch that we are the last in all this County, this shire the last of most in this kingdume, soe you have hear ancient rule and later practise. Now albeitt we had none, our owne discretions might herein be rules to themselfes, yeat knowing that men generally incline rather to example then precept and naturally are sociable creaturs, therfore have I made you a present of thes tow like Jacob's rodds in the water that you might bring forth semblable fruits, euen such as are most fitt for the state, most needfull for our selfes.

I now cum to the third which is our own obligation binding now more then euer. This will appeare most plainly in the person of our gracious and dread Souerain; I confesse my owne feeblenes to deale with such an immense greatnes of all regality and honor and therby acknowledge the habituall greatnes and accustomed goodnes adherent to his royall Maiesty *huius temperiem nescit mens, naturale decus fictæ ut commodet arti,* his rare perfection admitting noe expressor, but his owne excellent scill. Well the Frenche prouerb hearin shall perswade with me. *Qui trope embrase mal estrint,* say they, he that gripes much, holds but weakely; I then will fasten myselfe to a branche not able to compas the tree, leauing this royall stok to learneder pens and relating unto you the great happines our selfes have enioyed by his Maiesty's prosperous raine. Man's composition is twofold, of soule and body, unto the good and preseruation of which tends all our watches and cares, mouing upon these tow adamantin pillers of diuine and humain lawes. Which of this company that was in those times sensible of the world but knowes the danger of both, all men expecting upon the death of our late famous Queene Elizabeth that we should have bin forced like Rachel to haue fledd with our God and with Jacob to have bin fugitiues too with our wifes and families. I speake not unknowen things whear now we see by the bright arriual of his Maiesty to this Crowne, all thos mists happily dispersed and ourselfes in a fare and glorious sunshine. O let us neuer be unthankfull to God for soe great a blessing, asseuredly and safly to professe his holy Gospell and true service, or ingratefull to soe good a Prince that hath ruled euer since by our owne lawes with iustice, clemency, fatherly care and in peace, but lett us now plentifully and liberally fill his wants and with that famous Ronsard, *Aux cieux dressans les mains et soulevants les yeux, supplie a dieu qu'en santé tres parfaite viuiez cent ans en la paix qu'auez faite,* pray that he may liue many healthfull yeares enioying the sweetnes of that peace which himselfe hath effected and we contentfully tasted of, that soe his Maiesty, asseured of our loyalty and affection towards him, might be moued to call another parlament by the mediation whereof he may exonerate his subiects of the burdens that now presse them, if there be any such.

I descend now to the 4th and last which is our owne comfort and benefitt. Albeitt the forpast reasons are powerfull, yeat I know charity begins with it selfe, therefore doubt not but you will be most ready when you perceive the chefest benefitt to be yours, which I will shew unto you by two arguments *a converso.* The strenthe of a kingdome is the strenthe of the king, that of a king is his treasure; lett us then lay to our helping hands to make his Maiesty a glorious and feared monarche and ourselfs secure in that feare. Againe, the want of the Prince is the impouerishing of the subiect; lett us not then be soe tender ouer our coine as to beggar ourselfs, like those that kill themselfes out of the apprehension of death, *et certamen erat lethi,* but lett us yeald supplement to these necesities and make ourselfes the rich subiects of a riche Prince.

I draw to my conclusion fearing to haue been troublesum, had it not been upon this subiect, which I dare answer is soe agreable to you all. The Parlament then would have fullfilled the same I moue you to, had they been as we are. Our ancesters formerly and our neibours and frends lately haue dune the like; our King, the most meriting and deseruing of all his predecessors, lastly ourselfs therby liue in plenty and security. Whie trifle we any longer time, but we with you and you with us *impensis manibus* lay hold of soe happi an occasion and readily and willingly yeeld to that which is soe fatherly and louingly demanded, lest we might be iudged soe benummed as not to be sensible of the meritt of soe glorious monarch and our owne present danger. Not doubting but you will second my words with your actions and be as ready to giue as this worthy gentleman the Collector to receive for the king. I leave itt to your zeals to his Maiesty's seruice, to your desires of the euerlasting happines of his royall person and kingdume and of the quiett and prosperous estate of your selfs, wives and children, my poore self to your fauorable censures.

**30.** *Lord Sheffield, Lord President of the North, to Lord Chancellor Ellesmere. 15 Feb. 1614 (SC, xx/202).*[1]

It may please your good Lordshipp, I desired much to haue waighted uppon you myselfe to present an Informacon lately made unto me of the evell caryadge of one Sir John Savyle, a gent of Yorksheire, one of the principall in commission that maketh use of his authority to satisffy his owne ends, syth sundry complaynts be true which of late haue been made unto me. Touching one particuler which (in my opinion) is a matter of fowle condicon, I am bowlde to intrete your lordshipp to giue me leave to make knowne unto you by the relacon of Sir Thomas Fairfax, a gent of good worth, to whome the particulers of that matter is well knowne; not being able to attend your Lordshipp my selfe (as I much desiered) by reson of a fitt of sicknesse which nowe hath attached me. This gentleman shall waight your Lordshipps best leysure to inform this matter, which I most humbly commend to your Lordshipps graue wisdome and soe take my leaue, remayning alwayes redy to doe your Lordshipp any service, Sheffield. From Stratford at Bowe the xvth of Fe: 1613[/4]. To the right honorable my verie good Lord the Lord Ellesmere Lord Chancellor of England.

[*Endorsed*] Rec: 21th Feb: 1613 from the Lord Sheffield for the leaving of Sir John Savile kt. oute of the Commission of the peace in the Westryding within the countye of Yorke. A warrant dated to leave him out the xi December being his owne desyre 1615.

**31.** *Sir John Savile to Lord Chancellor Ellesmere, 6 December 1615 (Knowler, i, pp. 2–3; SC, xx/211) asking to be removed from the commission of the peace, owing to the subtle prosecution of a mean adversary. 9 December 1615, Ellesmere commends his request, but attributes his troubles to his disorderly and passionate carriage of himself.*

[1] Knowler, i, p. 2, prints the letter without the endorsement.

**32.** (*SC*, xx/213) [*Endorsed*] Instructions in a reference betwixt me and Sir Jhon Sauile whearin I used Mr Greenwood, 25 Dec. 1615.

First that by the relation of Mr John Tailer I understood that Sir John had imparted unto him a resolusion to leaue the place of Custos Rotulorum and had made itt knowen to my Lorde Chanceler desiringe his Lordship's fauour to giue him leaue to nomynate thre, one whereof might succeed him; in which number it had pleased him to name me. That therefore I could not, but be sensible of his freindly good meaninge towards me, nor doe lesse then send some trustie freind to giue him hartye thankes for the same, whiche was the occasion of your cominge to him att this time.

If he acknowledge the premisses and that his opynion to leaue the place and good will to me be still the same, then I desire that yow wold in my name renue my hartie thankes for this kindenes and to tell him that I neuer had thoughte or meaninge to affect itt without his resolution to parte therewith and absolute consente and good likinge and therefore I did so much relie upon his firmnes to me and iudge-ment in this matter, as to require his experiensed aduise in some pointes touching the same:

First, whether he thinke itt fyttinge for me to make meanes for itt;

Secondlie, what course were beste to obteine itt;

Thirdlie, what oppositions may be expected and what meanes to preuent them;

Fowrthelie, if Sir John Jackson or Mr Sargeant Hutton doe stand for the place then whether itt be fitting for me to oppose them, or likelie that I shold preuale.

If acknowledging such a discourse had with Mr Tayler, yett answear[s] doubtfullie as not fully resolued to parte therewith. Then seing that the first occasyon of parlie tooke roote from himselfe, I estemed itt conuenient to indeuoure to knowe his certeine resolution and intension which is still my desire he wold imparte unto me. But if he haue noe such purpos, then I am where I began and wishe itt might goe noe farther and that he maie longe enioy itt, as much more able and sufficient to dischardge itt.

If he say that sence his speach with Mr Tailer some other hath obteined itt, or proceeded so farre that itt will be hard for me to crosse itt. Then I desire as aforesaid that noe passages betwixt us touching this busines be at any time hereafter spoken of.

Yett I wold haue yow of your selfe to sownd him whether he be determyned absolutely to parte with itt or nott, what the parties name is that labors for itt, his affection towards him, how farre he hath proceded and what meanes he hath used and if yow perceiue him well affected towards me then what hope on my behalfe to obteine itt.

If he say itt be true that he had such speach with Mr Tailor, but now he is resolued to kepe itt, yow haue the answer in the 2 former answers.

Yett I wold haue yow as of your selfe to tell him what a speach yow had hard of his being putt owte of the Commission of peace and his place of Custos rotulorum and well to obserue his countenance and gesture.

**33.** *From Charles Greenwood. 26 Dec. 1615 (SC, xx/215).*

Worthy knight, I have (according to your appoyntment) beene with Sir John Savile att the Haghe. I found him verie merrie, still the same man *homo quadratus*, rather taking comfort by being eased of the late burden he had so longe borne in commission of the peace, then apprehending by it any touch of disgrace att all; and indeed I understood by his man Mooke that he made it his owne suite unto my Lord Chancellour. I gave him thankes in your name, for that he haveing libertie graunted unto him from his lordship to nominate three principall gentlemen his frends in the countie, of which nomber one should succeed him in the office of custos rotulorum (as you understood by Mr John Taylor from his owne mouth) he had pleased to thinke you worthie to bee named for one. He replied, he was sorie you understood so much, for that he would not have had itt knowne your name had beene used, untill you had beene sure of the place, so iealous doth he seeme to be of your reputation. His speaches (as I conceaue) give more hope of the place then assurance which I attribute to his wisdome who well knowes that *de futuris contingentibus non est certum individ'*. I find him unwilling to aduise for any course of prosecution, for that the Lord Chancellour had before that tyme resolved what should be done. He thought you should take no notice of this accident, but with patience expect the event. For howsoever you misse the place you yett (mee seemes) you gayne opinion by being rancked amongst those worthies and in this sense (take itt to be true) that *est aliquid prodiisse levus si non detur ultra*. When I left him I desired to know (if it should bee your happe to succeed him) what he would have done by you that might concern himselue or any of his, for that I knewe in this, or any other frendly curtesie you would not be a wanting. He answered, nothing. Yett after a short pause, their is (sayth he) Mr Cartwright that was my clarke of the peace a verie worthie fellowe and fitt for the place, but my Lord Chancellour hath (*sede vacante*) taken order it should be confirmed unto him. Thus with his frendly commendacons unto you he ended and with the humble remembrance of my dutie and service so will I praying God do multiplie his graces upon you and make me worthie the title of one of your faithfull servants, Ch: Grenewood. This 26th of Dec 1615. Thornhill.

**34.** *W. Cartwright to Wentworth, 26 December 1615 (Knowler, i, p. 3; SC, xx/214). When Sir John Savile was removed from the commission at his own request, the Chancellor allowed him to nominate his successor as Custos Rotulorum. He named Wentworth and had Cartwright confirmed as Clerk of the Peace, for which Wentworth's allowance is craved.*

**35.** *Edward Talbot, later 8th earl of Shrewsbury, to Wentworth, 2 April 1616 (Knowler, i, p. 3; SC, xx/216), about Wentworth's litigation on behalf of his Savile nephews and £1000 owed by Talbot.*

**36.** *From W. Cartwright. 1 Sept. 1616 (SC, xx/217).*

May it please you, Sir, I have of late bene informed that your worship is offended with me for a supposed report that is suggested to be given out by me of your self, which as it is strange to me to heare of, soe I thinke it should be incredible unto you. For I hope theare is none that knoweth me will hould me soe void of discretion, or imagine me so ile or blabbishe of tongue, as to give out that I would not serve under so base a man as yourself. For if I should so say, the world might condempne me as well for that I hould yow inferior to none under whom I served in that place, as also for that both by writeinge and often by word I haue published your honorable, kinde and worthy dealeinge with me towchinge the Clerkshipp of the Peace not only to my owne beste frindes, but alsoe to all others that I had occacon to speake thearof. And thearfore if I should so farr ouersee myself, or wronge yow, I ware not worthye to live. I beseach yow, Sir, to doe me so much favor as to lett me knowe an author for the same and then I shall make it appeare unto yow that I am wronged. For I protest unto yow upon my faith and creditt I never spake nor meant ill of yow in my life, nor had ever cause soe to doe. And thearfore I hope yow do not thinke me to be a man of soe ill breadinge as to wronge those by wordes that neuer deserved ill at my handes, much lesse my best frindes that haue bene beneficiall unto me; that is the first tyme I ever was taxed for misreportinge of any; and I doe protest that whosoever made that reporte unto yow did most lewdly belye me and I will iustify and maintayne the same against him whoesoever he be. I heard that Mathewe Feild should be the aucthor of this report and thearupon I sent unto him to know the truth thearof, but he absolutely denyeth it with soe many great oathes and protestacons as I have reason to beleave him. Thearfore I beseach you once more to lett me knowe an aucthor of this lynge report and then I doubt not but to give you such satifaccon as shall content you. In the meantyme my desire is that you will suspend your opinyon of me and think no worse of me then I deserve; for after I shall give you iust cause of offence either by word or deed, I will never be seene in England and yett I would be glad to knowe wheather you do give creditt to this lyinge report, or noe, which if you doe, I neither may nor will so farr presume your favour as otherwise I would. Thus craveinge your good oppinyon of me untill I deserve the contrary, I take leave, alwaies restinge your worships to be commaunded, W. Cartwright. Ebor, primo September 1616.

### 37. *From C. Radcliffe. 5 Oct. 1616 (SC, xx/218).*

Honorable Sir, the Sessyons being well ended, though something distractedly in regard of holdinge itt att seuerall places. For wee were driven to dispatch the rest of the busynes after your worship's departure in the church, which in my poore opinion was unseemly, and the like inconvenience wold hereafter be prevented by providinge a fitt place for that service which I doubt nott butt your worship will forsee, as allso for the placinge of some sufficient and learned in the law to be in commission in that part of the cuntry that is fitt to geue the charge and preuent censures which that omission may incurre; and therefore wold I be bold to putt you in mynde of Mr Cressye who (amongst others wherof I send here inclosed a note) wilbe comended to our Iudge for that purpose, being neere that place and of good meritt, amongst whome I hope you wil be pleased nott to forgett Mr Cha: Greenwood when you see the Baron att London. Cloughe was nott bounde over againe, though much urged, wherin Sir Henry Savile did with all confidence geue your worthie respect, as the iustice of the pore man's cause requyred. I think the places for the next sessions wilbe Knarsbrough, Leedes and Barnesley, which wilbe sett down now att Skipton whereof (if your worship dislike) I beseich you signifie your pleasure therin to mee by some that come to the Sessions there; all which I doe referre to your wisdome and humbly take leave, allwaies remayninge your worships most bounden, Cha: Radclyffe. 5 Oct. 1616. To the honorable and right worthie k$^t$

Barronett Sir Thomas Wentworth at Woodhous. [*Endorsed*] speake with Mr Baron Bromley touching the same.

**38.** *From C. Radcliffe. 20 Dec. 1616* (*SC*, xx/219).

Honorable Sir, that I may nott neglect my bounden duty, be pleased to accept some aduertisement of this tymes occurencs. There was a generall expectacon of thapparance of all the Iustics of the county att this gaole deliuery (my Lord President being there in person himself), butt his Lordship did honorably consider of the tyme and unseasonablenes of the weather and was pleased to admitt of my allegacon for your worship that you cold not well be heare in regard of your late coming from London, as for Sir Godfrey Rodes and Mr Wentworth being both nott well att this present whome (next) I held myself most bound to observe. The gaole was great, butt the causes noe more then ordynary, saving that an extraordinary imposicon is likelie to be chardged uppon the West-riding wherewith I though itt my part to acquaint you. For there was one Barker of Tadcaster that brought mee a commission from my Lord President directed to him for providing cariages in the Westriding for 500 chawder of lyme towards the erecting of new buildings att the mannor, presently to be done att v$^s$ iiii$^d$ euery chawder, which amounteth to the some of 192$^l$ or thereabouts as allso for a hundred chawder of coales att the same rate, all which either must be carried by the cuntry or this allowance made for the same; and Barker desired mee to make out assessments to the seuerall wapentakes to collect the same, which I refused to doe till I had warrant from the Justics in that behalf and therefore referred him to the next Sessions to receive further order therin, as the Justices would be pleased to consider when he purposeth to be with his commission. And for that I doubted whether your worship wold be at Wetherby Sessions, being the 7th of January (wher Barker wilbe), I thought itt my duty to advise you therof, farther to advise as best seemed to your wisdome; for happilie the Justics there may condiscend thereunto, I think Mr Serieant Hutton will be there, who happilie will not understand of thes till he be there.

Wee haue had some opposicon betwixt my Lord President and the high sheriffe[1] about the attachment office which my Lord expected to haue had, but the Sheriffe uppon some conceived grevaunce boldlie and absolutelie told him to face in plaine tearmes he shold nott haue itt. Whereunto my Lord replied that none but a clowne or a foole would make him such an answere; itt is said there

---

[1] Sir Michael Wharton.

was some contestacon betwixt them for commaund (the sheriffe being demaunded whether he wold attend him to the hall or noe) who stoutlie maynteyned his owne powr that by vertue of his letters pattents from the kinge under the great seale of England (duringe his yeare) he might command *Ducibus, Comitibus, militibus &c* and that he was nott to attend any man's person but the king's and his service which he wold not neglect. Butt even now this morninge all things are attunde and well againe: the Sheriffe hath bestowed the office att his lordship's appoyntment and pacificacon had of each side. Theis things [I am] bold to write unto your worship rather to expresse my dutie then taking delight to divuldge matters that concerne mee nott and so doe I presume of your noble interpretacon acknowledging your honorable goodnes which hath bound me euer to be, att your worship's commaund, Cha: Radclyffe. 20 Dec 1616.

**39.** *Wentworth to Lord Clifford, 9 January 1617 (Knowler, i, p. 5; SC, ii, p. 1), asking pardon for not meeting him at York.*

**40.** (*SC*, ii, p. 1) To the right worshipfull my very lovinge cozen Sir Thomas Fairfax knight at Walton. Wentworth Woodhowse. 16 January 1617.[1]

Sir, I haue receaued your letter and herein returne yow my answer. Where yow write that I promised yow should understand my determinacon concerninge the sale of my tenement and interest of common in Walton att Martinmasse last, truly I doe not remember the same, but I doe presently call to mind that I tould yow I would passe unto yow upon valewable consideracon my interest of Common, albeitt I should resolue to keepe the tenement which I am still purposed to doe and yow shall find mee willinge to giue yow all reasonable satisfaccon therin. Yet I must intreate yow not to mistake my delay of answer, seinge that by reason of my many important affaires, I cannot as yet attend truly to informe my selfe in this perticuler. And indeed seinge my resolucon is to pleasure yow therwith as aforesaid, I cannot see why yow should at all dislike this pause, when in the interim my selfe onely looseth therby. I will conclude therfore that if yow wilbee pleased to assure your selfe of all louinge respects and indeauours from mee to preserue future goodwill betwixt our howses and for this matter repose your selfe upon these lines, yow shall therby doe your selfe righte, haue your owne desire I hope in due

---

[1] The heading is here printed in full. The headings of the other letters in the letter-book have been abbreviated.

time fulfilled and the more encourage mee to apply my selfe constantly to perseuearance in remaininge, Your assured lovinge cozen, Th. Wentworth.

**41.** (*SC*, ii, p. 2) *To Lady Grace Cavendish.*[1] *Wentworth Woodhouse. 4 March 1617.*[2]

My much honored Lady, I am sorry that beinge unable to trauell I should therby bee disinabled to attend your Ladyship, which I much desired. In the meane time therfore I haue sent my servant and these lines to excuse my selfe and, assoone as I can endure to ride, I will, Godwillinge, waite upon your Ladyship's pleasure. My sollicitor told mee what your Ladyship required from mee, in all which at my cominge I shall giue your Ladyship full satisfaccon soe farr forthe as lyes in my power. He likewise related unto mee that your counsell informes your Ladyship that the inheritance is youres: I wish it were soe, but I much misdoubt it will proue otherwaies, wherin if a sight of the true coppy of the originall indenture (beinge all that I haue and which I formerly shewed your Ladyship) will satisfy yow, I shall bringe itt with mee soe that your counsell may view itt. I must conclude, Madam, with my former request that your Ladyship wilbee pleased to extend your fauour towards your fatherlesse nephues in such things as shall not preiudice your selfe and in other sort, nether did I nor euer will moue your Ladyship; in which kind I shalbee humbly bold to rely upon your honorable disposicon and affeccon towards them. Thus praying, Madam, unto God for your long life and happines, I take leaue and remaine, Your Ladyship's affecconate freind and servant, Th. Wentworth.

**42.** *To Mr. Francis Bristow. Wentworth Woodhouse. 12 April 1617* (*SC*, ii, p. 3).

Sir, being purposed to haue brought up your sonne in my owne company and to haue furnished him with such thinges as he wantes at London, I haue notwithstandinge sent him unto yow with this bearer sooner then I intended, as that which is best suteinge with his owne desire of late made knowne unto mee by himselfe. And indeed I found him soe ill contented with his stay here and soe little pleasinge unto mee that I iudged the lesse time hee staied here would bee better for us both. I hope in the future hee may proue more profittinge with

---

[1] Daughter of George, earl of Shrewsbury, and widow of Henry Cavendish.
[2] It has been assumed that this letter and no. 40 were entered in the correct sequence; if they were not, both should be dated 1617/8.

yow then in these parts where he hath had noe likeing to abide. I am sory out of my respect to your selfe I should bee constrained to part with him soe sone and yow shall but doe mee right to beleeue that I haue endeauored by all meanes to breed him in such manner as might most haue enabled him and contented yow. Therfore I must entreat yow not to beleeue your sonnes reports too farre, if hee enforme yow to the contrary, which I thinke hee will not been soe impudent as to doe. For if yow will let mee know wherin hee maie pretend not to haue bene well used, I will giue satisfaccon in each particular. I haue by reason of this suddaine departure deliuered to the bearer ten pounds, desireinge yow to receaue itt and to bestow itt for him as yow shall best like. I must for conclusion desire (that without discourageinge your sonne upon this occasion, for it may bee hee will fashion himselfe to your good liking hereafter) yow will with a fatherly care still respect him if hee merritt itt. Assure yourselfe I shalbee allwaies ready to deserue your loue and as oportunity shalbee offered, giue yow testimony of my beinge, Your truly affecconate freind, Th. Wentworth.

**43.** (*SC*, ii, p. 4) *To Sir Thomas Fairfax knight. Gawthorpe. 12 June 1617.*

Sir, there hath bene with mee this day, my freholders and tennants of Huby, by reason of a distress taken by your Baliffe of Rigton, for an amerciament of three shillings fower pence against Francis Atkinson, for cuttinge brakes upon the South side of Almistcliffe, within my bounder of Harwood, which goods hee hath loosed by replevin: yet in regard of the respect I beare yow, and as the poore man himselfe desired, I thought good to enforme yow how the matter stands, before there bee any further proceedinge in Lawe, hopeing that the matter followinge, will giue yow full satisfaccon. First the said inhabitants of Huby, haue had free use time out of mind, without restraint to depasture all their cattle, to gather maste, to cut downe brakes, digg and gett turfes, with other benefitts and easmentes, thorowout all the Moores within my bounder of Harwood, on that side the riuer; and secondly, and more particulerly, not onely the liberties aforesaid, in the woods and territories of Stainburne and Rigton, but also their reasonable estouers, howsboot and hayboote, within the said woods and territories. For the first, your tennants and officers may sufficiently satisfie yow, for the second, I assure you Sir I haue this day seene a very ancient and faire deed, fully warrantinge the said customes and liberties. Besides which, as I am enformed, yow haue noe freeholder, that is bound to doe suite and seruice at your Court of Rigton, wherby to warrant any such amerciament, if there were any iuste cause. Lesse then this I could not well write in respect the matter concernes my owne tennants in consequence as well as them; and that (if lawfully I may) it seemes to mee good reason, I should ioyne in the preservacon of our accustomed liberties. The premisses therfore considered, I am to moue yow, that this suite maye fall, and that things may bee hereafter continewed, accordinge to ancient right, and custome. And that yow wilbee pleased, to lett this bearer know your mind herein. Thus with my kind comendacons to your selfe, and service to your Lady remembred, I remaine Your very lovinge freind, Th. Wentworth.

**44.** (*SC*, ii, p. 5) *To William Cartwright Esq. Gawthorpe. 23 June 1617.*

Mr Cartwright, there is a fellon in the Castle for horse stealinge, his name is Richard Wildsmith, who besides hath confessed, that hee hath diuerse times stollen corne from his Maister William Spencer, by the inticement of Francis Cosse, who likewise receaued and paid for the same soe stollen. Cosse is bound ouer to the Sessions, and there to bee indicted as accessary. Now Wildsmith haueing not as yet bene examined before any Justice as concerninge this matter, I desire that yow would take the paines to send for him; take his examinacon, and try if yow can gett him to confesse any further matter, for his neighboures doe much suspect him for other pil-feringes. Itt is said Cosse hath sent him some money since hee was comitted, which hee would bee examined upon. The confession I desire that yow will send mee by this bearer my servant, who hath a note to shew yow concerninge this businesse. Euen soe I comend mee unto yow and rest Your very lovinge freind, Th. Wentworth.

**45.** (*SC*, ii, p. 5) *To Sir William Bambrough knight. Wentworth Woodhouse. 3 July 1617.*

Sir, I am to entreate your furtherance, that I may bee righted, as concerninge very unequall assessments wherwith as I conceaue my little Mannore of Thornton under Risberge hath bene more ouer-charged then any other. I perceaue that in some sessments, Thornton is rated at a full third to Sawton cum Brawby; in some, at a full halfe, in others as deeply allout, nay and somtimes ten shillings for the other eight shillings; yet it is well understood I doubte not by your selfe, that Sawton is worth 800[ll] per anum, and I know mine not to bee worth a fowerth part therof. Determininge with my selfe to send my servant to gett a remedy (if might bee) and beinge a stranger in the cuntry, I could address my selfe to none with better confidence, then your selfe. Wherfore Sir, I desire your good meanes in this cause, and that yow would bee pleased to acquaint the rest of the bench therwith, the messinger my servant beinge ready to make the matter appeare unto you in particuler. And lastly, I very much desire, that there may bee some indifferent course held, and accordingly setled; wherby I shalbee particulerly ingaged to doe the like for yow or them in these partes, as occasion shall serue. Euen soe wishinge yow longe life, and much happinesse in some haste I remaine, your very affecconate and assured freind, Th. Wentworth.

**46.** (*SC*, ii, p. 6) *To Sir Robert Anstruther knight. Wentworth Woodhouse. 9 July 1617.*

Sir, I should not satisfy my owne thoughts, if I did not hereby take notice of the kind remembrance, respect, and affeccon, which yow soe lately made profession of to mee, in a conferrence betwixte your selfe and Mr Radcliffe, clarke of the peace. And the rather must I needs acknowledge it, in regard I was there unknowne unto yow, and soe could in noe sort expect itt. The hope I haue conceaued to enioy soe worthy a neighbour, affords mee great content, yet shall I bee much more desirous that the title of unacquainted and straungers, may clearly bee remoued, and altered into the assured attributes of familiars and freinds; and that the nearnesse of our dwellinges, may minister occasion of often meetinges and conversings togeather. I will conclude, Sir, that yow may rest satisfied to find mee in the future, as your selfe desires, willingly ready to render yow the offices of a setled frendshipp with the respect due to soe meritting a gentleman, and that I remaine fully disposed to giue yow the testimonies therof, Your rightly affecconate freind Th. Wentworth.

**47.** (*SC*, ii, p. 6) *To Lord Keeper Bacon. Gawthorpe. 13 July 1617.*

Right honorable and my most honoured Lord, beinge at the Sessions in one of the deuisions of this Westridinge of Yorkshire, your Lordships lettere was openly readd, dyrectinge that one William Vessy might bee discharged from an high Constable's place, which was ordered accordingly by the maior parte of the Justics then present, yett my selfe and those that had formerly bene of another opinion, with all due reuerence to your Lordship dissentinge, in regard wee perceaued by the contents of the letter, your Lordship had not bene fully enformed of the truth of the matter; I thought it my part (fearinge the like measure might bee offered my selfe by unwarranted suggestions) humbly to present your Lordship with these lynes. I dare not enter into the particulers, least their length might in some sort seeme presumpcon in mee, soe much to trouble your Lordship, which neuerthelesse I thinke wee shall hereafter craue leaue to offer unto your approued wisdome. Onely somarily our opinion is noe other then such as hath bene formerly confirmed expressly by order from the Judges of Assizes, ratified by comon consent at two generall Sessions for the whole Rideinge, where Mr Justice Hutton and Sir John Jackson were both present, Vessy with [*p. 7*] his owne full good likeinge and consent sworne to execute the place, and the other that had but executed the place *quousque* discharged. On the other side, it was neuer thought unfitt, but onely at the Sessions for one deuision, beinge but a third part of those that mett at Easter, and yet still carryed with maior part of voices confirminge Vessie's eleccon: the manner it selfe much preiudiciall to his Maiesty's service in the example, beinge carryed with that contempt and play to the kings Comissioners, as in all my little practize I neuer saw the like, the man himselfe of a proud conceate scorninge to serue the cuntry in soe meane a plase, and one that I dare make good, hath misinformed your Lordship. The truth hereof, if your Lordship doubt, or desire present satisfaccon in, Mr Justice Hutton wilbee I thinke in towne, who can best enform yow, wherto I humbly craue your Lordship would bee pleased. The labour that now rests upon mee, is to signify unto your Lordship that I was humbly bold for the reasons shortly expressed (and seing your Lordship's letter was upon misinformacon to continew in my former mind) relyinge both upon the order of the Judges of Assize, and also the opinion of Mr Justice Hutton and Sir John Jackson; but yet with this caution till I should further receaue your Lordship's determinate pleasure, when your Lordship hath understood the seuerall passages: which I shall now and euer submitt my selfe unto, with that duty and observance, that I hold my selfe bound in unto your Lordship, more particulerly, then any other of the Comissioners. And thus humbly suinge that the apprehencon to bee wronged by report, and soe ecclipsed in your fauour, (beinge that which is most deare unto mee, and which I am most desirous to continewe) may obtaine my pardon for the length of thes lynes; I beseech God to blesse your Lordship with many honorable happy, and longe dayes, Your Lordship's humbly bound, in all duty and seruice, Th. Wentworth

**48.** (*SC*, ii, p. 7) *To Mr Christopher Danby Esq. Gawthorpe. 29 July 1617.*

Sir, my condicon free from medlinge in other mens affaires, and the nearnesse of blood betwixt us, may excuse my forwardnes and

freedome in writinge, and both of them assure yow of my harty good
meaninge towards yow; true freindshipp beinge indeed noe other
then upright plainnesse. I haue formerly bene acquainted with some
distrustfull jealousies yow haue conceaued against your wife,
which since not hearinge of, I was exceedinge gladd, verely per-
swadinge my selfe yow had receaued satisfaccon for those supposed
wrongs. But now to my great griefe, I haue itt credibly confirmed,
that yow openly disavowe your last child, passionately charginge
your wife with adultery. Hereby as I may say, yow arraigne and
question your iudgment and reputacon, in a complaint causelesse,
scandalous and very daungerous (p. 8). Causelesse, because in the
opinion of most, the gentlewoman is acquitt as inocent and wronged.
Scandalous, for bee it neuer soe plainly proued, yet in matters of soe
much tendernes and nearnesse, as are those betwixt man and wife,
part of the staine must of necessity remaine upon the blood and howse
of the husband; yet more particulerly in your case, both in regard the
world taxeth your selfe with frequent condicons in the like kind. In
respect also yow haue frequented her bedd and yet depriued her
of the rites of marriage; the former will much touch your creditt, the
latter make yow a tempter to, and procurer of, her pretended loos-
nesse; and in both of them all men will exceedingly much condemne
yow, very daungerous in respect of the proofe of your and her freinds,
and of the euent.

For the proofe that wilbee produced against her, I fully perswade
my selfe, it will fall short and bee found uncertaine, as grounded
upon the tales of idle ill-affected servants, or invented to please your
humour. But on the contrary call well to mind and thorowly waigh
with your selfe, what course yow haue held with her; whether you
euer indeauoured to haue procured her footman by large promisses
to haue charged her with incontinency; others of your servants to
attempt her; wherin notwithstandinge they neuer preuailed, which
might haue giuen yow good satisfaccon. Farr bee it from mee to
beleeue these things, that euer yow plotted soe indiscreetly, I may
say, to blemish your selfe, yet this is publiquely spoken abroade, and
generally in your owne house and amonge your owne servants. Yow
know how yow haue formerly bene questioned, by that wicked instrument Clarke, to haue practized her death. Take heed least these
new breaches cause a beeleefe, and confirme such odious slaunders.

Secondly your owne freinds wilbee forced to dissavowe these
proceedings, where those that bee hers are tyed in all honour and
other respects, to maintaine her creditt, which assure your selfe the
Lord her brother[1] will doe, by all the power and the meanes hee

[1] Edward, Lord Morley.

possibly can procure, and indeauour to cast those reproachfull disgraces upon yow, which yow desire to heape upon his sister.

Thirdly the euent (if it fortune to bee brought into the Starr chamber, or els where iudicially) is fearfull, deeply endaungeringe your estate, your children, your creditt, your life; and bee it neuer soe sutable to your owne wishes, yet all things considered I am confident it had better neuer bene attempted. And therfore your owne judgment must needs tell yow, your aduenture to bee strangly inconsiderate, where yow may loose soe much and cannott possibly gaine any thinge; and I am most earnestly to moue yow, not to second your errour in publishinge itt, with soe great a scandall and daunger in pursuinge itt. But in the name of God beseech his grace to giue yow better thoughts and safer (*p. 9*) undertakings; reconcile your selfe to your wife in loue and kindnesse, and apply your selfe to manage your estate with prouidence and aduantage, that now by meanes of these inward and domestique discontentments, is liable to many losses, impairinges, if not ruines.

Now, Sir, hearinge thus much, I could not answer the office of soe neare a kindred with lesse then once plainly to giue yow my aduise, which haueinge now done, I shall not importunatly pursew itt, but leaue yow both in this, and all other your affaires, to God's blessed guiding, and your owne serious consideracon. Your very assured lovinge Cosen, Th. Wentworth.

**49.** (*SC*, ii, p. 9) *To [Edward, earl of Shrewsbury].*

My much honoured Lord, whensoeuer I shall heare any thinge preiudiciall to your affaires, I shalbee right gladd to acknowledge my errour, and much contented to bee soe mistaken, that soe all may bee, (as I shall euer wish) both in the meanes, progresse, and effect, profittable, honourable and successfull to your Lordship. There is nothinge now to bee done, but with all industry and care, to labour the appearance of the Jury, which wilbee exceedinge aduantagious for yow, and most usefull when it shall please his Maiesty to enforme himselfe of the state of the cause; for noe doubt but by God's grace the verdict will goe with yow.

And truly if yow bringe the cause to hearinge before Michelmas, the stay till then will nothinge harme, but rather helpe yow, if God spare my Lady Grace life.[1] In the meane while, things standinge upon these faire tearmes betwixt your Lordship and my Lord C. and Lord A.[2] I hope the Jury will the more easily bee drawne to appeare;

---

[1] Lady Grace Cavendish.
[2] Lord Chamberlain and the earl of Arundel, see no. 50, p. 97 and n. 1.

and therfore I thinke it cannot bee amisse to haue it discreetly published by some of your agents abroad in the cuntry that now the difference is onely betwixt your selfe and sister in lawe, and that in all that concernes the Lords, your nephewes, they beinge referred to the kinge, his Maiesty will arbitrate; their Lordships beinge rather against, then any waies consentinge to the violences, and uniust sutes of your sister in lawe. Your Lordship may now very well put of in good and faire tearmes my Lord Cauendish, by reason of the stay of the recouery, and yet take the benefitt of his writinges at the hearinge of the cause; wherin your Lordship hath to walke warely, nether too farr to engage your selfe by promis, nor yet too much to distast him, but to bringe him on with a sweet hand as they say. [*p. 10*] Your treaties with him should bee allwaies (if possibly it may bee) before some witnesse, which would both restraine him from pressing your Lordship with earnestnesse, but rather in moderate tearmes, and bee a good safety to your Lordship that matters might not bee misconceaued as heretofore your Lordship knowes they haue bene.

My Lord, I made bold to write thus much to your Lordship in respect I am not certaine to see yow til yow come to London, crauinge pardon for these hasty scribled lines, and for presumeinge to deliuer unto your Lordship soe freely my opinion; which notwithstandinge I humbly submitt to your wisdome, hopeinge that what I write may dye in secret, which shalbee a greate incouragement to mee, to doe yow most affecconate and true service Your Lordship's to dispose of, Th. Wentworth [September 1617].

**50.** (*SC*, xx/83) Ouertures on the behalfe of the Earle of Shrew[s]bury whearby all future differences betwixt the lord Chamberlaine, the Earle of Arundel, the lord Ruthen and himself may be preuented and finally concluded.[1]

Wheareas the late Earle of Shrewbury, the aforesaid lords and ther ladies haue indeuoured by fines and recoueries to barre me, the nowe Earle, of att the least 20,000[li] per annum intended me by my father, as may appear by severall his conueyances, unto all which notwithstanding my title (as I hope) is still perfectly good and not in law to be auoided; yeat out of the good afection towards them and a peacible

---

[1] The daughters and heirs-general of Gilbert, the seventh earl, who died 8 May 1616, were Mary, married in 1604 to William, earl of Pembroke, Elizabeth in 1601 to Henry Lord Ruthin, and Alethea, married in 1606 to Thomas, earl of Arundel.

disposition in myself I thought good to make them thes respectiue offers following:

First, if the said lords will be content that my sister Grace (whose interest I haue bought upon valewable considerations) may perfect a Recouery in the Common-pleas, according to the usuall manner in all cases of like nature.

Secondly, noe ways disquiett me in the peacible injoying of such lands contained in two seuerall conueyances therof, made by my father, whearwithall I haue formerly acquainted the said lords and whearupon I haue fower seuerall times recouered before the Judges in the King's Benche.

Thirdly, that I may haue without sute possession deliuered unto me of the mannour howse of Winfeild in the county of Derby and of the mannour of Ashton Gifford in the county of Wiltshire, both which are contained in the same conueyances and as yeat withheld from me. I will be content that my right and title to all the lands within the great Intaile made by my father 15 Elizabeth maybe examined and determined by the mediation of frends and counsellors; as alsoe (if it please God I die without issue) to estate upon my neeces and ther heirs after my decease soe much of the said lands contained in the said conueyance of 15 Elizabeth as shall appear iustly and rightfully to belong unto me, which (as I think) wilbe treble in valew thos lands whearin I desire a freedume by means of my sister Grace her perfecting of the aforesaid Recouery.

Howsoeuer I doubt not butt itt will be iudged by all persons exceeding reasonable and necessary that a nobleman of my ranke, and borne to soe great an inheritance, should haue libertie in disposing of 2000ll per annum, or little more, whearwithall to be armed aganst casuall euents, to discharge his debts, to make a ioynture to his wife and to preferre his well deseruing kinsmen and seruants.

My lord Chamberlain's Answeare:

Your lordship's demands are soe great in desiring quiett possession of all such landes as you haue any culler to make claime untoo and your offers soe shortt in that you would referr soe much only to mediation to which your lordship hath noe title at all, that I can conceaue noe otherwise of these ouertures, butt that they are soe farre from reason or curtesy that I can naither make answear nor giue consent unto them.

Butt that which your lordship doth seeke to perswade by this conclusion I thinke all men that are either indifferent or that understand anything of thes differences between us will easily be perswaded otherwise.

For first, your lordship hath not shewed anything to intitle you to any inheritance at all; your lordship's own conueyances make you butt tenantt for life, soe that inconueniences which your lordship mentioneth doe necessarily follow such an estate.

Secondly, your lordship hath not heathertoo declared that you intend in case your lordship could recouer an estate of inheritance in this partt to conferre itt, either upon him that shall be heire to your name and dignity, or upon thos that are your heirs in blood. Butt it may rather be gathered that your lordship intends itt to strangers, which I thinke all persons will iudge exceeding reasonable that the Coheirs doe indeuour by all lawfull means to hinder.[1]
[*Endorsed*] 1617.

**51.** *Buckingham to Wentworth, 5 September 1617* (*Knowler*, i, p. 4; *SC*, xx/221); *the king is informed Savile yielded the Custos-ship voluntarily to him; he has received Savile into favour again and will take it well 'that you resign it up again unto him with the same willingness.' Wentworth's answer to this dated 15 September has been printed by J. J.* Cartwright, Chapters in the History of Yorkshire (*Wakefield, 1872*), *pp. 187–91, and in* The Fortescue Papers, *ed. S. R.* Gardiner (*Camden Society, new series i, 1871*), *pp. 23–27; a heavily corrected draught of the letter is SC, xx/11. Sir Thomas Savile's answer to this is also in* The Fortescue Papers, *pp. 27–28. Both sides regaled Buckingham with half truths. Wentworth's assertion (ibid., p. 25) that Savile had never told him of his alleged nomination to the place, is only true in so far as Sir John had not said this in the interview with Greenwood, but ignores the fact that he claimed to have named him with two others, as well as the circumstance of Cartwright being continued as Clerk of the Peace (see above nos. 34, 36). If Savile probably exaggerated his part in Wentworth's nomination and certainly misrepresented the circumstances of his own resignation, Wentworth's complete denial of knowledge was also a misrepresentation. It is worth noting that Wentworth appealed to the written testimony of Ellesmere, who was dead, while Savile appealed to the unwritten testimony of Ellesmere's secretary, who was alive.*

---

[1] *SC*, xxi/14, records Wentworth's opinion also in 1617 against settiing a half share of certain lands on Lady Ruthin and a moiety of other lands amounting to £1200 a year on Mr Talbot of Grafton, because both these settlements might enable the beneficiaries to trench into the future peace and safety of Wentworth's sister, Lady Anne Savile, and his nephew, Sir George Savile. Wentworth's suggestion that Edward should settle rent charges instead of land was not approved by the earl.

**52.** (*SC*, xxi/13) [*Endorsed*] Copy of a letter which should haue been deliuered to the lord keeper 1617.

My most honored lord, euer thankfully acknowleging to be continued in the place of Custos Rotulorum by your lordship's espetiall fauoure; understanding of late that Sir Jhon Sauill hath made some extraordinary means to his Maiestie to be therunto restored, much tending to my disgrace if itt should now be taken from me, hauing no wayes I hope miscarried my self therin. I haue thought itt my partt humbly to addresse this messinger together with these few lines unto your lordship, both fully to informe your lordship (if itt may stande with youre good pleasure) of the state of the cause and likewise to craue that comforth and supportt from your lordship, which, next under God and his Maiestie, I principally relye upon in my iust and lawfull causes. I will therfore humbly make bold to be a sutor to your lordship that such a course be not taken aganst me, butt that the same be stayed until I shall haue oportunity to answeare for my self which shallbe, God-willing, the beginning of this next terme. For which fauour I shal euer hold my self much bownden to your lordship, humbly pray unto God for your lordship' long life with all honoure and happines and assume unto my self iustly and uprightly the title of youre lordship's in all duty and seruice humbly to be commanded, Th. Wentworth. Gawthorp this 15th of September 1617.

**53.** (*SC*, xxi/12) [*Endorsed*] Copy of a letter which should haue been sentt to my lord Wotton.

My much honored lord, the confidence I haue growndedly taken of your honorable fauour and good opinion euer shewed unto me causeth me att this present humbly to desire your lordship to take information from this bearer of a matter that doth very nearly touche me in my creditt and to grantt me your countenance as occasion shallbe offered aganst soe iniuriouse a prosecution of my adversaries and espetially your commendations to my lord Keeper that soe I may haue his honorable supportt soe farr forth as my honest and upright cariage shall iustly meritt; the which I will lay up as a faithfull remembrancer of the humble thankes I shall owe to your lordship for the same and how deeply I am bownde to remaine Your lordship's humbly to be commanded, Th. Wentworth. Gawthorp this 15th of September 1617.

**54.** (*SC*, xx/222) [*Endorsed*] Coppy of a letter to be hearafter writt to his Maiestie by my lord of Cumberland if need be 1617.

May it please your most excellent Maiestie, whereas I understand by my sonne in law, Sir Thomas Wentworth, that he hath received a letter from my honorable good Lord, the Earle of Buckingham, signifyinge unto him that whereas your Maiestie hath bene enformed that Sir John Savile did voluntarile yeild to him the place of custos rotulorum that your Maiestie wold take itt well att his handes that he resigne it back againe with the same willingness,[1] for which your gracious dealinge with my said sonne, I geve your maiestie most humble thanks. Yett withall humbly beseeching your highnes wold be pleased to be informed that my sonne conceves nott that the same was by Sir John voluntarilie yeilded up, as he pretendds, butt Sir John beeing putt out by reason of some passionate cariage of his, complayned on in the starrechamber (my sonne then not in any sort either knowing thereof or labouringe for the place) was freely called thereunto by my late Lord Chancelor, in such sort as my sonne hathe written at lardge to my Lord of Buckingham. In the execucon wherof he hath (I doe well asseur myself) so caried himself both in respect of your Maiestie's service and in uprightnes towards the cuntry, as upon examinacon will geue your Maiestie full satisfaccon he hath nott in any sort neglected the one or misbehaved himselfe in the other. I am therefore (on my said sonne's behalf) to be an humble sutor unto your Maiestie that (with your good pleasure) he may be still contynued in the saide place. For the which I shall hold my self much bound unto your princely goodnes and trust your Maiestie shall heare the Cuntrye to be as orderly and peaceably governed and your service by my sonne's care (for so much as belongs to that place) as well performed, as if Sir John were againe restored and the rather am I humbly to move your Maiestie in respect my sonne conceves Sir John to be very ill affected towards him and, being thus taken from him without any cause of offence, ytt wold bee a great disgrace unto him in the cuntrye and very much to my discomforthe now in my old age.

**55.** (*SC*, ii, p. 10) *To Sir Gervas Clifton Bart. Gawthorpe. 10 Sept. 1617.*

Sir, I am to desire yow from my Lord Clifford that yow would write unto his Lordship by this messinger, therby takeinge notice of

---

[1] This letter was dated 5 September 1617. Buckingham's second letter of 23 September, acknowledging that he and the king had been misinformed about Savile's resignation, presumably made it unnecessary for Cumberland to write to the king; Knowler, i, p. 4.

his Lordship's being here with his Lady, and to moue that they would doe yow likewise the fauour to visitt your selfe and Lady, as they haue done Gawthorpe. The reason of this is, as I conceaue, that my Lord is willing to make my Lady see and beleeue how much his freinds respect her, which will cause her to increase in respect towards him, and content her. If please yow, Sir, to send it inclosed in a letter to mee, I shall take order it may bee sent to Skipton as my Lord desireth; but I conceaue my Lord would haue this done as of your selfe. Thus with my service to your Lady remembred, togeather with my wiue's kind respects to yow both, I remaine, your affecconate brother in law and servant, Th. Wentworth

Sir, I would haue writt more formally, but that my hast hath caused mee to bee briefe, and likewise to write ill, which it will please yow to excuse.

**56.** (*SC*, ii, p. 10) *Another to Sir Gervas Clifton, the same tyme and place.*

Sir, might not too frequent letteres proue troublesome, I could not set pen to paper often enough, to soe respected a freind as your selfe. Albeitt then I writt unto yow this very day by another messinger, yet must I needs by these latter lynes giue yow thanks both for your kind remembrance of mee, as also for the contentfull newes of the good health of (*p. 11*) your selfe and vertuous good Lady, and wish I may neuer receaue other notice of soe honorable freinds, then of their perfect recouery, which I shall pray for. Sir, I rest much beholden to yow for the booke yow sent mee, which I receaued not til this eueninge, and in regard I may the better performe promis with yow, I am to desire, findinge it is longer then I did expect, that I may haue it as longe as yow can conveniently spare itt; yet I wish yow wilbee pleased to write mee word when you desire itt, and I shall not faile to pursue your dyreccon in returninge it, with many thanks. I intend, Godwillinge, either before, or presently after Michelmas to remoue towards Woodhus. Thus, Sir, beinge ready to retribute the like effect of a true and upright freindship: as I shalbee fitted with an occasion, with my service to your honourable Lady remembred, I remaine your affecconate brother in law and servant, Th. Wentworth.

**57.** (*SC*, ii, p. 11) *To the Earl of Shrewsbury.*[1] *Gawthorpe. 22 Sept. 1617.*

Right honourable and truly honoured, wee are hereby to giue your Lordship and our honourable good Lady humble thankes, both for

---

[1] Edward Talbot, eighth earl of Shrewsbury, died 8 February 1618.

your noble remembrance of us, and the great dainty sent unto us by your footman, which I dare say was the first of that kind, that euer came within these walls. Wee shall both Godwillinge attend yow before your goinge to London, and my selfe bee ready to waite on yow that journey. I doe wish wee had any thinge worthy to bee esteemed or taken as a testimony of our thankfullnes for this great kindnesse; but haueinge nothinge equivalent to your many fauoures, but our dutifull respects, wee must end, with the tender therof to your noble selues, and with our humble praiers to God, for your eternall felicities, Humbly at your honour's seruice, Th. Wentworth, Mar. Wentworth.

**58.** *Buckingham to Wentworth, 23 September 1617* (*Knowler*, i, p. 4; *SC*, xx/223), *accepts that he was misinformed as to Savile's resignation and withdraws the request for Wentworth's surrender of the custos-ship.*

**59.** (*SC*, ii, p. 11) *To Lord Wentworth. Gawthorpe. 30 Sept. 1617.*

My much honoured Lord, it falls out oft times, that thanks for small services doe rather deeplyer engage the parties in their respects, then that there is any proporcon of desert to occasion such acknowledgment. Thus it is with mee at this present, your Lordship by your noble remembrance and ample thanks for my meane endeauours, in observance of your comaunds doe therby the more bind mee to your seruice, and adds to my obligacon. I am right gladd to heare of your Lordship's good health, which I beseech God may long continew (*p. 12*) with much honore and happinesse to your selfe and much content and comfort to your freinds. Lastly crauinge leaue hereby to present my wiue's seruice and my owne to your Lordship and noble Lady I will spare your Lordship's further trouble, and conclude with the constancy of good wishes, and truth of affeccon, which yow may both justly chalenge, and rest assured of, from Your Lordship's deuoted kinsman and servant, Th. Wentworth.

**60.** (*SC*, ii, p. 12) *To Sir Peter Freschevile knight. Hansworth Wood-house. 8 Oct. 1617.*

Sir, apprehendinge that my long absence from Stailey might seeme forgetfullnes of soe worthy a freind and kinsman as your selfe, I haue set my hand to paper hereby at the least in some sort to redeeme the same, which my urgent occasions and remoter dwellings haue longer delayed then I eyther did desire or could expecte. Nether haue I bene unmindfull of yow, for haueinge with some difficulty gotten the booke and songes of his Maiesty's entertainment att Broham,[1] I doe herewith send yow the same; hopeing that they will giue yow contentment both in the poetry and musiq, wherin yow soe much delight and can soe perfectly judge. And surely if they please yow, I am right hartely well pleased, for therin I fully enioy my end. I will conclude, desireinge that yow would admitt of these papers as an excuse, and keepe them, til I come my selfe and fetch them, and visite yow, which assure your selfe shalbee assoone, as with any convenience I may; and remembringe my true affeccon and harty good wishes to your worthy selfe, and good Lady, and sweet children. Your assured louinge cozen, Th. Wentworth.

I am enioined by my wife, and sister Sauile, to remember their true affeccons to your selfe and Lady, to the greatnes wherof, this little square paper is noe waies proportionable.

**61.** (*SC*, ii, p. 12) *To Mr Francis Bristowe. Fetter Lane. 15 Oct. 1617.*

Sir, your kind respects haue made mee much to seeke your satisfaccon in the educacon of your sonne, and to passe ouer in hope of amendment diuers things which were nothinge well pleasinge unto mee, and wherin I haue endeauoured to rectify him. But now findinge him unwillinge to liue in my howse, I must withall signify unto yow that I plainly see hee looseth his tyme with mee, and therfore must desire yow, as one desirous of his good, eyther to prouide him another Maister or to sett him in some other course, wherto hee may apply himselfe with more chearfullnes and (*p. 13*) willingnes, and consequently better answer your expectacon. Yett, least upon this suddaine, yow should not place him to your likeinge, I will not refuse (if yow allow of itt) to keepe him til Easter; against which tyme, or sooner upon notice, I will see him furnished with money and clothes. This which now is my motion to yow hath bene diuers times your sonne's to mee, which I was unwillinge to harken unto, being loth to part with him, beinge a child of soe respectiue a gentleman and in hope his accons might bee more conformable. But

---

[1] The king was at Brougham 4 August 1617. J. Nichols, *The Progresses, Processions and Magnificent Festivities of King James the First* (London, 1828), iii, pp. 391–92 and n. 4. The book may have been *The Ayres that were sung and played at Brougham Castle in Westmerland in the King's Entertainment given by the Right Honorable the Earl of Cumberland and his Right Noble Sonne the Lord Clifford. Composed by Mr George Mason and Mr John Earsden*, though it was not published in print until 1618. Nichols did not see a copy, but it is recorded by A. W. Pollard and G. R. Redgrave, *A Short Title Catalogue of Books . . . 1475–1640* (London, 1926), no. 17601.

beinge as it is, I am to entreat yow first not to conceaue hardly of your child, who may bee better pleasinge and profittinge elswheare and also not to take it as an unkindnes from mee, whome yow shall allwaies find ready to deserue your loue. Thus expectinge your answer and remembringe my kind comendacons to your selfe and wife I remaine Your very louinge freind, Th. Wentworth.

**62.** *From C. Radclyffe* (*SC*, xx/224).

Honorable Sir, beeing latelie in conference with a Justic of Peace in the Westriding, he demaunded of mee (amongst other things) whether it were true that there was a new custos rotulorum in the Westriding or noe and whether that letters were written from a great person to you for resignacon of that place unto Sir John Savile or noe. And (for that I was ignorant thereof) I answered that I cold nott satisfie him any thing therin other then I hard by publique report, butt I was sure that you were custos rotulorum at the last Sessions and as likelie so to contynue as any other man whatsoeuer and that I thought that was butt a flying report which was ended and done. Whereunto he replied that he thought itt was nott done, nor would be ended so, for that your aduersaries frends had engaged themselues so farre in that busynes for him as they cold nott with theire reputacons leaue ytt so. And whether this was spoken to me by way of a caution or otherwise I cold nott collect, but I thought ytt my part to signifie the same unto your worship to thend you may be prepared to prevent if anything shold be intended. And thus craving pardon for my boldnes, wishing myself able to accomplish that service your noblenes hath treblie bound mee unto, I humbly take leaue, beeing euer att your worship's commaundment, Cha. Radclyffe. 5 November 1617.

**63.** *Wentworth to Sir Henry Wotton at Venice, 8 November 1617* (*Knowler*, 1, p. 5; *SC*, ii, p. 13). *Secretary Winwood is dead, Buckingham expected to be made Admiral and Marquess Hamilton, who is well affected to Wotton, Master of the Horse.*

**64.** (*SC*, ii, p. 14) *To Mr Christopher Danby Esq. Wentworth Woodhouse. 10 Dec. 1617.*

Sir, I haue receaued your letter, and writt to Mr high Sherriffe, as yow therby required, and I desire yow would let mee heare what answer (*p. 15*) yow receaue from him. Assure your selfe there is noe kinsman yow haue which will more truly and faithfully wish and endeauour your happynesse and content then my selfe, wherin your beleefe shall doe both your selfe and mee but right. I am sorry yow shold fall into these extremities, wherin giue mee leue to say I know you are to blame, and let mee earnestly moue yow to bee more vigilant in your occasions hereafter. Yow haue a lordship called Oxenshawe that will sell the readyest and best of any lande yow haue, and beinge now upon the racke, and yow forced to sell, I see noe reason to keepe itt. And surely if yow doe not sell itt, there beinge noe pleasure that should make yow unwillinge to parte with itt, I shall conceaue yow doe not respecte the standinge of your howse. And soe in some hast I rest in the plainnesse and truth of beinge, Your assured louinge cozen, Th. Wentworth.

**65.** (*SC*, ii, p. 14) *To Sir Robert Swift knight, high Sheriffe of York-shire. Wentworth Woodhouse. 18 Dec. 1617.*

Sir, I am at the intreaty and in the behalfe of a neare kinsman of myne, Mr Danby, to desire a fauour from yow, the occasion is thus: Sir William Ingleby haueinge a Statute of 3000$^{li}$ from my cozen Danby for the security of 1500$^{li}$ which Sir William had formerly lent him, by reason of some difference betwixt them, as my cozen enformes mee, an extent is now forth intendinge to lay it upon my cozen's lands, which surely will much preiudice him. Therfore am I the rather moued, the gentleman being a stranger to your selfe, to intreat your tender consideracon herein, as also that yow wilbee pleased to extend your lawfull fauour soe farr forth towards him, that, if the Statute come to your hands, yow would make a stay of the execucon til the begininge of the next terme, giuinge also the like dyreccon to your under Sherriffe, in which tyme my Cozen hopes to end the matter in freindly tearmes with Sir William, which wilbee noe losse to your under Sherriffe; for my cozen will see the fees satisfied unto him, which shalbee due by reason of the extend-ing of the Statute. Restinge herein upon your worthy disposicon to a gentleman of his qualety, and ready to requite your kindnesse upon a like occasion I remaine, your affecconate freind, Th. Wentworth.

**66.** (*SC*, ii, p. 15) *To Mr Henry Withham Esq. Wentworth Wood-house. 18 Dec. 1617.*

Sir, reservinge in my hands 800$^{li}$ which should haue bene paid unto yow in Nouember last, by reason of a charge of 600$^{li}$ for rents arreare allready come forth against Ledstone, as yow know, and of as much more which is like to followe; as also lettinge yow understand by my servant, and sendinge yow word by youre's, that I was neuerthelesse willinge the profitt of the money should in the meane tyme bee bestowed to your use. I much marvaile I heare not from yow in a matter that soe much concernes yow. And therfore as the $800^{li}$ was ready at the day and place to haue bene paid accordinge to our articles, if yow could haue shewed my servant a sufficient discharge for the said $600^{li}$, soe is it, and shalbee still, when by acquittances, or otherwaies I shalbe sufficiently secured in that behalfe; and if yow can not presently cleare the said arrerages, notwithstandinge the money lyes here ready to bee lett forth to such persons for your profitt, as yow shall best like of; soe as I may haue good security for the principall wherwithall to saue my selfe harmlesse. I therfore wish yow would take some present course, that soe the money may bee ordered best for your benefitt, which as it is, doth nether your selfe, or mee any good, or otherwaies that yow blame your selfe and not mee, if yow loose any thinge by my detaininge of the money accordinge to our articles. For a bond of $1000^{li}$, which, as I heare, yow alleadge I haue from yow, yow doe mistake it, for I assure yow I haue none such. Thus much I thought good once more to signify unto yow, for your good and my owne clearinge and justificacon in the carriage of this busines; And soe expecting to heare from yow I remaine, Your very louinge freind, Th. Wentworth.

**67.** (*SC*, ii, p. 16) *To Mr Justice Hutton. Wentworth Woodhouse. 22 Dec. 1617.*[1]

Sir, the old matter for Vessy beinge againe sett on foote, by reason of a lettere from my Lord Keeper, which this bearer hath to shew unto yow; I thought it good to acquaint yow therwith, in regard my Lord may chance to haue some speach with yow concerninge the same. The Justices formerly of that opinion, haue (according to the letter) discharged Vessy, both of his office and fine, and againe authorized Peatinger. For my selfe, I did still continew of my former opinion, by reason I saw my Lord had bene misinformed, as will appeare unto yow by the coppy of my lettere to my Lord Keeper, which this bearer will shew yow, wherin I shalbee much bound unto yow, if yow wilbee pleased to tel him your opinion, whether it bee fittinge to deliuer it or noe; and if yow haue any speach with my Lord Keeper, yow may bee pleased to remember that it was twice ordered att Pontfract Sessions, and confirmed by the Judges' order,

[1] See no. 47, p. 93.

and at the Sessions within our owne deuison carryed by plurality of voices. And thus, Sir, wishinge yow a prosperous Journey, and safe returne, I remaine, Your assured and affecconate frend Th. Wentworth

My wife remembers her kind comendacons unto yow, and Mistress Jane Hutton her duty, desireinge your blessinge, who I thanke my Lady your wife, is heare now [to] beare my wife company part of this sommer.

**68.** (*SC*, ii, p. 16) *To Sir Peter Freschevile knight. Wentworth Woodhouse. 22 Dec. 1617.*

Sir, my longe (albeitt enforced) absence from Stavley doth in noe sorte merritt soe kind a remembrance of your loue, as I haue receaued by your lettere and venison, for both which, I must here retorne many thanks. Yet yow would haue too much aduantage in kindnes ouer mee, if I did suffer my selfe to receaue the contentment of your presence here, before I haue performed the longe protracted visitt I owe yow. I shall therfore in this (otherwaies free from contencon, and chiefely with my most respected freinds) soe farr emulate your affeccon and respect, as if I can get the start, I will Godwillinge see yow first. In the interim, Sir, I assure my selfe, your kind disposicon togeather with the consideracon of many affaires, and those tedious in dispatch to an unexperienced yong man, will mittigate if not deferre your (*p. 17*) censure, until upon some good occasion, I may both redeeme that which is past, and futurely giue yow testimony how constant and firme I shall remaine to the truth and fastnes of my beinge, Your kinsman in all assurance of freindship and affeccon, Th. Wentworth.

My wife remembers her kind respect to your selfe and lady, and I desire my service may bee remembred to her ladyship with much content to heare of the health of your little ones, wherin I beseech God continewe and increase your comfort.

**69.** (*SC*, ii, p. 17) *To the Earl of Cumberland. Wentworth Woodhouse. 18 Jan. 1618.*

My most honoured Lord, seinge that my occasions permitt mee not to attend yow before my going to the Tearme, I thought fitt to send this bearer towards your Lordship that soe by the tender of my duty and seruice, I might receaue at the least, the welcome newes of your good health, which I shall take as a fauourable aspecte on my journey ward; as also to offer my selfe a minister of your comaunds, if my good fortune bee such, as I may bee usefull unto your Lordship at London. I sett forward Godwillinge, Munday next, in the meane space I will waite for the honore of your imployments. I wish my Lord Clifford a safe retorne home to your Lordship with good successe in all which hee goes about. To conclude all in a word, I pray for your Lordship's longe life and happines, and in soe doinge I remaine firmly and observantly Your Lordships most obedient sonne in law to bee comaunded, Th. Wentworth.

**70.** (*SC*, ii, p. 17) *To Mistress Dorothy Hughes at Ledstone. Wentworth Woodhouse. 19 Jan. 1618.*

Good auntt, I am to thank yow and your sister for the good remembrance yow haue of us, unto whome I desire yow will remember my loue with kind thanks: yet before I stirr any further, I will desire Mr Justice Hutton to inqueare of the condicons of the party, and soe after the circuite, I will further proceed as occasion shalbee offered, wherwith yow shalbee acquainted. In the meane tyme I haue sent this bearer, to know how yow and your daughter are in your healthes, unto whome I shall wish all good fortune, and wilbee ready wherin I may bee usefull unto yow to testify my selfe to bee, Your affecconate and assured nephew, Th. Wentworth.

**71.** (*SC*, ii, p. 18) *To the Countess of Shrewsbury[1] at Rufford. Fetter lane. 11 Feb. 1618.*

My most honoured Lady, Mr Cookson hath acquainted mee with the contents of yours dated the 6 of February, and wee both haue bene with Sir John Jackson, to aduise with him therupon. For Buck's misdemeanours upon the distresse taken for his Lady, Sir John Jackson's aduice is that it is noe riott, but onely an affray and battery, and therfore if your Ladyship will question him for the same, then the parties greiued must in their owne names bringe an action of battery against him; yet aduiseth rather to let itt passe then otherwaies, matters restinge now as they are. Sir John Jackson likewise aduiseth us, rather to alleadge wee dayly expect your answer out of the Cuntry, touchinge the arbitrament betwixt your Ladyship and the Lady Grace, and soe passe it ouer till your cominge upp the next Tearme, then to acquaint them that your Ladyship hath retorned answer, yow will giue them satisfaccon at your cominge to towne, which may sauour of delay. For ioininge in

---

[1] Joan, widow of Edward, eighth earl of Shrewsbury, daughter and co-heir of Cuthbert, Lord Ogle, died without issue 1627.

Comission with the Lady Grace, Sir John Jackson aduiseth us therunto, nether indeed can it bee auoided; for the Lady Grace by her Counsell did yesterday moue in Chauncery for possession of the moytye of those lands shee pretends right in; and therupon an order conceaued eyther to shew cause the last day of the Tearme, or els an iniunccon to bee awarded; soe as wee must offer to ioine in Comission, least wee might seeme to seeke delayes. My Lord Chamberlaine rests noe waies satisfied with your Ladyship's last to him touching Emley lodge, seemeth to bee therwith much discontented, and in truth I thinke nothing will content him, but redeliuery of the possession.

My Lady of Exester's cause hath now bene heard [by] the kinge in person 4 dayes in the Starr Chamber, and is to bee sentenced on Satturday next, the particulers I shall relate unto yow at my cominge downe. Onely if I may bee bould to deliuer my opinion, I thinke the Countesse will come of cleare with her honore, that it will lye very heauy on the other side and that I neuer thought to haue seene matters of soe fowle and ignominious a nature soe weakly and meanly proued. Thus Madam, wishinge your Ladyship longe life, with all happinesse to enioy it I rest, as I euer haue, deuoted and faithfull in your seruice, Th. Wentworth.

**72.** (*SC*, ii, p. 18) *To the Countess of Shrewsbury at Rufford. Fetter Lane. 12 Feb. 1618.*

My most honored Lady, this day Mr Sergeant Richardson was at the Chancery barre, to shew (*p. 19*) cause why an iniunccon might not bee graunted as the Lady Grace desired; which was notwithstandinge ordered should bee awarded to giue the Lady Grace possession of an entier moyty, the Lord Deuonshire and Deane haueinge sworn the intencon was for noe more, and your owne letteres acknowledginge as much. My Lord Cauendish himself declared to Mr Cookson hee had bene a meanes to my Lord Chancellore for my Lady Grace, soe yow see how both father, sonne, and their dependants stand affected. How this can bee preuented I know not, except my Lord Chamberlaine will interest himselfe therin, joined with some such meanes of your owne, as I told your Ladyship of at my last beinge with yow. For my Lord Chamberlaine hee will not stirre, nor hold arbitrament with yow, unlesse hee may haue possession of Emley lodge againe, and itt is now too late for your Ladyship to contest with him. Therfore Madam under fauour I wilbee bould to deliuer my opinion unto yow, I would aduise your Ladyship to bee pleased to write to my Lord Chamberlaine, signifyinge that yow will not runne any course displeasing to his Lordship in matters of greater moment, and therfore yow will deliuer upp the lodge to such as hee shall appointe; and also by lettere to giue his Lordship and my Lord of Arondell to understand, that such an iniunccon beinge awarded, and by the Articles their Lordships and your Ladyship beinge to receaue the profitts indifferently til the arbitrament bee ended, yow desire that they would ioyne that the iniunccon may bee recalled, which otherwaies will equally turne to their preiudice as well as youres. Wherin Madam I likewise thinke fittinge that yow should use as much speed as yow well may that soe, if it can bee, the Iniunccon may bee dissoulued. And in the meane tyme, least yow might bee preiudiced by the tennants, to send presently to them all some of your principall servants, to let them know of the iniunccon, and that when the same is serued upon them they make noe attornment, alleadginge that there are noe rents due til Lady day, and that they will first acquaint your Ladyship; withall charginge them to behaue themselues with all circumspeccon and respect, and to giue mild answers noe way tastinge of peremptorines. This is a matter of great importance, and may not bee slept in; therfore good Madam aduise seriously, and speedily what to doe therin. Thus haueinge deliuered my poore and faithfull aduise, I submitt it to your wisdome, and wishing your Ladyship longe life with much happines, I remaine Your Ladyship's affecconate freind and servant, Th. Wentworth.

**73.** (*SC*, ii, p. 20) *To Sir Peter Freschevile knight. Wentworth Woodhouse. 22 March 1618.*

Sir, it might bee deemed a needles taske, to aduise a gentleman furnished with learninge and judgment, which inwardly affords him better rules, and sounder grounds of comfort, then can in any sort proceed from mee; were it not often seene that wiser men in the height of passion somtimes admitt of counsell from persons farr shorte; that wee find sorrowe easilyer borne, in some measure lessened, when freinds puts their shoulders to the pressure of affliccons; and that your loue to my howse, recomended by my father, your continewinge freindship approued by my selfe, might justly argue in mee a cold and dull forgettfullnes, if I did not (when I can noe more) render yet my dropp into the bottell. Omittinge then, or at least shortly passinge ouer the exhortacons to masculine vertue, in sufferinge these worldly and temporall crosses, which might seeme vaine repeticons of matters better knowne, and studied by your selfe. Surely, Sir, I may truly say there are not any of your freinds, more tender and sencible of your losse, or that doe with greater greife disburthen yow of some of yours, by bearinge their part, then my selfe: nether is there any that can performe this office with greater willingnes and affeccon. Wherfore I shall pray to God, to graunt yow the rich treasure of frankly submittinge your selfe unto his blessed will, which may deduce from his bountifull and all ministringe hand other fatherly comforts to supply this present discomfort, and that his goodnesse may protect, his mercies bee multiplyed upon yow and yours. Lastly, I am to entreate your pardon, that these lynes come noe sooner, nor hearinge thes heauy newes, til Friday last beinge then att Rufford, and that yow will excuse mee I come not my selfe, seinge my present occasions forcibly draw mee from yow; in both which reposeinge upon your kind acceptance, I wilbee found firmly and constantly, your assured louinge cozen and freind, Th. Wentworth.

**74.** (*SC*, ii, p. 20) *To Sir Henry Sauile of Methley. Wentworth Woodhouse. 26 March 1618.*

Sir, I haue this day receaued an order out of the Starrchamber, by meanes of the Bushoppe of Worster, importinge, that yourselfe beinge formerly named as Comissioner in the cause dependinge betwixt mee and (*p. 21*) the feoffees of the said Bishoppe; yet in regard your brother in law Sir Henry Goodricke made title to parcell of the lands in question and that there is now a sute dependinge in the dutchy; to decide that controuersy my Lord Chauncellor hath ordered that your paines should bee spared, and Mr George Ellis appointed to ioyne with Sir Thomas Tilsley for the sittinge of that Comission. To which purpose, there is a new Comission awarded, and a supersedeas to dissolue the former: soe there is nothinge remaines, saue onely to giue yow notice therof, and very kindly to thanke yow for your willingnes to undergoe that trouble for mee, which I shall both remember as a testimony of your affeccon and bee ready to requite it, soe soon as my good fortune shall afford mee an occasion. In expectancy whereof I shall remaine, Your very louinge freind, Th. Wentworth.

**75.** (*SC*, ii, p. 21) *To the Countess of Shrewsbury. Wentworth Woodhouse. 31 March 1618.*

My most honoured Lady, if your Ladyship haue as yet perused the euidence of Bryerley, I hope wee may haue a coppy of the deed made by my Lord to your Ladyship for life, the remainder to my nephewe; and if your Ladyship (findinge it noe preiudice to your selfe) wilbee pleased that I may haue the keepinge of the ancient euidence concerninge that mannor, which otherwaies may bee dispersed and lost, they shalbee allwaies ready to doe yow seruice, and I hold my selfe bound unto yow for the same. By reason of your Ladyship's intended journey to London, and my wiue's towards the Bathe, now presently after Easter, I haue presumed with your good leaue and fauour, to send for my sister and nephewes, fearinge that otherwaies, my wife haueinge the coach and horses, there might bee more trouble and difficulty in my sister's cominge heather, which I assure my selfe your Ladyship wilbee pleased to like well of for the present, seinge my sister and they shall upon your Ladyship's retorne into the country bee allwayes ready to waite your comaunds, and to bee disposed of, as your Ladyship shall thinke fitt. And in truth there should bee otherwaies great forgetfullnes on our parte, of your many honourable fauoures, which by God's grace Madam (whatsoeuer may bee suggested or conceaued) your Ladyship shall neuer find, or wee bee other, then ready to doe yow all humble seruice. I understand that my Lord hath nominated mee one of the superuisors of his will, a thinge I confesse very contentfull unto mee, as an assurance of his good opinion; which trust I wilbee found as faithfully to performe, when occasion shall serue, as any of your servants, and more then I can well expresse. I doubt not but there are many will (*p. 22*) perswade your Ladyship to the contrary, I will desire noe other tryall betwixt their upright meanings and myne, then our accons. I beseech yow therfore in your wisdome, if ther bee any thinge soundinge contrary to the contents of this letter, that your Ladyship wilbee pleased freely to imparte the same unto mee, and not to giue a facile eare therunto but first heare both parties before yow beleeue. Thus I doubt not but wee shall easily continewe unto us, your accustomed goodnes, and fauour, which wee chiefly and principally repose our selues upon, as wee shall truly continew our prayers to allmighty God for your longe life, plenty, honour, and happinesse. Your Ladyship's humble servant to dispose of, Th. Wentworth.

My wife presents her humble seruice to your Ladyship.

**76.** (*SC*, ii, p. 22) *To Mr Robert Pierrepoint Esq. Wentworth Woodhouse. 23 July 1618.*

Sir, I understand by my servant William Colebrand that hee hath taken for mee of yow, this yeare, your tithes of Wentworth, under the rent of 34$^{li}$ payable equally at Michelmas and Martinmasse next.

These are therfore to giue yow thanks, and this lettere to bind mee
to the just payment of your rent, and to performe the said agreement.
Itt is true, the rent reserued, is more then was giuen yow the last
yeare by nine pounds, and indeed more then they are worth to any
other then my selfe, yet if yow would graunt mee a tearme therin,
for 8 or 9 yeares, I would continewe the same, otherwaies the
bargaine is too hard. Nay your wisdome is such that yow know I
cannot bee a sauer at this rate, except I plow upp some of my owne
demaines, which it may bee I shall doe, if I take a lease. I doe desire
now therfore to bee assertained of your resolucon, beinge very ready
to deserue the kindnes and pleasure yow shall doe mee therin, and
to giue yow the testimony of a thankfull and harty affeccon for the
same. And soe I comitt yow to the proteccon of the Allmighty,
Your affecconate freind and servantt, Th. Wentworth.

**77.** (*SC*, ii, p. 22) *To the Lady Wotton at Canterbury. Wentworth
Woodhouse. 10 Aug. 1618.*

My most honoured Lady, the deuoted respect that deseruedly I
beare your Ladyship is such a faithfull and diligent remembrancer
unto mee of my obligacon, that (in expectancy (*p. 23*) of a greater)
I must not let slippe the least occasion, wherby to giue yow testimony
therof; and in the acknowledgment of your many noble fauours, I
must also giue your Ladyship humble thanks for the rootes it
pleased yow now laitly to bestowe upon mee. They are allready in
the ground, and by their flowers will put mee in mind that my
seruice ought to bee fruitfull and usefull unto your Ladyship wherin,
if my intencons and wishes (wantinge onely meanes of performance)
may fructifye into accons and demonstracons, surely I shall yeild as
great an increase of duty, as any whosoeuer and will esteeme my
selfe very fortunate, if I may as well bee thankfully executinge your
comaunds, as I haue bene hetherto an obiecte of your good opinion
and bounty. Madame, my pen is not able to answer the large extent
of my hart, but when I stoppe, meditatinge what were the best I
could wish unto your Ladyship, I can in this world wish yow noe
greater happinesse then that wherin I found and left yow att Canterbury. I must therfore pray for the full continewance therof, which is
both for the health and happinesse of my much honoured Lord and
your selfe, and endinge this letter, will continewe unto yow both, in
truth and plainnesse, a most humble and bounden servant, Th.
Wentworth.

**78.** (*SC*, ii, p. 23) *To the Earl of Cumberland. Wentworth Woodhouse.
20 Aug. 1618.*

My most honored Lord, I am to giue your Lordship most humble
thanks for the letteres it pleased your Lordship to send mee, and
beinge right gladd of the good successe of my Lord Clifford in the
Northerne Cuntries I may not conceale the great contentment I
receaued by the newes of your Lordship's good health, which in
duty I am bound to pray for. I beseech therfore God to blesse your
Lordship with multiplyed happines, and my Lord Clifford with
successfull proceedings in those thinges which hee shall undertake,
to both your full contentments, to the comfort of those that truly
honour yow, and that those that maligne yow may bee lookers on
with an enuious eye, wantinge power to stoppe the currents of your
contentments and honorable good fortunes. Lastly I must conclude
with the same hast that I haue writt the rest, which giues a sinceare
and free passage to my penne to stile my selfe in an observant truth
and plainnesse, your Lordship's most humble sonne in law to bee
comaunded, Th. Wentworth.

**79.** (*SC*, ii, p. 24) *To Mr John Hanson at Woodhouse. Wentworth
Woodhouse. 21 Aug. 1618.*

Sir, the possession of the nyne townes neare and about Hallifax,
which my brother Sir George Sauile enioyed, beinge now lawfully
and rightly setled in my nephewes, his children, or in the Comittees
to and for their use: to the intent that my sister and selfe may bee
better enabled to giue an accoumpt of our care and proceedings in
the manageing of their estate unto the Archbushoppe of Canterbury,
his grace being one of the said Comittees and our most honourable
lord; I am to desire that yow will deliuer unto the bearer Mr Charles
Greenwood to and for our use such writings court rolles, rentalles,
and other euidence as doe concerne any of the mannores wherof my
said brother dyed possessed; good store wherof, as wee credibly
heare, are now in your custody and keepinge and that yow will take
the paines to enforme us of such particulers, as your experience hath
found fittinge the owners of those lands should bee acquainted with.
For the which wee shall rest very much beholden unto yow, and
which I noe waies doubt yow will satisfy us in, when I call to mind the
good opinion my brother Sauile did euer conceaue of yow and the
long employment yow had under him. And soe comittinge yow to
God I rest, Your very louinge freind, Th. Wentworth.

**80.** (*SC*, ii, p. 24) *To Mr Edward Osborne Esq. Wentworth Wood-house. 4 Oct. 1618.*

Sir, this bearer cominge to tender his seruice unto mee at Londes-borowe, and withall hearinge hee was belonginge [to] yow, I did refuse to entertaine him unlesse first hee brought your letter to recomend his good carryage in your seruice, as also to assertaine mee that hee departed with your fauour and good allowance. Nether would the respect I beare yow, permitt mee to giue way unto his motion upon other tearmes. Seinge now then your desire is not suddainly to part from him, I doe freely remitt him unto yow, and shall in noe sort take him wherby yow may bee unfurnished; hopeinge that if hee chaunce hereafter to bee out of your seruice, and haueinge behaued himselfe towards yow as befitts him, I may with your good consent haue him as soone as another; and otherwaies I assure yow I will leaue him to his other fortunes. This is all that for the present I will trouble yow with, more then the assureance that I am Your very affecconate freind, Th. Wentworth.

**81.** (*SC*, ii, p. 25) *To Lord Clifford. Wentworth. 6 Oct. 1618.*

My much honoured Lord, I haue receaued your Lordship's pacquett and shall apply my selfe carefully and seriously to follow the dyrec-cons therin giuen mee by your Lordship, yet I shall not goe forward soe soone to London by two dayes as I intended. My Lord, for the true zeale I beare your Lordship and the desire I haue to doe yow any acceptable seruice that rests in the ability of my lower fortunes, I shall need to say noe more seinge your Lordship may bee pleased readily to beleeue soe much; wherin the more confidence yow bestow upon mee, the more right yow shall doe mee. I will therfore pray for your increase of all honore and happinesse, and praying continewe Your Lordship's most humble brother in law and servant, Th. Wentworth.

I shall craue leaue, that these lynes may present my humble duty to my Lord and my seruice to the two noble Ladyes.

**82.** (*SC*, ii, p. 25) *To the Archbishop of York. Wentworth Woodhouse. 7 Oct. 1618.*

Most reuerend father in God, and my very good Lord, Mr Benson beinge now with your grace, your piety and religion imboldens mee still to enforme your Lordship of the great neglect wherin hee holds his flocke here at Wath and Wentworth, and the rather by reason yow were graciously pleased (as this bearer enformeth mee) to write

your lynes unto him upon my last letter that the defects and strang
scandalls in this church, now comitted to his charge, might bee
supplyed and reformed; for the which my selfe in the name of all
the inhabitants am to giue your grace most humble thanks. Now
seinge that Mr Benson neuer (as it seemeth) bendeth his thoughts
hetherward, nether giueth any respect to your grace's letteres, adinge
the small regard of your Lordship's admonicons to the former
neglect of his charge, I am againe to renewe my sute to your grace,
that by your good meanes hee may bee made better to know the
duty of a pastor towards his flocke. For true it is that the parish of
Wath being very large, hath within itt (besides the mother church)
the Chappellry of Wentworth, indowed with parochial rights, where
there hath bene preaching ministers found by the Vickers of Wath
tyme out of mynd. That your Lordship may then know how both
the mother church and the Chappellry are at this present prouided
for by Mr Benson, these are to signify unto your grace, that here
within the (*p. 26*) Chappellry of Wentworth consistinge of 2 or 3
tounshipps, haueinge had noe minister to say diuine seruice since
Easter, Mr Benson not within these 8 weeks hath prouided a lycence
for one Goodere, formerly Clarke, to read seruice, which very
busyly hee performeth, conceauinge his fauore therby to bee largely
extended (as seemeth) towards us, for hee leaues us still unprouided
of any to performe the other great and misticall dutyes of the
ministery. Att Wath, the parish church it selfe, there is likewise one
Bishoppe, late (and now also as I take it) tith-gatherer for Mr
Benson, who hath the like licence to read, beinge for ability or
learninge as unable and ignorant as the other. Onely indeed Mr
Benson hath procured one Henry Tailor, the minister of Adwicke,
with a kind of superintendent power to post from mother church to
Chappellry, for burialls, christenings and such like, the said Henry
Tailor being belike a deacon; but sure I am hee was within these
3 yeares a comon informer, and now at this present an alehowse
keeper and soe farre engaged to his tiplinge howse, that being repre-
hended for the same, hee himselfe did professe in open Sessions to
bee soe unworthily affected to the ministery, that hee would rather
giue ouer that then his brewinges. In the meane tyme Mr Benson
hath thorowe your Lordship's bounty and goodnes, besides his
vickeridge here, a parsonidge at Carleton, worth by comon report
eight score pounds by yeare, as also money to lett to use (if I bee
rightly enformed) after the rate of twenty in the hundreth, yet hath
none to spare for the mantainance of able and well qualefied
curates to serue under him, albeitt therunto bound in conscyence
and religion. These demeanours being soe insufferable that wee may

not therwith rest content, seing our selues soe apparantly neglected in the greatest worke, euen the saluacon of our soules; I doe most humbly renew my sute to your grace and beseech yow in your goodnes to redresse the same, either that Mr Benson himselfe may furnish us with able ministers, as hath euer by his predecessors bene accustomed, or els that, takinge halfe of the profitt of the vickeridge cleare to himselfe, wee may haue allotted unto us, the other halfe to prouide our selues; which I noe waies doubt from your Lordship, beinge soe much to the advancement of God's seruice, and for which I shalbee ready to giue testimony of my thankfullnes, in obseruantly remaininge, your grace's humbly to bee comaunded, Th. Wentworth.

**83.** (*SC*, ii, p. 26) *To Sir Peter Middleton knight. Wentworth Woodhouse. 25 Dec. 1618.*

Sir, I haue here sent yow parte of the rootes which I told yow of att your last beinge with mee, but not soe many as I did purpose, by reason (*p. 27*) I found my store smaller, then I ymagined. Yet of those few, I haue sent yow a third part, and if myne prosper yow may hereafter if yow please bee better furnished. I thinke yow were best to sett them as soone as may be, for they will take the better. My wife desires these lynes may recomend her respects to your selfe and lady, not forgettinge my seruice to her Ladyship. And thus wishinge yow longe life and happinesse, the occasions wherin yow shall haue use of mee, shall approue my beinge, Your assured louinge cozen, Th. Wentworth.

**84.** (*SC*, ii, p. 27) *To the Earl of Cumberland. Wentworth. 29 Dec. 1618.*

My most honoured Lord, your Lordship's fauoures are dealt soe thicke upon mee that they busy mee in what sort and in what manner to returne my humble duty and seruice, seinge that my meanes cannot counteruaile the thankfullnes which I owe, the obligacon wherin I am bound by soe many honourable and affecconate respects and remembrances. In a word they make mee confesse my owne negligence in beinge thus ouertaken as it were with demonstrations of your loue, before I haue giuen (albeitt not a full requitall) yet some testimony how much I meditate of them, and prize them, and hold my selfe bound unto yow for them. Yet giue mee leaue to right the duty I owe yow, in it selfe perfect and firme, by laying the fault upon my many occasions, which at this present much importune mee and to blame my ill fortune, which amongst many other burthens, makes mee undergoe this, (the greatest of all to a generous mind) to bee ouercome (if I may soe say) with kindnesse. In sume yet my Lord, as there is none which receaues the earnests of your good opinion with more comfort, soe is there not any that shall more carefully lay them upp in memory, or answer (according to my ability) yow a more plentifull or sounder fruite upon all occasions and in all seasons. I am right glad to heare of your Lordship's good health, and albeitt (I doubte) I shall not see your Lordship before the Tearme, yet I will waite upon yow and see your good haulks fly before Shrouetide. Lastly I shall pray that all happinesse, with many happy new yeares may bee multiplyed upon yow, that soe I may liue to see the one setled in your person and haue the larger occasion by the continewance of tyme to giue your Lordship unfained and infallible arguments of my beinge. Your Lordship's most obedient sonne in lawe, Th. Wentworth.

**85.** (*SC*, ii, p. 27) *To Lord Clifford. Wentworth. 29 Dec. 1618.*

(*p. 28*) My much honoured Lord, I giue your Lordship humble thanks for your lettere, nether will I torment my selfe, or trouble your Lordship with writinge excuses, by reason I know your Lordship wilbee confident that it is greife enough to mee, that I cannott waite upon yow at this next Gaole deliuery, seinge I am still in mind and prayers with yow; this is a misfortune fallen upon mee, (which I hope God will disburthen me of in mine age) to see my selfe rentt from myne owne quiett, and performinge those duties which I am bound to by importune and wearysome imployments and in good faith my letts att this present are soe many and waighty, that it would bee irksome to mee to count them, and to your Lordship troublesome in the readinge. Pardon mee therfore I beseech your Lordship and the rather by reason that I must striue paciently to pardon my owne ill fortune, depriuinge mee of that, which I protest I did exceedingly desire, which was to haue attended yow this journey. Mr Radcliffe I doubt not but wilbee most ready to doe yow seruice, and my selfe shall euer pray that all honore and good successe may bee with yow and beare yow company. Your Lordship's most humble brother in law and seruant, Th. Wentworth.

**86.** (*SC*, ii, p. 28) *To Mr Anthony Eyre. Wentworth Woodhouse. 13 Jan. 1619.*

Sir, the inclosed will beare mee wittnesse, I haue not bene unmindfull of my promis, I am sorry I knew your mind noe sooner, seinge I

WP—I

cannot well moue him any further the bargaine allready concluded, and money prouided. Yet notwithstandinge upon further notice from yow, I will presse it as farr in your behalfe, as yow shall reasonably thinke it fittinge for mee to doe. This is all that for the present I will trouble yow with, more then the assureance of my beinge your very affecconate freind and kinsman, Th. Wentworth.

**87.** *(SC,* ii, p. 28) *To Sir Thomas Wharton knight. Wentworth Woodhouse. 17 Jan. 1619.*

Sir, I am desired by the bearer Mr Gascoigne, my kinsman, to recomend his sute unto yow, which is to haue a sight of the Coucher booke of Helaigh Abbay.[1] I understand soe well how dainty a matter it is to permitt a man's euidence to bee viewed, as if I were not as well assured of the condicon of the gentleman, I would bee farr from moueinge it; but I dare say the honesty of the person to bee such, that hee will not wronge yow in the least tittle, his curiosity beinge onely matter of pedegree. What curtesy yow are pleased to bestow on him therfore, I shall take it as done unto my selfe, wishinge yow and your honourable Lady the increase of all honore and happines, your affecconate freind and seruant Th. Wentworth.

My wife remembers her true loue and kind comendacons to your selfe & lady.

**88.** *To Lady Craven, Fetter Lane. 16 Feb. 1619 (SC,* xxi/15).[2]

Madame, I will with your good leaue presentt that motion now in writing which formerly I haue made unto you by worde of mouthe; as allsoe sett down in the inclosed paper, the reasons and other inducements which may perswade your ladyship to entertaine the same, for words slide away, butt letters remaine, soe as by this meanes you may more aduisedly consider therof. The person whom I moue for is my second brothere, now liuing in the Inner Temple and the next heire of my house, my self as yeat not hauing any children, allbeitt eight years married; the consideration whearof makes me desirouse to see him bestowed in some vertuouse stocke and family and that he may not only content himself therin but in some measure aduance his fortunes allsoe. To which end and purpose I confesse I rather wishe he may haue the happines to matche with M^ris Crauen youre ladyship's daughter then in any other place, if it may soe please God and stande with your ladyship's good liking.

---

[1] Probably Healaugh Priory in Ainsty.
[2] See below, pp. 323–24.

I exspect noe presentt answeare, I will make bold to waite on you myself the next terme to receaue your resolution; in the meane space I desire that, as the the motion proceeds from respect, soe your ladyship would therin use a respectfull secresy by keeping itt too youre selfe. For I doe not soe much undervalue my brother as willingly to haue itt published that he was a sutor and reiected. For allbeitt this motion proue not either well pleasing to your ladyship or well liking to the young gentlewoman, I hope in God neither of them shall be the worse for itt. And thus I committ your ladyship to the guiding of allmighty God, both in this and all other youre affaires, myself howsoeuer acknowledging your great kindnes which shall still putt me in minde asseuredly to remaine, your ladyship's affectionate frend to dispose, Th. Wentworth. Fetterlaine, this 16 of February 1618[9].

**89.** (*SC*, ii, p. 29) *To Sir Peter Middleton knight. Wentworth. 26 Feb. 1619.*

Sir, I am to giue yow thanks for your kind and respectiue lynes as one that receaues a great deale of true content in your freindship and loue. There is not any shall requite it in a more abundant and affecconate manner, nor endeauore more really to conserue itt and increase itt. For the euidence in Sir William Slingsbye's custody belonginge your mannore of Duffeild, such as hee hath beinge but poore stuffe, I haue deliuered unto your servant for yow; my desire and care to doe yow seruice was as much as if they had bene of more valewe. Hee affirmeth that (hee haueinge but an estate for life in Harswell, the inheritance his brother's, Sir Henry) his brother hath all the rest. Wherupon I spoke to Sir Henry to looke upp amongst his writinges and such as hee should find onely concerninge Duffeild, that hee would deliuer them unto yow, and coppies of such as concerned yow jointly, which hee promised that hee would willingly doe. Soe as now hee beinge in the cuntry, if yow please to put him in mind therof, yow may, I thinke, haue all that belonges yow for as much as in him lyeth. My wife and sister Sauile desire to bee very kindly comended to your selfe and good Lady, to whome I will hereby present my seruice and harty good wishes. Sir, there liues not any of whome yow may haue more assureance, or that doth more firmly or inviolably remayne, Your truly affecconate kinsman and servant, Th. Wentworth.

If yow goe in with the Sherriffe, let mee know, and I will either come to Stockhill the night before, or call on yow by the way as I goe to Yorke; soe as wee shall enioy one another's company.

**90.** (*SC*, ii, p. 29) *To the Archbishop of York. Wentworth Woodhouse. 1 March 1619.*

May it please your grace, wheras his Maiesty by a late proclamacon hath expressed his princely pleasure for all persons to keepe and obserue in their howses this fast of Lent and all other fastinge dayes. Now I haueinge by sufficient experience found that the eatinge of fish continewally is very harmfull unto mee, as also my wife, being at this present very sickly and weake and some of my brothers and sisters troubled with infirmities, for remedy wherunto their phisitians haue forbidden them fishe and milk meats: I am to bee an humble sutore unto your Lordship that yow would bee pleased upon thes just reasons to graunt unto mee, and such as sitt at table with mee, a lycence to eate flesh; to the intent wee may prouide for our healthes, without breach of his Maiesty's royall comaundements, which shall notwithstandinge bee used as sparingly as may bee, and for which your gracious fauour, I shall hold my selfe much bound to your Lordship. My Lord I wish that the continewance of God's blessinges may bee multiplyed upon yow, togeather with the increase of many longe dayes to enioy them, your grace's humbly to bee comaunded, Th. Wentworth.

**91.** (*SC*, ii, p. 30) *To Lord Clifford. Wentworth Woodhouse. 26 March 1619.*

My much honoured Lord, I shall pray for your Lordship's happy successe in your northerne journey, principally in your busines with your tennantes, which as it is the greatest, soe is it most carefully and circumspectly to bee regarded and dealt in. Yow shall find the nature of comon people to bee such, that they are easilyer carryed away upon a suddaine, then with longer gaininge of tyme, which makes them see their errour and fall back from that which at the beginninge they were desirous of. Therfore my Lord in my poore opinion, especially payinge use for soe great sommes, there would bee as speedy a conclusion made, as possibly may bee without apparant precipitacon, or els very great disaduantage. I conceaue your affaires in those cuntryes, will detaine yow there soe longe, as I shalbee at London a weeke or ten dayes before yow; if your Lordship please to imploy mee in any seruices, yow may comaund him, that most readily undergoes them. I set forward, Godwillinge, Munday cum fortnight. My Lord, I must still make bold to entreat your Lordship that Thomas Pickering may search upp for an indenture betwixt my Lord your grandfather and Dakins and Pollard touchinge the rent charge out of Pickering lithe, that soe I may either haue the originall, or at least a coppy therof. Lastly prayinge that your hopes may still bee confirmed, both to your owne greatest comforte and the continewance of your noble howse, I remaine both to your selfe and itt, an humble brother in law and seruant, Th. Wentworth.

**92.** (*SC*, ii, p. 30) *To Sir Thomas Fairfax at Walton. Wentworth Woodhouse. 3 April 1619.*

Sir, that yow desire the continewance of peace and kindnes betwixt our howses, I noe way doubte of, nether haue I giuen the least culler that my intencons should bee censured to tend to other purpose, then to the continewed unitye of our selues and howses, in a constant and setled freindship. My seruant Richard Marris informes mee that at the tyme of the bargaine made hee spoke of comon upon Thorparch More, belonging to your closes, and that his agreement was noe other then to passe all comon in Thorparch, if any did therto belonge, nether in truth was it materiall for yow to desire the like for the Wood close, by reason it was parte of Wycliffe's farme and soe included in grosse. Wheare yow alleadge (which I beleeue) that there is noe comon due upon Thorparch Moore for your closes, the lesse difficulty is it for yow to giue mee words for my money, being indeed a graunt of a thinge which is not, and soe fruitles to mee, noe hurt to your selfe; only I desire it to take away any shaddowe of difference hereafter.

For any aduantage that might bee taken by words in the assureance, I am free (*p. 31*) from itt, or if I might find any within my iudgment did tend to such a purpose, I would as forwardly and uprightly explaine my selfe, as any man liueinge. These books were engrossed before I receaued your last lettere, which are full to carry away all which was intended on both partes and noe more, as my counsell aduise mee; soe as I haue signed and sealed the one parte therof to your use, with a lettere of attorney for takeing possession, and desire the like from yow, which may therupon bee enterchangably deliuered, and seizin giuen, this bearer paying unto yow 40$^{li}$, which hee hath for yow and indeed to the best of my understandinge they are soe reasonable for us both, that I shall not giue any consent they should bee altered. Onely where in your last note, yow would haue the farme sett before the close, if yow desire any alteracon therin, if it please yow to drawe upp a new Indenture to passe the comon belonging to the farme, I wilbee content to passe it in as full and large manner as your counsell shall reasonably

deuise. Thus desireing yow wilbee pleased to consider whether yow
will goe thorowe with the bargaine or noe, with remembrance of
my seruice to your Lady and loue to your selfe, I remaine, Your
assured and affecconate cozen, Th. Wentworth.

**93.** (*SC*, ii, p. 31) *To Lord Wotton. London. 13 June 1619.*

My much honored Lord, I haue herewith sent unto your Lordship
Mr Seldon's history of tithes; I wish also I were by some good
occasion enabled to retribute the tenth of the obligacon your noble
fauoures doe justly and inuiolably bind mee unto, but indeed they
haue bene soe multiplyed, the burthen now soe greate, that it rests
not in mee to discharge my selfe of the hundreth part. Well my
Lord, your Lordship hath the comaund of a gratfull and entyre hart,
which as it is the best, soe is it all I haue worthy to present yow with.
I will conclude then with my humble thanks for your Lordship's
abundant entertainement, when I last attended your Lordship at
Canterbury, togeather with my prayers to allmighty God to graunt
your Lordship the blessinge of a contented longe life, Your Lordship's faithful freind and seruant, Th. Wentworth.

**94.** (*SC* ii, p. 31) *To Mr Yonge, fellow of St John's College in Cambridge. Wentworth Woodhouse. 26 June 1619.*

Sir, beinge intreated by this bearer my neighbour (intendinge to make
his sonne a scholler) that I would write my lettere in his behalfe to
some (*p. 32*) gentleman of mine acquaintance who might become his
tutore, I thought good to send these few lines to yow, that yow might
the rather bee pleased to take him for your peuple, and that for
my sake, yow might afford him an extraordinary respect and care,
which I desire yow very hartely to doe; that setting him in such a
course as in your judgment shall appeare fittest, the yong man may
bee therby bettered in his studies and his honest father bound to
pray for yow. I will detaine yow noe longer, but comitt yow to the
mercifull proteccon of God and rest, Your very louinge freind,
Th. Wentworth.

**95.** (*SC*, ii, p. 32) *To Lord Clifford. Wentworth Woodhouse. 2 July
1619.*

My much honoured Lord, soe equall goes the ballance with mee,
betwixt joy and a timorous sadnes that I cannott readily resolue,
whether I am to giue thankes to allmighty God for blessinge yow

with a sonne, or to administer (accordinge to my talent) comfort
to your Lordship for an untimely birth, and therby a suddaine
pryuacon of such a precious jewell. That which wee most desire,
wee most easily beleeue; which I must confesse (togeather with God's
goodnesse) induce mee to hope the best, nether without reason as
I conceaue. First I haue knowne weaker children to liue then youres
is; secondly I understand that the tender one (whome I beseech God
yow may long enioy) hath heare and nayles, which shew hee is not
borne much before the tyme. Thirdly hee cryes and takes some sus-
tenance, good arguments of strength; lastly, that my Lady hath had
an easy and safe deliuerye, which in abbortiue birthes are marvelous
painfull and daungerous. All which laid togeather, make mee trust
my Lady might reckon beyond her accounte and that God, who in
his mercy hath giuen yow the blossome, will in the abundance
therof nourish itt, prosper itt, and bring it to a mature and sollied
fruite. Therfore I humbly beseech your Lordship fix your confidence
on God, and reuerently waite the meanes and waies of his unsearchable workinge and wisdome, for hee that of stones was able
to raise upp seed unto Abraham, is in humane reason much more
able to giue your noble yssue a (*p. 33*) longe and healthfull life, which
hee in the richnesse of his compassion graunt. Howeuer, my Lord,
beare for a season with Christian pacience this seeminge affliccon
and the same supreame power, that laid it upon yow, to try yow,
will in his gracious goodnesse, crowne your pyous sufferings, with a
plentifull and vertuous ofspringe, to your owne greatest comfort
and the setled continewance of your noble family; wherinto I haue
the honour to bee matched, soe shall there allwaies abide with mee,
the faith and obseruance of Your Lordship's humble brother in
law and seruant, Th. Wentworth.

**96.** (*SC,* ii, p. 33) *To the Bishop of Lincoln, Dr. Mountayne. Wentworth Woodhouse. 20 July 1619.*

Right reuerend father in God and my very good Lord, the church
of Himsworth neare unto mee, by the death of the late incumbent
is become void, and the presentacon or guift therof by lapse or
otherwaies fallen into his Maiesty's hands. There is a gentleman,
Mr Thomas Carre, borne in Crauen, Maister of Artes and laitly
fellowe of Jesus Colledge in Cambridge, who since hath liued with
mee in my howse, which at this tyme is a sutore for that preferment.
I know his merritt, both in learninge and gouernmentt, deserues that
benefice if it were much better. I am therfore humbly to entreate your
Lordship (in case it bee needfull) that yow would bee pleased to

further his sute, by subscribinge on his behalfe the writinge drawne upp for his Maiesty's signature, which this bearer hath in readynesse and to graunt unto him your honourable fauour therin as occasion shall serue. For which I dare undertake hee will in all humble and thankfull manner acknowledge himselfe for euer deeply bounden unto your good Lordship and my selfe, on his behalfe, shall likewise rest very much your servant. Thus crauinge pardon for presumeinge to trouble your Lordship thus longe, I beseech God to graunt unto your Lordship longe life and happynesse, Your Lordship's humbly to bee comaunded, Th. Wentworth.

**97.** (*SC*, ii, p. 33) *To Sir George Caluert. Wentworth Woodhouse. 22 July 1619.*

May it please yow, Sir, the church of Himsworth, a towne not farre from mee is at this present void of a pastore, and the next presentacon is by lapse or otherwaies (*p. 34*) fallen to his Maiesty. I humbly desire your honours furtherance in the obtaininge his Maiesty's signature to a presentacon therof, which this bearer hath ready drawne. The gentleman, Mr Carre, a Crauen man borne, for whome this suite is preferred, hath taken the degree of Master of artes, beinge then fellowe of Jesus Colledge, since which tyme hee hath liued with mee in howse. His learning and gouernment I assure yow upon my creditt deserue a much better preferrment. Wherfore Sir, if yow wilbee pleased to take him into your proteccon, yow shall doe an acte worthy your owne noble disposicon; for which hee shalbee bound to pray to God to giue your honour the increase of all his good blessings, and my selfe bee ready to acknowledge your great fauour herein, with the constant and affecconate truth of beinge Your honour's humbly to bee comaunded, Th. Wentworth.

**98.** (*SC*, ii, p. 34) *To Sir George Calvert. Wakefeild. 4 Oct. 1619.*

May it please your honour, wheras wee are acquainted by the bearers hereof, that very many haue bene and still are wrongfully (as they conceaue) vexed and troubled for buying and sellinge of woolle to the clothiers inhabitinge within Hallifax and other townes neare adioininge, in such sort, as by the peticon will more at large appeare unto yow. Wee could doe noe lesse in a matter of soe great con- sequence as is the trade of clothinge in those partes, then craue your honorable fauour and furtherance in recomendinge their sute to the Lords, that soe they may hencforth, quiettly setled, followe their seuerall trades, as heretofore they haue done. And surely, Sir, it wilbee an acte worthy your honorable disposicon, to aduance that greatest and profittablest trade to the kingdome, to encourage them soe farr forth as may stand with the justice of their cause, especially haueing bene of late yeares much disturbed, greatly to the decay of that trade. All which wee submitt unto your wisdome and judgment beseechinge God to multiply upon yow, many happy, honorable, and longe dayes, Your honoures humbly to bee comaunded Th. Wentworth, H. Savile.

**99.** (*SC*, ii, p. 35) *To the Earl of Cumberland. Wentworth Woodhouse. 13 Dec. 1619.*

My most honoured Lord, I hope yow will not impute unto mee my late not writing to your Lordship; indeed the messinger's stay was soe shorte, my eyes soe drowsye, and my purpose of sendinge this bearer soe instantly ensewinge, as I did a little dispence with the duty I owe yow, wherin to gaine your Lordships pardon is one greate drifte of my letter, which I assure my selfe your noble disposicon will easily graunt unto mee. But chiefly my Lord, I am by the meanes of my penne to assure your Lordship of the continewinge testimony of my obedience and faithfullnes towards yow, til I may represent more liuely images therof, then my present ability doth bestowe upon mee. And lastly to praise God for your Lordship's good health, which I beseech him in his mercy to multiply and continewe, as the thinge that doth exceedingly much add to the joyfull comfort of Your Lordship's most obedient sonne in lawe to bee comaunded, Th. Wentworth.

**100.** (*SC*, ii, p. 35) *To Lord Clifford. Wentworth Woodhouse. 13 Dec. 1619.*

My much honoured Lord, Your Lordship hath by this bearer the oyle yow enioined mee to chuse; and if it bee a more probable way to iudge of the inward man, by the guidinge and gouerninge of ordinary accons, then by those of greater moment, wherin nature is forced aboue the simplicity of its owne inclynacon. Itt will not bee amisse then for your Lordship and I doe with good right desire yow would obserue the same rule, coniectture and esteeme of my deuoted affeccon and seruice, by the remembrance I had of this your petty comaund, wherin yow shall not bee deceaued, for assuredly I will not bee found forgettfull, or unwillinge in the greatest. Itt is the best I could gett, I take it to bee good, but I feare it is frozen this hard weather, yet it will come to himselfe againe. The latest newes I heard is that the kinge of Spaine hath receaued extreame unction, which if it bee soe, I wish itt may effecte his chearfull departure to God. I beseech the allmighty to graunt yow all his blessinge with the increase of all honour and length of daies, Your Lordship's most humble brother in lawe and servantt, Th. Wentworth.

**101.** (*SC*, ii, p. 36) *To Lord Scrope, Lord President of York. Wentworth Woodhouse. 19 Dec. 1619.*

May itt please yonr Lordship, retaininge with my selfe a gratfull remembrance of your noble fauoures towards mee, I find itt likewise accompanyed with a great readynesse and will, to doe yow seruice. Seeing then that my occasions drawe mee or rather fix mee here at home for the present, I cannott chuse but in blaminge the ill lucke of itt, craue your Lordship's pardon; for yow may bee pleased to [do] mee honour and right in beeleeuinge, that noe body did more earnestly desire to haue waited on yow, or shalbee found with more industry to labour the gaininge, the continewance and increase of your noble respectes. My Lord, your Lordship is like to haue before yow six or seauen of my sendinge; I iudge it part of my duty to enforme yow in the condicons of the persons. Crossley that by mishappe kil'd his father will merritt your compassion, for surely hee intended it not and besides hee hath the report to bee a painfull and honest person; for the residewe, they deserue noe more then the justice of their cause requires, for I feare mee most of them are incorrigible. All which I offer to your iudicious consideracon, and my selfe in the truth and observance of being, Your Lordship's humbly to bee comaunded, Th. Wentworth.

**102.** (*SC*, ii, p. 36) *To Sir Arthur Ingram, high Sherif of Yorkshire. Wentworth Woodhouse. 21 Dec. 1619.*

Sir, George Butler stayed here two daies in hope to haue waited on yow, but now that wee are both disappointed of our longinge, I will pray to God my Lady may haue here a jolly braue boy like the father. For yow I must affirme, yow are not soe bold a man, as I tooke yow for, that durst not hazard one night's ill lodginge with your freind. I owe yow a great respecte, yet giue mee leaue not to admitt of an excuse; onely I will quallefy the fault, til I see yow, and your Lady here, where it wilbee a —— in yow to bee found; soe shall yow bee accompanied with as free and freindly a welcome, as in any place whatsoeuer. Nether shall yow saue by this, for doe what yow list, I will waite on your person and eate of your meate the next Assizes,

God willinge. Sir, I will conclude with my prayers for my Ladie's happy arriuall att York and with my best respectes to your selfe; expecting the good hower wherin to giue yow the assured testimony of my beinge, Youres in all affeccon and freindshipp, Th. Wentworth.

**103.** (*SC*, ii, p. 37) *To Sir Edward Sackville knight. Fetter Lane. 26 Feb. 1620.*

Noble Sir, I am imboldened by these few lynes to put yow in mind of the curtesye yow were pleased to afford mee the last night; and (not beinge soe happye, as to haue deserued any thinge of yow as yet) I must ascribe both this and your former respects unto mee in the house, to the worth and noblenesse of your owne disposicon and nature and by the acknowledgemente of them now, bind my selfe to make yow as faithfull and fruitfull a returne as my poore fortune shall inable mee unto. The messinger (albeitt my sollicitore) knoweth nothinge of the matter, what yow please to deliuer him shalbe ready for yow, wheare or how yow shall please to comaund. Sir, there shall not bee any that honoures yow more truly, or more seriously indeauoures to merritt your good opinion, then Your affecconate freind to doe yow seruice, Th. Wentworth.

**104.** *Wentworth to Sir Henry Wotton at Venice, 8 April 1620 (Knowler i, p. 6; SC, ii, p. 37), thanking him for his favour to Wentworth's younger brother on his travels.*

**105.** (*SC*, ii, p. 38) *To Mr John Wentworth at London. Wentworth Woodhouse. 8 April 1620.*

Good brother, I haue sent yow by this bearer a nagge for your journey, I pray yow take care hee bee well looked to, that soe hee maie fitt yow the better, when yow shall haue occasion to make use of him; I haue likewise herewith sent yow other 25$^{li}$ which yow are to receaue. I hope it shalbee superfluous for mee to counsell [you] to circumspeccon in your expences, and soberly and constantly to liue of your allowance, seing the necessety of your owne estate, and judgment will more viuely represent them unto yow then my penne; yet let mee deliuer my selfe plainly unto yow; if yow faile therin, yow build without foundacon. For, besides the ruyne of your estate, it will bringe with itt, the shipwrecke of your creditt, and hopes; and therfore esteeme itt noe trifle, or matter of small momentt, for experience would teach yow the contrary when it were too late.

Secondly, yow must diligently apply your selfe to bee fitted in that course of life, and to that end, which yow intend to betake your selfe unto hereafter; and industriously to seeke out the meanes and make use of meet persons, places, and oportunities for the obtaininge therof. Wherin yow may reape much aduantage by the good aduise and experience of my Lord Ambassadour, desireinge his counsell and dyreccon how yow should imploy your selfe, and spend your tyme in these your trauailes, which I assure my selfe, hee will very freely and affecconately afford unto yow. I pray yow therfore bee very obseruant towards him, (and if yow can within 30 or 40 miles rideinge waite of him 2 or 3 daies in 3 or 4 monthes) impart unto him how yow bestowe your howers; and still in a ciuell and modest manner, reposing upon his dyreccons engage him to continewe and encrease his care and affeccon towards yow. Yow will present this lettere togeather with my seruice unto him, wherin specially I giue him thanks for his fauour and good respectes shewed yow. Good brother, carry a watch ouer your selfe and bee soe behaued both in your outward curtesie towards all his traine, obseruance to my Lord Ambassadour, and in temperance and moderacon both in meate, drinke and discourse; that not beinge offensiue to any (*p. 39*) yow may gaine to your person esteeme, approbacon of your good gouerment and loue and good likeinge of all the company. For the more sollid effectinge of all which, let the entrance and pursuite of all your accons bee begunne and followed with the unfained and constant seruice of allmighty God; calling upon him to bee pleased, in his infinite mercye and wisdome, to dyrecte and establish yow in all goodnesse and vertue that soe yow truly and reuerently seruinge him, hee may blesse your laboures with knowledge, wisdome and preferrment, and that soe disposed, yow may use the same to his glory, to your freinds' comfort, your owne advancment here and endlesse happinesse hereafter; which God graunt both yow and us all. I haue noe more to say, but to desire to heare from yow as soone as I may what course yow hold; and that yow would write mee downe the passages of the places where yow liue. And soe I comitt yow to the mercifall proteccon of the allmighty, wishing yow a happy and prosperous journey, and retaininge with my selfe the constant and sinceare truth of beinge, Your most affecconate brother, Th. Wentworth.

**106.** (*SC*, ii, p. 39) *To Lord Clifford. Wentworth Woodhouse. 19 April 1620.*

My much honoured Lord, I intended to waite upon yow as this day, but in truth my occasions inauoidably crosse my purpose. I will then hereby recomend my sute unto yow, for which I thought to haue bene an humble intercessor in person, that yow would bee pleased to set your hand to this pardon for Thomas Heaton, which, as I am enformed by persons experimented in these courses, your Lordship may very safely doe, beinge ordinary in courses of like nature. The reasons that moue mee are these, I am well assured hee had noe intencon to kill; he was prouoked by spea[c]hes and assaulted with blowes, before hee gaue him the wound. Hee is heir to 40$^{li}$ a yeare land, a towardly well gouerned yonge fellow, Richard Marris his owne nephewe, and light upon this mischaunce in my sister's seruice. If therfore your Lordshipp in your wisdome judge fitting to extend your noble disposicon and compassion towards a poore distressed yong man, soe farr forth as to signe the inclosed and retourne it mee backe by this bearer, (*p. 40*) (whose paines I will see satisfied) I shall esteeme my selfe very much bound unto yow for the same, and will add this, to other your noble fauoures, which haue fixed mee in abideinge, Your Lordship's most humble brother in lawe and seruant, Th. Wentworth.

I desire these lynes may present my humble duty to my Lord, my seruice to my Lady Clifford, togeather with my prayers to God, for her safe and comfortable deliuerye; not omittinge the deuoted seruice of a faithfull seruant to my little Mistress.

**107.** (*SC*, ii, p. 40) *To Mr John Carvyle Esq. Wentworth Woodhouse. 27 April 1620.*

Sir, to administer cause of comfort unto yow for the losse of your daughter, were now unseasonable, assureing my selfe it is by this tyme Christianly dygested, and your fatherly compunccon maistered by your pyous judgment and pacience. I will therfore make noe further mencon of itt, then to wish it may bee the last of your losses and the entrance into future blessings. To giue yow some reason why Mr Carre preached not, was partly the shortnesse of tyme, but principally the desire of my cozen Kay; for Sir Richard Saltenstall's cominge late occasioned him to wish itt might bee spared, the howers beinge soe farr spent. Soe soone as Mr Carre shall retorne from Yorke, I will cause him to write fully unto yow, as is desired in your lettere, which indeed he may justly doe, haueinge soe vertuous, discreete, wellgouerned and religious a subiect to worke upon; and in truth, there remaines nothinge (as concerninge her) for us to remember, but her goodnes and pyety, as examples for us to kindle our zeale to Godwards, and to glorify him in her, that hath in his kingdome glorified her for them. I shall wish that God may bee pleased to establish upon yow, my cozen your wife, and all youres, the assured and constant proteccon of his grace and goodnesse; and that hee may (by addinge to the number as yet left yow) make yow both a happy and joyfull father and mother. My wife remembers her kindest loue to your selfe and good Mistress Caruile, wishing that as yow haue bene both partners in this great losse, (*p. 41*) in respect of the world and your selues, (albeitt of greate purchase and endlesse happines to her blessed soule in heauen) soe hee will graunt unto yow long liues, to bee enioyers and pertakers of many his sweete comfortes togeather hereafter. As for the contents of the letter, shee will likewise see them obserued. And soe I comitt us all to the mercifull guidance and gouernance of allmighty God, your euer assured louinge freind, Th. Wentworth.

**108.** (*SC*, ii, p. 41) *To Sir Arthur Ingram, high Sheriff of the County of York. Wentworth Woodhouse. 3 May 1620.*

Sir, beinge on Fryday next to goe (by God's goodnes) towards London, I am very desirous to understand what answer yow haue receaued concerninge the chaunge of Kirkby Mallomdale's tenure, which hath bene the occasion that makes mee sett pen to paper. If your man bee not yet retourned, in regard I haue promised the tennants to effect it for them before Whitsontide and that Mr Carre tells mee yow intend not to sett forwards before my Lady bee brought in bedd, I desire that yow would let mee know by this bearer, whome yow use in this businesse, to the intent I may sollicite with him a dispatch (if possibly can bee) before Whitsontide and that by lettere which I shall deliuer, yow would recomend unto him the speedy effectinge therof, because in truth it doth very much concerne mee. Thus, Sir, praying to God to make yow a ioyfull father, and my Lady a stronge mother, with remembrance of my seruice to her Ladyship I remaine, your assured freind and affecconate seruant, Th. Wentworth.

**109.** (*SC*, ii, p. 41) *To Lord Wotton. Fetter Lane. 12 May 1620.*

My much honored Lord, being hindered in a resolucon I had put on to haue waited somtime this tearme on your Lordship I haue laid hold of this well suteing oportunity, to performe that duty, which your many respects bind mee unto, at least with my pen, til it may bee perfected with a personall attendance in some fitter season. I nether breath nor entertaine other thoughts to yow wards then honore and seruice; soe as I cannot bee estemed to haue buried your

Lordship's (*p. 42*) talent, soe affecconately lent mee, except there were abilitye, at least occasion offered, to breake forth of meditacon into action. Therfore (still relyinge upon your noble fauoures) I hope not to incurre the censure of an unprofittable or negligent seruant, beinge disfurnished of the meanes not of the zeale; and (in expectance of a better) make use of this way to fix my selfe to your constant and good opinion, as I am inuyolably in my hart Your Lordship's most humbly to bee comaunded, Th. Wentworth.

**110.** (*SC*, ii, p. 42) *To Sir Richard Hutton knight one of his Maiesty's Justices in the Comon pleas* [*Undated*].

May it please yow, Sir, I thought it might somthinge helpe mee to preuent a leaud knaue, if may bee. There is one John Parker, lately my seruant, indebted unto mee aboue 600ᴵᴵ, who, beinge (for secureinge therof) to passe unto mee certaine landes, hath fraudulently made an other conuayance of the same lands unto an other of his creditours the same daye. I heare that hee will endeauour to strengthen his title by a fine or a recouerye. And therfore, Sir, my earnest sute unto yow is, that if any such thinge bee offered, yow wilbee pleased (upon this notice) to make a stopp therof, soe farre forth as lawfully yow maye, in regard it is onely intended to circumvent mee, which I shall esteeme as a greate fauour and which the justice of the cause deserueth; for surely neuer was any man soe leaudly dealt with. Soe with my due respects to your selfe and Lady, I remayne, Your affecconate freind to doe yow seruice, Th. Wentworth.

My wife remembers her harty comendacons both to your selfe and Ladye. And when the said Parker cometh unto yow, I desire that yow would cause him to bee attached as a fellon; for (being my baliffe) hee hath feloniously runne away with my rentt; and bee pleased to giue mee notice therof, for I will see him to bee endicted for the same.

**111.** (*SC*, ii, p. 43) The Coppy of my answer to a message deliuered unto mee from Mr William Mallory by my uncle Trappes 1620.

In answer to Mr Mallory, I must say firste that (as at all times I desire friendship with all men) soe principally with my cuntrymen and gentlemen of his qualety. And beinge now to prepare my selfe for the receuinge of the Comunion, I know itt one of my principall duties to forgiue and forgett, as I hope my sinnes shal bee forgiuen and forgotten.

In this late businesse concerning the election of the knights for Yorkshire I perceaue my disgrace hath bene very earnestly and causlesly sought after; and therfore albeit I do freely forgiue them that prosecute, yet I cannot thinke them that interest themselues in itt to beare mee any good will. Some accons and words of Mr Mallorye haue giuen mee occasion to conceaue his affeccon ledd him that wayes, but nowe this message hath giuen mee full satisfaccon I was mistaken; and although I had some ground for my opinion, yet I haue more reason to beleeue his gentlemanly and respectfull assurance to the contrarye and soe shall firmly perswade myselfe hereafter.

Lastly Mr Mallory shall finde from mee such respect and usage as shall giue him occasion to beleeue that I desire not onely now a takeing away of all misconceauings from betwixt us for the present, but that there may bee a free and freindly entercourse of respect betwixt us hereafter.

**112.** *Sir Arthur Ingram, sheriff of Yorkshire to Wentworth, 6 August 1620 (Knowler, i, pp. 6–7, SC, xx/227). He thanks him for attending Assizes and encloses a letter from Baron Dona about a contribution for the Palatinate to be sought in the West Riding.*

**113.** (*SC*, ii, p. 43) *To Mr Thomas Wentworth Esq. Wentworth Woodhouse. 17 Aug. 1620.*

Sir, wee ought as Christians to reioyce ouer those that dye in Christ, death being indeed the onely happy end of worldly troubles and the perfect accomplishment of all our hopes and desires. Notwithstanding nature will haue the stroake and bee tenderly sensible of neare losses. Myselfe therfore as a kinsman and an affecconate freind to her that is with God and your howse cannot chuse but (*p. 44*) hartely lament the suddaine departure of soe vertuous, and discreet a gentlewoman; and yow as an indulgent and louinge father, I feare mee with more affliccon of spiritt. Yet in my selfe, haueinge found priuacye the best digester of sorrowe, I haue for the present rather made choice of this way to administer comfort, then by visitinge yow; the sight of freinds and persons equally interested in the losse, beinge rather renewers, then abaters of greife. Laying aside then as yow are a father, I must treate with yow as a Christian; consider that God hath many waies blessed yow and youres, that hee hath of his goodnes bestowed upon yow both children and grand children, to bee continewinge comfortes in your old age and therfore

yow may the better afford him part of his owne; that yow had more
true content in beinge pertaker of her goodnesse, and vertuous
carryage, the short tyme it pleased God to lend yow her, then if
yow had enioyed many children many yeares, that had bene ill
gouerned. But aboue all, remember, that yow haue brought upp a
child in God's feare, that yow haue seene her liue in her loue, dye
in his true religion, and consequently crowned in heauen with the
crowne of imortality. Let these meditacons abate the passions of a
fleshly parent, raise your thoughts to heauen, whether shee is allready gone before, and bee just motiues to cause yow with thankfullnesse and pacience to take this one crosse. Lett us remember noe
more of her, then to comfort our selues that shee dyed God's seruant
and liues now a gloryfied soule; and after her example in humble-
nesse and in expectance of God's best leasure prepare and fitt our
selues against hee call us, and then reueale unto us the endles joy
of his presence, and restore unto us againe her heauenly companye.
I will within a day or two by God's leaue see yow, in the interim
comitt yow to his blessed guidance, and to such thoughts as these
and others; which I assure my selfe your pyety and judgment, will
much more powerfully administer unto yow. Your assured and
affecconate freind and kinsman, Th. Wentworth.

**114.** (*SC*, ii, p. 44) *To Nicholas Waller Esq. Wentworth Woodhouse.
19 Aug. 1620.*

(*p. 45*) Sir, I am by this bearer to make a request unto yow, importuned therunto by many of my best and nearest freinds, which I
assure my selfe yow will easily graunte; yet I thought good to write
these lynes, the more effectually to moue yow therin. The matter
I will then leaue to Richard Marris his relacon, and onely signify
thus much, that I shall take the grauntinge therof exceedinge kindly
and bee euer found ready to deserue itt. And therfore I pray yow to
carry that respect therunto, as I protest upon the like occasion I
would bee found readye to shewe not onely to your selfe, but also
to any freind of youres for your sake. And soe I rest, Your very
louinge freind, Th. Wentworth.

**115.** (*SC*, ii, p. 45) *To Sir Arthur Ingram, high Sheriff of Yorkshire.
Wentworth Woodhouse. 3 Sept. 1620.*

Sir, I am to giue yow thanks for your paines in Mr Carre's businesse,
which still addes to my obligacon, and will purchase to your selfe
the comendable and Christian stile of peace-maker. I heare his title

WP—K

much undervallewed by doctor Fauour; wherin his little understandinge shall make mee beleeue, hee speakes as hee thinks. I must
therfore confidently affirme, that I know it by the judgment of as
learned comon lawyers (where it must bee tryed) as are in this
kingdome, to bee inavoidable; and dare well say, that albeitt they
may trouble him for a while, yet in conclusion the parsonage wilbee
his. The justnesse wherof then makes mee to entreate yow (consideracon had of the reasons deliuered by Mr Carre himselfe) to get
him forthwith into possession and to presse that he may haue his
first fruites and this next yeare's tenthes, as the lowest I can perceaue
him willinge to yeild unto. For obtaininge wherof, albeitt Mr Carre
will (as a louer of peace) thinke himselfe euer bound unto yow, yet
they (knowinge what I doe) haue double cause to thanke yow, as
freed from that which would haue fallen heauy upon them how
secure soeuer they are, or att least seeme to bee. Thus leauinge the
conclusion to your judgment and respecte as that wherupon Mr
Carre wholly relyes and freely referrs himselfe, with my seruice to
your noble Lady presented, I shall make an end with the continewance of my beinge Your very affecconate and assured freind, Th.
Wentworth.

**116.** (*SC*, ii, p. 45) *To Sir Peter Freschvile knight. Wentworth Woodhouse. 4 Sept. 1620.*

Sir, my seruant did not longe since by my appointment attend yow
with (*p. 46*) a Comission for findinge an office after my brother
Sauile, wherin presumeinge of your woonted kindnesse I had made
bold to nominate your selfe a Comissioner, at which time yow were
pleased to appointe the last of this month at Chesterfeild for sittinge
upon the said Comission. My seruant then likewise in pursuite of
your dyreccons went to Mr Bullocke, the feodary, to acquaint him
withall and to procure a warrant from him; which accordingly is
done, as this bearer will shewe unto yow. I must therfore desire,
that yow will likewise sett your hand and seale therto; to the end it
may bee deliuered to the Sheriff at Darby on Thursday next and
there to bee proclamed and entred in the county booke, as is prescribed by a late priuie seale. The escheator wee could not yet light
on, but hee shall haue notice in tyme, God willinge. And it beinge
an office to bee found by consent, I haue appointed the messinger
to goe of purpose to let Sir Francis Cooke and Mr Lassells understand the time and place. And thus with my seruice presented to
your Lady, til I see yow next (which shalbee, Godwillinge, the night
before the findinge of the office) I comitt yow to God's blessed

proteccon, remaininge Your very affecconate and assured kinsman and freind, Th. Wentworth.

**117.** (*SC*, ii, p. 46) *To Sir Godfrey Rodes knight. Wentworth Woodhouse. 5 Sept. 1620.*

Sir, the statute entred into by your sonne was deposited by both parties in my custody and the trust expressed under the hands of them all, as yow may see by that which is hereinclosed, which I conceaue to bee that which yow terme a defeazance; soe as for my discharge it had bene fitt I should haue had warrant under both their hands for deliuering it ouer unto yow; and let mee say truly unto yow, there is not that man almost in Yorkshire unto whome I would haue parted with it, saueing Sir Godfrey Rodes. Therfore I must confidently repose thus farre in yow, that yow shall ether deliuer back unto mee, both the statute and the trust expreste upon your retourne from Yorke, or els procure mee an acknowledgment of the receate therof by your sonne, with the good allowance and approbacon (*p. 47*) of my cozen Butler. And in the meane tyme to certefy mee back by lettere, (for which of purpose I haue sent this messinger) that yow haue receaued this statute and trust from mee upon these tearmes onely. Excuse mee if I deale strictly by reason it is the trust of a freind reposed in mee, which I must confesse makes mee more scrupulous it may bee then ordinary, and more indeed then if it did concerne my selfe. I neuer did the like before, therfore yow maie see what affyance I haue in yow, that takes all doubtes out of mind. I will trouble yow noe longer, more then to end this letter with the setled abideinge, Your assured louinge freind, Th. Wentworth.

**118.** (*SC*, ii, p. 47) *To Mr Charles Greenwood. Wentworth Woodhouse. 5 Sept. 1620.*

Good Mr Greenwood, I am sorry both that yow lost your labour your last beinge here, as likewise to understand that yow continewe still ill of your goute. Take heed of desireing wealth too fast, least your goute increase togeather with itt. That I was not at home was not my fault, for in truth I little looked for yow on Munday, but not at all the day yow came. It is longe since I saw yow here and therfore if [it] please God to blesse yow with strength (which hee graunt yow) I should bee right gladd to haue your company and speake with yow about two or three matters now when Mr Radcliffe comes ouer, who by the way I must tel yow plaies well at chesse. Yet if yow bee not perfectly well, I would not haue yow by any meanes to stirre, for the businesse requires noe great hast and wee shall (by God's grace) haue time sufficient hereafter. Comend mee I pray yow to your wife, tel her I wish her pacience and as for my infirmity (choller) I assure my selfe there will want none in the house, as longe as your gout holds. God bee with thee, good Charles, and giue thee health and long life to enioy itt and that yow may bee as thorowly hole, as my wishes are harty and as firmly, as my affeccon binds mee to bee Your assured freind, Thomas Wentworth.

**119.** (*SC*, ii, p. 47) *To Lord Darcy. Wentworth Woodhouse. 8 Sept. 1620.*

My much honoured Lord, (*p. 48*) this inclosed being brought yesterday by a messinger that told mee hee was dyrected in speciall to deliuer itt to mee, and perceauinge therby and the superscripcon, that it concerned some ordinary matter belonging the Sessions, I opened the same. But after I saw the contentes, I found my errour, being much more fitt both in respect of your quallety, as also of your experience and wisdome in these seruices, that the lettere should haue beene first deliuered and opened by your Lordship. I haue therfor sent the same (togeather with this excuse) unto your Lordship by this bearer and will to morrowe, Godwillinge, my selfe attend yow, to know your further pleasure what course wee are to hold in the execucon of this seruice. In the meane space I shall cease further to trouble yow, and rest in the due and constant obseruance of beinge, your Lordship's affecconate kinsman and seruant, Th. Wentworth.

**120.** (*SC*, ii, p. 48) *To Lord Clifford. Ledstone. 19 Sept. 1620.*

My much honoured Lord, I haue according to your lettere used the best meanes I could to enquire out a howse for yow here about Peckfeild, but as yet find none of sufficient receate, saueing Pontfract, which (being altogether without stuffe, and much decaied since the difference betwixt my Lady and Mr Pierrpointe) can nether bee furnished nor yet repaired. But I shall further imploy my endeauour and giue your Lordship an accounte therof, when this poore howse shall haue the honore to lodge yow. Thus presenting my humble duty to my lord, my suite to your honorable Lady, with your noble yssue, praying God to heape upon yow all (with a setled continewance) the richnesse of his bountie and goodnesse, I end in the unfained truth of beinge Your Lordship's most humble brother in lawe and seruant, Th. Wentworth.

**121.** (*SC*, ii, p. 48) *To Lord Clifford at the same time as no. 120.*

My much honoured Lord, giue mee leaue to walke your owne way, and to deliuer my poore, yet faithfull aduise in this letter. I doe wonderfully approue your (*p. 49*) course in seeming to giue passage to my Lord's humore and yet underhand useing all meanes to diuert him from these extrauagances. They that counsell otherwaies, or not afford their best helpe, either want witt or honesty. Likewise that it is the fittest and best for your selues and estates to liue to-geather, I haue allwaies and soe doe still esteeme itt. Therfore as yow cannot too much desire itt, soe, good my Lord, lett your meanes in accomplishing bee still (as they haue bene) filiall obedience and obseruance; which I doubt not will in tyme (albeitt may bee not for the present) constantly winne him to yow and allwaies bee your honour in the best judgments, to attaine to this end by following and accompanying him as it were whether hee will or noe. Certainly this is the best rec[kon]inge, nay I dare hardly assent soe farr as to admitt the use therof at all, but as yet surely I will neuer aduise itt, as in my conceate a course subiect to scandall, full of hazard and difficulties; my Lord's mind I feare mee being soe wonderfully bent upon liuinge apart (I cannot say from your Lordship) from your Lady. The reasons moueing mee to giue this judgment are shortly these: first yow should hereby blemish the obedience of a sonne to a father, which I know yow haue very tender, too great a losse to bee ventured, where the daunger is noe greater to your selfe or estate. For bee it graunted that letting him haue his mind, yow bee preiudiced fiue hundreth pounds, which is more then itt can bee, would yow for twice soe much endeauour to crosse, displease, or disquiett my Lord? I assure my selfe yow would not. Secondly it may bee well doubted whether (being your father and haueing the staffe in his owne power) yow shalbee able to constraine him to a way against his will, which is not lightly to bee regarded, soe yow shall not onely open your selfe to men's censures, but more hazard the peace of your howse then euer. Thirdly it is more then probable that my Lord must bee weary of this ramblinge once in a winter and then perceauing his errour, yow shall haue him more desirous then euer of your companye, which hee will best learne to vallewe by the want of itt and most likely to continewe more steadily therin hereafter. Wherby I am fully perswaded, yow will find your conquest much more honorable and more absolute and him more tractable to satisfy your desires in the future. Fowerthly to free your selfe from the blott of disobedience, it is requisite that yow first suffer out of your duty to your father, which, God bee praised, hetherto yow haue not bene putt to: and then if after aparient tryall hee should fortune to perseueare in this uncertaine and ill aduised way, a contrary course should bee better grounded, and appeare to the (*p. 50*) world to bee in a manner wrested and forced from yow, by the urgent reasons and necessity of preseruinge the honore of your selfe and posterity. Fiftly and lastly, as this is the last refuge, soe will it not bee too late to use itt the next yeare, which I hope in God yet yow shall neuer haue occasion to doe. Therfore out of all these premisses I will conclude and deliuer the resulate. I hold it good for your Lordship by all faire meanes, both open and priuate, to labour my Lord not to part and disperse your selues and families, as being indeed a great greife to yow, to thinke him weary of your companye, wherin my wife and my selfe will use all our Creditt and doe your Lordship by God's grace the best seruice that wee shall bee able. But if noe perswasions can preuaile, then referre all to God's good pleasure, prouide for your howshold as well as yow can upon this suddaine, giue way to his humore for a yeare and hereafter *dies dabit consilium*. My Lord, the truth, I perswade my selfe yow beleeue to bee in mee, will plead for my boldnesse and plainnesse and shall euer put mee in mind to pray to God, that both in this and all other your accons, yow may apply your selfe to that which shalbee most to his glorye and the preseruacon of your selfe and howse in honorable and prosperous estate; humbly submitting the consideracon hereof to your wisdome, and vowing my selfe, Your Lordship's most humble brother in law and seruant, Th. Wentworth.

**122.** (*SC*, ii, p. 50) Direccon for Christopher Steuenson touching a message to bee deliuered to Sir Guy Palmes, 12 October 1620.

Christopher Steuenson, I would haue yow to goe to Sir Guy Palmes, remember my loue to him and to lett him knowe that I understand hee hath taken from Christopher Knightson a setting dogg, which I assure my selfe hee would not haue done, had hee bene rightly enformed. Yow shall then proceed and relate unto him that Knightson is a man by mee authorized to hunt within my whole freewarren and mannore of Harwood as my meniall seruant, that such doggs as hee hath they are allwaies at my comaund and disposall, hee haueinge onely the use of them soe longe as I please. That hee doth not hunt within any man's libertie saue my owne, that if hee doe, let him bee punished as the law hath prouided; yet, howeuer, (*p. 51*) that there is noe law to warrant any man to take my dogg from him, or to detaine him being taken. And therfore yow are from mee to desire him to deliuer the dogge to yow, which yow are to receaue and dispose of as I shall further dyrect. Which, if hee refuse, yow may say I feare I will take the detaininge of the dogge in a verry discurteous manner, as an unneighbourly and an unwarrantable action and soe take your leaue quietly. After yow are departed, I would haue yow write mee word what answer hee giues and to stay somwhere about Gawthorpe, and learne out if yow can possibly what is become of the dogge. And if yow by any meanes get sight of him, that yow take him away, bring him to mee and I will satisfy itt.

**123.** (*SC*, ii, p. 51) *To Sir Guy Palmes knight. Wentworth Woodhouse. 12 Oct. 1620.*

Sir, I haue sent the bearers to attend yow, and acquaint yow with an accident wherin I conceaue yow are misinformed; not doubtinge but they shall receaue such satisfaccon as the case doth require. And so referringe my selfe to their relacon I rest, Your louinge freind, Th. Wentworth.

**124.** *Wentworth to Christopher Wandesford, 28 November 1620 (Knowler, i, p. 9; SC, ii, p. 51). Lord Clifford has promised Wandesford the seat at Appleby, if Wentworth is elected for Yorkshire. P.S. omitted by Knowler,* I hope you will take your part of a Christmas pye with mee at Yorke the day of seruice the meanetime farewell as preparinge for a hungry dynner.

**125.** *Wentworth to Sir Thomas Gower, sheriff of Yorkshire, 28 November 1620 (Knowler, i, p. 8; SC, ii, p. 52). He seeks his just and equal favour at the election.*

**126.** *Wentworth to Sir Henry Bellassys, 28 November 1620 (Knowler, i, p. 8; SC, ii, p. 53). He thanks him for his support and asks him to dinner on the election day (25 December).*

**127.** *Wentworth to Sir Mathew Boynton, 28 November 1620 (Knowler, i, p. 9; SC, ii, p. 53). He asks him and his friends to dinner on election day.*

**128.** *Wentworth to Sir Henry Savile, 28 November 1620 (Knowler, i, p. 8; SC, ii, p. 54). He promises to support him in getting a borough seat if he should fail at Aldborough.*

**129.** *Wentworth to Sir Thomas Fairfax at Walton, 3 December 1620 (Knowler, i, p. 10; SC, ii, p. 54). He thanks him for retiring from the election and promising his support.*

**130.** *Wentworth to Sir George Calvert, 5 December 1620 (Knowler, i, p. 10; SC, ii, p. 55). He urges him to ask the Lord President to be present at the election, and to procure the Lord Chancellor's intervention.*

**131.** *Wentworth to Sir Arthur Ingram, 6 December 1620 (Knowler, i, p. 11; SC, ii, p. 56). He suggests that Wentworth should stand for the first place instead of Calvert in order to counter Sir John Savile's influence with the clothiers.*

**132.** *Wentworth to Sir Thomas Dawney, 6 December 1620 (Knowler, i, p. 11; SC, ii, p. 58). He thanks him for his favour and asks him to be at York with his freeholders and friends for the election.*

**133.** *[Cancelled].*

**134.** *(SC, ii, p. 58) To Sir Robert Askwith [7 Dec. 1620].*

Sir, hauing bene enioined by some of my nearest freinds to stand at this eleccon for knights for the parliament with Sir George Caluertt, his Maiesties principall Secretary, and haueinge now declared our selues, are to try the affeccon of our frends, amonge which number I haue longe esteemed yourselfe for to bee unto mee well assured. I must therfore hereby moue yow very effectually earnestly to sollicite all your neighbours and freinds that yow haue interest in in Yorke to giue their voices with us at this next choice which is to bee made up on Christmas daie. Which your kind and respectfull indeauoures, as I shall euer bee mindfull to requite as an argument of your true affeccon towards mee and in the nature of an especiall curtesie. Soe will I undertake when I come to London (for I know wee shall haue yow a member of the howse) to carry yow to Mr Secretary, make yow knowen to him, not procure yow onely many thanks from him, but that yow shall hereafter find a readynesse and chearfullnesse to doe yow such good offices as shall lye in his waie hereafter. Lastly I hope to haue your company with mee att dinner that day, where yow shalbee most welcome and soe desiring answer I remaine, Your very assured and affecconate freind, Th. Wentworth.

**135.** *Wentworth to Sir Henry Slingsby, 8 December 1620 (Knowler, i, p. 12; SC, ii, p. 59). He hopes to have a thousand voices besides his friends, wishes for his advice as to standing for the first place and asks him to enter York with Lord Clifford on election day.*

**136.** (*SC*, ii, p. 60) *To George Weatheridde Esq. Wentworth Woodhouse. 8 Dec. 1620.*

Sir, beinge engaged by some of my freinds to stand with Mr Secretary knights of this shire for the next parliament, I am therby occasioned to moue my freinds for their good assistance, the more effectually in regard I understand Sir John Sauile purposeth to putt in to bee one, whereby he may crosse Mr Secretary it maie be. For as for myselfe, I rest well assured my cuntrymen knowes mee too well to refuse mee for him. I perceaue my Lord is nobly affected towards us, therfore I desire this fauor from yow; that yow will moue him thorowly to deale with Sir Henry Constable and Sir Thomas Fairfax of Gillinge that they will laboure their freinds and further our eleccons, togeather with my Lord of Rutland's and his Lordship's owne freeholders and other freinds, as alsoe to declare himselfe in some publique and effectuall sorte for us to the intent the cuntry may take notice therof and the better to represse some forward spirrits that will frame needlesse doubtes against Mr Secretary, to the intent men might perceaue they in their deepe iudgments foresawe more then other simpler persons euer dreamed of. I doe indeed assure my selfe of your sound endeauoures herein, both in respect of Mr Secretarie and my selfe. I will not therfore longer detaine yow from your other occasions, onely hereby lett yow knowe howe gratfull an offic this shalbee unto mee that I will (if able) make a free and chearfull requitall and soe rest your very assured and affectionate freind, Th. Wentworth.

**137.** *Wentworth to Sir Thomas Fairfax at Denton, 8 December 1620 (Knowler, i, p. 12; SC, ii, p. 60). He urges him to use all his influence for himself and Calvert and to join in the entry to York on the election day.*

**138.** *Wentworth to Thomas Wentworth Esq., 8 Dec. 1620 (Knowler, i, p. 13; SC, ii, p. 61). He asks for returns of freeholders and their promised votes from the constables.*

**139.** (*SC*, ii, p. 62) *To Lord Scrope, Lord Lieutenant of Yorkshire.
Wentworth Woodhouse. 8 Dec. 1620.*

My much honoured Lord, amongst your many noble and free fauoures
placed upon mee I maie not esteeme the declaringe yourselfe to
stand at this next eleccon of knights for the parliament for Mr
Secretary and my selfe of meanest condicon; nor can I in contem-
placon of them altogeather bee other then most ready (in some small
measure) to bee thought worthie of them by the uttermost of my
endeauors and seruices, which I shall freely and dutifully offer upp
to your Lordship in way of poore acknowledgment, being too meane
to beare the name of requitalls. Sir John Sauile, my good and ancient
freind, intends certainly to stand, workinge closely in these parts by
his instruments to supplant Mr Secretary, finding hee cannot drawe
them from mee (constant to himselfe, best beseeminge oposiccon,
which in him is nature). If this old vetteraine should carry it against
Mr Secretary (without whome nether will I bee), itt were some
touch to our owne estimacons aboue and therfore I must humbly
beseech your Lordship to afford your power and countenance as to
your wisdome shall seeme best and as has bene accustomed heretofore by our Lord Lieftennants. I should bee sorry to see such a
carriage of the commons I assure yow; it might breed ill blood in the
example and imbolden them more then wer fitt for this gouernment.
I purposed to haue waited on your Lordship this last weeke and
performed this duty in person, but being on my way this day seauennight my horse unluckily gaue mee a fall, since which time I haue
here lyen by itt. I will here cease your further troble, humbly submitting the consideracon hereof to your wisdome and my selfe euer
truly deuoted in all respectt and seruice to remaine, Your Lordship's
most humbly to bee commaunded, Th. Wentworth.

**140.** (*SC*, ii, p. 63) *To George Lassells Esq. Wentworth Woodhouse.
8 Dec. 1620.*

Sir, yow did mee the fauour to write a letter in the behalfe of Mr
Secretary and my selfe to all my lord's officers to labour the freeholders in Hallamshire to giue their voices with us this next eleccon,
which falles forth upon Christmasse daie, an unfitt time but cannot
be helped. I must entreate this further kindnes that yow would take
the paines to come ouer to mee Munday or Tuesday before Christmasse, upon the one of the daies I will expect your company here.
For Sir John Sauile, your good freind and mine, labouring the
cuntrye and haueing in a manner declared hee will stand, I am

wonderfull desirous to speake with yow. This I shall take as a very greate curtesie which yow shall find mee euer ready to meritt from yow and requite with chearfullnesse. Thus noe wayes doubting but yow wilbee pleased to satisfy my desire herein I remaine, your very assured louing frend and kinsman, Th. Wentworth.

**141.** *Samuel Casson to Wentworth, Leeds, 12 December 1620 (Knowler, i, p. 13; SC, xx, 229). He urges him to stand for the first place and promises him a hundred freeholders in and about Leeds, but reports that the country is not well affected to Calvert.*

**142.** (*SC*, ii, p. 63) *To Sir Richard Beaumont knight. Wentworth Woodhouse. 17 Dec. 1620.*

Sir, I understand from seuerall quarters how much paines yow haue bene pleased to take in the behalfe of Sir George Caluerte and my selfe and doubt not but yow will second itt with a constant pursuit therof which as I must entreate from yow soe shall I make it knowne to Mr Secretary and in my owne particular esteeme it a great curtesie and an argument of your good affeccon towards mee, which yow shall finde mee ready to deserue in performaunce of the best offices of friendshippe that shall lye in my power. I saw a postscript of yours in a lettere to Mr Sauile Radcliffe, wherin yow were misinformed, noe such matter hauing fallen from mee, or other desire more then to know the names of my freinds, to lay them by as remembrancers unto mee of my wellwillers, which I may lawfully doe without iust offence to any other, or daunger to myselfe. I am sure my lord Clifford would haue bene gladd hee might haue had your company on Christmasse eue at Tadcaster, but seeing yow goe in the daie before. Let mee desire yow to bee circumspecte there bee noe workinge underhand with your freeholders; for that end moues others to goe in that daie as I conceaue more then any other reason. I hope howeuer I shall haue your company at supper on Sunday and on Christmasse day at dynner, where yow shalbee most welcome and therby dowble your fauores towards mee. Thus, Sir, with the remembrance of my harty affeccon towards you, Your right assured and affecconate freind, Th. Wentworth.

**143.** (*SC*, ii, p. 64) *To Sir Henry Sauile Baronet. Wentworth Woodhouse. 30 Dec. 1620.*

Sir, I haue hardly in my life put pen to paper with a worse will, nether indeed had I euer the like occasion: what fruites my laboures haue brought forth at Londsbrough, the inclosed will certefie yow, my selfe takeinge noe great pleasure to relate them. Thus farr I must professe upon my faith, I haue sett my whole strength upon itt, soe farre as to part in some unkindnesse and yet cannott effect it for yow, the old man will not bee moued nor heare reason. Yow are beholden to my Lord Clifford, who moued very earnestly on your behalfe, and promised still to doe his uttermost, albeitt without hope of preuailinge. I pray yow, Sir, doe not misconceaue mee in this businesse, there is nothing happened unto mee these fiue yeares troubled mee soe much, as that it should bee my misfortune, thus to engage my selfe and disappoint yow. I must therfore very earnestly entreate your pacience, both in regard I had an absolute promise and soe thought I might haue relied therupon, as also because it is a thinge *extra me*. Your good acceptance of my endeauours herein shall put mee in mind how much I am behind with yow and to labour to free my selfe, in as good and as affecconate a manner, as my power will extend unto. I esteeme my selfe much beholden unto yow for your last fauour, which was soe really performed that I shall not forgett itt, nor yow find other dealinge from mee. If there bee any occasion wherin I maie doe yow or any freind (*p. 65*) of youres any good office, in the howse or elswhere, let mee I pray yow heare from yow, none shall more hartely and chearfully frame himselfe more fully to answer your expectacon then, Your very assured freind, Th. Wentworth.

**144.** (*SC*, ii, p. 65) *To Lord Clifford. Austin Friars. 8 Jan. 1621.*

My much honoured Lord, your departure from hence was soe lately, that the occurrents come to my knowledge since, would not bee worth the labour now to write them; such thinges being onely in a progresse towards a conclusion, as hadd their begininges dureinge their aboade here. Yet am I easily inticed to presume soe farre upon your noble nature, as to entreate yow to honore these lynes soe farre, as to giue them a readinge, which convayes my truest and most deuoted hart by this (in fault of a more demonstratiue expression and meanes) of opening it selfe unto yow; as also my prayers to allmightie God for the well grounded and encreasing happines and honore of your selfe and noble family, Your Lordship's most humble brother in law and seruant, Th. Wentworth.

I beseech your Lordship giue leaue to these lines to present my humble duty to my Lord; my seruice to my Lady Clifford, and to my sweet Mistress Elizabeth, praying God to multiply on yow his fairest blessinge in hopefull M^r Charles.

**145.** (*SC*, ii, p. 67) *To the Countess of Shrewsbury. Austin Friars.*
*8 Feb. 1621.*

My most honoured lady, accordinge to your desire signified unto
mee both by your Ladyship's owne lettere and by Mr Ogle, I haue
togeather with my brother William entred into bond for one thowsand pounds; which albeitt a great some, yet I should make noe
great difficultie to engage my selfe for a greater and confidently put
my selfe into your hands, could I (our fraile condicon considered)
bee assured of your life. But giue mee leaue to professe, I would not
willingly, in a matter of this nature and voluntarinesse, bee hereafter
thrust or enforced to sue and bee beholden to others for our securitie,
if such a mishappe should befall us, which God of his goodnesse
diuerte. (*p. 68*) Therfore I assure my selfe the discerning justice,
and noble uprightnesse of your mind to bee such, as your Ladyship
will not misconstrue mee, in that I send herwith by Mr Ogle and
desire that yow would seale and deliuer to the use of my selfe and
brother an assignement of Pontfract for our counter securitie, as
once yow were pleased upon the like occasion to passe Rufford unto
mee, which act neuer preiudicated your Ladyship, noe more then I
trust this shall. What wee haue done herein, I maie truly affirme this
further merritt, to proceed from as much chearfullnesse and respect,
as is possible and therfore I rest assertained your Ladyship will see
that such a willingnesse to serue yow shall not suffer or sustaine
any losse. But that yow will arme us against any unexpected accident
that maie befall us, and use as much readynesse and speed to prouide
for us by the aforesaid counter security, (accordinge to Mr Ogle's
ingagement) as wee did of zeale and contentment in performinge
this dutie. Now Madame, touching Malhamdale, yow mencon an
offer made of 3500[11], which seemes most strange to mee, and (with
your pardon) I rest full well grounded, if any such bee, it comes
from those, who either understand it not, or meane not to performe
roundly and uprightly with yow. Yet albeitt (with much hazard to
loose my chapman) I will expect the issue of that proposicon til
midd March, hopeing your ladyship doth beleeue I should bee sorrye
to sell it soe much under the vallewe. And on the other side, that it
behoues mee to sell it in such conuenient tyme, as the moneies maie
come in seasonably to discharge the debtes which I am engaged in
my creditt to paie, a course too indeed (as I judge) most for your
profitt and honore. And therfore if I heare not from your Ladyship
before that time, I resolue to conclude the bargaine Godwillinge upon
such tearmes as I haue acquainted Mr Ogle with. There remaines
nothinge but to present my wiue's seruice to your Ladyship and my

Lady Ogle, togeather with my sister's and my owne. Which done, I comitt your increase of sound health, and happinesse to the good grace and blessinge of the allmightie. Your Ladyships affecconate kinsman and deuoted seruant, Th. Wentworth.

**146.** (*SC*, ii, p. 69) *To Lord Clifford. Austin Friars. 8 Feb. 1621.*

My much honoured Lord, I haue put my pen to paper, albeitt noe newes now stirre, to aduertize your Lordship that upon conference had betwixt Sir Arthur Ingram, Mr Tailor and my selfe concerning your cloth business,[1] wee were of opinion that your Lordship might doe well to write soe soon as may bee to my Lord Tresorer that at your beeing here yow had in good discreccon forborne to moue his lordship in that your sute referred unto him as then well discerning his imployments to bee ouer many and waighty to giue him leasure to take the same into consideration; that in your absence yow had desired Sir Arthur and my selfe to putt his lordship in mind therof when wee found a seasonable occasion, which wee haue as yet likewise forborne out of the same reason; that your desire is when wee moue him you may present his noble fauour towards yow, soe far forthe as the justice of your cause shall beare, which yow will take as a particular engagement of yow and your howse to serue and honor him. All which yow frame in such wise, as yow know many degrees better then I am able to suggest, if I wanted soe much good manners as to offer itt. Only under reformation I could wish that your letter might bee soe warily penned as to bee void of excepcion although itt came to the view of my lord of Buckingham, least he might conceaue that yow doe not soe absolutely depend on him, as it maie bee he expects, and soe take that occasion to grow cold in the matter. Your Lordship will present my duty and seruice where I owe itt, crauing pardon for my breuity in regard I will write more at large to yow the next week Godwillinge. God take yow and yours into his blessed keeping, Your lordship's most humble brother in lawe to commaund, Th. Wentworth.

**147.** (*SC*, ii, p. 69) *To Michael Wentworth Esq. Austin Friars. 20 Feb. 1621.*

Good cozen, I haue receaued your lettere wherin yow write yow will not chide mee, albeitt yow thincke yow haue some cause, being nowe a yeare since yow desired mee to preferre your sonne to Mr

---

[1] The renewal of Cumberland's patent for licensing the export of white, undressed cloth.

Secretarie's seruice and since Michelmas last yow desired that, if I fownd difficultie to place him there, then in some (*p. 70*) other seruice where I thought conuenient. That yow will not say that I haue not since thought of yow nor itt, but yow may truly saie yow have not heard of mee nor itt. That this delaye unto yow is a double greife, your sonne's losse of time in his educacon and that yow hauing said unto some of your freinds that I would place him in seruice very shortly, that they thinke I either cannot or will not doe it for yow; but yow are loth to haue any such thought of mee, the one being too great a disabling of mee, the other an unkindnesse in mee, this being but an ordinary curtesie amongst comon acquaint-ance. Those your owne words I haue set downe that soe they and my answer might appeare togeather.

I conceaue then yow haue noe cause to chide mee at all, the meanes to satisfy yow not absolutely restinge with mee, but depend-inge chiefly upon others, and when yow think better of itt yow will perceaue that with persons of such qualetie it well befitts mee to obserue and waite times and leasures, to moue thinges with ciuilitie, not to presse with importunity, by this meanes rather hindering then furthering my desires. And to write to yow howe I proceeded before the businesse had bene done would haue bene troublesome and in itselfe a vaine expence of time. Nor yet, by your leaue, haue yow iust grounds to charg mee with delay, in regard my stay (indeauouring to bestowe your sonne where I imagined yow would haue best liked) can bee noe fault, unlesse it bee one to labour not onely the matter it selfe but the place to your contentment. Againe, the time your sonne hath lost since Michelmas in his educacon is not soe great, but maie by God's grace easily bee repaired. Yet the blame in that too is altogeather your owne, your selfe desireinge mee when I came out of Yorkshire, being three weeks after Michaellmas, to stay some time expecting Mr Secretarie's answer, before I should seeke elswhere. That the not effecting of this matter for yow might by others bee iudged a disableinge of mee, that consideracon moues mee nothinge; for I seeke my selfe within not without in other men's notes or table bookes. But it shalbee much against my will to giue yow, or any soe neare a freind, iust occasion of unkindnes; howsoeuer hee that shall without ground take one wronges himselfe much more then any other.

But the truth is, finding Mr Secretary conceaued himselfe ouer-charged with number of seruants allready (*p. 71*) and that hee intended to lessen them, I haue moued and obtained with my lord Treasurer for your sonne to attend upon him in the quallety of a gentleman with allowance both of a man and a horse. Now albeitt yow valewe this as an ordinary curtesie done for a comon acquaintance, let mee assure yow I found itt not soe in other men's opinions and for myselfe I iudge it farr otherwaies, neather would I haue done thus much for many in the kingdome. For to tel yow plainly I right well knowe how small thanks men receaue many times for doinge offices of this nature, nor would I make a custume to lay my discretion and creditt at stake upon the staied and sober carriage of an unexperienced yong man, as well foreseing (if hee behaue himselfe not well) I must suffer in both. And therfore (my lord takeing notice that hee is my kinsman) I will looke that yow will allowe him such meanes yearely as wilbee expected, to witt forty pounds by yeare at least that soe hee maie serue in the fashion of a gentleman; also his capacity and understandinge to bee such as, beinge noe preiudice to them that comend him, may sufficiently enable him to make use of his breedinge to his owne preferrment. After Easter hee wilbee expected, in the meane time yow may aduise what yow will doe and let mee knowe your resolucon when I come downe into the cuntry which wilbee within that time, Godwillinge. My wife, my brothers and sisters kindly salute yow, your sonne and his wife. My selfe wish to yow and all yours much happines. And soe I rest, Your assured and affecconate freind and cozen, Th. Wentworth.

**148.** (*SC*, ii, p. 71) *To Lord Clifford. Austin Friars. 26 Feb. 1621.*

My much honoured Lord, the sadd relacon of Mr Charles's departure, much afflicts all that loue yow or your howse and most sharpe noe doubte to your selfe, more nearly and deeply touched in nature and interest; yea alasse it may bee, as a tender father, yow were more delighted in that goodly and hopefull braunch then yow ought and by building the future strength and continewance of your howse too much upon him, haue drawne this heauy hand upon yow; yet obserue how itt is (*p. 72*) tempered and praise God euen in his judgmentts. It befalles yow not in your old age, but in your youth, soe as hee maie repaire your losse in a few monthes. Hee hath not punished yow in the rebellion or disobedyence of a sonne, as Dauid in Absolom, nor taken him from yow in a whirlewind eatinge and drinkinge as to Job, but (by a most blessed and peacfull end) hath sealed him to eternall life. My Lord, in the feare of God then moderate your passion and (inwardly humbled under his allmightie hand) your Christian pacience assuredly will turne him from his displeasures to his mercies, cause him to blesse your latter daies more then your begininges; instead of sonns, to giue yow sonns, sonns; and soe fill and stuffe your quiver with them, as yow shall not bee afraid to meet your enemies in the gate. Which of his infinite grace and goodnesse

hee graunt yow that onely in his wisdome knowes bringe us both by
affliccons and blessings to the true acknowledgment of the richnes
of his compassions. Your Lordship's most humble brother in law to
bee comaunded, Th. Wentworth.

**149.** (*SC*, ii, p. 72) *To Thomas Wentworth Esq. Austin Friars. 18 Mar.
1621.*

Good Cozen, my Cozen Will his unlooked for coming hether to mee
is the occasion of my present writing and albeitt the respect I beare
yow made mee giue him noe encouragement at all, in soe ill aduised
a waie and caused mee not to doe for him that, which most readily
I would, if hee had taken your allowance with him. Yet being your
sonne, (to whome I doe beare soe true and cordiall an affeccon)
meethought it did not befitt mee to bee altogeather carelesse or
diserting of him, in soe greate a daunger both of his person and
future fortunes; especially when I found in him a true sence of his
owne indiscretion and a sorrowe that hee had giuen yow soe just an
offence, by his undutifull and youthful departure from yow. In what
sort then I haue (after aduizement taken with my Cozen Wandesford)
admitted him into my howse, till yow otherwaies dispose of him, for
preuenting of a greater daunger, I must leaue it to the relacon of my
Cozen Wandesford; and in the (*p. 73*) interim I assure yow, I wilbee
farre from hardening him in his forgettfullnes towards yow. Onely
beinge desired by the yong gentleman himselfe to mediate with yow
for his pardon, I must confesse I promised I would. My motiues
were these: first his demeanore here in my howse, which in good
earnest hath bene verie discreete; such indeed, as I should bee loth
to see miscarrie with a stranger, much lesse with my kinsman.
Secondly, that parents must often pardon the omissions of their
children euen in true judgment; for wee are none of us borne at the
first able to gouerne ourselues, but gained it by time and obseruacon.
Therfore truly, Sir, if yow would bee pleased upon this his humiliacon, in such a sort to forgiue him, as maie well stand with the distance betwixt a father and a child; and (seing I find him soe willing
to take his fortune abroade) to allowe unto him some such meanes of
liuelyhood, as yow in your wisdome shall thinke fitt. In good faith I
hope hee will soe behaue himselfe and waigh his accons hereafter, as
that yow will not repent yow descended one steppe from your seueritie
towards him. And as I shall in particuler thanke yow that yow were
the more inclinable therunto at my request; soe I doubt not but the
future comfort in him wilbee youres. I will write unto yow shortly by
Richard Marris, and therfore for the present I will end with my

WP—L

paper, wishing from my hart the increase of happinesse and many daies to you and youres. Your most assured and affecconate freind and Cozen, Th. Wentworth.

**150.** *Wentworth to Sir Edward Sackville, 26 March 1621* (*Knowler*, i, p. 14; *SC*, ii, p. 73), *introducing his brother.*

**151.** *Wentworth to Lord Darcy, 31 March 1621* (*Knowler*, i, p. 14, *SC*, ii, p. 74). *He will use his influence to get Sir Richard Wynne elected for a borough, possibly Pontefract.*

**152.** [*Endorsed*] A Speache spoken by Sir Thomas Wentworth upon taxing of the subsedy at Rotherham. 23 April 1621 (*SC*, xxi/17). [*In Wentworth's hand.*]

Gentlemen, I neuer liked to spinne out howers that might more properly be imployed in dispatche of the king's affaires and ease of the cuntry, I say to trifle such time away in long discourses. Yet before I should abruptly fall to the businesse of the day, the seruice I conceaue you weare pleased to impose upon me doth first aptly administer occasion to presentt you with a shortt accountt what hath been acted in this presentt Parlamentt and that the rather, in regarde I perswade my self the declaration therof wilJ much conduce to our chearfull proceeding and effectuall conclusion and his Maiestie's graciouse goodnesse be alsoe made abundantly appeare, whearin we haue as great reason to reioyce as any people possibly can haue and for which we ought as much to, praise God, as for any other thing thorow his mercy bestowed upon this nation.

You may be pleased then to understande that the Commons howse of Parlamentt, in contemplation of the manifold blessings appropriated to this estate and commonwealthe in the royall person and under the piouse gouernment of his Maiestie, haue out of ther bownden duties and ample thankfullnesse presented him with tow intire subsedies, as faithfull wittnesses and free oblations of ther loyalties and loues; the first wherof is to be paide att one intire pay-ment upon May day next, which haue thorowe God's especiall fauours produced a most happy union twixt the king and his people, as the asseured ancor hold whearunto to fasten the wel setled peace and quiet of our selues and posterities; which union upon the break-ing up of the last Parlamentt being much scandalised gaue great hope of exultation to the enimies of our religion and cuntry.

For his Maiesty, being faithfully informed of this our chearfullnesse, out of the good liking whearwith he entertained the same and out of the largenesse of his royall hartte benignly vouchsafed to returne this most princely answeare that our noe marchantlike dealing with him should worke tow notable effects, reputation to his affaires abrode and a presente readinesse to ease his louing subiects of all ther iust greeuances att home, which he would be most willing to heare, more ready to reforme then wee to desire and meet us therin more then the halfe way, thus comes he downe upon his people like raine upon the mowen grasse and as showers that refreshe the earthe.

Since which, as a witnesse of his reall meaning, wee haue founde a free and speedy passage to what euer wee might require of reformation. Wheare I must needs obserue to the immortall praise of his Maiesty that searching into the sores of the commonwealthe, itt plainely appeares none of thes patents which in the execution haue vexed the people past his royall hande before a certificate first made from sum of his grauest and greatest ministers, both for the conuenience and lawfullness therof; and therfore as a remonstrance that he hath hated thos with a perfect hatred that haue (as I may terme itt) thus interloped betwixt him and his people, seperating them from his intended grace and care, he hath been well pleased to shew himself forwarde in this Parlamintary proceeding aganst Sir Giles Mompesson and his complices and to leaue the censure of him and thos which are like to followe as liuing monuments of his iustice and as documentts too such licentiouse spiritts from hearafter attempting upon the sacred power of a king, upon the peace and quiett of a people. Thus deliuereth the needy when he crieth, the poore allsoe and him that hath no helper; thus hath he broken in peeces the oppressor, redeeming your soules from deceite and violence.

Butt it may be obiected that we haue giuen away your money and made noe lawes, which are the true sure and parlamintary means whirby to redeme and secure the subiect. Both indeed by reason of time straightened and Parlamentts long discontinued, we could not, amidst soe many considerable matters fitt to be prouided for, readily settle our selues whear to beginne first. Soe as we haue not as yet brought any thing too a perfect birthe, yett I asseure my self we shall by God's grace as wee laboure of diuers wholsum lawwes, soe in his due season haue strengthe to bring forth to the contentment of you all and happinesse of the whole kingdume.

Neuerthelesse that itt may appeare unto you we haue not been idle in performance of our duties towards our greatt mother, tha commonwealthe, I will shortly declaire unto you sum of the lawes which are allready past our howse. First, by one it is inacted that noe certioraries or supersedeas for the peace or good behauioure shall hearafter be granted forth of the Chancery or King's Benche, butt all be tried and had in the cuntry; by a second, that noe common informer, neither the atturney general himself, shall informe upon any penall lawe, sauing upon such as concerne Popishe recusantts, but only in the proper county whear the offence was actually dun, in the Sessions or Assisses of the same and not else whear. By a thirde, which is one of the bills of grace, that 60 yeares' possession shalbe allowed a good plea aganst the king; by a fourthe, that all actions of trespasse upon the case for words and such like shall be brought within a certaine limited time and that the plaintiffe shall recouer noe more costs then damages. Soe as noe oppressor shall passe thorow you any more, the extortioner as formerly shall not catche what you haue, nor the strainger spoile your labours, a right iustice and reposed quiet, being by means of thes lawes conueyed and brought home to your own dores.

Now allbeit thes lawes are not fully inacted, yett to giue you a taste what asseurance we haue that in ther time they shall passe as compleate lawes, I will euen reade his Maiesties owne words, full of grace and goodnesse touching as they haue been lately printed, *viz* 'I heare allsoe that ther is an other bill amonge you against informers, I desire you, my lords, that as yee tender my honoure and the good of my people, yee will putt that bill to an end, soe soon as you can and att your next meeting to make itt one of your first workes.' This I haue reade unto you, as the best means in my opinion to settle your iudgmentts and beleefes for all the rest, as allsoe to shewe you the beames of his Maiestie's grace breaking down upon you like a bewtifull sunshine thorow a dusky cloude. And heare by the way giue me leaue to do right to Mr Secretary Caluerte, which is due unto him for his excellent seruice in Parlamentt, as in many other things, soe in this particulare: this bill for informers att the first contained in itt a sauing to the Atturney Generall to informe as formerly he might, which being reade, Mr Secretary moued that prouisoe might be alltogeither left out, lest itt might proue a backstaire to conuey away and robbe the people of the fruites of soe beneficiall and needfull a lawe. This gaue me occasion to obiect in priuate to Mr Secretary that I doubted the king would not passe the lawe soe generall, he made me answeare I need not feare that, for he well knew his Maiestie's tender affection towards us to be such that, weare he rightly possest, he wuld neuer stoppe itt, which, sayth he, I will not faile to doe both out of my seruice to him and the common wealthe. Thus became I a conuertt and the prouisoe strucke out. How faithfully the Secretary performed promise hath appeared unto you by that which I haue redde, soe as I may truly giue him the honoure to be the means, next under his Maiestie's one princely disposition, of making this lawe perfect; which I dare say, as itt is more then any your neibours could haue been able to doe for you, soe is itt better seruice then hath been dun by any of your knights in Parlament thes twenty yeares. Thus I hope you will hearby see the peruerse and depraued nature of such as indeauored to perswade you the chusing of this noble gentleman to be little better then a betraying of the cuntry; and the naked sincernesse and faithfull affection of thos be made abundantly appeare towards the good of you all that moued you in his byhalfe and soe much for him to whom you haue ioyned me, allbeitt unworthy, whearby indeed you haue much aduantaged your selues and I confesse much honored me.

What shall I say more then of the hopes, nay asseurances, of the happy issue of this Parlament, or rather who might I not say, the very censure of Sir Giles Mounpesson in itt self, being of more safety to the Commonwealth in the example then 6 of the best lawes that haue been made in 6 of the last Parlementts. Yett moreouer, beleeue me gentlemen, ther is nothing that can be thought of for inritching of the state which is not intertained with feruency of zeale, prosecuted with watchefull and restlesse diligence and I doubt not thorow God's grace wilbe finished with uprightnesse and iudgement. You shall receaue ease in all your iust greeuances, your traffic and commerce in forraine partts florishe with increase, your trades att home be gouerned with right order, the faire streame of iustice purged from the leauen and sowrnesse of extortion and bribery. In a worde what maybe hoped for from an harmoniouse union betwixt the kinge, the nobles and commons, what iustly to be desired by a loyall people from a gratiouse Soueraine, euen that and noe other, are you too expect, I say againe with asseurance.

My necessary lengthe hath not been tediouse I hope, relating unto you such tidings of ioy and comfortte, as I protest they cause the bloode springe in my vaines, as I speake. Neither will itt be by you thought impertinentte when I asseure my self the true relation of thes passages will stirre up your ready minds and inlardge your cheerfull hartts to giue to his most excellent maiestie with all alacrity sum small partte of your substance under the pleasing shade of whose greatnesse and goodnesse you inioy all that you haue.

Now I beseeche you giue me leaue to putt you in remembrance of sum few points which I haue noted needfull aboue the rest for our more equall proceeding and the bettering of your understandings in this present seruice, plainly and freely likewise to deliuer my minde unto you therin and soe an end.

For soe much as concerns the leuying and paying in of this sub-sedye, itt is only our chardge that be Commissioners and we shall Godwilling without your trouble take care and giue order for itt. Butt you that be Assessors itt is for you most requisite that you call to minde what espetiall trust and confidence is reposed in you by his Maiestie, by us his Commissioners and by your honest neighboures whom in true Christian charity you ought to loue as your selues, to doe unto them as you would that others should doe unto you and therfore you must not thorowe fauoure or mallice partially seeke to ease the better able by laying pressures and unreasonable burthens upon your innocent and shiftlesse neiboures, butt rather putt them quite out, if there be iust cause, and lett the wealthier supply that want in God's name. If you finde any deade, remoued, or decayed, you must notwithstanding (as no doubt you well may) lay the chardge of sum other amongst you and soe make your bills as good or better then formerly, otherways we must, for example sake and the king's profitt, sett what wants on your heads, or fine you for your misdeameanours.

If ther be any amongst you, whose estate consists in money hidde from the open sight of men, hauing itt may be ten pounds a yeare in lande and one thousande pounds in money and goods, or an other sortt of people farr worse then thes which grinde the face of the poor by selling corne and cattell too a day att cruell and unconscionable rates, thes men in speciall fauoure with the assessors, perhaps assessors themselues, must forsoothe be sessed in lands peraduenture att twenty or forty shillings; well a poore man hath noe lands, butt may be three or fower kine and a wife and small children, his cattell sumtimes miscarrying, his wife or himself diseased, he must be three poundes in goods, for lesse he cannot be, if inn att all, soe is he as much as the other tow great ritche men that are of threscore times his substance. O my Masters, lett not thes men scape soe easily as formerly they haue, butt sett them deepe a God's blessing, neither suffer his Maiestie to be thus deluded, his pore subiects oppressed, or your own consciences chardged.

Allsoe whear ther be in subsedy sum ten groates or nobles odde, it weare good if by raysing of sum and abayting of others, whear reason requires that you would make all euen pownds, or angells att the leaste for the mor ease of the Commissioners' clerks, the collectors and the exchequer allsoe.

I must likewise giue you to understande that all moueable goods, as cattell, corne and such like, except apparell, all somes of money upon bonds or contracts, which are like to be paide, are goods liable to this paymentt, that all aboue the yearly valew of twenty shillings which a man hath either in fee simple or fee taile, for terme of life, or in ioynture with his wife, which he hath in execution for certaine yeares, or by vertue of any wardshippe, all yearly annuities or fees, as allsoe all coppyholde lands, are liable to this subsedye.

I am unwilling farther to presume upon your patience and therfore I pray you haue in espetiall regard thes things, lay before your eyes the confluence of grace whearwith his Maiesty presents himself unto you, lett not one droppe therof fall in vaine, butt treasure itt up in your hartts that soe itt may in all eache of you bring forth the pleasing fruites of deuotion to his Maiestie's person, obedience to his gouernmentt, chearfull readinesse to expresse your thankfullnesse in this seruice, which I recommend to your staide discretions and good consciences.

**153.** (*SC*, ii, p. 75) *To Mr Dixon at Beamley. Wentworth Woodhouse. 10 Aug. 1621.*

Good Mr Dixon, I am moued by this gentleman, my good freind, to renew the offer I formerly made unto yow on his behalfe now at your beinge in this Cuntrie. His desires are first to know whether the treatie with your kinsman bee as yet either consumate or otherwaies determined; and secondly, if that succeed not, that yow wold then doe him a good office for his sonne, as (thorow my mediation) yow were content to assure him yow would. For his estate, hee wilbee able to giue yow satisfaccon and make it appeare to bee as good, as hee hath undertaken. Soe as that graunted, I perswade my selfe yow will hardly better the fortune of your daughter-in-lawe in these partes, all thinges considered. The kindnesse and good respect yow shall afford and shew unto him in this affaire, I shall take it as an argument of your loue towards mee and as such requite itt when occasion shall serue. I should bee very gladd my acquaintance in these partes might in any sort bee useful unto yow; if it may proue soe, I pray yow let mee know; if yow addresse your selfe to any other I will take it unkindly, for I will therin assuredly approue my self, Your very affecconate freind, Th. Wentworth.

**154.** (*SC*, ii, p. 76) *To the Lord Treasurer Viscount Mandeville. Wentworth Woodhouse. 27 Sept. 1621.*

Right honourable and my very good Lord, not onely the discharge of the comissioners for the subsedy within the Westriding of the County of Yorke, but also the duty I owe to the aduancement of his Maiestie's seruice and my owne particuler obligacon unto your

selfe, imbolden and perswade mee humbly to signifie unto your
Lordship that in these partes, albeitt wee haue receaued letteres of
direccon from your Lordship and others of his Maiestie's most
honorable Priuie Counsell concerning that seruice, yet wee haue not
hetherto seene any comission for assessinge the first payment of this
latter subsedy, which surely must bee imputed to some miscarriage,
not (I hope) in any of the comissioners. And therfore trust wee shalbee held excuseable, if our payments proue not soe speedy, as in
others our neighbouring shires, where they haue alreadie dispatched;
seing our forwardnesse is as much as theires, yet forced against our
wills to attend for our warrant. If your Lordship would bee pleased
to enquire out in whome the fault rests, it might proue a good meanes
to preuent the like hereafter; the last comission likewise being but
negligently looked after, the last time. All which I humbly submitt
to your wisdome, resting in the due mediacon of your many noble
fauoures towards mee, Your Lordship's most humbly to bee comaunded, Th. Wentworth.

**155.** (*SC*, ii, p. 76) *To the Earl of Cumberland. Wentworth Woodhouse. 30 Sept. 1621.*

My much honoured Lord, that which I haue to write is not much,
yet haueing rested now soe long in this kind, and haueinge soe fitt a
meanes to conuay these lines to your Lordship I find the dutie and
true affeccon I owe your Lordship in my most retired thoughts and
that deseruedly desires to lay itt selfe downe before yow in this
paper; and imperfect as it is in effecte, (*p. 77*) though not in intencon
and purpose, humblie to present it selfe unto yow. The fruites for this
time which yow may expecte or they bringe forth, are my true praiers
for the increase of your health, your daies, your honour, and that
of your most noble and ancient familye. Those in the future shalbee
by God's grace a chearfull hart to doe yow seruice, and an assured
faith to approue my selfe to bee honestly and plainly, Your Lordship's
most humble and obedient sonne in law to bee comaunded, Th.
Wentworth.

**156.** (*SC*, ii, p. 77) *To Lord Clifford. Wentworth Woodhouse. 30 Sep.
1621.*

My much honoured Lord, I neuer hunted after newes, and indeed it is
not the least pleasing to imploy a mans selfe in his owne occasions;
yet I confesse I know not how, I doe very much desire to heare how
the squares goe with your new comonwealth at Londesborowe. My
Lord, I know yow are wise and although I can add nothinge unto yow,

as indeed I cannott, yet bee pleased that I may with your good leaue in part satisfie the zeale I beare yow and your howse. I beseech yow then, (as wee shall all labour to hold my Lord to our last determinacons) to bend your thoughts and to imploy those faire gifts God hath giuen yow, to the full accomplishment of soe good purposes, with chearfullnesse and perseuearance. If the course seeme at the first strange and perplexed, let it not amaze yow, but oppose (but for a while) all such apprehencons, or the desire of your quiett or recreacons with a masculine vertue and they wilbee found in time easy that now appeare most difficult. If my Lord (as I feare hee will) startle or mislike your endeauours, beare itt with an obseruant pacience and yow will easily calme and reduce him in all your distastes (which it may bee before this worke bee effected) which yow are to encounter which haue recourse unto noble Mr Charles, which will still incite yow to perseueare. Consider with your selfe the honore and contentment the end wilbee; what a blessing it is to bee the restorer of your howse and posteritie and that your worke is not of an age, but of a few yeares and then assuredly the bitternesse yow shall meet with in the way wilbee easilie digested. But alasse, my affeccon hath runne mee out of my paper and now good manners makes mee craue pardon for my boldnesse seing I must acknowledge your owne judgment hath allready deeply imprinted these consideracons in yow. I shall therfore pray unto God more and more to strengthen them in yow and crowne them with contentment and long life in your selfe, with continewing honore and happinesse to your howse. Your Lordship's most humble brother in law and seruant, Th. Wentworth.

**157.** (*SC*, ii, p. 78) *To Sir Thomas Fairfax knight. Wentworth Woodhouse. 8 Oct. 1621.*

Worthie Sir, I haue indeed understood somethinge of the late differences betwixt those of Huby and Rigton, which seemed the more strange unto mee, in regard I conceaued your selfe rested satisfied with shewe of our euidence upon the like occasion the other yeare. Now albeit the difference touch mee in myne inheritance, as well as my freholders, and reason requires mee to haue the more regard unto itt; yet will I haue noe difference with soe worthie a freind as your selfe, especially there beinge soe neare an allyance approachinge betwixt your howse and the nearest and dearest braunch of my owne. In a word therfore I desire that there bee noe farther proceedings, which I will undertake on our side (albeit indeed the ryotte will appeare to bee in those of Rigton) til such time as

my cozen Wentworth of Woolley, as an indifferent man betwixt us
both, haue heard the cause and then I assure my selfe there wilbee an
end betwixt us. If this like yow not, then I yeild very willingly to your
owne motion, that 2 lawyers may heare and end the businesse,
thinges resting in the same state that they are now. This is all that
for the present I will trouble yow with, more than the assurance of my
beinge your very affecconate freind to serue yow, Th. Wentworth.

**158.** (*SC*, ii, p. 78) *To the Countess of Shrewsbury. Wentworth
Woodhouse. 8 Oct. 1621.*

My most honoured Lady, the time of your sicknes appeares to your
freinds to draw into length and great comfort would it bee to us all
to heare now of your perfect recouerie; and that the rather because
of the various reports in these partes, which if they bee true, as
indeed I hope they are not, I would haue seene yow before my going
to London. But I could not with a quiett mind remoue out of this
cuntry, til by a messinger of my owne, I might receaue the welcome
newes of your certaine and good recouerie. And soe shall I thinke
itt the best journey that euer the bearer went for mee. God is my
judge (*p. 79*) there is noe man should bee more sorry, if it should
please God to call yow; but wee are all in his hands; and as it will
howeuer bee a great preiudice unto your nephewes, yet it maie bee
much more if itt happen (which God of his goodnesse diuerte)
unlooked for, and in my absence out of these partes. Therfore I doe
most humbly beseech yow Madame, as I haue euer found from your
Ladyship plaine and free dealinge, soe that now I may certainly
understand, how yow stand in the strength and recouerie of your
bodye, that soe accordinglie I may giue some direccon touchinge
your little nephews, who haue bene infinitely happie by enioyinge
your presence amongst us, and in loosing yow shall (God knowes)
receaue a heauy crosse and stand in need of the assistance and good
aduise and foresight of their freinds. Whatsoeuer I shall receaue
from your Ladyship I shall by God's grace keepe to my selfe, without
makeing any use either to the preiudice of yow or youres; but I trust
I shall receaue good and happy tideinges of your health, which
shalbee a great contentment to Your Ladyship's most humbly to bee
comaunded, Th. Wentworth.

My wife remembers her seruice to your Ladyship and wee both of
us desire these lines maie present our seruice to the Lady Ogle.

**159.** (*SC*, ii, p. 79) *To Robert Wentworth at Rouen. Wentworth Woodhouse. 8 Oct. 1621.*

Deare brother, I receaued your letteres dated from Rouen and therin tooke noe small contentment both to understand of your good health, and also of your improuement both in your hand and stile. Good brother, haue a care to proceed and to enable your selfe daily; which wilbee, as to yow the greatest profitt, soe to mee one of my greatest comforts. Bee sure in all companies and places to carry your selfe as in the presence of your utter enemies, which wilbee a meanes to cause moderacon and circumspeccon in all thinges, from whence ariseth judgment and wisdome. For bee yow well assured that mallice and enuy are of subtill condicon and will search and try out all a mans accons, and many times by that meanes the most secrett thinges are published and made comon to the eares of all men, where men may think they had bene buried in an utter obliuion. Bee therfore (*p. 80*) soe well aduised in all which yow doe, as that the slipps of your youth bee not laid in your dish, when yow haue both forgotten them and your selfe growne upp into more yeares and nearer your preferrments. As for my selfe, rest assured I will neuer bee a wanting in the uttermost of my endeauours to bee as carefull of your occasions and person, as of my owne; and for your moneies, there shall want noe care on our parts; your Michelmas quarter was long agoe retourned, soe as yow wilbee prouided til your journey beginne, against which time yow shall receaue satisfaccon as yow desire. Soe soone as I come to London (which wilbee (Godwillinge) within these 3 weekes) yow shall againe heare from mee. Comend mee to my brother Michaell. All your freinds are in good health (God bee praised) and often remember yow. God of his goodnesse blesse both your trauailes and persons, unto whose blessed proteccon and direccons I shall with my humble praiers comitte yow, euer remaininge Your most assured and truly louing brother, Th. Wentworth.

**160.** (*SC*, ii, p. 80) *To the Executors of Mr Hanson. Wentworth. 26 Oct. 1621.*

Hearinge of the late death of Mr John Hanson, for which I am sorry and being made acquainted both by others and himselfe in his life time, of diuerse writings in his custodie, concerninge the inheritance of my nephew Sauile, in the nine townes and other places, as also of a booke wherin hee had digested and collected togeather the principall matters which were in his knowledge and longe experience discouered unto him, touching those lands, with a purpose to present them to mee, for my nephewes' use, as his last seruice to that howse, wherunto hee did esteeme himselfe very much beholden. I am therfore hereby to desire your care, that the same maie not in any sort fall into wrong hands, but that yow will permitt Mr Greenwood to peruse them in your presence and that hee maie haue both such writinges as concerne my nephewes' inheritance, as also the said booke deliuered (*p. 81*) unto him for his use, giueinge yow an acknowledgment under his hand for the receate therof. This beinge indeed noe more then is just for yow to performe and which Mr Hanson would haue done, had not death preuented him; yet I shall receaue itt as a speciall curtesie from yow, bee very thankfull for writing ouer the booke; and rest mindfull and ready to requite your kindnesses, as occasion shalbee offered. And soe I rest, Your louinge freind, Th. Wentworth.

**161.** (*SC*, ii, p. 81) *To the Countess of Shrewsbury. Wentworth. 26 Oct. 1621.*

My most honoured Ladye, since my last lettere to your ladyship I haue bene offered for the tithes of Malhamdale, two thowsand and fower hundred pounds, and the purchaser not to enter before Lady day next, the payment in a yeare and a halfe. I stood upon more, but since upon speach with James Ward and my owne seruantes, I am perswaded if I can drawe the price to fiue and twenty hundreth, not to keepe them. The tennants (I am of opinion) would giue 200$^{li}$ more, but then itt wilbee indeed at least 2 yeares before it could bee effected, their payment bee much longer, and (as I haue found allready by the gleabe) come in by peece meale and not in any conuenient time to discharg the debtes. Soe that as all now stand, I conceaue it wilbee a better course to sell them to one, then to waite the delaies and troubles, which will of necessitie followe the other. I craue to receaue your aduise herein, soe soone as yow maie, and in the meane time I will hartelie praie unto God, still to add strength and longe continewance to your daies; retaininge to my selfe, the zeale and truth of beinge, Your Ladyship's most affecconate and humble freind and seruant, Th. Wentworth.

**162.** *Speech in Wentworth's hand about privilege and the arrest of Sir Edwin Sandys, possibly 23 Nov. 1621* (*SC*, xxi/211) [*Endorsed*] Sir Edw Sandes.[1]

Consultations which after due debate terminate in resolutions ought in hearing to be seated as the midle betwixt the tow scales of the

---

[1] See Notestein, ii, pp. 440–41, but the arguments would also have been appropriate for the debate on 5 December, *ibid.*, p. 504.

ballance, declining only too that side wheare ther appeares greatest weighte and sowndnesse of reason and experience. This iust and considerat manner of proceeding hauing euer been constantly and grauely practised by this howse, I shall with your good leaues examin the presentt staite of the question which now moues amongst us and which in itt self is soe considerable by thes tow rules, reason and experience.

1. To imagine that his Maiestie will now either not allow, or giue an account of, or not iustifie, what hath been acted in the person of this gentleman, or passe more in the future then hath been already graciously granted in the beginning of this presentt session, weare in my poore opinion without all grownde of sadde iudgmentt. Seing then we are not to exspecte any further inlardgmentt or warrantt for our speatche then our owne aduised staidnesse in what wee speake; whie should we in reason by complainte refreshe our griefes, wheare ther is soe small hope of remedy, or stirre wheare our indeauours are soe like to proue fruitlesse?

2. I conceaue we inioy by ancientt and well decided right as greate a libertie of speache within thes walls, as can or ought be granted, soe as for my owne partt I professe that when we had obtained what we now desire, itt should not incourage me to speake any thing wherin otherwayes I shold be silentt, nor yet shall I, in the condition we now stande, forbeare to utter what in the truth of my hartte I conceaue. Whie should we then in reason trouble ourselues aboute that whearof wee haue noe neede or drawe the pointte into dispute, which we soe undeniably possesse soe soon as wee enter thes doores?

3. Butt admitt ther weare sum probability to preuaile, yet me thinks this motion weare now sumthing too much hastened and mistimed, our affaires being not yett brought too such a maturity to beare soe long a digression as this would drawe us unto. Seeing then that *intempestiuis remediis accenduntur delicta* and that a wise man should not only be maister of his words, butt of time allsoe, fitting itt too his purpose, wee weare better in reason waite an oportunity, when we had dispatched our other businesse and re-moued all colourable pretentions, as if we might not, as moderately and modestly, use our liberties, soe should we make our motion more reasonable, more probable to receaue good acceptance and successe.

Now in experience I haue obserued and soe assuredly haue many more that discourses of this nature betwixt the king and his commons haue heartofore been allwayes ill accompanied with distrusts and iealousies without any asseurance to our persons, or increase of power att all to the howse. And indeed in my poore iudgmentt ther is not any thing we ought with more warinesse decline the dispute of, then rights of priuiledge and iurisdiction with his Maiestie. For still me thinks in arguing, wee rather loose ground then inlardge our limitts, reducing our liberties within narrow boundes which before weare in themselues att least in opinion of a very lardge extentte. Therfore weare itt much better, for the good of the subiect and honoure of the howse, moderately and soberly to use them, leauing them (such as they are) wrapte up in a sacred and questionable doubtfullnesse then with ouer precise curiosity to raule [ravel] too farre into such misteries, thus ther power without doubte would not be lesse apprehended, butt ther respect and esteeme the more venerable.

I wishe with all my hearte this occasion had not been giuen, yett euen in this ther are tow points greatly considerable: his Maiestie's iustice, our owne innocency. One of us was questioned, butt his Maiestie layed not a heauy hande upon him, noe sooner soe, butt was presently inlardged, as being cleare and in him the howse, which is a faire argumentt to his Maiestie of the faithe of his Commons whoe are soe vigilantte as not to suffer any thing deliuered heare, without due regarde to his gouernment or royall person to escape uncontrouled, unpunished; whearof his Maiesty, once well asseured, will not easily lend his sacred eares to thos that woulde indeauoure to possesse him to the contrary, if such ther be any.

Seeing then matters proceed, God be praysed, in noe seuerer a course then such as is sutable to the accustomed and habituall clemency of his Maiestie, whie should wee create vaine terrors in ourselues, like the Burgundians before Paris, apprehending that the topps of soe many thisles had been the heads of soe many lances. Lett eache of us much rather stande ferme upon the squaire of his owne loyallty and discretion, carry ourselues without further dispute confidently (yett with reuerence too his Maiesty) and faithfully in the trust committed to us, according too the preciouse freedume, used and taken by our ancestors in this place. Lett us not suffer soe many good bills too lie weatherfast, whilst wee ride it out in such a passage, as on eatche side casts us upon the rockes. The session is not like to be longe, lett us worke whilst itt is day, or euer the siluer corde be unloosed, or the wheele broken as the cisterne. Lett us speedily apply ourselues to perfect thos matters wee are allready possest of, whearby we hope the subiecte shall receaue ease and protection and we haue good reason to rest satesfied with our laboure and seruice, least being surprised with straitnesse of time, as upon our last recesse, the ill affected abrode to the state and us may cast this false shadowe upon our proceedings, as if our care wrought

more tenderly towards the safety of our owne persons then for the
good of the Commonwealth and least we may (with a repentance to
our selues, a preiudice to the publicke) be assimulated to the hinde
in the prophett that calued in the feilds and then forsooke itt, unto
the little ones that weare sentt unto the waters that came to the pitts,
butt returning with ther vessels empty, weare ashamed and couered
their heades.

**163.** *Speech, possibly 12 Dec. 1621*[1] (*SC*, xxi/209) [*Wentworth's
hand*].

May it please you Mr Speaker, did I more regarde the outwarde
then inwarde man, I would now in truthe be silentt, but euery man
heare ought to dischardge his conscience. Out of this stronge motiue
then I shall be bold to contribute my poore and humble aduice in
this weighty matter now in proposition amongst us, resting fully
asseured, you will with indifferentt and untrubled affections heare all
men patiently; a iust and considerate manner of proceeding constantly and grauely practised and euer best beseeming this great and
numerouse counsell. The true state of the question (as I conceaue) is,
wheather we should lay aside all businesse till wee receaue his
Maiestie's graciouse answeare, or wheather effectually to proceed
and prepare to conclude and shutt up this session before Christmas,
reposing our selues in the meane space upon the inherentt rights and
priuiledges of our howse, upon the habituall goodnesse and iustice
of his Maiestie.

The opinions inclining to the first haue heathertoo been very
possitiue, the reasons which might binde and perswade therunto
being reserued and not made patent, which, I must needs say, is
sum thing magistrall and in sum sortts amountts too an *ipse dixit*.
To be thus carried away in an implicite faithe, I neither like in diuine
nor yet in ciuile causes, therfore I professe opinions thus deliuered
moue me nothing att all. Butt let us forsee in our iudgmentt the in-

[1] This may be a draught relating to 11 or 12 December 1621. The reference
(below, p. 166) to the precedent of Henry IV appears to refer to Coke's speech
of 10 December (Notestein ii, p. 509 and n. 11) and would date this speech to
11 December. Wentworth spoke on both 11 and 12 December (*ibid.*, ii, pp. 512,
515; vi, p. 233). The speech would seem rather more appropriate to the context
of the debate recorded on 12 December than that of 11 December On the other
hand the reference to three subsidies having been granted (below, p. 167) could
only apply to 1624, not to 1621 when two subsidies only were granted. But the
references to concluding the session by Christmas, the questions of privilege and
to the king's messages would only fit the context of 1621. Either the reference
to the three subsidies is a slip, or an attempt to revise a draught originally made
in 1621.

conueniences arising from doing nothing, which will appear soe many argumentts for our going forwarde in the businesse of the howse. First, a cessation, as is propounded, argues an inconstancy in our selues and implies a contradiction too our petition, wherin wee sue for a session before Christmas and yet, by trifling away our time in this sortt, wee shall render the worke and our owne desires impossible. Secondly, itt amountts allmost too a quitting and diserting of our liberties which are soe deare and tender unto us. For God forbid, wee had soe loose hold of them, as that they weare to be wrunge from us by one letter. Noe, Mr Speaker, they are better fixed then soe; neither can any power take them from us, yet let us dispute them lesse frequently, least it proue *curiosum potius quam reale officium.* And seeing for my owne partte, I professe I will speake as freely and clearly in the condition we now stande, as if the letter had neuer been writt. Lett us more boldly and confidently use and take what belongs unto us, as well warranted therunto by the noble example of our ancestors in this place, which doing itt shall allways be more safe to suffer our liberties to rest wrapte up in a sacred and misticall mannere then with ouer precise curiosity too raule to farre into them. Thus noe doubte ther power and extent would not be lesse apprehended, butt ther respect and esteeme the more venerable.

Thirdly, our forbearance att this presentt might incurre the danger of a scandall and by the ill affected abrode be misnamed a sullennesse in us, which, as itt is farre from the sense and iudgment of the howse, soe is itt an humore more excusable in women then men. This indeed is of dangerouse consequence and such a false aspersion cast upon us may reflecte farther upon his Maiestie's affaires abrode then wee are as yet well aware of, or then weare indeed conuenientt in thes darke and gloumy dayes, whearin we haue good cause to pray that the mists which hang ouer our heads may be by the beames of his Maiestie's timely wisedume and prouidence happily dispersed and our selues sheltred from the iminent storme under the well pleasing shade of his greatnesse and goodnesse.

Now I will, with your good leaues, ask this question, what doe wee loose by goeing on in a Parlamentary course? I protest before God nothing att all that I see, sauing (I speake itt with all duty) a supercilieuse forme only and that, soe farre as I haue yet hearde, unwarranted by any antient presidentts. For as for that president yesterday urged in the time of Henry the 4, itt is most excellent to warrantt our second humble declaration to his Maiesty, yett I did not heare that, allbeitt the king was misinformed and itt seems offended with sum perticulars, that therupon the house staide ther parlamentary proceeding, soe as in the second place itt strongly perswades us likewise to goe on with our businesse; and as for the actions of the last Parlamentary conuention, I see noe necessity whie they should be introduced as binding rules for us to guide our selues by, except the issue of ther counsells had been more successfull.

And seeing wee are in good discretion, not only to looke upon men of refined iudgment, butt to indeauoure the contentment and satesfaction of the common sortt likewise, into whose capacity (God knowes) the consideration of the liberties of this howse neuer fall [they] only exspecte a good pardon, sum beneficiall lawes, an ease and dischardg of ther greeuances and pressures. I desire we may be furnished with sum fitting answer to such obiections, as they, being men wise in ther owne generatione, they may bluntly and shrewdly make; as thus, you haue giuen three subsedies to be paide all in a yeare which was neuer before, what is the reason wee haue not our pardon, our lawes, and greeuances remoued? doe you delighte your selfs to heare one an other talke, to giue away our money and bring home nothing! Weare you straitned with time upon your last recesse and will you still laboure of the same disease? Did not his Maiesty offer you a Session att your last departure and now alsoe signified itt should be in your owne default if you had not one before Christmas, how chanceth itt then you are still (like thos indiscreet and improvidentt virgins) unprouided of oile in your lampes upon the call of the bridgroome?

I beseeche you therfore, lett us lay thes things to our hartts and with alacrity sett ourselues seriously and setledly too our worke, putting our selues in remembranc that itt concerns us most deeply in our creditts and reputations, not now to relate unto our neiboures what wee haue said for them heare, or what they may hope for, butt to be able to shewe what we haue dun for them which will certainly produce thes happy effects; first that they will rest satesfied with our laboures and seruice, but cheefly stirre them up and that iustly too in the faithfullnesse and cherfullnesse of ther contented hartts to power forth ther praises and thanks giuing too allmighty God, in acknowledgmentt and true sense of his Maiesty's piouse and fatherly gouernmentt ouer them.

Finally I desire that, either wee may heare the reasons of thos which are of a contrary minde wherunto itt maybe when they are understoode, I shall submitt and becume conuertt, or else that wee may lay aside any further dispute, which doth spinne out time, and roundly indeauoure speedily too effect that wee can. For the better to expedite which, my humble motion is that such bills as are allready ingrossed may be this morning putt to the question and that

WP—M

the committees for preparing the bills of repeales and continuances may meet this afternoone and fall into mature consideration therof.

**164.** *Wentworth to Lord Darcy, 9 January 1621/2 (Knowler, i, p. 15; SC, ii, p. 66). He sends him the proclamation dissolving parliament and news from abroad.*

**165.** *From Cranfield. Chelsea. 23 April 1622 (SC, xii/2).*

Sir Thomas Wentworth, upon a duble clayme made under seuerall deputacons of the Receauor's office of Yorke-shire, which yet depends in controuersie undecided, I haue thought fitt to make choice of a good man for the king, euen yourself, into whose hands to recommend the care and chardge of that greate receipt, amounting to about 9000[li] per annum. This I pray you take not unkindlie at my handes, for I know not many gentlemen there unto whome I would comitt such a trust; my meaning being that the allowances belonging to the place shall beare all chardges of executing it, without any burthen or further trouble to you then for your care of appointing good deputies, the Commission enabling them to dischardg the busines for you, as they shall much the better doe by your countenance and direction. Wherin I haue appointed this bearer James Jackson (by whome I sende you the Commission) to make tender of his seruice unto you, as being well acquainted with the course of the office both in the last Receauor's tyme and since, if you shall thinke fitt to employ him.

And so, not doubting but you will easily conceaue I reserue better busines for you then this, wherby to shewe my respect unto you, I commend my self verie hartelie unto you and remayne, your assured loving frende, L. Cranfeilde. Chelsey 23 Aprill, 1622.

**166.** *(SC, ii, p. 82) To Lord Clifford. Austin Friars. 31 May 1622.*

My much honoured Lord, if my endeauours in your seruice make not that profittable retourne which I did well hope and most hartely desire they might; yet my trust is, yow will make a faire construccon and esteeme of my zealous intencons. I waited the other daie upon my Lord Treasurer, and deliuered your lettere, whereunto hee made this answer; that hee must deale plainlie with mee, least otherwaies hee might seeme to trifle, which in short must bee, that your Lordship might not haue any enlargement of tearme graunted yow in the Cloth office, it beinge allready promissed to a great person in Court, protesting that it was past by a strong hand much against his will.

For if hee could haue preuailed, nether your Lordship nor the other should haue had itt, being most fitt to haue bene reserued for his Maiesty's owne best aduantage. Sir Arthur Ingram replied hee was sorry to heare soe much, yet seing the office was gone, if your Lordship might otherwaies haue some satisfaccon for your losse sustained it would (as hee thought) moderately content yow. My Lord made answer that if yow could find out any sute, where his Maiesty's profitts and youres might goe hand in hand, hee could like it very well. But therupon I tooke hold, and tould my Lord that I feared, not without cause, that this was occasioned by some displeasure taken against yow by his Maiestie through some misinformacon secretly had against yow and til that cloude were dispersed, I hoped not for any good either in this or any other sute yow could haue at Courte. Therfore, and in regard I well knewe, there was nothinge wherin yow more joyed then in his Maiesty's gracious fauore towards yow, nether any thinge could soe much trouble yow, as to suffer the least diminucon of his princly good opinion, I must bee an humble suitore to his Lordship that by his good meanes, yow might haue some light, wherby to take notice of his Maiesty's darknesse towards yow and soe bee brought in the face of your accusors to your justificacon. Wherby as his Lordship should bind unto him both your selfe and all that honoured (*p. 83*) your howse; soe if there appeared not in yow, that accustomed loyalty and ancient zeale to his Maiesty's affaires, which was euer found in your howse, and which I haue allwaies obserued to continew firme and inuiolable in yow, I should neuer open my mouth more. But if yow cleared your selfe, as I rested most assured yow would; then it might bee seazonable to moue his Maiestie in your behalfe and this rubbe unremoued, I did judge all proposicons of that nature fitt to bee forborne, which his Lordship approuinge, hee promised to speake with the king to search out a ground if hee could and to let mee know more shortly. Soe I departed, affirminge as soone as I could learne out matter for yow to fix upon, I would write to your Lordship of itt, which would forthwith upon notice I assured my selfe bringe yow upp post hether, to answer what euer could bee obiected and to make the sincerity of your hart appeare through the vale of callumnye and detraccon. Since which time I haue found out that the duke of Lenoux is indeed the person who hath gotten an engagement for a lease upon your terme expired; which whether it bee judgment or noe for a man to fall twice upon one stone, hee may perhaps find by experience, but surely had I bene of his counsell, I would haue found out somthinge els.

Now my Lord, this beinge the true state of the businesse, wee

intend first if wee can to gett some good ground, wherupon taking
notice that his Maiestie hath misunderstood yow, yow may presse
to come to your justificacon. But I very much doubte this fauour
will not be allowed yow; howeuer wee all judge it most necessary
for yow to come upp hether sometimes before the next tearme, to free
your selfe from under this burthen, if maie bee, and therfore haue
sent yow downe these by pacquett that soe yow maie haue time to
prouide your selfe; yet wee wish yow would bee pleased not to set
forwards, till yow receaue other letteres from us. And this resolucon
of your cominge uppe hath made us all resolue to staie Mr Tailore
here til your ariuall, who otherwaies purposed to haue attended your
Lordship before Whittsontide, hopeing that in your judgment yow
will well approue of this alteracon, grounded upon this suddaine
accident. I doe also (under fauour) thinke it good, my Lord of
Cumbreland should know noe more (*p. 84*) of this matter, saueinge
onely that the duke laboures to take a lease ouer your heades and
therfore wee esteeme it high time now for your Lordship to come to
towne, to assist your cause by your owne presence and to put it to
a finall issue, one way or another. My reason which moues mee is
that I haue euer obserued my lord to make use of the badd successe
of his affaires, as slippes, wherwith to upbraid those which endeauour
to doe him seruice and, not applying them to his owne fortune, as
hee ought, nor takeing them as indeed hee should, for demonstratiue counsells to settle his uncertaine and unstable humores and
to informe his judgmentt that the lesse fauore hee finds abroade,
the more it behoues him carefully to labour, rightly to order and
dispose of his owne priuate estate at home and seriously to recomend
himselfe and posteritie to the good guidance and blessinge of allmightie God, which, God graunt, hee maie doe in some good and
seasonable time. For your selfe my Lord, I rest assured yow will
beare these and all other crosses, as a wise man should. *Flagrantior
aequo, non debet esse dolor viri, nec vulnere maior:* yow will not make
them soe greate, as to suffer your thoughts to bee therwith too much
opprest, your sences benumed, or mind too much deiected, nor yet
make them soe little as to bee carelesse of them, or improuident how
to auoide the stinges and bitternesse of them, but constantly paceinge
the middle waie (which in the most is wisdome) remoue euery
stone and still cast about, as one not beaten downe with affliccons,
how to fix your selfe againe in his Maiesty's good opinion and to
settle the priuate fortune of your noble howse, wherin yow must not
bee weary before yow beginne, nor grow hopelesse by framinge your
case in your owne retired debates, more desperate, or more lowe,
then indeed they are; still comforting and chearinge upp your spiritts,

that it is admitted to an innocent mind to defend it self stoutly and
strongly and that yow may, I dare saie, with a great deale of ease,
though the kinge doe nothinge for yow, in three yeares time well
imployed discharge all your debts honorably and leaue a braue fortune of 4500$^{li}$ a yeare beside your game, not in leases and offices
depending upon others, but in good land of inheritance dayly im-
prouing upon the expiracon of your leases in Crauen. I haue now
done my taske; the other for newes (*p. 85*) beinge distributed by
consent of us both to my brother Clifton who knoweth as much as I
doe. Soe there remaines nothinge for mee, but to craue pardon for
my boldnesse, beinge ledd on in the plainnesse of a faithfull and
unfolded hart; and to wish unto your Lordship the increase and
firmnesse of all honour, long life, and happines. Your Lordship's
most humble brother in law and seruant, Th. Wentworth.

**167.** (*SC*, ii, p. 85) *To Michael Wentworth. Austin Friars. 31 May
    1622.*

Brother, albeitt yow neuer consider seriously with yourselfe of your
owne businesse, as should seeme in that yow neuer aduise any course
to helpe us in the returninge of your money to soe obscare a place as
that where yow now are, nor yet in the troubled state of Fraunce as it
now stands. Yet at all aduenture I haue according to your letter
returned thirtie pounds to Towers, as yow may perceaue by the
lettere of exchange here inclosed, being the nearest place I could
possiblie send this same unto yow. I must plainly tel yow I am noe
waies satisfied with the course of your trauaile, for I perceaue your
hand mends not, being indeed soe passing badd as itt is altogeather
unworthie a gentleman of your breeding and birth and your endite-
inge a degree worse then that and shewes plainly (which I like
worst of all) yow endeauour not your selfe to mend, for much negligence and carelesnesse appeares in them. And for your expence that
showes it selfe as little ordered or regulated as either of the other,
yow hauing (as should seme) in such a priuate place, as a man would
haue imagined yow had retired your selfe unto to saue your money,
runne your selfe out of all compasse. Therefore in good faith either
looke to your person and accons with more circumspeccon and
prouidence, or I shall haue small comforte to take paines for yow,
or trouble my thoughte about him that soe little troubles himselfe
with those thinges that most concerne him, both in his creditt and
estate. For it is fitt yow should remember your selfe that the time
of your trauaile is not a time of ease and idlenesse, but to bee im-
ploied laboriously and discreetly in selecting forth and learninge those

qualleties and gifts which may not onely grace your person, but also enable and informe your iudgement in that course of life which yow intend hereafter (by God's grace) to take upon yow.

But I will lay aside this theame, confidently hopinge that yow wilbee soe vigilant ouer your selfe hereafter that I shall haue cause to take comfort to see yow soe desirous to improue your selfe and to make soe vertuous an use of the faithfull counsell and aduice of your freinds which most truly loue yow and desire your good. I wish yow should (if yow haue the meanes to learne when he passeth by) to cast to meet your brother about Toures and soe to goe alonge with him. If yow cannot conueniently doe this, then I iudge itt fittest for yow to remoue presently to Parris and there remaine til your brother come, that soe when yow are togeather yow may seriously and deliberatly take such a course as may the most profitt yow and aduance towards the end yow direct your selues unto. And let him know, I pray yow, that there is a letter for him at Mr Randalls, the marchantt, with a letter of exchange for 20 pounds. This is al that for the present I will trouble yow with; more then that I remaine, Your very louing brother, Th. Wentworth.

**168.** (*SC*, ii, p. 86) *To Christopher Danby Esq. Austin Friars. 2 June 1622.*

Sir, I understand that Mr Secretary Caluerte hath a buildinge in hand att Kiplinge and that hee wantes timber sufficient to serue the use hee hath for itt; againe, that your wood of Thorpe Hollinges is the nearest, where yow haue soe good store, that a small number will not bee missed. I am therfore to recomend (*p. 87*) a desire of Mr Leonard Caluertt's unto yow, in the behalfe of his sonne, that yow wilbee pleased to let him haue thirty choice trees out of your said wood for his money, towards the furnishinge and finishinge his worke; which in truth is a request soe faire, as I should not well tel how to denye any neighbour I haue. But now haueing recomended his, which I assure my selfe yow will not denye, let mee make one of my owne, which is that yow would freely bestow them upon him, seing their valewe cannot bee greate, and I will promise yow, yow shall haue power to comaund a greater matter from mee. Besides, I know the last yeare Mr Secretary did yow a kindnesse, deseruinge a greater matter at your hands, which hee did for yow most carefully and affecconatly, (as I came to know casually after). This curtesy therfore frankly and generously performed for soe noble a gentleman shall make yow a fruitfull and double retourne, the one by the fauoures and countenance of soe honorable a freind, the other by an

office of freindshipp of equall valew from mee, whensoeuer yow
shall challenge itt. Soe as I noe waies doubt of the performance, but
that yow will readily and freely doe itt, out of your loue to mee and
out of your discretion too, as one glad of soe good an oportunity in
some small measure to settle your selfe in the faire respects and good
opinion of soe honorable and able a frend as Mr Secretary This is
all that for the present I will trouble yow with, more then the assurance of my beinge, Your most assured and affecconate freind and
cozen, Th. Wentworth.

**169.** (*SC*, ii, p. 87) *To Leonard Caluert Esquier. Austin Friars. 2 June
1622.*

Good Sir, I shall neuer thinke it any trouble unto mee, to doe Mr
Secretary any seruice, but shall euer joy my selfe, when such a meanes
shalbee offered unto mee; and therfore I must thank yow for put-
tinge this occasion into my hands, albeitt (God knowes) a very poore
one, wherby to giue yow some small tast of my affeccon and zeale
to him and his affaires. I haue according to your desire used the
uttermost of my power both with my aunts and cozen Danby (*p.
88*) to satisfy your faire demaunds of thirty trees, which may much
pleasure yow and cannott at all preiudice him, soe as I hope itt wilbee
forthwith graunted and that the rather in regard I would haue done
as much as this comes to for a meaner freind of theires upon the like
request unto mee from them. The letteres are both open to the
intent yow may read them, which done, yow wilbee pleased but to
droppe a little hard wax under the labell, and then they are closed,
and fit for deliuerye. I wish these lines may ariue yow in seasonable
time, howsoeuer yow wilbee pleased to excuse mee, for I receaued
your lettere dated the 25 of May but this morninge, beinge the second
of June, and tomorrow Godwillinge they shall moue towards yow
by a trusty messinger, soe as I hope they will ariue yow att the
furthest before Whittson Munday. Thus wishinge yow the continewance of many daies, with good health to enioy them, I remaine,
Your very assured and affecconate freind, Th. Wentworth.

Sir I pray yow bee pleased to let mee to know from yow how yow
speed; that accordingly I may proporcon my thanks.

**170.** (*SC*, ii, p. 88) *To Mrs. Danby. Austin Friars. 2 June 1622.*

My very good auntt, I am out of that mutuall interest that remaines
in mee to wards yow and in yow to mee, to entreat a fauour from
yow, which I shall not onely take most kindly, but your selfe haue

occasion to rest much contented yow had meanes to pleasure soe noble and worthy a gentleman. Itt is shortly this, that yow would use your best meanes with my cozen, your sonne, that hee would bee pleased to let Mr Caluertt haue (towards his sonnes building Mr Secretary Caluertt) thirty good timber trees, out of his wood of Thorpe Hollinges, which hee desires noe otherwaies, then for his money, a curtesy which one neighbour will not deny another. But if I might aduise my cozen, hee should freely giue him his choice where hee would (*p. 89*) take them; the price of them nor his preiudice in them cannot bee greate; and of my knowledge (which I came to casually) Mr Secretary did my cozen a fauour deseruinge as great or a greater matter, then that comes to the last yeare. Therefore, good Aunt, deale effectually with your sonne in this businesse, which I shall take more kindly tenne times ouer, then if itt were for my selfe and it shall meritt from mee a requitall of as great worth whensoeuer yow shall haue occasion to desire the like from mee. God graunt yow (my best auntt) many and good daies. Your euer most assured and affecconate nephew and seruant, Th. Wentworth.

**171.** *To Marris. Austin Friars. 3 June 1622 (SC, xxi/19).*

Rich. Marris, I haue upon the intreaty of Sir Arthur Ingram giuen direction under my hande unto Charles Ratcliffe and James Jackson for the paymentt of two hundreth pounds forth of the receit, if itt could be spared, which he hath promised to repay me heare att London. This I might not deny as things now rest, neither doe I hope will itt be any dangere. Yet I pray you write to Mr Radcliffe to giue me notice soe soon as itt shall be paid that soe I may call for itt backe as occasion shallbe offered. You may likewise signifie unto him that I thanke him very much fore his paines and care in the looking to the execution of the place which I must desire him for a while not to grow weary of. I will procure, you may allsoe tell him, a constat of such moneys as are paide hear into the Receite and send itt unto him that soe theruppon they may take a presentt course for leuying such of the king's rentts as are yett behind. I pray you informe yourself what moneys will remaine, pentions and other duties paid; if ther doe appear an ouerplus, I would you take itt into your custody and cast aboute how to putt itt to the best aduantage, seeing itt is not to be paide in, as I take itt, till Lady Day next. For my petition touching Bardsey, my lord Treasurer, promised me on Satterday last that he would dispatche itt for me to morrow, telling me that I stood soe right in his Maiestie's opinion and thos about him that I could moue nothing to misse. I perceaue by your letter to Peter Man that my meadowes att Ledstone are ouerflowen; looke you send me all the men's names who in right ought to repaire the goules and I will instantly send you downe processe for them and commence my sute; the longer itt is driuen, I shall be the greater loser and the banks further from repairing. Soe I rest, your Mr and frende, Th. Wentworth. Austin Friers this 3 of June 1622. Remember Watson. I pray you take a course that none of my letters writt to you upon any occasion be opened in your absence; ther may cum much inconuenciency of it.

**172.** (*SC*, ii, p. 89) *To Lord Clifford. Wentworth Woodhouse. 17 Sept. 1622.*

My honoured Lord, I shall proue (I feare) a miserable comforter, my grief still encreasinge, as one depriued of the greatest treasure, this world could afford mee; soe as mee thinks sadnesse and sorrowe best beseemes and befitts mee. This passion soe distracts, that it will not giue mee leaue to thinke upon my owne affaires, albeitt very pressing and urgent, the tast of all earthly thinges (as to one oppressed with a vehement feauore) is loathsome and flatt; the salt now a wanting which seasoned them all; yet reason tells mee, and religion too, it should not bee thus, nor ought wee thus to sorrowe, as without hope. I shall then I trust by God's goodnesse ouercome itt by degrees, in the meane time comforting my selfe in thes, that whome hee correcteth hee loueth, and as to that blessed woman in the ghospell much was forgiuen because shee loued much, soe I perswade my selfe doth hee chastize us much and seuearly, because hee loueth us much and tenderly. Therfore God forbidd our affeccons should corrupt our thankfullnesse, duty, or obedience towards him; but that wee should chearfully restore him his owne, which God graunt wee both may doe. I shall, Godwilling, attend your Lordship's pleasure att (*p. 90*) Ledstone, on Weddensday cum seuen night, except I heare from yow to the contrary; or sooner, or later, as shall best sute your occasions upon notice of your further pleasure therin. God giue us both the full and lasting comforts of his holy spiritt which cannott bee taken from us. Your Lordship's most humble seruant to bee comaunded Th. Wentworth.

**173.** (*SC*, ii, p. 90) *To Lord Clifford. Wentworth Woodhouse. 24 Sept. 1622.*

My much honoured Lord, I shall, God willinge, attend your pleasure at Ledstone on Munday next accordinge to your Lordship's direccon,

where as euery where els, I shall doe yow faithful seruice and the best
that a poore distressed man, both in his passions and understandinge,
shalbee able to performe. The world is strangly fashioned new to
mee, that where rested the fountaine of my comfort, from thence
should now springe my greatest anguish and torment.[1] This is
God's doinges and albeitt wonderfull in my eyes, yet I haue learned
to submitt both my selfe and all myne to his gracious pleasure and
freely to giue and (as I may say) to convay them backe againe to his
most wise and blessed disposall.

*Sic ego defunctus iam viuo, mihique superstes*
*et vite amisso, manere fata moror.*

Well my Lord, I will dwell noe longer upon this sadd and mournfull
subiect, least I therby renew your greife; this onely I will add as a
request of mine to your Lordship that haueing (God knowes) soe
many other occasions of sorrowe, yow will in some measure transmitt
that for your sister ouer unto mee, soe shall it be deposited with as
true and faithfull a storer, as euer had charge comitted unto him, and
helpe to fill upp the measure of my teares, albeitt not both sufficient
to lament my unspeakable losse in my most obedient and louing
wife. The good God of heauen and earth guide and blesse all your
affaires, preserue your person in all honore and happines, Your
Lordship's most humble seruant to bee comaunded, Th. Wentworth.

**174.** (*SC*, ii, p. 91) *To Lord Clifford. Wentworth Woodhouse. 8 Oct.
1622.*

My much honoured Lord, I haue herewith sent yow Buchanan's
Scottish history, which I shold haue brought with mee to Londes-
borowe, had my memory bene as good as formerly; I perswade myselfe the stile will delight yow and soe bee a meanes to passe ouer
some sad howers with contentment. If this or any other thing in my
power maie doe yow seruice, itt shall much comfort mee. And now
my Lord, albeitt my dearest wife bee in heauen, yet her memory and
vertue still liuinge, togeather with my true and faithfull zeale to yow
and youres, I shall assume my wonted boldnesse to write frely unto
yow my poore opinion and that with more confidence in that otherwaies I should not uprightly (as I conceaue) discharge my duty to the
defunct, a consideracon which must euer bee before myne eyes. I
haue seriously thought upon your last speaches, which occasions
mee as then soe now, to presse your Lordship with the care and

[1] The death of Wentworth's wife, Margaret Clifford.

repect yow owe your howse, which it hath pleased God to blesse soe many generations and whose hand I doubte not (if his tyme bee piously and paciently attended) will still bee enlarged towards itt. I urge itt to this purpose that the due consideracon hereof will make it appeare unto your judgment necessary to persist and walke on in your purpose begunne, for freeing your estate, with a constant reso-lucon not to bee tourned aside or discouraged, albeitt yow find not that sinceare meaninge in others, which yow might justly expect. And surely, my Lord, it is their endeauour to stoppe yow in the fountaine and therfore your vertue should bee whetted on the more sharply by such opposicon, especially when that if yow should fainte, or grow remisse, itt will not onely blemish yow in your reputacon, soe soone to bee weary of well doinge, but in good faith threatens your howse with a fearfull ruyne. Pardon my plainnesse, the worke of it selfe is a worke of tyme and therfore, if yow meete with some rubbs in your passage, it is noe more then befalles all men in affaires of like nature. But my lord, if yow (*p. 92*) wilbee pleased to goe on confidently and boldly without dwelling too much upon offences by the way, which will but detaine yow longer from your desired end, and without suffering them to take too deepe impression in your thoughts, I rest assured, by the grace of God, yow will (with more ease, then upon the first view yow imagine) ouercome all these letts and hinderances and bee in all more then a conqueror. And if at any tyme yow find your selfe opprest, recomend your person and affaires by harty and feruent praier to allmighty God, bee sure that in these fiery times of your tryall, yow neglect none of those duties which hee hath comaunded; and then I doubt not but hee will sensibly comfort yow and still giue yow courage, chearfully againe to take upp your burthen, til your shoulders bee altogeather eased, enioying (after all your labour) a peaceable and plentifull old age and drawing unto your selfe motions of thankfullnesse to his eternall Maiestie euen out of the remembrance of these euill daies and troubles of your youth. God of his goodnesse guide and blesse yow in all your waies and send yow full contentment at the last, which none shall see with more comforte, then Your Lordship's most humbly to bee comaunded, Th. Wentworth.

My humble duty to my lord and my seruice to my Ladye, and little Mistresse, I beseech yow.

**175.** *From James Jackson. 27 Oct. 1622 (SC, xx/234).*

Sir, according to our last speaches yow shall here in brief receiue that direccon and satisfaccon for the true valewacon of that particuler

we then spoke of, as I will iustifie to be good, saue onelie the allowaunce for Barwick which maie with a little charge made as absolute
as of the rest following, *vizt.*

> *Feodum Receptoris per annum*    C$^{li}$
> *Portagium monetae tam in rure quam super Comp[utandum]*
> Cxx$^{li}$
>
> *Regard Receptoris venientem ad Computandum*    x$^{li}$
> *Expensis tempore Auditi*    xl$^{li}$
> *Annualis Pencio pro solucione de la Garrison*
> *apud Barwick*    lxvi$^{li}$ xiii$^s$ 4$^d$
>
> CCCxxxxvi$^{li}$ xiii$^s$ iiii$^d$

This last, as I haue said before, maie be made as good as anie of the
rest, if the proceedings be with my lord Treasorer's approbacon and
noe question but his lordship will further that allowaunce, in regard
he is soe carefull to haue the pencens there duelie performed withall.
Other aduantages maie happen for the bettering of the offics, as
payment out of moneyes by warrant whereupon is allowed vi$^d$ at
pound, whereas for euery hundred paied into the receipt there is
onelie but xx$^s$ allowed. By all meanes if yow contract, gett in all the
intrest in the 3 pattents, *viz* Lassells', Lepton's and Mr Scudamor's
and renue yt for 3 liues in leiw of them, as I told yow (as I apprehend yt) the more sudenlie and quicklie it is performed the more
easier will your passage be; I told yow which waie I held the best.
And soe in haist with the remembraunc of my hartie loue to yourself and my uncle Mr Man, I rest in great haist, Yours assuredlie to
his power[?], James Jackson. 27 Octobris 1622.

If yow goe forward make noe words untill yow be fullie concluded
by constraint &c. Remember my last words, which wear that
Lepton would not be compounded with except he was called to
bringe his extent before the kinge and ther commanded, seinge he
cannot giue satesfaction for securitye to take a composition &c.

**176.** (*SC*, xx/231). An estimate of such fees as are incident and
belonginge to the Receauer generall of the Counetye of Yorke.

| | | | |
|---|---|--:|--:|--:|
| The Receauor's Fee | 100$^{li}$ | 00 | 00 |
| *it.* 6$^d$ in the pownde for paiment of the some of 206$^{li}$ to survayors, stewards &c amounting to | | 5 | 03 | 00 |
| *it.* 6$^d$ in the pownde for paiment of 1029$^{li}$ for anuities amowting to 25$^{li}$ 14$^s$ 6$^d$ | | 25 | 14 | 06 |
| *it.* 12$^d$ in the pownde for the paiment of 62$^{li}$ to the Churche of Yorke amownting to | | 1 | 11 | 00 |

*it*. for paiment of 65$^{li}$ to the poore *nil*

*it*. 6$^d$ a pownde for paiment of 17$^{li}$ for allowancs of
Tenthes is                                                                00   08   06

*it*. for the Chardges of the Awditt 40$^{li}$ and for
Chardges in passing the account att 10$^{li}$ *in toto*                    50   00   00

*it*. 20$^s$ for euerie C$^{li}$ paid to Barwicke and into the
receate with 12$^{li}$ 14$^s$ 6$^d$ for paiment of the Lord
President amounting to                                                     66   10   00

*it*. 6$^d$ in the pownde for paiment of 30$^{li}$ odd money
by debenter to Mr Trigge and amounting to                                 00   15   00

*it*. 6$^d$ in the pownde for paiment of 146$^{li}$ od money
to Sir James owter lorne [?] imprested for the
annuities at Christmas last past                                          04   13   00

*it*. due to the Receauore for making the pay to
Barwicke 66$^{li}$ 13$^s$ 0$^d$                                            66   13   04

                                                           Total[1]      340   13   04

                                                    besides acquittancees &c

**177.** *Passport* (*SC*, xii/3).

Whereas the bearer hereof, Sir Thomas Wentworth of the Countie
of Yorke, knight and Baronet, hath made earnest sute for leaue to
trauaill into the partes beyond the Seas there to continue the space
of one yeare the better to enable himselfe in language and otherwise.
These are to will and require yow and euerie of yow whom it may
concerne to suffer him with twoe seruants and his and their Trunkes
with apparrell and other necessaries for their iourney, quietly and
peaceablie to passe by yow and embarque themselues at any place
where they shall thinke most convenient, without let, hindraunce,
or molestation. And this shalbe your sufficient warrant. At Whitehall, the twentieth of Nouember 1622.

To all Mayors, Sherifs, Justices of the peace, Customers, Con-
troulers, Searchers and all other his Ma$^{ts}$ officers and Ministers
whom it may concerne

[*Signed*] Carlile, Kellie, H. Grandisone, Jo. Suckling, Geo.
Caluert, J. Cæsar, T. Edmondes.

**178.** (*SC*, ii, p. 92) *To the Earl of Cumberland. Fetter Lane. 7 Dec.
1622.*

My most honoured Lord, as an humble seruant to your Lordship
and your howse, I shall euer bee ready and ambitious to execute

---

[1] The correct total is £331–8–4. Another estimate (*SC*, xx/233) gives a total
of £316–13–4.

your comaunds and hold it to bee part of my duty I owe yow, hereby
to giue yow an accounte of the businesse concerninge Mr Greene,
wherwith it pleased your Lordship I should bee acquainted. Surely,
my lord, yow haue made a passing good choice and (*p. 93*) I doubte
not but yow will receaue passing good contentment in his seruice.
For in truth I haue knowne him out of long experience to bee very
religious and sinceare inwardly, to bee of a chearfull and sweet
conuersacon outwardly. But this is not the occasion of my writinge,
but much rather to signify humbly unto your Lordship how exceeding chearfully my Lord Clifford did embrace him upon your Lordship's recomendacons; and how sencible hee was of that perticuler
where yow were pleased to expresse, that Mr Greene was such an
one as your Lordshipp could well like to liue with. Soe as I may
truly say, hee tooke a greate deale of comfort in rendring backe to
yow the presentacon to bee soe disposed of to your good likeinge
and did therupon soe farr forth enlarge himselfe in acknowledgment of his faithfull and filiall obedience and obseruance, as I
protest it would loose much of the force and strength under the
expression of my penne, and therfore I will leaue it to the more
certaine and cleare testimony therof, which I rest most assured will
abundantly sheadd forth it selfe in his future accons. In the meane
time my self as euer deuoted to your family, doe rest much satisfied
to see your affeccon and respect discending upon my Lord Clifford,
and his duty and thankfullnes, as a sweet incence humbly ascending
upp back to yow againe. And doubt not but God's blessing wilbee
soe upon yow both that yow may long liue, to enioy one another in
this sweet and comfortable manner without breach of the least
stringe, which might in the least degree interrupt or trouble soe sweet
and well pleasinge a harmony both to God and men. I beseech God
to blesse yow with long life and good health, your howse with increase of all honour and happines wherin I shall euer much and
unfainedly reioice, my selfe as remaininge in all firmnes and truth
Your Lordship's most humbly to bee comaunded, Th. Wentworth.

**179.** (*SC*, ii, p. 93) *To Sir Arthur Ingram. Fetter Lane. 22 Dec. 1622.*

Sir, I haue in my absence directed this bearer to attend yow who
hath from mee to present his Lordship with a poore New-Yeare's
gifte, as a small testimony of my duty and thankfull-(*p. 94*)nesse, for
his many noble fauores and curtesies extended towards mee farr
aboue my deserts, I haue not any sute to trouble his Lordship with,
which the rather imboldens mee, otherwaies I should haue forborne.
And therfore I pray yow to afford the messinger your direccon in the

way and meanes how it may with most decencye bee deliuered, who
from mee hath noe other appointment saueing onely to doe as yow
shallbee pleased to comaund him. Your paines herein I shall file upp
in a gratefull remembrance amongst the rest of your kind and
freindly offices, which haue bound mee iustly and uprightly to
remaine, your very assured and affecconate freind, Th. Wentworth.

**180.** (*SC*, ii, p. 94) *To the Countess of Shrewsbury. Wentworth
Woodhouse. 29 Dec. 1622.*

My most honored Lady, to repeate what it hath pleased God to lay
both upon your Ladyship and upon my poore selfe, since I saw yow
last were but a fruitlesse renewinge of our greifes; and somthing
mistimed in regard soe much space is since runne upp as maie
suffice, laying aside the passions of nature and blood, to produce in
us an obedient and rectified will to the good pleasure of the allmighty.
Bee pleased then, Madame, to consider how long God lent yow the
comfort of a noble and pious mother, which truly and rightly
waighed, will doubtles stirr upp in yow a thankfullnes for soe lasting
a contentment and a chearfullnes in rendring upp to God his owne,
which now at the last hee requires from yow, after soe pacient and
long forbearance. I was moued by Mr Ogle at London to bee bound
for yow, for three hundreth pounds, which I was well content to doe,
as also any other seruice which shall rest in my power. I onely desire
your Ladyship would bee pleased by your lettere to mee, to take
notice of itt as done with your priuitie and allowance and that the
money was taken upp for your occasions and soe imployed. Wee
now conceaue hope wee maie by God's grace see yow once more
(*p. 95*) in these partes, which the sooner it is, giue mee leaue to say,
I think will proue better both for your health and estate. I must
acknowledge indeed I doe much desire itt shold bee soe, not out of
any end of my owne, but as a person that doth truly honore yow and
wish these cuntries and your freinds, might find the light of your
presence amongst us and bee comforted by your setled abode with
us. Your Ladyship's most humble and affecconate seruant and kinsman, Th. Wentworth.

**181.** *Wentworth's account of his relations with Lord Scrope* (*SC*,
xxi/20).

Upon Munday the twelfte of January 1622 [3], cumming to Yorke I
sentt Richard Marris to Mr Whethered to desire to knowe from
him when I might cum conueniently to tender my self to my Lord

Presidentt. Which Richard Marris doing accordingly, about an hower after Mr. Wheatheride came unto me to Kayes howse and ther relating unto me, how he had made my lord Presidentt acquainted with my desire, was therupon directed by my lord to deliuer this messuage unto me, *viz*:

That my lorde did not expect my cumming unto him out of respect to him, considering how things did now stand betwixt us, best knowen to my self. And therfore if I had anything to acquainte him with concerning his Maiestie's seruice, I might then or att any other time cum unto him; otherwayes I might spare my labour. The rather in regard that during all my lord's being att London, I had neuer cummed unto him, being a place wher I might haue shewed my particular respect more unto him and a fitter place to discusse the matters which weare then betwixt us. Wherunto my answeare was as followeth:

Thatt itt was true, being in towne upon other businesse, I thought itt fitt for me to presentt my self, as a poore seruant of the king's in thes parttes, in case my poore indeauoures might proue any wayes useful in his Maiestie's affaires and being one of his Maiestie's Counsell in thes parttes to him the Presidentt therof. Butt perceiuing by this messuage that his lordship [had] had nothing to impartt unto me of that nature, nor my self neither any thing to informe his lordship of att this time concerning the same, I would very willingly forbeare. That I knew nothing of any matters betwixt us butt such as I was very well able to giue a good accountt of that neuerthelesse itt was besides my intention to make any apologies wher I had made noe fault, yett if [it] pleased my lord to giue me my chardge, I would then giue him my answeare.

That meeting my lord att Hinchinbrooke in Michelmas terme laste and offering my self with due respect unto him (as I conceaued was then well befitting me) it pleased his lordship with much neglect (as I did conceaue) to turne himself aboute from me, which was the occasion that moued me att London to take unto my self the libertie of a gentleman and not to intrude myself into company wher I thought I should not be wellcume.

Mr Weatheride therupon asked me wheather I would giue him commission to returne this answeare, I replied he might with all my hartte. Then Mr Weathered proceeded (therby as he affermed to auoide mistakes) to repeate my answeare, which he did punctually and directly, sauing in that part wher I had said that if itt pleased my lord to giue me my chardge, I would giue him my answeare. Mr Weatheride repeated itt, as if I had desired my chardge from my lorde. Wherin I told him he did mistake itt, for I did not desire itt, butt if itt pleased his lordship I might haue the one, he should haue the other.

Att parting Mr Weatheride desired me that howeuer the messuage might be displeasing unto me yeat the messinger might not; wherto I replied that in good faithe the messuage was not att all displeasing unto me, butt, howsoeuer the first had been, the second should not, himself being a gentleman whom I had allways loued and well respected and soe would doe still.

**182.** (*SC*, ii, p. 95) *To the Earl of Cumberland. Wentworth Woodhouse. 29 Jan. 1623.*

My most honored Lord, I am right gladd to heare by Mr Greene, of your Lordships good health, as also to understand by your letter the good acceptance and approbacon yow haue of his seruice; neither doe I doubt, but the more yow shall know him, the more yow will like him. I purposed as this day to haue sent my footman ouer to Lounsborowe, but now I will craue pardon to make use of Mr Greene and hereby to desire that if I may doe your Lordship any seruice at London, I may receaue the honore of your comaunds before Tuesday next, being the day I intend, God willing, to beeginne my journey. In good faith the necessity of my affaires haue all this while detained mee from waiting upon yow, much against my mind, and therfore I assure my selfe of your pardon; yet howsoeuer I may (beinge, thus pressed) make bold to dispence with respectes and obseruances of this nature, I will neuer bee a wantinge when I shalbee to giue reall and sollid testimonies to yow and your noble howse, of my unfained beinge, Your Lordship's most humble and obedient seruant, Th. Wentworth.

**183.** (*SC*, ii, p. 96) *To George Butler Esq. Wentworth Woodhouse. 29 Jan. 1623.*

Sir, I am much to thank yow for your last letter which I receaued at Yorke, but had not then time to answer yow with the like respecte, coming to my hands iust as I was getting to horse. Surely I will in all occasions which shall present themselues unto mee, giue yow good proofe of my harty affeccon towards yow and of the neare and large esteme I must allwaies haue of yow. I am sorry I shall not see yow this time of my being in the cuntry; yet I pray yow, if there bee any thinge yow would haue mee doe for yow at London, that I may know your mind therin before Tuesday next and I will not faile by God's grace to see it performed. I desire my seruice may bee presented to your worthie good Lady. And I wish yow maie liue long

WP—N

togeather, with much happynesse and contentment your very assured and affecconate freind and kinsman, Th. Wentworth.

**184.** (*SC*, ii, p. 97) *To the Earl of Cumberland. Wentworth Woodhouse. 25 April 1623.*

My most honoured Lord, after a wearisome and tedious journey from London, one of my best refreshmentes wilbee the newes of your Lordship's good helth espetially understanding by Mr Greene that the state therof hath these hollydaies bene somthing ill desposed and uncertaine. I could therfore retaine this bearer noe longer with mee, nor deny my selfe any further the comfort and contentment to heare by this meanes (I trust) of your perfect recouerie, as that which I both wish and pray for; and which I hope shalbee confirmed and established unto yow for many yeares, with a constant and fruitfull encrease of honore and well setled contentment. Which God of his goodnes graunt and take not onely your person, but howse & affaires into his blessed proteccon and guidance. Your Lordship's most humbly to bee comaunded, Th. Wentworth.

**185.** (*SC*, ii, p. 97) *To Lord Clifford. Wentworth Woodhouse. 25 April 1623.*

My much honoured Lord, if there were any other demonstratiue way for a poore sick man to present himselfe unto yow, I would haue att this tyme attended your Lordship in person, rather then to haue moued towards yow in a few weake lynes. But in this (as the case is now with mee) yow haue the uttermost of my (*p. 98*) strength, as it wilbee to mee the highest cordiall these or any other parts can yeild mee, to heare of your lordship's content and health. The newes of London happening since my brother Clifton's departure, haue bene but cold and barren; onely two shipps were appointed to goe presently into Spaine to fetch my Lord Marquesse as was generally beleeued, but in truth as I take it to bring the Conde de Gondomar hether to conferr with the kinge touching his negociacon into Germany for which hee is designed. As for my Lord Marquesse, it is said hee returnes not before the marriage bee fully consumate, which for any thing I can learne, is not like to bee til towards midd June. They saie the cleargie of Spaine haue undertaken to paie the whole porconn, beinge a marriage soe much tendinge to the honore and safetie of Spaine, the good and aduancment of the Catholiq faith. It beginns to bee whispered that the yong Palsgraue shall marry the Emperour's daughter, that the Palatinate shalbee forthwith restored, but not the Electorate, yet that dignitie after his death shall by sollemne decree and act of diett bee established on his sonne also. Further that the kinge will make peace betwixt the king of Spaine and the Low Cuntries. These thinges once done, hee blaspheames that will not saie *beati pacifici*. My Lord, I am your Lordship's humble seruant, Th. Wentworth.

**186.** *Wentworth to Sir Geo Calvert, 28 April 1623 (Knowler, i, p. 16; SC, ii, p. 96), on country pleasures.*

**187.** *From Sir Arthur Ingram (SC, xx/236).*

Worthi Sir, I hop now you ar gott home to your own howse and country ayrs, that you haue recouered your helth and ar becom a strong man, the which I shall bee right glad to hear of. Sines your departur Mr Fotherly hath made greatt means to my Lord thatt hee mytt bee the present receauuer and thatt hee would putt in such security as should giue his Lordship good contentt. Understanding of itt, I tould his Lordship thatt hee had appoin[ted] you to r[eceive] itt and yf ther should be any chans[g] now itt mytt [bee a tuch to your reputacion upon which my speach I found my Lord very senssibell and synned a letter which I had prepared redy for him, the which hear inclosed you shall r[eceive] withall. Att thatt tym hee tould me thatt hee must wright to all the receiuors to intrett them to pay in som monny this term, in regard of the king's greatt and presentt wantt. Butt yf hee dow wright, I hop you will bee so wisse as [to] bee spuring in the dowing of itt. For the nott you sentt me to gett sined by my Lord and Mr Chansellor, I moued my Lord in itt and his answer was thatt hee had appointed a messenger to attend upon you with a scedule of such debes as was owing and thatt hee would intrett your car and direccion therin.

I moued you when you wear att London that you would pay for me ther 200[li], the on 100[li] the last of this montt and the other 100[li], the last of the next mont, the which I pray you appointt itt to bee paid unto my brother accordingly and to both a nott bee taken for the recept of the same for my use and, God willing, I will see you paid the sam iustly again, when you shall call for the sam; and so I rest, yours euer faythfully to loue and serue you, Ar. Ingram. This iiiith of May 1623.

**188.** *Wentworth to the Earl of Middlesex, 5 June 1623 (Knowler, i, p. 16; SC, ii, p. 98), recommending Mr Wetheridd for the place of Receiver of Yorkshire.*

**189.** (*SC*, ii, p. 99) *To Mr James Jackson. Wentworth Woodhouse. 5 June 1623.*

Mr Jackson, I am sorry your occasions and mine suite noe better, for the meeting at Ledstone would haue stood as well with my leasure, as any other time ( I feare mee) wee shall light of hereafter. Yet seing yow must of necessity goe presently to London, it must bee put of til some other seazon; howeuer I will expect yow here some tyme before Weddensday next in your passage, to the intent I may conferre with yow touchinge the haueinge of a newe and better warrant both for your discharge and mine, for the payinge ouer of the seauen hundreth pounds to mee forth of the colleccon which yow hold under the Bishoppe, as also that I may shewe yow the duplicate of my account which is now come downe, and bee enformed whether it bee right as it ought to bee for my discharge. Besides there is som-thing els, which I desire yow to doe for mee at London, which I will acquaint yow with at your cominge; and therfore let mee entreate yow not to faile of seeinge mee, as yow goe onwards on your journey. I trust yow will haue in a readines your money for Barwicke pay and take some substantiall course, that wee may not bee therin dis-sappointed and soe my selfe lyable to their renewed clamour, which in truth I shold take very ill from yow. Therfore I assure my selfe yow will looke to itt and as for any (*p. 100*) moneyes part therof, which yow shall pay to Charles Radcliffe and take his acquittance for the receate, I doe hereby giue yow to understand, I my selfe wilbee answerable for itt and discharge yow therof. Soe in some hast I rest, your lovinge freind, Th. Wentworth.

**190.** (*SC*, ii, p. 100) *To the Archbishop of Canterbury. Wentworth Woodhouse. 10 June 1623.*

Maie it please your Grace, a good space since, there was an agrement made with my Lord of Arrondell and the rest of the coheires of Gilbert, Earle of Shrewsbury, concerning diuers lands in Darbyshire and Oxfordshire, to which his Maiestie is intitled by office and of which your Grace and my sister are lessees. Neuerthelesse (chiefly occasioned by my sicknes) the same continewes hetherto unperfected, the indentures unsealed. I haue made bold therfore, (as unable to take such a journey my selfe) to appoint this bearer my sollicitore to waite upon your Lordship therwith and by these lynes humblie to moue your grace that somtimes this tearme yow would bee pleased to seale the same; wherupon wee shall proceed (as indeed doth much import) to the findinge of other lands in pursuite and full accomplishment of the said agreement. I will noe longer presume upon

your leisure, but here conclude in the true and bounden acknowledgment of your many gracious fauoures, both to my sister and to
my selfe, I beseech God longe to preserue yow with encrease of all
honore and happinesse, your Grace's humblie to bee comaunded,
Th. Wentworth.

**191.** (*SC*, ii, p. 100) *To Sir Edward Leech knight. Wentworth Woodhouse. 15 June 1623.*

Sir, I would haue bene well contented this tearme to haue spoken
with yow my selfe, but this being denied mee, I am (*p. 101*) forced to
convay my selfe unto yow partly by these lines, partly by the bearer,
my sollicitore, to whose further speach I referr my selfe. The agrement
long since made with your good helpe, betwixt the lords, the lady of
Shrewsbury and us, hee hath in a readines to shew unto yow, sealed
and signed by my lord's grace of Canterbury, the Countesse of
Shrewsbury, and my sister Sauile, according as yow haue often
required of mee; I am now therfore in exchange to desire the like
maie bee (thorowe your good meanes) done by the lords. But in
regard I know not how it maie stand with their lordship's leasure, yet
how unfitt it is for us to prescribe them any sett time (which I hope
neuertheles wee shall haue soe soone as conveniently maie bee) wee
shalbee well content, that in the meane space our part thus sealed
may remaine deposited in trust with my brother Clifton, to bee
deliuered back to yow, when wee shall receaue our counterparte
also from their Lordships. Further in pursuite and accordinge to the
couenants of the same agreement must I become a sutore, that wee
may with the Lords good likeinge and priuity proceed this long
vacation to the findinge of his Maiesties estate in right of Sir George
Sauile, his ward, to one half of Rufford and Langford, which I assure
my selfe will not bee denyed, seing all is perfected on our parts
roundly and really. And therfore haue I directed the bearer to moue
that a Comission maie bee sued forth this tearme for that purpose;
wherin I trust and humbly desire the Lords would ioine and further
us. Lastly I pray yow, when yow are pleased to acquaint my Lord
Chamberlaine with these contents, that yow would then likewise
present unto him my very humble dutie and seruice, which I shall
take as a very speciall curtesye and remaine, your very affecconate
freind, Th. Wentworth.

**192.** *Wentworth to Sir Edward Conway, 16 June 1623* (*Knowler*, i,
p. 16; *SC*, ii, p. 101). *He recommends his fifth brother for a place
in Conway's son's company.*

**193.** (*SC*, ii, p. 102) *To Sir George Calvert. Wentworth Woodhouse.*
*16 June 1623.*

Sir, I giue yow humble thanks for your noble remembrance of mee,
and under fauore must still auowe my selfe truly taken with a
cuntry life, wherof the more I haue, the lesse am I satisfied; the more
I valewe itt. I might too entertaine yow this season with a fresh
ofspringe of flowry delights, roses, pinks, woodbines, lillies and such
like, and set your teeth on edge it maie bee as much with these
sweetes, as some others with their sowers. But as (*p. 103*) for your
great Goddesse her altars are soe perfumed and smokinge with whole
haulocosts of honore and greatnesse, as meaner people may not
presume to approach them with their rurall and homely sacrifice.
*Sacer hic locus est extra me[i]ite*; as the Satirist hath it. Yet with your
leaue is the materiall wherupon they proiect, how goodly soeuer
outwardly, but copper intrincecally, and soe I comitt that shrine to
the proteccon of their Demetrius and his craftsmen. I understand our
local superintendent of these quarters hath certefied that hee hath
noe deputies within his dominion, but that the charge is comitted to
the justices of peace in generall; which is true. Yet it is (with his
leaue) as true, that it was neuer soe before his tyme, that the gentlemen
of the best ranke refuse to sitt upon that seruice, haueing most of
them formerly beene deputie Lieutennantes, and soe the businesse
dispatched by those of the meanest, or at the best, but of the middle
degrees. By meanes wherof that seruice with the comon sort looseth
much of the countenance and reputacon it formerly had, which I
conceaue stands not with his Maiesty's good likeinge. Therfore in
my poore opinion, it is more then high time, it were againe reduced
back into the ancient channell and not thus left to flowe at large,
makinge it euerie man's charge in shewe, but indeed noe man's care
or regard. Which particuler state of oures may bee made knowne to his
Maiestie, if it shall seeme soe good; and then I must still bee bold to
renewe my sute for my cozen Wandesford, whose discretion and
capacities euerie waies for that imployment is such, as I dare saie will
allwaies approue of his choice. Sir, I feare I am too liberall beyond
good manners, of that which is none of my owne, your time taken
upp with more urgent affaires. I will here then sett a periodd to my
selfe, beseeching God euer to preserue yow in his waies and to blesse
yow with all other worldly contentmentes. Your honore's euer most
readily and humbly to bee comaunded, Th. Wentworth.

**194.** *George Wetheryd to Charles Radcliffe* (*SC*, xx/127).

Good Sir, being confidently assured by seuerall reports both at Donkaster and Wentbrigg that Sir Thomas Wentworth was yeister-night gonne to Ledston, I hastened thether this morning, where to my grieff I fownd him not. Nowe I am inioyned to be this night at Yorke (yf God giue leave) about speciall businesse with my Lord, whoe goeth from thenc to morrow morning to Bolton. Thus am I forced to intrete you (in course paper, the best in Abberford) your kynd paynes to make my excuses to that noble gent to whome I owe much service and will study to performe what he shall please to command me. These inclosed from my Lord Tresorer will acquaint him with the setling of the Recyuership, wherein his honorable letters made way for my dispatch, which, good Sir, acknowledge on my behalfe. And nowe be you plesed to knowe for me what course Sir Thomas will direct to be obserued towching the arerages and what else he will. For I doe assure you I will indeuor the obseruacon of his comands in all things and when I maye heare of his being at Ledston, or at any other place neare York (for as yet I cannot leave my master's occasions aboue one daye), I will then waite uppon him as I nowe intended.

For occurrents aboue, the Lord Bellsasse is stayed from his intended voyadge to the Emperor.

The 4 shipps which were sent from the Erle of Rutland's fleet to releiue the Dunkarker uppon the coast of Scotland are (by post) recalled and those with the rest of that fleet hastely prepared for the Prince; I cannot perceyue that the marradge is like to be solembnised before his coming, but the contract is alredy past. I need not tell you that his Maiestie was sworne to performe the Articles uppon Sundaye was sevennight in the chappell at Whitehall after the sermon, the Spanish Ambassador being present in a traverse purposely made for him, nor that all the Privy Councell (then at Court) did take the same oath after dinner. For I suppose you haue alredy hard thereof; but you haue not hard and therfore I will tell you that a grete papist, witty and learned, did protest (in some passion) that the businesse of that daye had giuen the gretest blow to theire religion that euer was giuen in England.

Diuerse letters are come to sundry grete persons of twoe defeats giuen Count Tilly by the duke of Brunswick, at the last theye all agree of 7000 slayne, 6 peeces of ordinance taken, with cariedges, waggons and grete store of municon. I will troble you no longer, but shall thinke the tyme long till I see you that I maye knowe the plesure of that noble gent and haue the happenesse to se you that I am and will stryve to be approued, your faythfull true freind to be com-an[ded], Geo: Wetheryd. Abberford, this Tuesdaye noone 27° Julii 1623. I haue a suite to Sir Tho: Wentworth which my man will tell you.

**195.** (*SC*, ii, p. 104) *To Lord Clifford. Wentworth Woodhouse. 28 July 1623.*

My much honoured Lord, I can by noe meanes stay Mr Caluerte any longer here and soe am ready to sett him 2 or 3 miles upon his way towards Rufford, where hee will meet yow to night, sorry that I my selfe cannot attend yow there also, and soe waite on your Lordship alonge to Clifton, by reason of the neare approach of the Assizes, where now unluckily I haue some businesse requiringe my presence, which I hope will excuse mee too for this time at Clifton, where I desire these lynes maie present my loue and seruice. I thank your Lordship for the letteres I euen now receaued by your footman and hereinclosed returne, but (*p. 105*) wonder that the heat of Spaine hath noe more warmed the blood of an English wooer, thus coldly to decline halfe a yeare's good sport at least, when hee might haue it. Yet by my faith I like the choice well, it beinge to us of more consequence here, to haue againe his person in health, which God preserue, then them there to haue their royall donzella well and merrily wrought. I purpose Godwillinge to waite upon your Lordship in the Assize weeke at Londesborowe if yow bee there. In the meane time God haue yow in his keepinge. Your Lordship's most humble and faithfull seruant, Th. Wentworth.

**196.** (*SC*, ii, p. 105) *To Christopher Wandesford Esq. Wentworth Woodhouse. 30 July 1623.*

My diligent and expedite Ambassadore resident with his Maiestie of greate Brittaine, your newes were to mee in this out angle, as new and fresh as oisters in September. I haue euer obserued in my read-inge that in the accons of great states, wherin there is a mutuall worldly aduantage to bee had on both sides, that in such exorbitant cases it appeares to both partes commonly sufficient onely to keepe good quarters in point of religion formally without pressing on either side matter of reallity, which would of necessety bee a touch and blemish to one of them. And I pray yow, Sir, in this, what could bee lesse either demaunded or graunted, then a bare and single promise of indulgence, to bee enlarged, to bee straitned too upon any emergent occasion. Well the hartes of Princes are unsearchable, unfitt obiectes for cuntry swaynes to contemplate in; yet in some proporcons it may hold in Comon wealthes, as in gardens, and then sure wee neuer faile to pluck upp the weedes in our owne groundes, albeitt in hope therby to reape the dainty and pleasant fruites of our neighboures. Againe in some seasons wee make more account of our plantes, then att other times; wee remoue, wee water, wee tend that in sommer, which is pulled upp and withered in winter. I protest, I verely beleeue their fauninge hopes and flatteringe will bringe forth noe fruite, and soe their tree entirely (by that great (*p. 106*) and judicious planter) in his fitt time bee hewen upp and cast into the fire; the branches wherof (as that other in Daniell) whose haight reached upp into heauen bee cut of, his faire leaues shaken, his much fruite scattered, and the fowles (or if yow will the fooles) of the aire upon this fall gotten away from under itt, who now seeme to dwell and pride themselues in the boughes, yea euen the stumpe therof, bound upp with a band of iron and brasse neuer to spring forth or budd againe; and soe let the dreame bee to them that hate us and the interpretacon therof to our enemies. If this proue true, deny if yow dare that I haue good skill in the tearmes and art of gardeninge. For the present, that yow may haue a tast too of my insight into armes, I proceed now from the spade to the lance. I must thank yow for your good remembrance of your absent freind, and I doe right hartely wish my selfe upon the place, that I might bee reuenged upon yow in the same case. Meethinks, were I there but for 2 or 3 daies, I should make the gaininge of your end to appeare to bee the worke but of an easy witt and then I hope yow would haue confessed mee to haue also bene a boone cauallier, but on the other side yow haue leadd mee upon the breach, *guerra, guerra, usque ad capillos*, and soe would I haue it or not at all: a pretty spiritt (if yow marke itt) in a gardner. I wish with all my hart that yow maie make your word good and your selfe (soe farr at least) a man at armes as to appoint mee for godfather to a boy; beleeue mee yow can battle upon noe man's head more freely nor that will with more chearfullnes and truth, auowe what his deputy shall performe in that kind, then my selfe. I shall truly pray for itt and expect the welcome newes of itt, and I pray yow soe let my cozen knowe. And now haueinge acquitt my selfe in answer of your lettere, partly with morrall discourse befitting a Spaniard, in parte also with *Gailliardire*, as the Frensh hath it, I will conclude in good and sober English, with the reall profession of my abideinge, your euer most assured and affecconate kinsman, Th. Wentworth.

**197.** (*SC*, ii, p. 107) To my very loving freind Mr Peasley, at Mr Secretary Caluerte's howse in St Martin's lane. Wentworth. 1° August 1623.

Mr Peasley, I will hereby make bould with yow and desire a curtesie from yow, which may afford mee much pleasure in this place. Mr Robert Mynne was pleased to promise mee some pinke seeds a good while agoe, which I tooke as an especiall fauoure. If therfore yow would put him in mind therof (this beinge now the season to receaue them in) soe as I might call for them the next tearme at my cominge upp (Godwilling) I should thinke my selfe much beholden and giue yow both many thankes; such innocent delightes as these beinge to us in these quarters more studied, then how yow more soaringe spiritts wind upp towards an end (which God graunt maie bee both succesfull and speedy too) of your high designes in Spaine. And now I pray yow to the former add this latter curtesie likewise, as to present my humble and faithfull seruice to Mr Secretary, whose comaunds I shall euer chearfully answer both here and euery wheare, with a constant northerne plainnesse, and with a more sowtherne actiue quicknesse. I wish yow all in St Martin's Lane the continewance and increase of all happines, retaining in these cold climates a propertie suteable with that compleccon, the truth of beinge, Your very affecconate freind, Th. Wentworth.

**198.** (*SC*, ii. p. 107) *To Sir George Calvert. York. Friday in the Assize week, 1623.*

Sir, I haue sent my Sollicitore to attend and acquaint yow with a busines that somwhat concernes mee and very much Mr Carre, a neare freind of mine; and to beseech yow that as it tooke his first life from your selfe, soe it may in the conclusion haue imprinted upon it the fresh caracter of your fauore also. I dare saie it is most just and that which hath bene last gott from his Maiestie very surreptitious; the particulers wherof, as also my humble request, I comitt to the relacon of my seruant, whome I beseech yow to heare in respect it maie require a speedye dispatch. Sir, God haue yow euer in his blessed keepinge, your honor's humbly and readily to bee comaunded, Th. Wentworth.

**199.** (*SC*, ii, p. 108) *To Christopher Wandesford Esq. Wentworth Woodhouse, 15 Aug. 1623.*

Sir, the inclosed is the occasion of my writinge unto yow at this present, which I must desire yow (with what speed may bee) to deliuer to my lord Treasurer, and that yow might know what yow deliuer, I haue here before sent yow a coppie. Yow wilbe pleased to let mee know what answer yow receaue, soe soone as conueniently yow maie, and with that I hope to receaue the good newes of my cozen's deliuerye, which I beseech God maie bee unto yow both with all safety and full contentment. The stormes here blow not soe mercilessly as they haue done, for the sunne of this Orbe now offers his aspect, and to bee seene if please us. But wee are soe benumed with those former bitter blasts of his disdaine, as wee are not yet sencible, or our knees suppled, or reuiued with these blessed gleames. And when the planetts thus beginne now to stand in soe faire and goodly a coniunccon, is it possible that yow should longer stray out of this soe harmonious a spheare? *Redeunt Saturnia Regna*, for shame make hast home then and loose (*p. 109*) not your part. Well in sobernesse now, and yet in stomack too, noe peace nor harkening to itt from hence for the present, wee will see the strength of Appolloe's bow, the distance and compasse hee shoots too, soe shall wee bee able to discerne what armes will serue our turnes and what ground to trauers. Proceeding now then out of this Cabalisticall relacon, wherin God give yow grace, witt, and understandinge, I come to that which shall without vaile, or mistery to disguise itt appeare to yow and all men, the assured truth and faith of my beinge your most affecconate freind and kinsman, Th. Wentworth.

All here are in good health, remember their loues etc., as I my seruice to my shee cozen.

**200.** (*SC*, ii, p. 108) *To Sir Edward Conway. York. Assize week 1623.*

Sir, I must first giue yow humble thanks for your remembrance of mee in the Comission of Lieutennancy for Yorkshire, wherin albeitt I know nothinge of the particulers further then I gather upon uncertaine report, neuerthelesse I haue chosen rather to render in thes lines an imperfect acknowledgment of your noble fauore, then to incurre an opinion of too much dulnesse and coldnesse in that actiue dutie of gratitude. My seruant hath (with your good leaue) to acquaint yow with a businesse much concerning my selfe, because shrewdly pinching a neare freind of mine, one Mr Carre; wherin I am the more bold to resort to your proteccon, because I know the cause to bee most iust and honest. The particulers I shall comitt wholly to the relacon of the bearer and humbly beseech I may herein still tast of your woonted fauore. Sir, I shall euer wish unto yow the setled continewance and increase of all honore and happinesse, remaining your honore's humbly to bee comaunded, Th. Wentworth.

**201.** (*SC*, ii, p. 109) *To the Earl of Middlesex, Lord Treasurer. Wentworth, 15 Aug. 1623.*

My much honoured Lord, itt pleased your Lordshipp by your letteres of the 24th of June, to disburthen mee of the great charge I was trusted with under yow, by assigning Mr Wetheridd Receauor in these parts, and further therby to direct mee that my deputies should acquaint him with the state of their receates and payments since the declaracon of the last accompte. For the first, I am to render your lordship humble thanks, in the latter, I haue readily obserued your comaunds; soe as Mr Wetheridd, being priuie how all things stand, maie forthwith now proceed to the leuyinge and payinge of what is behind of the last yeare's reuennewe, in such sort, as your Lordship hath appointed. Moreouer it seemes by your Lordship's lettere it is conceaued that such monies as remaine in my deputies hands (with aboue 600$^{li}$ new supers[1] made upon the last declaracon as is alleadged) maie amount to a good some, and returne therof expected into the Exchequer with all conuenient speed. I beseech yow therfore my Lord to pardon mee a few lines, wherby I maie enforme your Lordshipp the truth, justifie, and free my selfe from blame. First for the last yeares supers, which in the totall were 1000$^{li}$, your Lordshipp will find, that since the last account, neare 400$^{li}$, therof (*p. 110*) haue bene paid into the Exchequer by Worsley and other under collectores; bond taken for payment aboue of 200$^{li}$ and odd more, by the purseuants coming imediatly from your lordshipp after Easter last, two hundreth pounds and better part also therof behind by seuerall noblemen; and the rest (being under a couple of hundreth pounds too) uncollected, saueing onely fower score and odd pounds therof, which wee haue taken into the receate here. Soe as I marvaile at those which should enforme that six hundreth poundes remaineth still answerable to his Maiestie upon those supers; yet much more that my deputies should bee charged therwith, when as they being especially scheduled out to those purseuants which came from aboue, wee conceaued here the principall care to bee taken of our hands and that your Lordship would expect the particuler accompt therof from them. Onely giue mee leaue then to assure your Lordship that these supers were not fraudulent or fained, the purseuants finding them all (saue such as had bene in the interim respectiuely paid into the Exchequer by those from whome they were due) unleuyed at their cominge, except a matter of 20$^{li}$, and that too plainly shewed to haue bene brought in by the ordinary messinger attending the office here, since the accompt declared, consequently

---

[1] Amounts charged to the accountant at the ending of his account.

at that tyme justly super'd as well as any of the rest. Now for the last Lady day rents, the receate is but small, scarce halfe soe much as that which is due at Michaelmasse, but the payments, pencons and other ordinary issues full as great; soe as that present reuennew will hardly reach to discharge them, espetially consideringe there is at this instant 400$^{li}$ of these rents behind likewise, which indeed are not leuied as yet, but forborne til haruest bee gott, therby to auoid the hubbubs accompanying distresses in these needy and miserable times. Wherein, if wee haue bene too remisse, wee humbly craue pardon, the some being noe greater and haueing soe done, (as wee under fauore still doe conceaue) for the best, and that without any daunger of losse, more then in a short forbearance. Thus your lordship sees by this time I haue made a long narration of a short accompte, yet I hope yow will hold mee excused, being constrained therunto in our owne just defence (I meane my selfe and deputies) that soe wee maie bee sett apart in your (*p. 111*) noble iustice from the aspersions of such as it seemes would faine haue beleeued wee are in fault or negligent in our duties. My lord, I beseech God long to preserue yow with increase of honor and happinesse. Your lordship's most obliged and humbly to bee commaunded, Th. Wentworth.

**202.** *Wentworth to Sir Gervase Clifton, 20 August 1623* (*Knowler* i, p. 17; *SC*, ii, p. 111), *to say that his coach will bring the earl of Cumberland and Clifton to Woodhouse.*

**203.** (*SC*, ii, p. 112) *To Lord Clifford. Wentworth Woodhouse. 25 Aug. 1623.*

My much honored Lord, I haue euery daie this weeke expected a messinger from Lownsborowe with newes of your continewinge purpose to haue mett my lord at this poore howse; and now find us heare, (whether in remembrance of what it pleased God once to lend us, or for want of your noble company or both) soe sadd and heauy, as I protest, I know I shall tast that humore, and relish noe other for some dayes: yet I can saie to my selfe *Quid frustra?* and when I haue done, practize it as ill as any man in England. I receaued last night a lettere from Mr Secretary wherin there was noe newes, saueinge of a defeate giuen to Brunswicke by Tylly and that a very great one as should seeme; togeather that it is now written from the duke of Buckingham and related euerie where, soe as it is sure enough, that the Prince togeather with his Princesse sett both from Madridd towards England the nine and twentieth of this month *stilo nouo*. Our nauy presently to hoise saile, attend them, and take them aboard at Anderas and by God's goodnes bringe them both safe hether before midd-October. My Lord it is late and my pen verie neare slippinge out of my paper; I will therfore wrappe upp all this and whateuer els is in mee, in the sollidd and eternall truth of beinge your Lordship's most humblie to bee comaunded, Th. Wentworth.

**204.** (*SC*, ii, p. 112) *To Sir George Ellis knight. Wentworth Woodhouse. 27 Aug. 1623.*

Sir, there beinge in the seuerall rights of my Lord of Northumberland and my selfe tenne oxen distrained *damage faisant* upon our grounds within Withington wherunto Mr Stephen (*p. 113*) Norcliff's widowe uniustly pretends title; I understand (thorowe misprision of the clarke) an order to bee conceaued and entred touchinge this difference in the Court att Yorke upon the ninetenth of August last without any ground at all. For it seemeth to establish a possession, which is not prayed in the bill, and it is also menconed to bee made with the consent of both parts, whereas nether my Lord nor my selfe haue, nor will assent to any such preiudiciall order, nor yet giue authoritie to any other soe to doe for us. I haue therfore sent the bearer, my seruant, to attend yow and to desire for us both that yow wilbee pleased to bee fully enformed in the cause and right us in the premisses. Howeuer I hope yow will presse noe contempts against us, or our seruants, if wee chaunce by the aduise of our counsell to proceed fairly and peacably in preseruinge our iust possessions and inheritance, soe longe as wee comitt nothinge against the statute of forcible entries; for surely wee maie not soe easilie waue our possessions in a matter of such consequence. Thus comendinge my selfe kindly unto yow I remaine your verie louinge freind, Th. Wentworth.

**205.** (*SC*, ii, p. 113) *To Sir Talbott Bowes and Sir Tymothie Hutton knights. Wentworth. 30 Aug. 1623.*

Gentlemen, haueinge by the bearer receaued a lettere from my Lord Treasurer to yow and mee directed, concerninge as it should seeme his Maiesty's tennants within his Mannore of Middleham. I thought good forthwith to send it to yow, and in regard that beinge a meare stranger in the businesse, I expect to receaue my light from your better knowledge both of the persons and places and to gouerne my selfe by your sounder opinions. I doe desire that (if it maie stand with your occasions) wee maie all meet on Friday next by nine of the clocke at the furtherest in Rippon, when (*p. 114*) I will not faile by God's grace to bee with yow there to aduise and resolue togeather what course to hold in the discharginge of our duties in that seruice, wherin I must againe professe my selfe to bee a meare *messciant*; and therfore seeinge it falles to my lott, am right gladd yet that I am matched with two soe worthie upright gentlemen. This is all that for the present I will trouble yow with more then the assurance of my beinge your verie affecconate and assured freind, Th. Wentworth.

**206.** (*SC*, ii, p. 114) *To George Butler Esq. Wentworth Woodhouse. 30 Aug. 1623.*

Sir, I am gladd to heare of the good progresse of your health, which I desire maie soe proceed from strength to strength as that your freinds maie enioy yow a perfect man againe, and that yow maie there settle and bee confirmed (to use the phrase of the courtly progresse) duringe pleasure. I should haue bene gladd to haue seene yow under this poore houell where yow may make accompt to find allwaies a plaine and harty welcome, if your body would haue as yet permitted the hazard of soe tedious a iourney. Therfore as I comend in yow at this time the care yow haue of your selfe, and your holesome warinesse before yow bee perfectly established, soe must I thanke yow for your promisse that wee shall see yow, soe soone as yow are able, which I shall expect with earnestnes, as one much desireinge to see yow both here and sollidly recouered. Yow will giue thes lines leaue to present my seruice to your worthie Ladie, my loue to Mr Christopher, who it seemes is as nice of his paper, as daintie of his presence. To morrowe I (*p. 115*) goe from hence towards Stockhill, where I purpose to waite upon my lord Clifford, where if yow bee not yet, yow shalbee remembred and I pray yow both then and all-waies doe as much for your verie assured freind and affecconate kinsman, Th. Wentworth.

**207.** (*SC*, ii, p. 115) *To Sir Peter Middleton knight. Gawthorpe. 18 Sept. 1623.*

Sir, I dayly find the wisdome of our forefathers in their prouerbs and in this one amongst the rest that ladies' thoughts and lords' purposes change ofte. Not to search then into the reasons of their resolucons, for the harts of Princes are unsearchable (and these are petty ones) I will onely saie that hee is a wise and prudent seruant that knowes their wills and doth them; yet I am not sorry of this alteracon which will occasion my longer stay at this place, and soe giue us a better leasure to enioy one another's companie. Wee shall at our meeting laie our jests soe as wee maie see the best sport of haulkinge that two or three daies will afford us. I will expect yow and Mr Hodgsons at

Harwood stanke to morrowe morninge about nine of the clocke and
here at dinner, where yow maie bee as assured of a chearfull welcome, as of sharpe comons, and if yow bringe your haulks I can
shew yow the covy wherat I flewe my lanner when I lost her, God
bee her good speed. My seruice to your Ladie and soe I shall with as
perfect a hart (as I now convay the profession therof unto yow in
badd paper) approue my selfe to yow and all men to abide in the
perseuerance and truth of beinge your most affecconate kinsman
and assured freind, Th. Wentworth.

**208.** *Wentworth to Christopher Wandesford, 2 October 1623 (Knowler,
i, p. 17; SC, ii, p. 116) on the birth of Wandesford's son.*

**209.** *Wentworth to his brother Michael, 3 October 1623 (Knowler,
i, p. 18; SC, ii, p. 117). He urges him to keep a journal of his
military experiences.*

**210.** *(SC, ii, p. 118) To Francis Burdett Esq. Wentworth Woodhouse.
10 Oct. 1623.*

Sir, I send yow hereinclosed two orders; the one of the Judge of
Assize, the other of the late Sessions at Doncaster, both tendinge
to the endinge (in his due place and season) of a little difference of
opinions in the grantinge and stayinge of an assessment touchinge
Burham bridge in Crauen. Notwithstandinge both which and the
substanciall reasons therin expressed, the bench at Wakefeild gaue
a dyreccon in Court for the payment therof presently to the high
constables of that middle diuision. Neuertheles I see noe cause why
wee should not keepe our slow and graue motion within our orbs
here, as indeed more sutable with the course of payments in
these needy tymes and more neare the sober Spanish garbe, which
maie in tyme become in fashion too. Therfore I desire yow would
send the order of the Sessions to the high constables of Staincrosse,
to whome I beleeue our doctrine will appeare as plausable as theirs.
The order of Assize yow will returne mee by the bearer. This is all
that for the present I will trouble yow with more then the assurance
that I am your right affecconate freind, Th. Wentworth.

**211.** *(SC, ii, p. 119) To Lord Clifford. Wentworth Woodhouse. 12
Oct. 1623.*

My much honored Lord, amongst many other noble fauours which
yow are daily pleased to place upon mee, I rest much bound unto

yow for this last relacon of the good and hopefull successe of your
affaires, God graunt them good speed; it doth I protest cheare upp
my spiritts as that wherupon rests great part of my comforts. Nether
shall your Lordshipp impose any comaund upon mee tendinge to
that end which I will not readely and obseruently betake my selfe
unto, makinge upp the foote of the accompte with truth and zeale,
which must couer a number of my other defects. And beleeue mee,
my Lord, it behoues yow to perseueare in this worke, in regard not
your estate onely, but your iudgment also are at stake and your
neighboures all generally at gaze what will become of your howse,
that as your compasse moues, they maie shape their course there-
after, if the weather fall forth sereane, they will embrace the rocks
for want of a shelter; yet I must tel yow a storme hurrles them out
of their roome, they hoise saile and wilbee noe more fownd neare
the place of daunger. Surely your owne eye is the onely pole starre,
which must (under God's assistance) bring all to a peacable and
quiett harbore, yet in my opinion there wilbee required a great deale
of temper, naie yow must bee content for a seazon to winke at small
faults, for soe spreading a defeccon as it seemes is in your affaires
cannot bee repaired all at once. Faire words, yet by their leaues
betwixt mee and my money they come not; or as Dick Wodroue
I haue heard replied to my Lord Stafford that, haueinge receaued
foule language, threatened to sue him upon a *scandalum magnatum*;
'*Scandalum* (*p. 120*) *fartum*' (quoth Richard) 'paie mee the twelue
pence yow owe mee'. Pardon soe homely an appothegme, because
it is to the purpose; your rents to the kinge til yow see what becomes
of your suites aboue may bee trifled ouer, but hereafter they would
bee orderly paid, the aduantage of tyme driuen beinge but a toy,
where the scandall and noise accompanyinge the deteanure are very
great and lowd. Our gentle Lindamore is now wee saie safely returned, haueing killed two hares with the hownds since his ariuall,
hare enough but noe conny. My iourney to London wilbee later
then I purposed, in regard I must of necessitie take the paines to
goe to Yorke this weeke to gather upp a ward or two for my Lord
of Northumberland and my selfe, which soe disappoints mee here
at home, as I thinke it wilbee Satturday cum seauen night before
I set my selfe sowthwards, by which tyme I expect to receaue your
comaunds, and in them and all the rest approue my selfe your
Lordship's most humble and ready servant, Th. Wentworth.

I desire these lynes maie present my humble dutie to my Lord,
my seruice to my little sweet mistresse.

**212.** (*SC*, ii, p. 120) *To Mr John Tailore. Wentworth Woodhouse. 12 Oct. 1623.*

Sir, I should bee right gladd of soe good company to London, but where yow feare your stay wilbee too longe, I am sorry it is noe longer, for Satturday cum seauen night I feare wilbee the soonest that I shalbee iogginge; if yow bee a good fellow stay the tyme, and then in faith haue with yow. Yow maie indeed bee assured (*p. 121*) that whateuer concernes my Lord Clifford or the howse of Cumbreland, I make it my owne, and I esteme not much lesse of it where it concernes Mr John Tailore, if yow know such a gentleman. Bee merry man and leaue whimperinge, for albeitt the daies of payment bee longe, yet I thinke yow cannot but haue use of much ready money. Well in good sober earnest yow maie recken mee your right affecconate freind, Th. Wentworth.

I pray yow comend mee to your sister, and put her in mind of my pinke seed shee promised mee.

**213.** (*SC*, ii, p. 121) *To Lady Clifford. Wentworth Woodhouse. 12 Oct. 1623.*

My much honored Lady, purposinge Godwillinge to moue towards London about Satturday cum seauen night, I haue dispatched this bearer humbly to signifie the same unto your Ladyship as one ambitious of your comaunds; and, Madame, great personages albeitt seldomer seeme, yet are they for the most part oftener heard of then meaner people. Giue mee leaue therfore to let your Ladyship know, that it is now a great space since yow haue stirred all tongues in your praises for your sweet and judicious carriage towards my Lord and his estate, nether wax they coole but much encreased euen since yow came to Skipton. Beleeue it, Madame, itt will more valewe yow with my Lord's freinds, with your owne freinds, with all good men, then yow can ymagine. And what an honore will it bee unto your Ladyship that where some haue reported this remoue to Skipton would tend to the weakeninge of my lord's estate, and yow allready charged as the occasioner, when that (with the assistance of your care and gouerment) it shalbee the cleare source of order and reformacon (*p. 122*) streaminge forth towards a happy settinge uppe againe of that noble howse in his woonted vigour and lustre. Witt and iudgment barely of themselues are noe great matters, but their power effectually workinge upon a right obiect, is that which attracts from all, respect and reuerence. My Lord and his estate is your (pardon my boldness) proper obiect; lett those greate gifts which God hath giuen yow aboue your fellowes bee still lent and setled therupon, which as it will infallibly add to your honore soe doubtles will it multiply your earthly comforts which God graunt with all other blessings fitting for yow your Ladyshipp's most humble and obleiged poore seruant, Th. Wentworth.

**214.** (*SC*, ii, p. 122) *To Sir George Reresby. Wentworth Woodhouse. 15 Oct. 1623.*

Sir, I understand by my seruant Marris that according to your desire hee hath deliuered yow a trew note of the accompt as itt now stands betwixt us; an accompt indeed of soe longe a dependance, that it is now more then tyme it were brought to a finall conclusion: and that much the rather in regard my occasions for money are at this present more pressinge then ordinary. Wherfore I must now entreate yow, that in requitall of my long forbearance yow would a little straine your selfe that I may haue all my money by Martinmas wherupon I will boldly relye and giue order here in my absence both for the receate and imployments. Then will it likewise bee fitt (the accompt beinge perfected) that both your writings from mee and mine from yow, maie bee absolutely drawne and executed. I desire my seruice maie bee presented to your Lady, and truly wish to yow and youres all increase of health and happines, your very assured freind and affecconate kinsman, Th. Wentworth.

**215.** (*SC*, ii, p. 123) *To Mr Carver and Mr Gamble at Doncaster. Wentworth Woodhouse. 29 Oct. 1623.*

After my harty comendacons to yow both, Wheras I understand that by the late death of Sir John Jackson (for which badd newes I am right sorry) your towne is for the present unprovided of a Recorder; I did embrace this occasion of putting yow in mind of my cosen Mr Rowland Wandesford, that the fittnes and abilitie of the person might bee a future argument of the good and true affeccon I will allwaies beare to any thing that maie bee for the good and benefitt of your corporacon. Itt beinge therfore a place which I assure my selfe my cosen will both kindly accept and uprightly execute, let mee entreate yow to make your freinds in his behalfe, which will I beleeue need little perswasion, in regard I protest in true judgment I hold it to bee the best course they can take in their eleccon to select out soe prime and worthy a gentleman in his profession. Your paines and goodwill herein I shall take verie kindly from yow and bee ready to deserue itt both of yow and all the rest when it shall lye in my power. Soe I rest your right affecconate freind, Th. Wentworth.

**216.** (*SC*, ii, p. 124) *To Thomas Wentworth Esq. Thornhill. 18 Jan. 1624.*

Sir, I am first to craue your pardon, that haue envited yow abroade this bitter unseasonable morninge wherin neuertheles I hope I shall not appeare altogeather inexcusable when the bearer shall lett yow know how hee was dispatched from mee yesternight before super and had bene with yow by one a clocke at night, but that unfortunately hee mist his way in the night. I beseech God yow haue not gott could, which I so much feare, that in good fayth I shall not bee at quiett with my selfe til I maie receaue the certainty from yow therof, the reason which makes mee send this lettere unto yow; nether shall I fully rest satisfied til I see yow my selfe, which shalbee Godwillinge on Tuesday next at night. Sir, I must acknowledge my selfe infinitly much beholden unto yow for your loue and chearfull undertaking (*p. 125*) this journey at my entreaty; but soe haue I bene in a great number of other occasions, which shall iustly challenge (accordinge as they haue deserued) from mee, not onely to your selfe, but (I vowe it too) to your howse, the uttermost of my power and meanes in all tymes wherby I maie testify to your selfe and the world the inviolable truth of my beinge your most assured freind and affecconate cosen, Th. Wentworth.

**217.** (*SC*, ii, p. 123) *To Sir Richard Beaumont knight. Thornhill. 18 Jan. 1624.*

Sir, I came hether with a purpose to haue gone to York upon a sudden noise in the cuntry of an intencon in some to haue elected persons suspected in religion, which to us all would haue beene full of daunger and scandall; which rather then wee shold haue repented when it had bene too late, I would haue bene there as a freeholder to haue giuen my voices to such as I shold haue conceaued to haue bene entyre that waie; albeitt accompanied with a suspicon that might haue bene had of mee, as if I desired the place, which in good faith shold haue bene as farr from mee as I am now from Yorke and soe I writt them (*p. 124*) word to Pontfract truly yesterday. But cominge hether, I perceaue the father and sonne are the men, whose soundnes in religion beinge so well approued to us all, I haue at home here fully my end, and so here haue sett a period to my journey; haueinge no more to say but ride they on with their honore, yet not because of the words of meeknes, for this attempt appeares to mee a point of high courage. Sharpe weather are they like to haue, but I hope they will keepe the freeholders warme with shoutinge and good clarett, and then all wilbee well by the grace of God (as my uncle Blythman's phrase is). I shold haue bene gladd of such a partner at Pontfract as your selfe, I would I were able to make us both, but I feare my selfe, albeitt they haue promissed mee with all assurance; howeuer I shalbee well content and loose noe great labour. I am gladd to heare of your retorne hether amongst us, and will approue my selfe to rest in the truth of beinge, your verie affecconate freind, Th. Wentworth.

**218.** *Wentworth to Lord Clifford, 23 January 1623/4 (Knowler, i, p. 19; SC, ii, p. 125). He urges him to become a member of the Commons.*

**219.** *(SC, ii, p. 126) To Lady Clifford. Wentworth Woodhouse. 23 Jan. 1624.*

My much honored Lady, soe soone as I haue some ayme when I shall beginne my journey sowthwards, itt doth euer well beseeme mee to tender my seruice to your Ladyship and to desire I maie receaue the honore of your comaunds. Munday seauennight then being the daie I intend to moue from this place, I shall humbly craue pardon herby to signify the same to your Ladyship, being most readily and chearfully prepared to execute whatsoeuer yow shall giue mee in charge. I desired to haue presented your Ladyship with some pheasants, but my haulke is sicke and will I thinke within few howers breath her last, a noble death since shee gott it in your seruice, seinge my selfe shall think mine well spent for soe noble a lady, who am imutably Madame your Ladyship's most humbly to bee comaunded, Th. Wentworth.

I beseech yow giue these few lynes leaue to present my faithfull seruice to my sweet, noble, little Mistresse, upon whome I trust God will power forth his fairest graces.

**220.** *(SC, ii, p. 126) To Sir George Calvert. Wentworth Woodhouse. 20 Feb. 1624.*

Sir, not beinge so fully confirmed in my strength as that I am yet able to present yow with a personall attendance, yow will admitt mee to creepe unto yow at least with my lynes; and giue mee leaue (once more (*p. 127*) taken forth of the jawes of death,) to ioye my selfe in the thought that I possesse some place in your respect and to cheare upp my languishinge spiritts by this liberty which I assume of writinge to soe noble and (if I may use a word of soe neare a distance) soe deare a freind. Truly, Sir, the greatest trouble I mett with in my

sicknes was a dreame I had yow were dead, and my greatest reioice-
ment upon my wakinge to find my cheeks full of teares togeather
with my happy errour. Soe moderate were all other affeccons in
mee, eyther concerning my fortune or my life: for hauinge before
setled my estate I thank God to my owne contentment, as one
nether ashamed to liue, nor yet afraid to dye, I did chearfully submitt the whole man to the good pleasure of my maker. I am to giue
yow humble thanks for the remembrance and care yow were pleased
to haue of mee upon the report of my sicknes, and to pray to God to
shower down upon yow and youres, the richnes of his best blessings
and graces, your honore's most humbly to bee comaunded, Th.
Wentworth.

**221.** (*SC*, ii, p. 127) *To Arthur Ingram. Wentworth Woodhouse.
20 Feb. 1624.*

Sir, I sett my pen to paper in regard (the report going at London of
my beinge past hope of recouery) I conceaued it would not bee
altogether displeasinge unto yow to see my owne hand testimony for
the daunger (I praise God) now escaped; soe as I maie now with his
good blessing hope yet to liue to giue yow demonstracon of that
truth and freindshipp, which I haue professed and beare yow, and
before it bee longe to see yow at Westminster. Yet yow must giue mee
leaue to chide with yow concerninge some particulers, espetially that
yow would upon the false report of a disaffected knaue distrust the
integrity and soundnes of that freind, who when the rule of triall
shalbee laid unto him wilbee found as square as the corner stone.
This is the first letter I writte since I was ill and in troth I find my
hand not very steady and by this (*p. 128*) tyme very wearie, I will
therfore make an end, and wrappe upp all in the perseuearance of
my beinge your most assured and affecconate freind, Th. Wentworth.

    Sir, I must still entreate that I maie bee heard before Grice bee put
in the Comission and, if it bee pressed farr, that yow would bee
pleased to present my humble seruice and duty to my Lord Keeper,
relateinge unto him the occasion of my long stay, sicknesse. And that
I make this my humble suite unto him, as beinge well able to make
Grice appeare unworthie to bee in the Comission and that the keepinge him out shalbee a betteringe to the king's seruice in these parts.

**222.** (*SC*, ii, p. 128) *To Christopher Wandesford Esq. Wentworth
Woodhouse. 20 February 1623.*

Gentle Mr Wandesford, the assurance that thes lines will giue yow
of my recouery, praised bee God, will I conceaue bee no unwelcome

newes unto yow, which moued mee by this meanes with the first to
giue yow notice therof. This inclosed after yow haue readd I pray
yow seale downe the labell and deliuer it unto Sir Arthur Ingram. I hope
I shalbee able by Munday cum fortnight to sett forward towards yow,
but I am in great doubt with my selfe, whether I had not better stay
til after Easter before I come, in regard it is likely the howse wilbee
adiourned within a week after my cominge, albeitt I should beginne
my journey so soone as my strength and health will giue mee leaue.
I desire therfore by the bearer that yow would let mee know your
opinion what I had best doe, and that yow would take Sir Arthur
Ingram's aduice therin, as also Mr Secretary Caluert's, unto whome
yow will deliver (together with my seruice) the inclosed. I pray yow
that I maie understand by your letteres the effect of the king's speach,
for upon the perusall of that, togeather with your aduice, I shall
ground my resolucon what to doe. This sicknes, I thanke God, was
much more moderate then that I had in sommer was tweluemonthes,
for my sence and understanding were (*p. 129*) not taken from mee
and in the whole course of it, as little daunger appearinge, as could
bee expected or hoped for in soe acute a dissease. Well, it hath pleased
God in a short tyme to visitt mee with a great deale of sicknesse,
and yet of his goodnesse to deliuer mee out of all, turninge all to
my good; for they haue humbled mee and made mee know my selfe,
which I hope will make mee the better man, and put mee in mind to
serue him more carefully then formerly I haue done. Of his grace
wee liue then and the greatest comfort must bee from our freinds
and the mutuall and true loue wee shold beare one to another, in
which number I esteme your selfe a principall one and assure my
selfe to receaue from yow in exchange the like demonstracon of your
loue and affeccon, wherby noe man shalbee better pleased then your
most assured freind and affecconate kinsman, Th. Wentworth.

I would haue faine writt to yow with my owne penne but my hand
was so weary with writinge these other letteres, as itt would not
wagge. My seruice to my cosen, God's blessinge and mine to my
sweete godsonne.

**223.** (*SC*, ii, p. 129) *To George Butler Esq. Wentworth Woodhouse.
22 Feb. 1624.*

Sir, the sendinge of your lines to my brother Robert hath produced
these, with my many thanks too for your entendment at Hodsocke,
which I heard of, and your actuated kindnes now in sendinge to enquire of my health. Yet aboue all the rest I thanke yow for your
praiers, the incertainty of my health and the sence of my sinnes

makinge mee see that my owne humiliacon under the hand all-mighty of my maker, yea my owne supplicacons for his pardon, are too too imperfect and therfore require the praiers of my freinds to ioine in my assistance; but aboue all, passing ouer other helpes as too weake, these consideracons make mee flee to the sauinge name of Jesus, that being once dipped in the blood of that Lambe slaine from the beginninge and hauinge his righteousnesse imprinted upon my soule, I maie, notwithstandinge that other scarlet dye of my owne transgressions, yet appeare acceptable in the sight and justice of the great and terrible judge. For the state of my present health beinge once more taken out of the graue, it is I praise God better then could bee expected; but consideringe how my body is habituated to (*p. 130*) sicknesse, what maie bee determined upon mee, life or death is I thinke a disputable probleame. For my owne part I am most indifferent, submittinge all to the best pleasure of my good God. In the meane tyme receauinge these visitacons upon the bended knees of my hart as his fatherly correccons to call mee home to his sheepfould, to assure mee too that I am a sonne and noe bastard; yea, valewinge them and judginge them to bee his infinite great mercies enlarged upon mee, for I hope of his grace they will bee the meanes if hee send life to make mee the better liuer, if death that I shalbee the better prepared Christian, prepared with a modest and humble confidence in the truth of his promisses, that there is now noe condemnacon to them that are in Christ, which liue not after the flesh but after the spiritt, which God graunt I maie doe. But alasse whether doe I extend my selfe upon this subiect? Yow are my freind which makes mee the boulder, the more open. My hart is full, which will I hope draw from yow my easier excuse. God blesse yow, God haue yow in his keepinge and send us Heauen at the last, for the things of this world are transitory, not considerable, your euer assured freind and affecconate kinsman, Th. Wentworth.

I pray yow present my seruice to that vertuous good ladie your wife.

**224.** (*SC*, ii, p. 130) *To Lord Darcy. Fetter Lane. 26 April 1624.*

My much honoured Lord, the neare and unexpected losse of your noble sonne hath soe distracted my thoughts with such unquietnesse that I found it a difficulty to settle them in any reasonable temper, or to make use of my penne. I confesse my selfe to beare a great share and burthen of the stocke, and that the greatest comfort I can for the present present to your Lordship is that I am participant, and that deeply, in your iust greife and sorrowe and that I (*p. 131*) iudge

(I protest) my owne losse in him that is now with God, the heauyest next after your Lordship's. Itt is easie for a man in health to counsell one that is sicke, but for one sick man to counsell another more sicke of the same dissease, I now find in my selfe a worke of labour. Surely my Lord, flesh and blood are unapt councellors herein, much lesse my selfe that haue not the imperfeccons therof onely, but the affeccons too sadly workinge and boilinge within mee. I can then say noe other to your Lordship, then that which I hold by my selfe, the wisdome, the goodnes of God, disposeinge all in his determinate counsells for our good, if wee were able soe to apprehend itt thorowe the disordered organes of our soules. That God therfore bee to us all, not onely a God of wisdome and goodnes, but a God of comfort too, that in all these wofull assaults, wee may (thorow him) bee more then conquerours. Hee praies it for your Lordship and for himselfe, that will most obseruantly and deuotedly remaine your Lordship's affecconate kinsman and seruant, Th. Wentworth.

**225.** *Wentworth to Sir Edward Osborne, 4 June 1624* (*Knowler*, i, p. 19; *SC*, ii, p. 131), *giving news of the Amboyna massacre and the French marriage treaty. Postscript omitted by Knowler,* Pray you if you see his lordship present my humble services to my lord Darcy to whome I will write shortly.

**226.** *Wentworth to Sir Gervase Clifton, 5 June 1624* (*Knowler*, i, p. 20; *SC*, ii, p. 132), *giving news of the French match, the treaty with the States General and moves for a breach with Spain.*

**227.** *Wentworth to Wandesford, 17 June 1624* (*Knowler*, i, pp. 21–23; *SC*, ii, pp. 134-38). *He sends news of the dissolution of the Virginia Company, the troops for the Netherlands, the French treaty, the breach with Spain and the charge to the judges to enforce the recusancy laws.*

**228.** (*SC*, ii, p. 138) *To Lord Clifford. Thornhill. 7 July 1624.*

My much honoured Lord, The last letter I writt to any was to your Lordship yet I am now I praise God in hope it shall neuer bee deliuered; for indeed as I was then it might well haue proued the last I should euer haue writt in this world, *homo bulla.* I receaued the other daie a strange message from Sir John Sauile, togeather with a late letter writt to him by your Lordship, which with all his circumstances I shall breifly relate in this paper. Sir John came on Munday last to Ledstone to see mee as hee affirmed, but not findinge of mee there, hee desired to speake to Richard Marris and, after askinge how I did, hee willed him to remember his loue unto mee: 'and tel your Maister, I haue receaued here this letter from my Lord Clifford, which I haue here sealed upp (*p. 139*) with my owne seale; I cannot answer it my selfe, by reason my hand shaketh and the matter is such, that I may not trust a secretary therwith; therfore tel your Maister I pray him to open and read itt and to retorne my lord this answer from mee; that for the matter sett forth in his letter, there was in mee noe such intencon nor euer so much as a thought in mee that waie. That George Clapham is my kinsman indeed, but that hee neuer had from mee any such comission as is menconed in his Lordship's letter and, if hee haue done any such thinge of himselfe, I shall let him know hee hath not dealt well with mee; all which I desire your Maister from mee to assure his Lordship to be true.' This is that and asmuch as I was desired to signify unto your Lordship and yow wilbee pleased to consider what I shall of your mind returne by waie of reply to Sir John by word of mouth, or whether yow wilbee pleased to write your answer to himselfe, or such a letter to mee, as I maie comunicate with him; wherin I expect your dyreccon, and that receaued shall readily apply my selfe unto itt. But thus much if it maie please yow, for my owne opinion: I did neuer thinke Sir John soe unwise as to attempt any such matter, or to bestow soe unaduisedly three thowsand pownds with his daughter. Besides, my Lord's mistakes in reportes are soe frequent, and such the power of beleife in matters which men themselues greedilie desire, (and such I take marriage to bee to your father that which I will warrant yow hee is (for the present) most intent upon) as in truth I doe beleiue there was noe reall designe in Sir John that waie, nether is it I protest allmost credible beinge such a contradiccon in itselfe, unlesse yow haue better demonstracon and argument for your suspicon, then my Lord's various reportes and chimeraes in this kind. My Lord, I shall heare from yow by this bearer, in the meane tyme and euer I shall wish your Lordship the encrease of all honour and happines, in your selfe, in your Lady, in my little Mistresse, and which is more in a fruitfull and rich posterity, your Lordship's most humblie to bee comaunded, Th. Wentworth.

**229.** *Wentworth to Sir George Calvert, 14 August 1624 (Knowler, i, p. 23; SC, ii, p. 140), sending compliments and describing the king's hunting at Rufford.*

**230.** (*SC*, ii, p. 141) *To Christopher Wandesford Esq. Gawthorpe. 31 Aug. 1624.*

Sir, as I was purposinge to answer one of your letters, in comes your last by poore Peter, who noe marvaile though his staie as yow saie made him scratch his taile when as hee came home with neuer a penny in his purse, but this is not strange yow will saie (beinge turned southerne man) beinge the comon case of the North, and soe put us of with a frumpe for our pouertie. Goe too leavinge your former, I will now betake my selfe to your latter letter and William Sommers-like strike him that is next mee. Your charitie it seemes partakes nothinge of the temper of the climate where yow now are, when it is soe cold, as that the ingenious confession of a plaine cuntryman can worke noe beliefe with yow, yet your iealousie and distrust sauoures of a sowtherne crafte, rather then of northerne innocencie, soe as I maie saie, yow haue an anagrame of an honest man, as the English poett (*p. 142*) said of the wenche, the yellownesse of her haire was in her teeth; the warmth which should bee in your charitie, is fallen and kindled in your braine, which causeth your suspition and mistrust to bee so actiue and the other so little feruent. But as it had bene more gracefull for the wench if the cullours had bene right placed, so were it in yow better Christianity this heate, this subtilty, this coldnes, had wrought upon the contrary obiects. Yow charge mee that I writt of stagges and foxes from Rufford where yow say I might haue sunge of secretaries displaced, messages dissavowed. But, by your leaue, that was not so sutable to my low condicon, nay if yow had bene so well readd in my domesticke Ouid as yow might, had yow but grace, yow might haue found a quaint art in that for-bearance *Triste petis munus, quis enim sue proelia victus commemorare velit*? God helpe yow man there is aswell Cuntry as Court crafte; But that yow may know wee liue not here altogether in a palpable, in an Egiptian darknes, bee yow aduertized that the French Ambassador came back to Darby with a fresh alarume that all should goe on with all persuearance, onely that the hands were to bee changed thorowe which it is to passe and so the match presently to bee concluded. What your more refined witts will make of this, as workinge upon your proper subiect the affaires of Princes and Potentates, I know not, but wee plaine Swaines after our ordinary manner resort to an old adage and cry out that there is art in daub-inge. One saieth hee cannot beleiue such a rubb can bee the prog-nosticacon of a speedy dispatch, but rather of a slow march *Et incessis passu de vulnere tarde*, as the Poett saieth of Euriciden fol-lowinge her husband Orpheus out of hell. Another hee saieth, that surely this suddaine change is not produced, actuated by any reall intencon firmly to knitt againe, but entertained a while with a *souplesse du main* (to use their owne phrase) that soe the matter may rather fall in peeces gently by degrees, then abruptly to fall in sunder at once; els what meaneth dissauowinge of ministers and comittment if (*p. 143*) there were any meaninge to performe that which by them was promissed? and that which is worse to bee liked, those seeminge agreements made whilest there might bee some feare of sowtheringe with Spaine, but now the blame laid upon seruants when all hope is cut of from that (so much by the French apprehended) coniunccon. *Passato el periculo, Gabato el sancto.* Others saie, that these are vailes cast ouer the affairs of great states, to delude our sightes that looke after them at a distance, which the looser is well enough content too should passe, and take them for payment, rather then that their losse and preiudice should draw a prophanacon upon them, if all were laid open and plaine to vulger eyes; Archelouslike when Hercules had pulled of one of his hornes, *Capitis quoque fronde saligna, aut super imposita celatur arundine damnum.* Yow blame mee that I am not so well readd in Ouid's *Arte amandi*, as in his other more excellent works and by that tyme I had readd your post script I found yow your selfe in the *Metamorphosis*, well passer [sic], these matters are but apparitions, shadowes; in which case Narcissus gaue good counsell if hee could haue followed it when hee had done, *Tecum venitque manetque, tecum discedet si tu discedere possis.* 'Soe sigma for that, and black and blew for all the rest', quoth Sir Arthur Ingram. Yow haue hereinclosed a letter to the Secretarie, where yow will see I know how to write to euery man in his kind; to yow as a statist, to him as a good cuntry gentleman of Thistleworth. God haue yow and all youres in his blessed keepinge and that I maie find yow all in health, that by yonge expression remaine, your most assured freind and affecconate kinsman, Th. Wentworth

I pray yow tell Mr Peasley that Mr Minne promissed mee some pinke seed the last yeare; if I might haue some this, I shold hold my selfe beholden unto them both, one for the gift, the other for his good remembrance.

**231.** *Wentworth to Sir George Calvert, 31 August 1624 (Knowler*, i, p. 24; *SC*, ii, p. 144). *He sends uncertain news of the French match.*

**232.** (*SC*, ii, p. 144) *To Sir Peter Freschvile. Wentworth Woodhouse. 7 Sept. 1624.*

Sir, I might not let passe this oportunity unaccompanied with these few lynes, without a tacite acknowledgment of omission, which I shall (euen in the least) vigilantly avoid to yow wards, seinge I owe not to yow alone, but your howse too, an accompt (*p. 145*) of freindshippe, not onely stirringe within mee by reason of blood and kindred, but also convaied unto mee by dissent, yea recomended. Yow will admitt this paper then to giue yow a short yet true testimony how gladsome the newes of your health wilbee unto mee, how much I desire the constant continewance of it and how readily I shall performe those upright duties, which euery man expects from those which are to them, as I shall euer appeare plainly to bee to yow, euen your affecconate kinsman and assured freind, Th. Wentworth.

Yow wilbee pleased to present my seruice to your noble Lady.

**233.** (*SC*, ii, p. 145) *To Sir Edward Osborne Bart. Wentworth Woodhouse. 7 Sept. 1624.*

Sir, I doe allwaies unwillingly heare of any occasions that hinder mee from the companie of my freinds, but am more then ordinarily affected to bee seperated from such as your selfe whome I respect (to say no more) in a much stronger degree then others; and that too by reason of my Ladie's indisposicon, which in good fayth causeth mee to apprehend it with much greife and that albeitt I honore her truly more in relation to yow then her; for in my beliefe the daunger of losse is more on your side then hers, who if God should visitt with that incurable malady yow write of, at the last shold make exchange of a momentary contentment at the best for an ymortall crowne, a great waight of glory. Yet I trust God will send her perfect health and yow the blessinge of enioyinge many happy yeares with her, which I shall pray for and for the present haue sent this bearer to bringe mee the good newes of both your good healthes I trust, which shalbe to no freind yow haue more welcome, then to your verie assured affecconate freind, Th. Wentworth.

**234.** (*SC*, ii, p. 146) *To Sir Henry Vane. Wentworth Woodhouse. 11 Oct. 1624.*

Sir, I heare that there is a comission on foote within the honore of Pontfract for assessinge the coppiholders' fines there, wherin Sir

Henry Sauile is a comissioner. I take it to bee an old one, longe since issued out from the Prince's Counsell, but I maie bee mistaken, forbearinge to bee too inquisitiue for the present, least it might bee obserued; yet by reason of Sir Henrye's goinge upp instantly to London, I doe a little misdoubt hee will endeauore to renew if not enlarge his employment and trust in that affaire. Therfore I must make bould to entreate yow (itt beinge one of the principall flowers of the Stewardshippe and wherin if I bee not mistaken I shalbee able to doe his highnes service) to stay all matters concerninge that honore, til my cominge upp to London, which shall by God's grace bee before the second of Nouember, that soe I maie haue tyme more fully to speake with yow and to use the best meanes I can for my selfe. Yow see how your former respect and kindnes towards mee draweth on this your further trouble, which yow wilbee pleased to accept of, in regard there shall not any (in truth) bee more vigilant to meritt it from yow, or that shall more truly and sincearly approue himselfe to bee your very affecconate and oblieged freind, Th. Wentworth.

I thanke yow for your pacience since yow were last with us.

**235.** (*SC*, ii, p. 146) *To Sir Walter Pye knight. Wentworth Woodhouse. 11 Oct. 1624.*

Sir, I am to bee a sutor to yow in the behalfe of a yong kinsman of mine, who by the late death of his father, my full cosine germaine, is now in ward to his Maiestie and that with the more earnestnes, in regard I conceaue both the good of himselfe and subsistence in his estate are deeply engaged and at the stake. There are two great parties which will put in for the wardshippe, his mother, sister to the late Lord Morley and her freinds on the one side, (*p. 147*) the ward's grandmother and my antte, my lord Darcy, my selfe and other of his father's kindred on the other side. Now, Sir, my humble request unto yow is, that yow wilbee a meanes that noe writt of *Diem clausit*, nor comission in nature thereof, maie goe forth before the second of Nouember, by which tyme Godwillinge I shall attend yow; which I doe well trust yow wilbee pleased to graunt mee, in respect his Maiesty is no waies preiudiced by soe short a stay and for that (trust mee) there are such maine obiections against the mother (hauinge spedd herselfe allready of a second husband not beinge two monthes since my cosen died), as I doe more then assure my selfe, shee shall neuer bee thought a person capable of such a trust, which will apparantly (should shee preuaile) bee an utter ouer-throwe to the poore child and his posteritie. The onely motiue which could haue stirred mee to interpose in this busines, of my selfe rather tendinge to my owne home affaires, then to put my selfe into such thankles offices, except strained thereunto aswell by necessitie, as (in this) by the naturall obligacon I haue to so neare and fatherlesse, I maie saie too, motherles kinsman. Sir, I feare I grow tedious; God therfore haue yow in his blessed protection, your verie assured and affecconate freind, Th. Wentworth.

**236.** (*SC*, ii, p. 147) *To Sir Arthur Ingram. Wentworth Woodhouse. 11 Oct. 1624.*

Sir, I writt to Sir Henry Slingsby not long since what answer I receaued from my lord Clifford concerninge your sonne Sir Arthur, which to doe him right was in truth as good as could be desired; which to effect before my cominge uppe I doe the rather now desire, in respect of the strange false reports that fly here of yow interpretinge euerie thinge to the worst. Therfore I praie yow quietlly send mee downe a new writt and I wilbee answerable unto yow for it, Godwillinge, when I shall next see yow. As for the Stewardshippe, I pray yow let no tyme slippe, but dispatch it assoone as yow can; and in regard I doubt your name will not soe well passe with the Prince as myne, I doe much desire yow would moue my Lord Chamberlaine in that regard, that yow might use my name in trust (*p. 148*) for yow, least it might receaue some rubb that waie. Yow see how plaine I am with yow, but I doubt not but yow will rightly interprett mee, the inwardnesse of freindshippe betwixt yow and mee assuringe mee it can admitt no badd one. I praie yow do nothinge for Leedes til I speake with yow, I can tel yow more then yow yet know. Yow wilbee pleased these lynes maie present my seruice to your noble Lady and the rest of your good companie. God strengthen yow and blesse yow, your most assured affecconate freind, Th. Wentworth.

**237.** (*SC*, ii, p. 148) *To Christopher Wandesford Esq. Wentworth Woodhouse. 11 Oct. 1624.*

My Ambassadour resident, I heare soe slowly from yow, that I conceaue yow are at ease, and therfore will by these my fresh instruccons sett the wheele a goinge, least it might grow reasty and rustie for want of use. These letters (when yow haue readd) yow will do mee the kindnes to close upp and deliuer and gett mee an answer from Sir Walter Pye; and I pray yow now duringe my absence haue an eye upon that busines, that all maie rest in peace til my cominge and then I assure yow I shall ringe such a peale, as I perswade my selfe, will not bee verie tunable in their eares that do so much study themselues how to make a praie of the innocent poore child. Beleeue it, my hart is much upon it and I will trie all the freinds I haue in England before hee haue any such mischiefe befall him, as to light into his mother's hands or her freinds' who haue allwaies so much nelgected and disrespected his father. Yow will deliuer this letter to Sir Henry Fane, and returne mee his answer. This other letter to Sir Arthur and presse him, I praie yow, to dispatch with Sir Edward Leech and that the graunt maie bee renewed in my name upon such pretence as is more fully expressed in my letter unto him. Yow maie aduise herein with Sir Henry Fane, who is acquainted with the busines, and (if I bee not farr wide) will giue yow all the helpe and furtherance hee can; but bee close, for this is I tel yow *El mio secreto.* Here yow haue a little sprinklinge of Italian, but as for Latine not a word, since it seemes your store in that language is (*p. 149*) all spent and know except yow afford mee some in your letter, yow gett none in myne, reservinge it for more sublimated spiritts then moue in your heauy fatt carcaise; yet beginne assoone as yow dare, I will a warrant yow haue as hott as yow bringe and soe yow shall find itt. My Lady Osburne continewes still sicke, little hope of amendment, for which I am right hartely sorry, a word or two in the other side if yow turne ouer. Somethinge I must write here to performe my promis on the other side, albeitt I know not well what more then that yow will admitt these lines to present my seruice to my cosen your wife, togeather with my blessing to my tender godsonne. Wee haue here his corrivall Thomas Radcliffe, who hath allready learned to call mee Tom, and was this very morninge laughinge, gapeinge and dauncinge in his father's armes to a piper that was playinge, to the great joie and comfort of the spectators, especially his father I will assure yow. These are such narrations as yow are to expect from us in these cuntry tabernacles, but wee looke there should bee wouen in your loomes aboue stuffe of a more pretious kind, more gayish and glitteringe at least, albeitt in truth not so rich, nor of soe vallewable a mettall. Therfore yow maie pride your selfe in those misticall constellacons, wee please our selues more safely in these naturall plaine coniunccons and marke anon who proues the wyser men. I haue allmost finished my this yeare's building, which dun, I shall then apply my selfe with such sages as your selfe to build upp the polliticall walles and repaire the ruinous breaches of the comon wealthes and I trow shew yow too that deseruedly I hold my selfe a maisterpeece in architecture and turne 2 or 300 of yow to scoole againe, like a companie of poore

fellowes as yow are. Am I not now as good as my word? and haue I
not enlarged my penne ouer this side too and draw out my lynes
as lastingly as a silke worme? Beleeue it, I thinke few men could
haue made so much of so little and so fare yow well, your euer most
assured freind and affecconate kinsman, Th. Wentworth.

I had no sooner writt that on the other side, but in comes your
letter of the first of this month and in it the newes of a prorogacon,
a great argument in my weake judgment that the French match
proceeds. This hath changed my resolucon, for I intend now (*p. 150*)
to staie here a fortnight longer in attendance upon my owne priuate,
except I heare somthinge from yow which alter mee and in the meane
tyme send yow here againe poore Peter to scratch his taile at your
seruice. I like no deale at all these Spanish streames which runne like
those of Siloa, so calme, so slowe, so still, wherin I feare wee shall
find our selues ouer head and eares before wee bee aware, encreasing
upon us like those waters in the Prophett, that were first to the
ancles, then to the knees, so to the loynes, and lastly hee measured
and the waters were risen, waters to swimme in, a riuer that could
not bee passed ouer. Naie, I thinke the praier that was made for the
daughter of Erisichthon hath beene made and graunted for us: *Sic
mare compositum, sic sit tibi piscis in unda, Credulus ut nullos nisi
fixos sentiat hamos.* This is othergesse [*sic*] stuffe then your threed
bare *Nil mihi rescribis.* But *quid moror externis*, espetially haueinge
so much to doe at home? The Stewardshipp of Pontfract lyes very
conueniently for mee and is a thinge I verie much desire, togeather
with the maistershippe of the game within that honore and keeper-
shippe of the Parke. Sir Henry Sauile is encroachinge on the one
side, endeauouringe to gaine an imployment in assessing of the
coppiholders' fines and Sir John Sauile, niblinge on another side,
laboures to gett a superintendencie ouer the game; his meanes is
Sir Henry Fane. To preuent both these is my ayme, the waie wilbee
to passe the Stewardshipp with all speed possible with large words,
and therin I pray yow presse forwards and aduise with Sir Arthur
Ingram, and secondly to stopp all graunts in the meane tyme, which
must bee by Sir Henry Fane, wherin I praie yow to sollicite him,
especially to slacken his course in gettinge Sir John his comaund ouer
the game; how that I doe wholly relye upon him and that it would
bee preiudiciall to mee if eyther should preuaile. If this busines could
bee any waies furthered by my cominge, let mee know, and I will
not bee longe from yow; it beinge indeed a thinge most conuenient
for mee in these parts. For my cosen Danby I pray yow haue a
speciall care that nothinge stirre; deale effectually with Mr Attorney
therin and let him know that I so much (*p. 151*) trust in him (this

WP—P

being a thing which may bee respected without any preiudice at all
for three weeks or a month) as that I shall stay in the orderinge of
my affaires here so much longer then otherwaies I would haue dun.
But if I needs must, I will instantly come upp rather then faile in
the duty I owe to so neare a kinsman and therfore that I maie by
yow receaue his aduise and dyreccon, letting him know notwithstandinge, that hee shall doe mee a most especiall curtesie, if hee
cast the busines so that I maie stay here a month before I come upp,
without preiudice to the ward. Let mee, I pray yow, heare from yow
and receaue your opinion in both these matters with what speed
yow can. Poore Peter will stay for it; some conscience yow should
use, least hee leaue himselfe no skynne upon his breech, which is
sure to paie for it if yow make him stay longer then ordinarie. What
yow doe for yong Danby shalbee deserued by him (I trust) hereafter; and the comittees will (if yow please) make yow the maister
of the game in Massamshire dureinge his minoritie, a simple pleasure
for the Squire of Kirklington, if yow well obserue itt.

**238.** (*SC*, ii, p. 151) *To Elizabeth Danby. Wentworth Woodhouse.*
11 Oct. 1624.

My good Antt, I was upon Thursday last with my Lord Darcy and
had full conference with his Lordship touchinge my cosen your
grandchild, whome I find verie carefull ouer the child and his estate,
verie desirous and willinge that your selfe, my cosen Wentworth,
and I should ioyne in the procuringe of the wardshippe and comittment of the lands, whatsoeuer others cunningly haue pretended to
the contrary. Soe as this daie seauennight wee shall meet againe
and agree of all these things. And for my owne part when I consider
the manie obieccons which are against the mother and his freinds
on that side, I cannot doubt the obtaininge our desires both for
body and lands. In the meane tyme I haue writt to Mr Attorney of
that Court, to stay all proceedings til my cominge upp (a curtesy I
perswade my selfe hee will not deny mee) and in all his other affaires
approue my selfe (by God's grace) a faithfull freind and (*p. 152*)
vigilant kynsman to him and his estate. For your so suddaine a
sale of Swinton, beinge a Mannor which lyeth so conueniently to
the rest of the estate, under fauour, I can in no sort approue of; it
beinge first fitt to consider thorowly with your freinds whether it
bee to bee saued and preserued for the heire by some other good
meanes before yow part from such a conueniencie. And beleiue it,
Antt, those that presse and aduise this hasty saile, study themselues
much more then the good eyther of your selfe or grand child, and

so as their mouthes bee made, care not what become of all the rest
and surely sleights on the poore men yow mencon in your letter to
importune and sollicite yow by their clamours to enforce yow to this
present resolucon of settinge your selfe at quiett by present payment
in any fashion, before yow should haue the oportunitie and benefitt
to aduise with your freinds. I like well your purpose of payment and
that none of his seruants, or others engaged, should loose a penny
by your sonne; God forbid I should thinke or counsell otherwaies,
but I doe not like this waie of theires to wind yow to it. I desire
your actions herein maie bee made plainly to appeare to bee proceedinge from piety in your selfe, rather then out of any legall duty;
rather induced unto it by the franknes and noblenes of your owne
nature, then subtlely wrought unto it by their witt and craft. Surely
in things of this nature hee that giues himselfe leaue to understand
fully what hee hath to doe, before hee bringe it unto action, hath
allwaies most thanks of the parties whome it concerneth and most
comendacons from forrainers. But the truth is yow maie in no sort
sell those lands before composicon bee made, for so yow shall
precipittatedly take away a maine motiue of abatement in the
valewe aswell of body as lands by shewinge the greatnesse of the
ancestor's debts. Therfore I pray yow, Antt, consent not to this sale
at this tyme, let the creditors know, they shall in fitting and due
tyme, bee honestly and really discharged, but they must bee contented to leaue the way and season to your owne election. And
rather then yow should part from such a flower of the estate, take
upp money (*p. 153*) at use and lay mee to stake, for letting mee haue
but collateral securitie upon your Mannore of Swinton, I wilbee
bound with yow for 1500[li] and hereafter once within a yeare, wee
shall by God's grace haue tyme at leasure to debate and resolue how
all turnes maie bee serued in order, honesty and honore. Yow wilbee
pleased to pardon my length, my scriblinge, for indeed my tooles
are not good. The allmighty haue yow in his blessed guidance and
keepinge; your most affectionate nephew to doe yow seruice, Th.
Wentworth.

**239.** *Wentworth to Sir Geo Calvert, 12 October 1624* (*Knowler*, i,
p. 24; *SC*, ii, p. 153), *about the Prorogation and French Treaty.*

**240.** (*SC*, ii, p. 154) *To Sir John Sauile knight. Thornhill. 23 Oct. 1624.*

Sir, the warrant yow write to mee of I cannot call to mind, my clarke
being at Woodhus. It is true indeed that I did not longe agoe signe

one or two of that nature, as I doe twenty in a yeare, beinge thinges of ordinary course, but I doe not precisely remember this perticuler; yet I am well assured, if there were any such, that I did as little imagine it had concerned yow as the kinge of Spaine; and when it had appeared unto mee to relate to yow, I should haue done nothinge that yow could haue taken amisse from mee. Now for the other part of your letter, which indeed is fitt I answer. In good fayth I neuer spake with any man in this matter, nor with Elmhirst in all my life, beinge one I know not so much as by sight, nor was I in any the least kind made acquainted with the meritts of the cause, nor whome it concerned. Yet do I not wonder if such meane fellowes sow such tares betwixt gentlemen of qualety, thinking to wind themselues closer upp to their owne ends by such opposicons. For I haue found the like by experience and your selfe by reason of your yeares I doubt not much more. And therfore I do well assure my selfe yow are too iuditious to regard what they say and farr from doinge mee the iniury to beleiue I should deale so indiscreetly or unworthily: for I must (*p. 155*) needs saie I should take such a beliefe as a great wronge unto mee from any man aliue. I will detaine yow no longer from your other affaires, but here rest your assured freind, Th. Wentworth.

**241.** (*SC*, ii, p. 155) *To Countess of Shrewsbury. Wentworth Woodhouse. 28 Oct. 1624.*

My most honoured Lady, when I last attended your Ladyship yow were pleased to dyrect mee to enforme yow how my sister Sauile made her demaund of one hundreth pounds of your Ladyship out of Bryerley; which writings I haue since perused, and I find that my Lord your husband did by his indenture convaie all the lands in Brierley then in the tenure of Marshall and Norton unto my sister dureinge her life, if my brother Sauile should dye in his father's life tyme, as will plainly appeare unto yow, if yow please to looke upp the counterparts. So as there beinge (by that deed) due unto her fifty pownds at Pentecost was tweluemonthes, as much at Martynmas last, and as much at Pentecost last, yow wilbee endebted to my sister at Martynmas next two hundreth pownds, which I hope your Ladyship (out of your woonted goodnes) will presently giue direccon for payment, my sister beinge in truth much straitened by reason shee wants this, the greatest part of her yearly meanes to mantaine her selfe by. And wheras your Ladyship did thinke the whole lands beinge now in my sister's owne possession, there was reason this rent should cease; under fauour it holds not in any conscience, my sister not haueinge (to her owne use) any penny out of that estate, but is accomptable to my nephew and (in the word of an honest man) rather worse then better in her owne poore priuate, by the death of ould Sir George Sauile. Now further giue mee leaue to trouble your Ladyship with a few lynes concerning my selfe. I doe stand bound for yow at London in two seuerall bonds, one for 1000$^{li}$, another for 300$^{li}$ principall debte, (*p. 156*) wherin I well know it is not your mind I should bee preiudiced, yet I haue no counter securitie sauinge onely Pontfract parke, farr short in valew of such a some. Therfore I must desire yow would bee pleased to giue mee further securitie, or (which I had much rather) that yow would pay in the money this next Terme, or at least a full halfe therof. And since my pen is thus farr dipped in matter of money, I shalbee bould to put your Ladyship in mind of a hundreth pownds which was due to mee Whitsontide last and as yet unpaid; wherfore I humblie beseech yow to dyrect Mr Baldwine that hee pay itt presently, for in good fayth my occasions are so pressinge that I maie want it no longer. Lastly, Madame, not long since Sir John Sauile and I fell in speach as touchinge his beinge last in Pontfract parke; I told him I wondered much at him that hee would giue iust cause of offence unprouoked by your Ladyship. His answer was that beinge trusted by the Prince, and there seeinge such shamefull spoile of wood, hee could not but say somthinge. Yet by what hee spake at partinge they might well understand hee meant to doe your Ladyship no ill office, for that hee willed your seruant Babthorpe or Booth to remember him to yow, and to assure yow hee would bee as ready to doe yow seruice, as any gentleman in Yorkshire, which if yow please to accept, hee is willinge yet to make appeare unto yow and so wished mee to signify unto your Ladyship from him, with desire that hee might heare (by mee) how yow tooke it. Now Madame I know yow are best able to aduise your selfe and that nothing can bee added by mee, yet in my poore opinion, it were no judgment to prouoke further a man of his spiritt, but rather (upon his ouerture) to close faire with him againe; espetially when I assure yow, your keepers are verie obnoxious to complaints in that kynd, I meane for spoile of woods. And which is worse, they haue iustified to Sir John that they doe it with your priuitie and that they haue told yow they were not able to pay so great a rent, but by such fall and sale of woods; which beleiue it being (*p. 157*) pressed by such an aduersary who both can and will doe it, (if matters bee not calmed betwixt yow) would sound ill at the Prince's board and might produce the like effect. Therfore if yow would bee pleased understanding thus much by mee, to giue mee leaue, or whome els yow think more fitt, to take knowledge of this faire waie of giuinge yow satisfaction, and seinge yow now perceaue yow had not bene enformed of all the truth, yow are willinge to accept of his respectiue offer; and as a farther testimony of it from him, yow expect that hee should forbeare to meddle with putting in any keepers there to the preiudice of your lease, (which yow might not endure), or to draw any thinge concerninge the same into question, beinge well able to iustify yourselfe in each perticuler; which not doubtinge (as well beseeming him) but hee would obserue, your game and keepers should bee free for him in all decent and fittinge manner. This in good fayth I thinke would free yow from a great deale of disquiett and therfore I beseech yow thinke well of it, and let mee know how or whether I shall proceed any further herein. Your Ladyship will pardon my length, which putts mee in mind to conclude this letter with my praiers for your health and happines, Your Ladyship's affecconate kinsman and humble seruant, Th. Wentworth.

**242.** (*SC*, ii, p. 157) *To the Earl of Holderness. Aston. 1 Nov. 1624.*

Right honorable, wheras by the late death of Mr Danby his sonne and heire is fallen in ward to his Maiestie and your Lordship (as wee heare) become a sutor for the same. Wee, beinge the freinds and neare kynsmen of the ancestors unto whome hee in his life tyme desired the (*p. 158*) trust and care of the child and estate might bee comitted, assuringe our selues, if yow were rightly enformed of the true valewe of his body and lands, your Lordship would neuer cast your eye, or trouble his Maiestie in soe small a matter, haue desired the bearers to attend yow, truly to make knowne the meannesse therof, both in regard of the grandmother's iointure, the mother's thirds, the lands of best vallewe in lease duringe the mynoritie, the debtes and the yonger children's portions, which are all to bee discharged and in some manner prouided for out of a poore surplusage. Wherin as our principall end is to doe your Lordship seruice by diuerting yow from a sute of so triuiall a nature, so yow will bee pleased to giue beliefe thus farr unto us that wee would not use these gentlemen to abuse yow, but that wee wilbee ready to make appeare unto your Lordship the truth of that, which by their good meanes wee shall for the present comunicate unto yow at any tyme hereafter, when yow shall require it from us. Thus leauinge it to your better consideracon and desireinge yow would bee pleased to let us know your further purpose herein, wee rest Your Lordship's humble seruants, John Darcy, Th. Wentworth.

**243.** (*SC*, ii, p. 158) *To Lord Darcy. Wentworth Woodhouse. 2 Nov. 1624.*

My much honoured Lord, I haue herewith sent your Lordship a draught of a letter to Mr Beckwith for yow to signe, as your Lordship dyrected mee to doe yesterdaie, which will I hope gaine us six monthes tyme of aduisement, without any preiudice to my Antt, who was to haue sold it for fifteene hundreth pownds outright, two parts in hand and a third part at halfe yeare daie. I tould your Lordship that some of her seruants presse her to sell other of her lands also, as Pott, which lyes in the very hart of his estate in (*p. 159*) Massomshire; some others moue her to lease them, which will much preiudice the child and aduance their sinister ends, if they bee not tymely preuented. Maie it therfore please your Lordship to write your letter to my Antte, as I shall doe one also to the like effect, that shee would neyther resolue to sell or lease those lands, without some of us, her freinds, priuitie and aduise, but seasonably discerne those that would thus worke their owne plotts upon her and auoid their snares and traines. I assure yow I heare, if Pott were sould, Massamshire were utterly maihmed. I haue taken a course that such persons as wilbee materiall wittnesses may bee sent upp to London and bee there against the daie (Godwillinge), onely Mr Hopton is now in Westmerland and will not retorne before Andrewtide, so wee are like to want him. I found here yesternight another letter from my cosen Wandesford wherin hee writes that Mr Attorney of the Wardes hath allready shewed his respect to us, in disswadinge my lord of Holdernesse from labouringe his sute and hath to my lord's sollicitor professed his auersnes unto my lord therin. I trust in God his goodnes to the child wilbee such as shall dyrect and guide all his affaires to his future comfort and preseruation of himselfe and howse. This is all that for the presente I will trouble yow with, more then the assureance that I am Your lordship's affecconate kinsman and seruantt, Th. Wentworth.

**244.** (*SC*, ii, p. 159) *To Mr — Beckwith. Aston. 2 Nov. 1624.*

Mr Beckwith. Wee are to thanke yow for the respect yow haue showen us in forbearinge to conclude the purchaise of Swintonn without our priuitie, seinge it cannot (as wee conceaue) bee (*p. 160*) presently sould without apparant preiudice to our cosen Danby, the ward, in his composicon with his Maiestie. Neuerthelesse, haueinge a iust care that his father's debtes shold bee paied, as is for his honour and creditt, wee shall giue our consents and thinke yow deale

soe with the ward, as wee in his behalfe shall iudge our selues
to bee beholden unto yow, if takinge a morgage of the thinge, yow
would laie forth upon it 1000$^{li}$ for six monthes, condiconed that at
the six monthes' end, eyther yow to haue your money paid with
consideracon, or els payinge 500$^{li}$ more, to haue the inheritance in
fee. Which, as it would bee (wee assure our selues) noe losse to yow,
soe would it giue us tyme to aduise what were best for the ward and
bee a meanes to preuent any suddaine or hasty resolucon. Which,
consideringe the wardshippe is not yet disposed and that there are
other competitors, might bee very inconuenient to the child and verie
blameworthie in us. Thus desiringe by the bearer to receaue your
answer herein, wee bidd yow hartely farewell, your louinge freinds,
John Darcy, Th. Wentworth.

**245.** (*SC*, ii, p. 161) *To the Countess of Shrewsbury. Wentworth
Woodhouse. 10 Nov. 1624.*

My most honoured Ladie, beinge pressed by the occasions of a
neare kinsman, my cosen Danby, to enter my appearance at London
before Satturday cum seauennight and neuertheless (which I did
not so much as dreame of) importuned exceedingly to bee at Gains-
brough on Munday next, where I happen to bee named a comissioner
betwixt the Lady Willoughby and her brother Sir George Manners,
I am soe exceedingly and unexpectedly strained in tyme, that I shall
not possibly bee able to see your ladyship at Rufford before my going
sowthwards, as in truth I had fully purposed and as was most (*p. 162*)
fitt I should haue done. Therfore trustinge to gaine (upon these iust
grounds) your Ladyship's pardon, I haue notwithstandinge thought
good hereinclosed to send yow a coppie of the deed examined by the
originall, wherby my sister claymes the hundreth pounds from your
Ladyship forth of Bryerley. And seinge I shall not in person attend
your Ladyship's pleasure and comaunds that I may receaue them
by this bearer, togeather with an answer of those particulers, wherin
I was bould by my last letters to moue yow unto. My sister remembers her humble dutie and seruice to your Ladyship, my selfe in all
assureance remaininge Your Ladyship's most affecconate kinsman
and seruant, Th. Wentworth.

**246.** *Archbishop of Canterbury to Wentworth, 28 November 1624*
(*Knowler*, i, p. 25; *SC*, xii/238). *Mr. Greenwood is well suited
for the place of Dean of Ripon, but the archbishop may not be a
suitor on his behalf.*

**247.** (*SC*, ii, p. 162) *To Lord Darcy. Fetter Lane. 1 Dec. 1624.*

My much honoured Lord, wheras in my last letteres I menconed an agreement not unlikely then to haue bene made betwixt my cosen Danbie's freinds of both sides, yet afterwards there was an absolute breach upon this pointe, that they would not consent, unlesse they might haue an equall number of comittees of their nominacon. Soe then yesterday the matter was heard before the Counsell of the Court of Wards, where first the Earle of Holdernesse makinge his pretence by his learned counsell was absolutely secluded, and then after a longe debate betwixt us and them, the resultate of the Court was that Mr Henry Parker and two others, whome my lord Morley should name, (wherof Richardes now the father in law must bee none) your lordship, my selfe and my cosen Wentworth of Woolley should haue the comittment of the body and lands and Satturday next assigned (the competition thus setled) to proceed to the composicon; this, albeitt wee pressed earnestly against, yet wee were ouerruled and forced to submitt ourselues to their order. As for newes, there are not any stirringe, so there remaines nothinge but in few words to expresse how gladd I am to heare your Lordship is now become a married man, as one which shall euer much reioice in the con- (*p. 163*) tinewance and enlargment of your noble howse and therfore doe hartely pray for God's good blessinge upon yow both that it maie in your owne persons bee a well grounded and lastinge meanes of comfort and in your noble yssue, of fruitfullnes and vertue. Your Lordship's most affecconate freind and kynsman, Th. Wentworth.

**248.** (*SC*, ii, p. 163) *To Sir Edward Leech. Fetter Lane. 4 Dec. 1624.*

Sir, I purposed to haue bene with yow this afternoone, if my occasions had not called mee to the Court of Wardes, which seinge they are like there to detaine mee til night, yow will admitt mee by these lynes to signify unto yow that this morninge I did attend my lord at Whitehall and, giuing his lordship humble thanks for the noble answer hee gaue to Mr Secretary Caluert's proposicon on my behalfe, I did further beseech him that I might know his lordship's pleasure therin, so soone as might stand with his lordship's good leasure. Wherunto his lordship gaue mee a very noble answer, sayinge hee would speake with yow in itt, and then I should know his resolucon. Sir, I will goe no further nor other way in this busines then as yow shall dyrect mee; for, as the first motion without so much as a thought of myne proceeded from your selfe (for which howeuer itt proue I hold my selfe much beholden unto yow), so is itt upon yow I doe and shall principally relye for the perfecting and finishinge of this worke. And therfore I haue giuen yow an accompt of this morning's discourse, I must leaue itt to yow to make such use of, as in your better judgment yow shall thinke meete, wherin albeitt I will not bee so unmannerly as to presse yow byond your owne pace, yet I shalbee modestly desirous to understand what wilbee the end, to the intent I maie giue some dyreccons to such of my affaires as doe in some sort depend hereupon; which to confesse the truth to (*p. 164*) yow is a purpose to make a park of my owne, if his lordship will not part with this for a terme. I trouble yow to longe, in a word therfore I shall euer hold my selfe bound to deserue your fauour and acknowledge my selfe to owe unto yow a good part of my health (which in good fayth I thinke this wilbee a meanes to preserue) and is the onely reason why I desire itt, Your very affecconate and assured freind, Th. Wentworth.

**249.** (*SC*, ii, p. 164) *To Elizabeth Danby. Fetter Lane. 7 Dec. 1624.*

My good Antt, I am very sorry that my occasions enforce mee to bee soe longe absent from yow, when it is so fittinge I should attend yow, which yow wilbee pleased for a season to excuse mee for and by God's goodnes, I will make yow amends upon the first oportunity. As concerninge our proceedings here, Michaell Hopwood will giue yow a perticuler accompt for your affaires and those of your grandchild, my cosen, in the Cuntry. I haue writt at large to my cosen Wentworth of Woolley, whome I haue desired to take the paines to visitt yow and both to make yow acquainted and take your aduise therin. My best Antt, let nothinge eyther concerninge your selfe, your sonne's children, or estate trouble yow, for I doubte not but God will giue such blessinges to our endeauoures, as that all will succeed to your owne hart's desire and bee happily ouercome with a little tyme and pacience, wherin I assure yow I shall trauaile with the same care, as if it did concerne mee euen the most importantly in my owne fortune, as indeed it cannot chuse but doe, when it doth soe nearly touch persons soe neare unto mee in blood, in affection. I shall wish unto yow the continewance, the increase of good health and all happines and for the present assume onely unto my selfe the true and rightfull tytle of your most assured nephew to doe yow seruice, Th. Wentworth.

**250.** (*SC*, ii, p. 165) *To Michaell Wentworth Esq. Fetter Lane.*
*7 Dec. 1624.*

Sir, by reason of the absence of the feodaries' certificate for the East
and North Rideings wee could not proceed to composicon for my
cosen Danbye's wardshipp, but are putt of til the third sitting of the
next Terme. For any thinge I can perceaue the mother's freinds will
by little and little disert the cause, at least lay all the burthen and
trouble of itt upon us. Therfore it behoues us to bee more carefull
and I must entreat yow to take a little paines to supply both your
owne and my part, til my occasions permitt my beinge in the cuntry,
which I shall requite when the like occasion falleth to my turne.
I haue written to my Lord Darcy, that hee would (by his letter)
moue yow to goe ouer to receaue the rents and that hee would take a
course to returne them upp against Candlemas Terme for then there
wilbee use I feare of all wee haue. And I pray yow take this upon
yow and make a journey to my Antt soe soone as conueniently yow
maie to aduise with her what there is presently to bee taken order for
in the estate and to settle it in some good waie, till wee haue an
oportunity all to meet togeather and to grow to full and absolute
resolucon in the managinge of this yong gentleman's fortune, wherin
I thinke Michaell Hopwood may bee a fitt instrument. For the euidence, good Sir, see them putt into safe hands, where they maie bee
deposited til wee further resolue how to dispose of them; in espetiall
let Michaell Hugganson deliuer upp all such as hee hath, whome
albeitt wee maie speake freindly to for a while, yet is hee one shall
haue noe ymployment under us. As for my cosen himselfe and his
yonger brother and sister, it would bee seene what they want for
meate, board, learninge and apparell and then, these things decently
prouided for out of the rents, returninge upp the remaindure as
aforesaid. As for the creditors, I pray (*p. 166*) yow speake to as many
of them as yow can, desiringe their patience and that there wilbee
such a course held, as they shalbee no loosers, but honestly and iustly
satisfied in conuenient tyme. Good Sir, deale effectually with them
herein, that so my Antt may bee quiett from their clamour. The
office cannot bee ouerthrowne without a trauerse, for the office
menconinge Nelson to haue beene present and his hand set to,
albeitt counterfaite, yet noe verball averrment wilbee admitted against
a record. So as wee must proceed to composicon upon the office
allready taken and therfore Pott and Swinton, beinge found as lands
wherof my cosen Danby dyed seized, wee must of necessity haue the
conveyances to shew in disproofe of his undew findinge, wherby itt
may appeare those lands are indeed my Antt's owne inheritance and

therfore I must haue them carefully sent upp before the next Tearme
to the intent I maie cleare the matter more effectually for my Antt
and iustly shew them that wee are not eyther in body or lands to bee
raised for those lands. And by any meanes gett in the estate made by
my Antt of Swinton to Hugganson and others. Here is one Windsor
presseth much for 100ˡⁱ, pretendinge if it bee not paid him hee is
undone, soe as to stopp his outcry I will take order hee shall haue it
paid him. Finally, what euer other fitt thinge which will require to
bee done in the estate which I haue eyther forgotten, or know not of,
yow wilbe pleased in your judgment and discretion to supply. And
so I rest your very assured freind and kinsman, Th. Wentworth.

Itt were verie good if yow would make a iourney to my lord Darcy,
to conferr with his lordshipp about those things (as I haue bene
bould to write to him yow would) and so to take him along with us,
as also to sound him how farre hee will meddle in the (*p. 167*) estate.
The feodaries must bee dealt withall to make their certificates and,
good Sir, take an accompt of Hugganson how hee hath disposed of
the personall estate, of those which haue the charge of the colepitts
at Farneley, and in Massamshire, and receaue of them the moneyes
appearing to bee in their hands and lastly to take Michaell Hopwood's bill of disbursments this Tearme.

**251.** (*SC*, ii, p. 167) *To Lord Darcy. Fetter Lane. 7 Dec. 1624.*

My much honoured Lord, for want of the feodaries' certificate within the East and North Rydeinges, wee could not proceed to composicon for my cosen Danbye's wardshipp, but are put of til the
third sittinge the next Terme, which I dislike not, for by this meanes
I shall haue tyme to receaue your Lordship's opinion what is fitt to
offer as I humbly desire I may. I did moue that the last office taken
at Richmond might bee damned, as beinge indeed illegall, nether of
the feodaries beinge there (albeitt one of them was to haue beene
of the Quorum) and this the rather because there is a dyinge seized
found of Swinton and Pott, albeitt (as your Lordship knowes) they
are my Antt's owne rightfull inheritance. But I could not bee
admitted to make any verball averrment against a record, that the
office could not bee ouerthrowne without a trauerse, albeitt one of
the feodaries' hands was counterfaited, and lastly that wee must
therfore goe to composicon upon this office. By reason of my
absence, I haue written to my cosen Wentworth of Wooley that hee
would attend yow to acquaint your Lordship with some things
presently to bee done, as I conceaue, and to receaue your dyreccon.
As for the rents, itt is fitt they were paid into safe hands and returned

upp hether against the next Terme, where there is like to bee use of them all, and therfore, thinkinge not fittinge to trouble your Lordship therwith, I haue moued that by (*p. 168*) order of the Court my cosen Wentworth may receaue them and bee accomptable to your Lordship and the rest of the Comittees for them. As concerninge other things I must leaue them to my cosen Wentworthe's conferenc with your Lordship, therby auoidinge your trouble in reading a longe letter. I desire then my seruice may bee remembred to your noble Lady, my selfe in all obseruance remaininge, Your Lordship's most affecconate kynsman and seruant, Th. Wentworth.

**252.** *To Marris. Westminster. 7 Jan 1625* (*SC*, xxi/33).

Richard Marris, I am sorry your hurt hath ben soe long a lett unto you and allbeitt I confesse I desire much to haue you heare as soon as might bee, yett in noe sortt would I haue you stirre till you be well able to indure trauell, soe as then I expectt to see you heare as soon as you well may, in the meane time patience. The matter I last writt to you of and which is the principall reason which makes me desirouse to speake with you aboute hath had an entrance made in itt; yett soe as itt is without any binding ingagement and we shall be by me with all cercumspection keept for at the least fourteen dayes longer, allbeitt I am strangly pressed by Sir A. Ingram, which in trothe makes me I know not well how to understand his end therin. Butt howeuer I shall doubte the worste, as for the best, itt will saue ittself and shall wholy repose and rest myself upon the staffe of God's goodnesse, which as itt hath heathertoo, I humbly thanke him, preserued me, soe in this action I well trust to finde itt my monitor and director to apprehend and lay hold of that which shalbee best for me and my howse. For other things I can write noe more, saue only to tell you you must be sure to returne up money as much as may be well spaired, for if I chance to conclude for Pontefracte ther will wante a great deale which willbe necessarily required for my occasions. Soe, wishing you perfect healthe and recovery, I remaine Your maister and frend, Th. Wentworth. Westminster, this 7th of January 1624[5]. To my trusty seruant Richard Marris att Wentworth Woodhowse.

**253.** (*SC*, ii, p. 168) *To Christopher Wandesford Esq. Ledston. 26 March 1625.*

Sir, accordinge to my promise I now sett pen to paper, the rather to giue yow a notable example how carefull yow should bee of your words, wherof itt is to bee feared (by mee being your freind) yow

with the rest of the world are but too much forgettfull. I haue fully
considered of the tyme I haue to spend and of my occasions, and find
directly I cannot come to Kirklington and keepe my daie at London;
yeatt that the Esquier of that place maie see how much I desire to doe
him seruice, I will for his sake breake my second promis which I
made to my wife and not beginne my iourney til Munday in Easter
weeke. Another notable example that somtymes upon very good
grounds a man maie breake his word. But this I need not indeed to
obserue unto yow, the malignity of your nature beinge I doubt too
apte to frame upon this modell, bee itt upon or without cause.
Howeuer at this tyme I would haue yow beginne to apply this rule
(bee not as good as your word). Yow tould mee I should find no good
beere; I giue yow faire warninge, lett us haue therfore good drinke
and call yow lier that dare. An other aduantage I gett by this (for
reason requires a man should haue some ends to himselfe and stands
current I know with your owne practize) I shall tymely shew my wife
what shee maie trust to. My first vow (by God's grace) I (*p. 169*)
will faithfully keepe, but for appointments of coming home (notwithstanding any thinge to the contrary) I will enioy my Christian
liberty and therfore will not now foster an ill use least shee prescribe
in itt. Well then, gentill Sir, if God spare health, I wilbee at Stockhill
on Palme Sunday night where (if yow haue any manners) yow will
meet mee; howeuer on Munday night followinge beinge in the
Passion weeke I come forwards to the great and portly stemme of the
musters whose least twigge (a legg or soe) might stand and bee taken
for a whole branch (a middle or soe) in an other, albeitt well likinge
stocke. God send yow grace and health and then for your mirth and
wealth I take no great care or thought. Your most affecconate
kinsman and assured freind, Th. Wentworth.

**254.** (*SC*, ii, p. 169) *To Mistresse Dorothy Hughes. Leadston. 26
March 1625.*

My good Antt, I thanke yow for your good wishes, which I vallew the
more because I know they are harty ones. I haue writt to Mr Cressy
wherof I send yow heareinclosed a coppie and if I doe not heare by
the middle of the next weeke from yow, as I desire I maie, that hee
hath bene with yow and giuen yow satisfaccon, I will take good aduise
in the busines and doe for yow with the same care as I would were it
my owne case. And that wee may goe upon safe grounds, put
Richard Marris in remembrance, who I know will see yow this
Assizes, that hee bringe your writings alonge with him from hence
to Woodhus, for here they are, but I know not how to come by them.

Thus in some hast I rest, my good Antt, Your affecconate freind and nephew, Th. Wentworth.

**255.** (*SC,* ii, p. 170) *To Christopher Wandesford Esq. Wentworth Woodhouse. 4 April 1625.*

Sir, my liberty is my owne and I must use it with yow and all the world and therfore tel yow plainly, take itt as yow list, I will not bee with you at Kirklington on Munday; yett by God's grace I wilbee with yow in your musters [at] Pott on Teusday in the Passion weeke. Nature and greatnes delight themselues in varietie and change and could the death of the kinge work lesse upon mee consideringe my pretences and hopes at Court, then one daie's intermission and pawse for aduisement how to sett my cards upon this new shuffle of the packe? Or weare it reasonable, think yow, for a man of my iudgment and valew rashly to abandon my selfe and high designes to stand bare and bleake, like a beacon on the topp of a hill without con- sultacon, without counsell? Farr bee it from yow (yow will now saie) soe to ymagine, farther from mee so supinely to sleepe, whilest all others are awake. Well, if my phisick worke this effecte, it is more of your curtesy then my deseruinge; for the plaine truth is nor soe nor soe. But (now a little to supple your stiffe and steely sinewes) being neuer more pleased then in your contentfull conuersacon, neuer soe much in that, as when I possesse and enioy it the freest from interup- tion, interposition of any other body, any other matter; I conceaued I might suffer in both, if I did not first doe all that I had to doe with my good Antt. Soe as I wilbee at Pott on Munday night, beinge this daie seaven night, expect yow there the next morninge being Tuesdaie and hauinge by that tyme disburthened all other waight or thought, like a man entier, neate and briske, apply my (*p. 171*) selfe chearfully obseruantly to your service. By this tyme (if any thinge will make your great lordly knees to bend) Sirra your legg low with dutie and humble thanks to his worshipp, if there dwell in yow eyther gratitude or ciuilitie. And now, Sir, for your salt peeter, that stuffe is such a comodity as is not to bee bought, for had it beene to haue beene purchased, I perswade my selfe thou hadst not by this tyme beene worth a groate; at least thie whole patrimony had but stood upon a tickle point and therfore bee frugall of your poore bald store. Soe shall yow appeare some waies oeconomick yet, albeitt the worst politick that euer was; neither can I indeed pardon yow this fault hauing beene trained upp in the passages of kingdomes and comon wealthes. For yow know that states deale not soe improuidently as to arme others out of their magazines espetially with warlike, martiall prouisions, but now to dreame of such a matter, when the French lady comes instantly ouer, I protest the drunken impertinent (my lord Baltimore told us hee mett with) could not haue stammerd, nodded forth a more forraigne incongruous conceate. Alasse, alasse, they are soe farr from hauinge any to spare that unto mee and understandinge men like my selfe, it is noe marvaile though at this tyme and upon this occasion the salt peeter men straine the prerogatiue to the highest; they are wise and know full well all wilbee little enough for themselues I will warrant yow. And are yow not now a wonder to your selfe how your braine (that fatt Minerua) should produce so misshapen, disproportioned a birth? Good fellow, good fellow, busie your selfe no longer with these misteries, leaue them to Sir Humphrey Maie, lately sworne of the Counsell; think how to secure your selfe of old Aldborowe (whome thes thinges would better haue becomed) and your burghesshippe, and whether it wilbee fitt for mee to stand to bee knight of the shire, for this beinge nearer your leuell, I expect some sober sadd aduise. I loose too (*p. 172*) much tyme upon yow more indeed then Richmondshire is worth. Farewell. Your most assured freind and affecconate kinsman, Th. Wentworth.

**256.** *Wentworth to Sir Francis Trappes, 6 April 1625 (Knowler,* i, p. 25; *SC,* ii, p. 172). *There will be a new election and he asks him to engage his friends to give their first voices for Wentworth. Postscript,* I pray yow lett all bee done as yett as of your selfe &c. [*Omitted*]

**257.** (*SC,* ii, p. 173) *To Sir Peter Middleton. Wentworth Woodhouse. 6 April 1625.*

Sir, I purposed to haue bene with yow on Sunday next, but now I am enforced much against my will to alter that appointment and to deny unto my selfe the contentment of seeinge yow a few weeks. The reason is my departure to London on Satturday next, occasioned by the now intended Parliament and consequently a new election for knights of the shire. Soe as the election fallinge out to bee on Munday come month, I cannot stay soe longe in the cuntry and yet, resoluing (Godwilling) to bee at the eleccon, I am thus constrained presently to goe upp and after a fortnight stay or soe to come back againe. Now, Sir, to yow, my deare and assured freind, I will open my selfe, which is that I intend to stand for a place at Yorke. But til yow heare further from mee (which assuredly yow shall doe in tyme) I must desire yow to keepe it to your selfe and onely to deale with your freinds in the present thus farr, that yow understand of a new election and that for certaine I wil bee at the same in person; then yow maie (if yow thinke mee so worthie) let them know how fitt it wilbee for them to chose mee the prime and lastly to deale effectually with them all to bee there and not to engage themselues any where els til they heare further from yow. Thus yow see how bouldly I chalke yow out a waie, but it is the more excusable in regard it proceeds from a grounded assurance I haue in your loue and a full determination I haue to deserue itt by all the meanes my mind or fortune shall enable mee with. God haue yow in his blessed keepinge, Your most assured freind and affectionate kinsman, Th. Wentworth.

Sir, I pray yow deale effectually with Sir William Hungate to this purpose, letting him understand that I haue earnestly entreated yow soe to doe, with the remembrance of my unfained respects towards him. My seruice to your lady; all happines and health to yow all.

**258.** *Wentworth to Sir John Jackson, 6 April 1625* (*Knowler*, i, p. 25; *SC*, ii, p. 174), *as above no. 257, he is writing to the Mayor of Pontefract for seats as in no. 259 below.*

**259.** *Wentworth to Mr. Cowper, Mayor of Pontefract, 6 April 1625,* (*Knowler*, i, p. 26; *SC*, ii, p. 175). *He asks the borough to elect himself and Sir John Jackson; or if Wentworth is elected for the shire, Sir Richard Beaumont.*

**260.** (*SC*, ii, p. 176) *To Henry Stapleton Esq. Wentworth Woodhouse. 1 May 1625.*

Sir, beinge by the opinion of some of my verie good freinds ledd to stand for a place in this next election at Yorke, I am hereby to entreate yow, as a gentleman I conceaue who respects and wisheth mee well, that you will take so much trouble upon yow for my sake, as to labour your freinds and freeholders to place upon mee their prime voices; which trust as I shall uprightly discharge towards them and the cuntry, so shall I for this fauour thinke my selfe much beholden unto yow and bee ready to make yow a faire returne of your kindnes in as much as shall rest in the power of Your verie assured and affectionate freind, Th. Wentworth. If I had come sooner home, yow had sooner heard from mee, &c.

**261.** *Wentworth to Sir John Hotham, 1 May 1625* (*Knowler*, i, p. 27; *SC*, ii, p. 176). *He thanks him for the promise of his support in the election and hopes to see him at York.*

**262.** *Wentworth to Mr. Melton, 1 May 1625 (Knowler,* i, *p.* 27; *SC,* ii, *p.* 177). *He asks him to be means for the prime voice of the earl of Northumberland's freeholders.*

**263.** *(SC,* ii, *p.* 177) *To George Butler Esq. Wentworth Woodhouse. 1 May 1625.*

Sir, some of my good freinds, I beinge at London, haue first ouerperwaded and then engaged mee to stand for the knightshipp of the shire once more. I haue bene therby somthinge slower in writeinge to my freinds (reseruing that til my cominge downe) then in truth the case (the opposicon considered) did require. To yow neuertheles I thought now good to addresse thes few lynes to entreate your best endeauoures with your freinds for the first voice and moue them to reserue themselues in the second place til their cominge to Yorke, where wee shall aduise togeather and resolue upon that which shall appeare best for the cuntrie. Perticulerly I pray yow present my humble duty to my lord of Cumberland, desiringe his pardon hee heard no sooner from mee for the reason abouesaid and now to entreate his letters to his officers in Crauen to labour his freholders for their prime voices in my behalfe, which I must take as the *(p. 178)* continewance of his fauour towards mee. But if his Lordship stand upon any former engagment, I would not haue this sute of mine in any wise pressed upon him; but, interpreting this quicknesse of his Lordship in the best sence, will rely upon my owne strength and other my noble kind freinds, which I must tell yow I pray God I find I want not. I praie yow remember my seruice to your good Lady and then, wishinge unto yow both many happy contentfull howers, I close upp this letter with the truth of my abideinge, Your verie affecconate kinsman and freind, Th. Wentworth.

**264.** *From John Grymesdyche. Knottingley, 20 May 1625 (SC,* xx/241).

Worthie Sir, as the cuntrey out of theire confidence in your wisedome and worth hath made speciall choyse of your self and that nowble knight (your associate) for the knights of our sheire this Parliament. So wee are assured you will allwaies be forward in the performance of such good offics for the good of your poore neighbours as may free them from such insufferable oppressions as are not to be endured in a comonwealth, amoungst which I conseaue none to be more offensiue then that graunt of the Greenewax of the duchie made by his late Maiestie unto Sir Roger Aston deceased, the interest whereof is in the Lady Peyton, late wife of Sir Samuell Peyton, one of Sir Roger's daughters and in Sir Gilbert Houghton, Sir Robert Wingfeild and Sir Thomas Perient, who married his other 3 daughters, and is by them demized unto Mrs Redhead, whose ministers and substituts so harrie the cuntrey hereabouts that they make men wearie both of theire lands and estates and this day haue distrained the goods of Mrs Jackson (a widow, Sir John Jackson's aunt) for 2 severall somes of x$^s$ a peece and caried hir goods away, though theire estreat be neyther in hir name, nor is she possest of the mannor or lands for which the charge cometh out. For the charge is for the manor of Knottingley, which mannor hir husband before his death 15 yeares agoe sould away to Mr Wilbore and is now in the king's possession, younge Wilbore being in warde for divers yeares yet to come for this land onely.

I forgot, Sir, to expres that the estreat is not in Mrs Jackson's name, but in the severall names of Thomas Jackson and John Jackson, the one of them hir husband (dead eight yeares since) and the other hir sonne, who during hir life possesseth not a foote of land. About 6 months since these Baylifes weare here in like manner and with the like estreat had of hir xl$^s$ at least and of others in this place allmost xx$^{ll}$.

This (Sir) I conseaved to be very iniuriose and therefore haue bound over hir Baylifs to answer it before the Judgs at the Assize and thought good in the meanetime to acquaint you with it and do hope that the cuntrey shall haue cawse to acknowledge your favour in procuring them such redres, as to your wisedome shall seeme good. For though I onely enforce this one particuler, becawse I conseaue it to be most tortiouse, yet the same baylifs haue at this time levied upon 7 or 8 more in this towne, some for respit of homage and others for non appearance at Assizes. And this, Sir, is the generall greevance of the cuntry that when they shall pay so many taxes and subcidies as they did the last yeare and hope to receaue some ease by the Pardon and then his Maiesty's grace and favor which his H[ighness] intends to the comonwealth shalbe in lease for the enriching of private men so that when the Pardon comes forth they haue little or no benefit by it; which (I assure you Sir) is a very great greevance and oppression to the cuntrey people, who liue in hope that the wisdome of this honorable Parliament will free them both of this and many other uniust exactions, whereby they are impoverished and made unhable to do his Maiestie service if there shalbe cawse.

Sir, if you please to take this particuler of the greenewax into your consideration, I would intreat you that the intimacon of it may not appeare from mee, becawse (as you know) I was Sir Roger Aston's servant.

Likewise, Sir, the Statu[t]e of xii$^d$ a Sunday for absence from church is very defectiue in one poynt, as I conseaue it. For if a man haue eyther frends or servants that liue in his howse and come not to church, the Mr of the family can be distrained for none but himselfe, and if the other persons (being likewise of his howshould) haue no goods, then the poore (to whom that forfaiture is due) lose it and no punishment is inflicted uppon the offendor, but imprisonment, which if wee should execute, thenn such gaoles as the castle of Yorke would not hould them. So that in my opinion (which I submit to your better iudgment) it weare fit that the Mr of the family should answer for all he keepes in his howse whether servants or frends. For if they be servants, theire wags may satisfy him againe and others he ought not to harbor against law, all which I leaue to your consideracon.

A third thinge is, Sir, that the iustics of peace may haue power to punish such pettie filchers as shall steale small trifles and not (as wee are forced to do now) to send them all to the howse of corr-[ection], which both puts the cuntrey to a great charge in conveying them thether, where they lye and learne much vilanie, and when they come to the Sessions (through the Sherif's negligence) often scape without punishment. Whereas if they weare punished where they comit those pettie offencs, the punishment would both be more bitter and more exemplarie, but yet not to ty the iustics to punish them in that manner, but to leaue it to theire discretions as they shall see cawse.

Sir, I intended to haue come to London this terme and I wish my self there at this present to haue testifyed my knowledge (if I weare called) concerninge the late election of the knights at Yorke, wherein as Mr Sherif carried himself very worthily doing all right to all the competitors with all possible indifference, neyther denying the poll when it was required (but that Sir John Savile by his owne act prevented it) nor forbearing to view the companies with a great deal of paines before he gaue iudgment. So I doubt not but you are sufficiently provided of frends there to manifest unto the howse of Parliament the iust and equall carriage of that busines. Wherein, Sir, if I may do you any service, I shalbe ready uppon any notice from you to leaue all occasions whatsoeuer and in the meane time with the remembraunce of my loue and service I rest, Yours euer to be comaunded, John Grymesdyche. Knottingley, the 20th of May 1625.

**265.** *Michael Wentworth to Wentworth. Dungen in Brabant. 17 May 1625* (*SC*, xx/240).

Sir, your letter you sent by Sir Henrie Fane I receiued last night, wherin I understand that Huh: Husband hath played the foole and

hath caried himselfe too proudely, for which I am verie sorie; not
soe much for the boy as for the good I entended him for my deare
brother's sake, whome I know loued him withal his hart and was the
onely means I had to exprese my loue to the vew of the world; and
yet, though I would not regard him but follow your opinion, the
remembrance of his master and the wordes he last spake to me
concerninge him will not diuert me from my entended resolution.
Therefore excuse me and iudge it for what you please, for I had
rather be condemned of tow much loue then other wise and that
monie you haue giuen him I will cast it up and will allow him fiue
pound a yeare, and when that monie is rund out I will still continue
that pension for his life.

Sir, the 12 of May two companies of euerie regiment was commanded to see if they could force the enime's quarters at Trahay
[Terheyden] and the English, hauinge the van, fell on and bett the
enimie for tow hours and toke 3 workes and was assailinge the fouert;
then, our amonistion failinge and not beinge seconed, was forced to
retraite, we lost and were shot togeth[er] — [m]ost of them — we
lost — of — — Captaine C[ ?L]euet and Tub and Sir Thomas Win with
a canon and 5 more shot, but not anie scared but Turwhite and —
leuetenant Corbut and another and 4 antients by [? my] lords of
Oxfords beinge the chefe;[1] my lord Vere and Oxford commanded in
chefe and gained a great dele of honor; and Sir Edward Holleis led
us on and caried himselfe soe valianly and assolted euerie worke him
selfe and did soe encourage the shoulders that all the chefe commanders
reported to the prince that in there lifes they had neuer seene soe
resolute and soe truly valant, and the generall report went that if his
exelence had let us bene second[ed] we had relieued the toune
[Breda]. But that designe is frustrated and we expect some other,
which I hope God will giue better successe then he hath yet. All this
is true for I was an actor in it. Sir, I am sorie that I cannot giue you
content as yet, by reason we are in the fielde, for I am forced to
wright on the ground lyinge of my bellie, but assone as I can get a
fittinge place I will be more carefull. Sir, I would entreat you to
remember me in this imployment of shippinge, for I like it better
then anie and, though I am all to gether ignorant of the knowledge
and guidinge of a ship, it is not the captaine's office, but his mareners

---

[1] This agrees better with the account of the casualties given by Dudley Carleton, cited by C. Dalton, *The Life and Times of General Sir Edward Cecil, Viscount
Wimbledon* (London, 1885), pp. 87–88, than with those given by C. R. Markham,
*The Fighting Veres* (London, 1888), pp. 427–28. The former gives Oxford,
captains Dacres, Tyrwhitt, Cromache and Sir Thomas Winne and lieutenant Bell
wounded, with ensign Stanhope killed.

who is charged with that care, and the commandinge of the shoulders I may doe that as well as anie, if I haue wrightly applied my time, and I will learne the other by my industrie. I intreat you to present my seruice to my ladie and the rest of my friendes and excuse me that I doe not wright to them for I haue nothing to doe it withall but as I below [?] and there fore I deare not be to boulde lest they d— wayes hereafter still prayinge for your health and happines, I shall euer striue to continue, Your louinge brother to doe you seruice, Mich: Wentworth. From the leager at Dungin[1] the 17 of May 1625, *sti. noua*. To my most respected Brother Sir Thomas Wentworth knight and barronnett at the signe of the Maiden Head in Fetter Lane near Temple Bar these dd. in London.

**266.** *Sir Richard Beaumont to Wentworth, 9 June 1625 (Knowler, i, p. 27; SC, xx/242); he will assist in the shire election, but will not sit for Pontefract, suggesting Sir Henry Savile or Mr. Shillitoe in his place.*

**267(a).** *Undated speech, probably for the Oxford meeting of the 1625 Parliament*[2] *(SC, xxi/212) [Wentworth's hand].*

May itt please you to beware, Mr Speaker; take heed how you proceed soe suddenly to propounde the question, the consequence is greater then I imagine by your hast you forsee; itt hath euer stoode with the wisedume of this howse not to suffer the question to passe in thes cases till all be cleare and serene, euery man satesfied and exspecting with earnestnesse and chearfullnesse to giue both with harte and voyce a free assentt and acknowledgment of the great goodnesse and grace of ther Soueraigne and that not without weighty reason. For the manner in granting thes supplies is of as great importe many times as the matter itt self; the unanimouse mindes, consents and affections of a people breaking forth in thes demonstrations, being the strongest and most irresistable treasure of a kinge and which giue princes the greatest reputatione both att home and abrode.

I purposed when I came inn this morning to haue been a tacite hearer, butt I finde myself now transported beyonde my intention and itt may be beyonde my iudgement too, for which I must craue

---

[1] Dungen in Brabant.

[2] Probably related to his speech on 10 August; *C.J.*, i, p. 814; *Debates in the House of Commons in 1625*, ed. S. R. Gardiner (Camden Society, new series, vi, 1873), p. 113. British Museum Add. MS. 48091, the other main account, does not record any speech by Wentworth.

your pardons, but sure I am not out of my faithfull and upright meaning to the king and his people.

Itt must be granted that wheather you haue relation to forraine states, or too ourselfs att home, ther depends as much upon this daye's debate as upon any other that euer moued in this howse. Therfore lett us first betake our selues to God, beseeching him to guide and direct our consultations and resolutions for the best. Secondly, laying aside all sudden passion, either of too much opposition or too much easinesse, retire our selues to untroubled and setled iudgments.

Itt is to be urged that we ought with all due circumspection to keepe our selues in the antient wayes and stepps of our ancestors, especially in the manner of granting subsedies, in noe sortt too create new presidentts which be stronge in the case of princes and in successe of time produce such effects as weare neither forseen, nor yett dreamed of, by the most iudiciouse in prospectiue. That wee cannot be intirely faithfull to the king being the heade, not hauing due regarde to the subiects being the members, nor truly liberall to his Maiesty, if wee appeare wanton dispensers of ther purses; that wee should not decline from the institutions left us by our ancestors, the obseruing whearof hauing been profitable to the commonwealthe, nor depart forth of tried and approued paithes, except ther weare an euidentt asseurance of good without all shadow to the contrary.

Reasons in themselues I confesse of great power and strengthe to perswade, yett before wee giue an absolute answeare,[1] itt is to be considered that the troubled and cloudy face of Christendume, into which I perswade myself the sharpest sightes perce butt neare att hande and darkly, requires and inuites us more then euer to a well established union att home, that otherways our religion, persecuted euery wheare, leaues us to exspect only the curtesy of Poliphemus to Ulisses, to be deuoured last. That the greatnesse and power of his Maiesty being our surest comfort and protection, both at home and abrode, the consideration therof ought to be held by us in as tender and deare a recommendation as any other thing whatsoeuer. That we cum not hether, as I take itt, to be partiall on the subiect's partte, butt as free and indifferent to prouide for the florishinge estate of this kingdume, which consists ioyntly and indeuisably in the happinesse and prosperity of the king and his people. Lastly itt is to be considered that this Parlament thus farre hath (to the abundant contentment of all honest men, to the apprehension and affright of the ennimies of God's sacred worde and this kingdume) been an

[1] The rest of the speech is also repeated in *SC*, xxi/213, but with a different opening, given below, p. 239.

incoation of a right understanding betwixt the kinge and his people and that itt is to be desired the acts therof may remaine to posterity as *firmamenta stabilitatis et constantiae*, euen as a couenantte of salte, to be betwixt his Maiestie's seed and our seed for euer. Now fearefull I am least thes faire fruites, appearing white for the haruest, might be blasted with any maleuolent winde, or least our too stiffe deniall might proue a rocke of offence and hinder the smothe passage of thes happy beginnings too a more blessed conclusion. Soe as indeed sustaining a greate conflicte in my self which way to turne, I am ledde from both the extreames too the consideration of a midle way, which I shall withall humility presentt and submitt to the wisdume of the howse, which is thus:—

That we (protesting our ready and good affections to giue satesfaction in all iust and fitting mannere) should humbly declaire unto his Maiesty that this demande, being without all presidentt, may be dangerouse in the example, that wee feare the granting therof willbe esteemed by his subiects noe faire acquitall of our duties towards them, or returne of ther trusts reposed in us and therfore humbly to beseeche him, hauing regarde unto our creditts and reputations, to take in good partte our declining an absolute answeare till an other session that soe we may (this session ended before Christmas) be enlightened by the beames of his grace in a free and princely pardon, as allsoe carry sum good bills downe with us to his people. With this assurance neuerthelesse that when itt shall please his Majesty to call us togeither againe, be itt within a day, and to propounde supply, wee shall intertaine itt with all chearfullnesse, make itt our first worke and answeare itt in such a proportion, as may giue his Maiesty iust cause of content. Lastly to auoide all miscarriage and misunderstanding, the intention of the howse being faithfully and clearly conuayed to his Maiesty, that a committee be appointed to consider in what manner to presentt of the same and who to be the messingers.

This, as I iudge, under reformation, the most discreet and safe for us, soe I protest doe I hold itt most honorable and advantageouse for his Maiesty. Honorable in that, as his goodnesse hath appeared unto us by many graciouse messages deliuered in this howse, we shall itt breathe forth to the whole kingdume in finishing and crowning them by his publicke and royall acte. I confesse noe man well bredde can doubte of this performance, yett itt will giue satesfaction to the vulgare, who out of a rurall and unmannerly distruste believe nothing till itt cum forth in printt after the end of the session. Aduantageouse too, in that partte of the seconde subsedy being yett to collecte, the payment of such others, as we shall present to his Maiesty, willbe as speedy into the Exchequer, granted the next session, as if itt weare presently yielded unto. In that again our promises are soe certaine that they may in truthe be valewed as matters acted, soe soon as we promise. And lastly in that the whole kingdume, seeing this blissed harmony betwixt the heade and the members, his Maiesty as a father putting himself back upon his people in the end, as his people putt themselues upon him in the beginning, of the Parlamentt, the spiritts of all generouse-minded men will melt, our guifts be more cherful and in a better proportion, and considering the straitnesse of the relation betwixt King and people, all men would be ready, I perswade myself, to feetche itt out euen of ther shinne bones and ancles to doe his Maiesty seruice.

**267(b).** *SC*, xxi/213, *is another version of this speech with a different beginning.*

The strings of Souerainity (not like those which slacken with use) still winde into themselues an addition of strengthe and power, seldum or neuer remitting [or] departing from a possession or custome. Therfore wee ought with all due circumspection to keep ourselues in the antientt wayes and stepps of our ancestors, espetially in the manner of granting subsedies, in noe sortt to create new presidentts which are stronge in the case of princes and in successe of time produce such effects, as weare neuer dreamed of, nor forseyn by the most iuditiouse in prospectiue.

I haue not reade (wherin if I be mistaken, I submitt to the more leardned) that euer ther hath been tow grantes of subsedies in one session. What accountt can we giue them that sentt us, whie wee should now leaue the beaten tracke? How can wee be intirely faithfull to the kinge being the heade, not hauing due regarde to the members which are his subiects, or how truly liberall to his Maiesty, if wee appeare wanton dispensers of ther purses? Confessing therfore that I lacke the deipthe of iudgement to consider how farre this presidentt may be drawn into consequence hearafter, my aduice is that we should not digresse from the institution left us by our ancestors, the obseruing whearof haue been profitable to the Commonwealthe, nor decline from tried and approued pathes, except ther weare an euidentt asseurance of good without all shadow too the contrary.

Yet before wee should giue this demande an absolute refusall, itt is to be considered [*continued as above, p.* 236].

**268.** *Sir Arthur Ingram to Sir Thomas Wentworth, 7 November 1625* (*Knowler*, i, p. 28; *SC*, xx/243). *They have lost a friend with the removal of Bishop Williams from the Chancery; Buckingham is more powerful than ever, Sir Humphrey May is hostile to Wentworth and Sir Richard Weston friendly. Wentworth likely to be made sheriff.*

**269.** *From Sir Arthur Ingram* (*SC*, xx/254).[1]

Nobell Sir, God giue you joy, you ar now the greatt officer of Yorksheir, butt you had the indeuours of your poor frind to haue preuentted itt. Butt I thinck yf all the counsell thatt was att courtt had joynned to gether in request for you, itt would nott haue preuailled. For itt was sett and resolued whatt should bee donn befor the greatt duk's gowing ouer and from thatt the King would nott chang a tittell. You gow along with good company: fyve Parlimentt men besids yourself and a seauenth cometh in to preuentt him from dowing hurtt: Sir Edward Cock is Captain, you folow, Sir Francis Seamor, Sir Robartt Phillips, Sir Guy Pallmes, Mr Edward Allford and the last, which was nott of the last parlimentt, is Sir William Flettwood. The Judges proseaded in ther ould courss and so wentt itt to the King, butt when the names cam to the King, the King declared him self thatt hee had the names of seauen thatt hee would haue shereffs and so named them him self and my Lord Kepper sett them down. Itt was tould me by tow counsellors thatt in the naming of you the king said you wear a honest gentellman, butt not a tittell to anny of the rest. This much aduantadge haue you thatt way for your being chossen. My poor opinion is thatt ther did nott on which befall you in the whole courss of your lyff thatt is and will bee mor honor to you; in the publick who speak most strongly of itt; ther is no mor to say now to itt, butt to undergow itt cherfully. Myself and my howss and whatt I can dow is att your comand. I thinck you must send up on abought itt presenttly. Sir John Gibson and my self will enter bond for you and so I rest your faythfull frend, Ar. Ingram. Abought the begininge of Feburary you will haue a parlimentt: aduiss your frind Arthur Ingram whether you would haue him stand then or no, dow itt by tow lynes, butt I pray you lett no man know.

To his worthie and nobull freind Sir Thomas Wentworth knyght baronitt geue thes; let this letter bee sentt by a fottman from Doncaster to Sir Thomas Wentworth howse att Woodhowss.

---

[1] Printed in Knowler, i, p. 29, without the postscript and with the date November 1625 added.

**270.** *Wentworth to Sir Walter Pye, 13 November 1625 (Knowler, i, p. 29; SC, ii, p. 178), asking that Wandesford should take over the wardship of Thomas Danby. For details of the history of this wardship, see J. T. Cliffe,* The Yorkshire Gentry *(London, 1969), pp. 130–31, 370–71.*

**271.** *From Sir Arthur Ingram. Reading. 21 Nov. 1625 (SC, xx/245).*

Nobell Sir, sines the last letter I wrott to you, the which I hop is cum to your hands befor now, I haue r[eceived] a letter from you for the which I thanck you; butt I perceaue att the wrygtinge therof you had nott the newes of the greatt office thatt was fallen upon you, butt by your letter you shew a braue and a dyscrett ressollussion; and lik your self, fynding no way to help you outt of itt by any way or means thatt I could thinck of, your sarvantt, Mr Man, and my self haue entred into the courss of preparing thos things thatt are to be dunn. Wee haue allredy entred bond into the excheq[uer] for you. Mr Man is sewing outt your pattent and ther shall bee a *dedimuss* to tack your oath in the country. This is all I can dow hear for you, when I cum into the country my self, my howss and whatt I haue [will be] att your command. The jaylor which is now in the castell, whose name is Blanch, I thinck to bee a uery honest man and as fitt a man for thatt place for your saffty as any you can make choys of. Butt I know in your wyssdom you will as other shereffs haue dunn before, tack good securyty then for ther particculers you ar saff. Yf you intend to haue an undersheryff, lett me recommend Mr Hunttly to you, who is an abell man, a skillfull man and an honest man, butt [if] you intend to keep itt in your own hands thatt I leaue to your own wyssdom. Thus outt of my lou to you I make bould to wrygt unto you of thes tow men, butt leue to you to dow what you will therin and so I rest, yours euer most faythfully to lou you, Ar. Ingram. Reading, this 21th of November 1625. I dow the rather commend Blanch unto you, because hee hath byn on thatt hath stod for the cuntry very honestly and is a tru man to his fame [? frends].

**272.** *Sir John Jackson to Wentworth, November 1625 (Knowler, i, p. 30; SC, xx/253); he recommends his kinsman George Clay as under-sheriff, will recommend any friend of Wentworth's to Pontefract.*

**273.** *From Sir Richard Cholmley. Nov. 1625 (SC, xx/252).*

Noble Sir, this bearer, my undersheriff, beinge laytly returned from
his apposall at Ridding, hath for certayne informed me of your
beinge elected Sheriff of this countye in the succeeding yeare. As
my hearte shall euer wishe all increase of honor to your deservinge
worth, so giue it leaue in the freenes of that dispotision to wishe
unto you therin the success of your owne deserts.

I knowe assuredly, Sir, you are suffetiently able to aduise your
self in the course of maneging the place. If therfore you resolve to
disburden your self of the cayre and troble by conferring the whole
busines upon an undersheriff, giue me leaue, I beseetch you, Sir,
yf all redye you haue not disposed it, to commend unto you the
service of Mr Cantby in that kinde, of whome, although in this my
yeare I must confess I haue at sundrye tymes receyved many informations to occation matter of distrust in me agaynst him, yet
upon my honest credit, having curiously sownded them all, I haue
fownd them light, him most reall and iust in all my occations. In
that course you can deale with no man more honest, more suffetient.
In conclusion, Sir, I haue so mutch approved him as I darr and
will (yf you weare pleased to mayke stay of the place till his returne
from the tearme and that you weare agreed upon fitting tearmes)
ingage myself in 500[11] for his discharge of the place.

Those I haue approved servants most faythfull to me, in my
respect to you I cannot but commend to you, leaving the consideration to your self. For your geole you can deale with no man
more reall then Mr Blanch, nor any clark more honest, mor suffetient
then Francis Turner. Fearing I haue alredye been too troblesome
to you, with comendment of my best respect and service to you,
I will tayk leaue and remayne, faythfull to do you service, Richard
Cholmely.

**274.** *From Lord Scrope. York. 16 Nov. 1625 (SC, xx/244).*

After my very harty comendacons, I understand his Maiestie hathe
bene pleased to make choyse of yow to be highe Sheriffe for this
county of York for this next yeare. And whereas heretofore my
predecessors in this place and my self ever since I came to this
government haue bene beholdinge to the Sheriffes from tyme to
tyme to haue the nomynacon of one to supply the place of breaking
upp attachments yssewinge from the court held before me and his
Maiestie's counsell here established. Therefore in good assewrance
to fynde the lyke respect from yow which heretofore hathe bene
afforded to my self and others upon request who have enyoyed the

place whereunto yow ar elected, I have thought good to desyre yow to nomynate to the exercise of that offyce my sarvant Edward Hutton, who I will undertake shall sufficiently discharge yow in the execucon thereof. And for which curtesy yow shall fynde me redy to make requytall as occasyon shalbe offered. And thus nothinge doubtinge to receyve your kynde answeare herein, I rest your assured loving freinde, Em. Scrope. At York, the xvith of November 1625. Post, I pray yow be pleased to send your seale to my said servant as formerly hath bene accustomed for the execucon of that offyce.

**275.** *From the earl of Clare. Haughton. 22 Nov. 1625 (SC, xxii/53).*

Sun Wentworthe, thoughe I perswade my self that this enclosed, for so muche as concernethe yourself, is no news to yow, the ill we would not comonly soner cuming to us then the good wee couet. Yet for your better comfort by your associats you shal by this paper fynd owt the humor that preferred yow to this dignite and methinks it putts a mark of estimation uppon you and your fellowes. For perseqution is oftner a simtome of vertu then reward and this is a glass for my masters of this studied Parlament, to understand themselfs that I fear me by the better spirits of that house yow wilbe rather enuied and that them selfs, as good erl John, disualued, haue the more cause to look about theme and so may this parlament proue a wurs hobgobling then the former. Such is the guilt of thear conscience that know thear cause bad; witnes Alsibiades that dared not to trust his mother with his triall. But let this pass; yow are no more hurt thearby then he that is confined to his house and hath no lust to stir forth of it; and I hope in God the man of power shal neuer hurt yow more. I haue sent this messenger hearwith to see yow and to bring me wourd of my daughter's good healthe, of which I hope wel, thoughe yow spoke nothing thearof in your last letter. The lord of heauen bless yow both and fill your days with mutual comforts. Amen. Haughton this 22 of 9br. 1625. Your very louing father in law, Clare. To my very loving sun.

**276.** *Sir Peter Middleton to Wentworth, 23 November 1625 (Knowler i, p. 31; SC, xx/247); about the possibility of those nominated as sheriffs being elected burgesses.*

**277.** *From Sir Thomas Fairfax. Denton. 26 Nov. 1625 (SC, xx/249).*

Worthy sir, I wish you much happines in your honorable office. I am to entreate you in the behalfe of the bearer hereof, Thomas

Barker, for the bailiwicke of Skiracke, a man who by former experience I knowe very fittinge for the place and hath supplied the same very effectually, which makes mee more willinge to write in his behalfe. I hope he will giue you satisfacion in aney thinge you shall demaund of him. Soe referringe the premisses to your good consideracon, remembringe mee kindly to your selfe and my lady, I take leaue, your assured louing frinde, T. Fairfax. Denton, Nouember xxvith 1625.

**278.** *From Sir Ferdinando Fairfax. Denton. 27 Nov. 1625 (SC, xxii/55).*

Noble Sir, giue me leaue to entreate your fauor for a near kinsman and freinde of mine, Mr Humfrey Brooke, who has executed the office of County Clarke under diuers Sheriffs and so carried himselfe in itt, as I thinke ther is none of them but will giue a good attestation of his honesty. If you wilbe pleased to make a triall of him as they haue donne, I make no doute butt he wilbe the same to you and what you shall thinke fittinge for him to doo, I will (if you shalbe pleased so to require itt) ingage my selfe for the performance. Sir, if he were nott a meere stranger to you, I suppose his fittness would enable him without a testimoniall from his frende for your acceptance. Yett if this may preuaile with you for his better esteeme, I must acknoledge the fauor and rest much behoulding. I desire, Sir, my humble seruice may be presented to your Ladye and I shall remayne, Your affectionate frende to doe you seruice, Fer: Fairfax. Denton, this 27 of 9$^{br}$ [1625].

**279.** *Clare to Wentworth, 27 November 1625 (Knowler, i, p. 31; SC, xxii/54). He discusses the proposals that the leaders pricked as sheriffs should be elected for boroughs. If these succeed they would secure Parliament and the subject, but he agrees that it is better to be a spectator than an actor. He desires Wentworth to forbear repayment of money which he owes him.*

**280.** *Sir Peter Middleton. Stockeld. 28 Nov. 1625 (SC, xxii/56).*

Sir, I shall now (I feare) giue you occation to thinke mee too presumptius, hauinge soe lately beene troblesome in the lyke kinde allredie, but my desyres shall allwaies be limited accordinge to your owne good pleasure and conueniency. This bearer (Arthur Godfrey) hauinge been this diuers yeares past bayliffe of Claro hath importuned mee to moue you in his behalfe that he may retaine his place still under you and his sufficiency to undertake that office makes mee the bolder to recommende him unto you; that upon such conditions as you admitt of others you wilbe pleased to accepte of his seruice before an other, wherin I shall take ytt as a great fauor to mee, whoe shall euer be redie with my best indeuors to giue you satisfaction how much I am Yours euer to honor and to serue you, Pe: Middleton. Stockell, 28 Nouember [1625].

**281.** *From Geoffrey Bilton. Selbye. 29 Nov. 1625 (SC, xx/251).*

Myne humble dewtie remembred, your kindnes shewed me at my being with yow hath emboldened me to write at this instant and to praye your wor[ship's] fauor on this bearer my sonnes behalf. Bothe he and I ioynes in desire that he might perform unto yow som acceptable seruice this yeare in execucon of th' office of the bailiffe of Barkeston; yf the same be not already graunted, I besech your worshipp that he maye haue yt before an other, yelding that gratuity which to your goodnes shall seme mete. And so in hope to spede the better for theire remembrance which are gone and for young Sir George Sauile sake, to whom with your self I wishe all honorable health and happynes, I humbly take my leaue. From Selbye the xxixth of Nouember 1625. Your good wor: humblie to commaunde, Geoffrey Bilton.

**282.** *From Richard Tempest. Waddow. 29 Nov. 1625 (SC, xx/250).*

Sir, this bringer, Mr Henry Somerscales, intendinge to be a suytor unto yow for the collection of the issues of grene wax and other fynes within our countrye of Craven, hath desired me to commende this his suyte unto your consideration that yow be pleased he might execute the place as your depute for this yeare. Wherein I am perswaded he will careye himselfe honestlie and discretelie, having formerly in the tymes of other sherifes giuen good content to the countrie in the dischardge of this service. So, leavinge it to your good consideration, with my best commend[ations] I rest, your kinsman and frend assured, Rich: Tempest. Waddow the xxixth of November 1625.

**283.** *Wentworth to Wandesford, 5 December 1625 (Knowler, i, pp. 32–34; SC, ii, pp. 181–85); he will execute the under-sheriff's place through his own servants and writes about the county election and Sir John Savile's strength, Danby's wardship; Wandesford must sit in the parliament. Wentworth has granted the attachment office to the Lord President's servant Mr. Hutton.*

**284.** (*SC*, ii, p. 186) *To Sir Henry Savile. Ledstone. 22 Dec. 1625.*

Sir, the companie of my respected freinds I euer much comfort my selfe in and soe desire it, as maie bee least with their trouble; and so it holds with mee in this new office of a Sheriffe (which I must now weare it seemes for this yeare) and therfore if yow will afford mee the same at the Assizes, as yow intend your great reuerend cousin at this next election, I must kindly thank yow. As for liueraies I purpose to charge none of my freinds with [them], purposinge to hold my selfe precisely to the order made in the tyme of Sir Guy Palmes, best becominge my modesty and as I take it my discretion to carry it soe, as to make this redoubted office heretofore lesse to bee apprehended hereafter by the gentlemen of this countie, to whome I find my selfe soe much bounden that I wilbee gladd to doe them some seruice, as in this I think I shall doe, albeitt with sufferinge in the vulger's opinion. I know right well the supremacie of Agbrigge and Morley will scorne to haue any partners in an eleccon of knights for the shire and therfore if yow come, our part wilbee little, and that yow maie come, yow frame imaginacon of an opposicon, wherof there is little ground. Yet can yow doe lesse then offer your selues? For alas what will els become of us and your trades, consequently our rentes, why els the Sessions at Leeds? Well, I wish yow all accomplishment of honour, much ioying my selfe in beinge a poore ministeriall instrument therin as Sherif, gladly beholdinge it in Agbrigge as being your neare neighbour in Strafforth, which must needs participate of some heate from the brightnesse of your beames. The continewance of all good health to yow, and soe I rest, Your very affecconate freind, Th. Wentworth.

**285.** (*SC*, ii, p. 187) *To Sir Edward Leech knight. Wentworth Wood-house. 3 Jan. 1626.*

Sir, I had beene too too forgettfull of the deserued respect I beare yow, had I not perticipated with yow in this greatest and nearest losse yow haue laitly sustained. Yet I for[b]ore to trouble yow with my lynes, purposinge to haue yow at my last beinge in Darbyshire, where the suddaine newes of the hoples sicknes of my lady Shrews-bury ariueinge mee, I was not onely by meanes therof drawen from that intendment, but mett with your letters before I had made it appeare unto yow how much I was touched where yow suffered soe deeply: which I pray yow excuse, for I protest I was hartely sorry when I heard the sadd relacon of your noble Ladie's departure and may sure chalenge too as great a share in the sence and thought

of your iust greife (by the right of my true affeccon towards yow)
as any other of your freinds. I know my counsells, as in themselues
weake, soe to yow are works of superarrogation, being much better
able to aduise, and I doubt not with a Christian piety to temper
and moderate the heate and sharpnes of your owne passion. Shee
is now a blessed saint in heauen, and wee that are left, *feneramur
mortis indies moras morbis, periclis, luctibus, molestiis*. I will therfore
from my hart pray to God that as children wee maie improue upon
this chastizement and that in his good and acceptable tyme, hee may
repay yow with many lasting comfortes for this, which hee hath
bene pleased to depriue yow of. Sir, I desire in pursuite of what
yow writt to mee, that yow will appoint some tyme and place wherin
I will not faile to obserue yow (soe as it bee not before Friday cum
seuennight) to mediate in such matters as maie happen questionable
betwixt the lords, my sister Sauile and her children. And since I
haue nothinge in this world so neare my hart, as to see all things
composed and wrapped upp in freindshipp and peace betwixt those
I so much and so truly honour and loue. And that wee shall come
in all duty to offer our selues at (*p. 188*) their feete, let mee entreate,
nay euen presse in season and out of season, for your good and
noble endeauoures in effectinge it, which in all assurance I repose
my self upon and shall acknowledge as the greatest obligacon I can
haue from any man aliue. My nephew Sauile hath taken possession
of Brearley, by reason I heard nothinge from yow on Sunday
last, but if there bee any thinge yow shall not approue, I wilbee
accomptable so farre forth unto the seruice and duty I owe the
lords and my perticular respect and affeccon to yow, as there shalbee
noe use made of itt to their Lordships' preiudice. Thus desiringe to
understand how yow will dispose of mee herein by this bearer, I
shall retaine with my selfe all constancie and assurance of abideing
Your euer most affecconate freind, Th. Wentworth.

**286.** (*SC*, ii, p. 188) *To Lord Clifford. Wentworth Woodhouse.*
*11 Jan. 1626.*

My much honored Lord, I am to giue unto God all praise, and
unto your lordship humble thanks for the newes yow were pleased
to impart unto mee by Mr Greene of my Ladie's beinge with child,
I shall continew them unto the same giuer, that hee may blesse it in
the budd and fruite to the enlargement of the honour and happy
estate of your honorable name and familie, wherin no man liuinge
out of your owne bowells shall take more comfort, more reioyce to
see then my selfe. Wee shall (as I laitly heard from London) haue a

Coronation the second, a Parliament the sixt of the next month. My Lord of Holland and Sir Dudley Carleton sworne Counsellores, the firste sent into Fraunce to disperse some little clouds (*p. 189*) or darknesse betwixt the two kings, so that their thoughts and designes maie reflect cleare and faire upon each other, without any interposicon; the latter shalbee vicechamberlaine. The Earle of Kelley is suspected to haue held some undue intelligence with Spaine, his papers haue bene searched, his secretary comitted to the Gatehowse and a Scottish Jesuite frequenting his howse sent to the Tower. I do not beleiue they beginne with him in iest, but that they will fully pay him the old score, for what can bee expected lesse from such true and mindfull paymaisters? The oath of Alleagiance hath bene offered and taken by the Queene's seruants without any refusall, sauinge a while by her secretary, which (if shee had not interposed) had lost his place onely upon the circumstance of tyme, in that hee did it not so soone as hee should haue done; another pronostick of a Parliament. Count Tilly being before Newbourg, a towne in the king of Denmarke's proteccon, gaue upon it and was beaten of by a sally forth of the towne with a losse of 2000 men, but after beinge againe reinforced by the Emperour gaue on againe and hath slaine the kinge of Denmarke's generall of his horse, a great many of his chiefe comaunders and of his souldiers to the number of 6000, for which good fortune bonefires and great iollity at Brussells. Surely if this kinge should chance but to stumble, it is to bee feared our hopes will fall flatt to the ground in Germany and dangers arise upp in their place nearer home and ourselues. God, that guideth all to the accomplishment of his determinate counsells, dispose for the best, if it bee his blessed will, and send your lordship many happy new yeares. Your lordship's most humbly to bee comaunded, Th. Wentworth.

I beseech these lynes may present my humble duty to my lord, my seruice to my lady and my little mistresse.

**287.** *From Sir Henry Savile of Methley. 11 April 1626 (SC, xx/255).*

Sir, you knowe I promised to sende to you upon seuerall occasions, but for the Inquisition for the busynes of Recusants ytt ys lyke to be sent you upp to London. This bearer, your tenant, Jo: Clough of Rigton, comes to you to auoyde the double chardge in the sub-sedies by recusancye of one Oglethorpe of Thornor, who upon his conformitie in religion certifyed under the Archbishoppe's seale ys for any thinge I knowe to be dischardged of his double burthen, though formerly conuict. I haue sent you the order of the Exchequer

Chamber in the case of Mr Gascoigne, to rectifye that judgement in poynt of seazure of the goods of Recusants where they haue leases of theyre landes from the kinge. I haue alsoe sent you the pamphlett, sett out by dyrection of the Lords of the Counsell, touchinge trayninge and disciplyninge of souldiours,[1] of which subiect I haue noe other treatize and therefore I pray you sende me all back agayne that I sende you in the boxe, exceptinge the paper that conteynes Sir Thom: Sauile's gloues, due to you upon the wager of the Judges' opinion at the Assyses. He ys this day gone towards London in some haste, pretendinge his father did hastelye send for him; he came yesterday for his 200[li] in golde, whiche when I had layde downe upon the table he called in for Mathew Feilde to tell ytt, who, he told me, should paye ytt agayne to me on Satterday next att the returne of Tutburie marte, which I take for good payment. Hee hath undertaken to exchange some that are in priuy seales for some that are out upon my certificate to my Lord Treasorer, wherin yf he prevayle Richard Marris and Wm. Colburne shall escape absolutly. I haue sent you herein his *petit poulet*, which he sent me this morninge before he put foot in styrope, whereby you may perceyue what skirmishe was att the Counsell table the last Thursday with my Lord President about the priuy seales; wherein he ytt seemes ys desyrous to gratifye the cuntry, after all his deuyses of advanceinge the Duke's desygnes in parlement, to complye with the complaynt of the cuntry att least in somthinges. Lastly I haue sent you all my parlement papers to peruse and what you knowe more of a latter date I pray you communicate to your assuredly affectionate frende, H. Savile. 11° April 1626.

[*In Wentworth's hand*] A coppy of Sir Tho. Sauile's letter mentioned in Sir Henrye's on the other side.

Sir, my foote in the stirrup makes my letter sutable to my paper, *more Laconico*. You shall be sure to understande with speed my successe with my lord Tres: and the new Priuye seales, if I obtaine them shallbe safely deliuered you. A letter last night tells me that the last Thursday in the afternoone my father and my Lord President mett att the Counsell table about the Priuy Seals. My father in the behalfe of the cuntry complained and shewed the presidents out of Sir Robert Pie's office that this County of Yorke was neuer aboue 3300[li] and now it is 10,000; noe cuntrye of England exceedes ther old proportion but ours; he desires an abatement and a Commision to others besides my Lord Presidentt. What effect itt hath I knowe not, because my letter came on Thursday morning away, but

---

[1] This probably refers to *Instructions for Musters and Arms . . . 1623;* see L. Boynton, *The Elizabethan Militia, 1558–1638* (London, 1967), pp. 240–41.

I am sure my lord Scroope hath the king's profitt on his side, which is a shrewde weighty argumentt. The Duke hath publickly renounced any hande in placing my lord Scroope heare, but that he bought itt of my lord Sheffeilde. The Corporation[1] is not as yet passed, neither is itt soe forwarde as I thought, for unlesse itt may be a burgesse towne they will haue none, which is not in Sir Arthur Ingram's power to effect. If any in our notes should cum unto you with ther money in the mean space, you will giue them day till you hear from me; and soe in hast I kisse your handes and rest, yours euer asseured, Tho. Sauile. I haue sent your papers.

### 288. *From Sir Thomas Fairfax. Denton. 16 April 1626 (SC, xx/257).*

Sir, I haue diuers occations of a littell stay, thoughe I sit upon thornes til this bill be answeird and one other in exchange; the [?] tould my sonne that he intendid not to serue subpenurs upon you or me, but I would not haue such a record lefte unanswerid and he goe scoutfre. I haue latlie found a myne of coole and I desier yow would send me a skelfull man to hew it; we haue none in thes partes, you haue many, I would set som to worke bycause now the time is fitt. If your stay were till the middest of the next weke, I should be redie to wate upon yow at Newarke what day yow would, but that wilbe the sownist of my goinge. I know not how to send to my Lord President befor that time; if I can, I will. I haue sent you the bill and desier you will giue it the carage to London, if the smell of such stinkinge lyes be not dangerus in thes times of infection. Thus in your messinger's hast I take leaue. Denton, 16 Aprill 1626. Your frind to doe you seruiss, T. Fairfax. My lord Clifforde wilbe with me on Teusday night.

### 289. *From Sir Henry Savile. Methley. 1 May 1626 (SC, xx/258).*

Sir, ys there noe remedie but that my olde kinsman must thus gallantly affront first my lord president and then us two in surveying *de novo*, thus our actions through the whole Westrydinge, as under pretense of seruice to his cuntrie by way of abatement of the priuy seale moneyes. The newe assessinge and dispensinge must be wholly lefte to him and his sonne alone and to Sir Jaruis Cutler, George Claypham and John Harryson heare belowe; my brother and I displaced out of our collection for a matter of 1800[ii], that by the same lordes were once thought fitt to collect fyue thousande and

---

[1] This probably refers to the charter for the incorporation of Leeds.

the worse of us beinge better in estate then all the other 3 put together. I put the Collectors in the ranke of disposers, because they haue more fauours and trust then my brother Goodricke and I had; for they haue blankes to insert *ad placitum* and they deale betwixt theyre frendes and theyre ennemies of the inferior ranke *quod libet licet* (I meane for such as the olde gallant and his sonne were ignorant of att London) stoopinge farre lower euen in the towne of Leedes then I did, especially to such as haue not the fauour of Mr Harryson, Medcalfe and Benson who, I suppose passe all *gratis* by speciall dyrection, as Dan. Foxcrofte and Jo. Clough with other of his speciall frendes doe. Thomas Whitley before readylye and willingly, as you can witnesse, 50$^{li}$ payde, nowe in regard of seruice done and to be done 10$^{li}$ to the great shame of all such curmogians.

The olde man himselfe and his sonne and sonnes in law, now I verily beleeue nothinge, before (they 3) 90$^{li}$. My brother and I for the fyue hundred myles rydinge to disperse the priuy seales and asmuch more to be ridde in the recollectinge of them by our seruants, requyted with eyther of us a newe priuy seale, his 15$^{li}$, myne 30$^{li}$, and must needes be deliuered me by the handes of John Harryson when I came to sitt for the poore att Leedes. I made shew upon the deliuery to esteeme ytt light in regard of the somme, sayinge I would haue giuen twyse as much willingly to haue bene ridde of my collectorshippe. Harryson sayth he ys as well pleased as yf Cristall Abbey[1] had bene giuen him and that he hath by this office saued 40$^{li}$ for himselfe and 20$^{li}$ for his sister Gledhill and thus Sir John payes the cuntrie as he beleeues 3000$^{li}$, which they haue spent in his elections, out of the kinge's purse, but whose doinge is this? the grand Duke's, his master, or hath he had the good luck to befoole a whole counsell of state to the kinge's preiudice?

I could not well be sylent as the case standeth, the rather because you are att the fountayne and therefore attempted Mr Chancellor of the Exchequer by this enclosed, wherof I haue sent you a coppie and to be further proceeded in as you shall advyse. Yf you thinke any good ys to be done in ytt, I hope you may without preiudice deliuer my letter to the Chancellor, who beinge a wyse gentleman will upon the readinge of the letter giue you satisfaction in what course further to proceed or not proceed. Att least I hope he will take order for dischardge of our priuy seales in regard of the preiudice wee haue alreadie sustayned by the busynes. Yf you fynde anythinge fitt to be done herein, you may in my name acquaynt the Master of the Rolles with the copie of my letter to the Chancellor,

---

[1] Presumably Kirkstall Abbey in the parish of Leeds.

out of which and this present to yourselfe you may reasonable fully understande this affayre.

Michael Wentworth ys nowe as I heare 20$^{li}$ and my uncle of Elmsall 15$^{li}$, soe as in effect this newe levye ys layde eyther upon theyre unbeloued frendes or upon such as they knowe not, but little or nothinge upon themselues or theyres. There ys 600$^{li}$ nowe readie unrecalled in Robert Kaye's handes, readie to be payde in upon your appointment yf that may worke anythinge; and though my lordes haue requyred me to pay back all I had formerly receyued, yet can I pay none hastily, hauinge yesterday receyued answer from Anthony Foxcroft, who had 500$^{li}$ to be payde into the Exchequer the 10th of Maye, that ytt wilbe 5 weekes before he can pay me back the same money in the cuntrye. Soe as til I gett that I am not lyke to pay much, which wilbe an occasion that these newe ones will not euer be soe readylie payde, as Sir John S. hath made the lords beleeue when he drewe them to the abatement. Ytt may be Harryson will certyfye att the 12 dayes' ende, yf I pay not and the old Cauallero (yf his grand Duke stands good, which I perceyue now grows very doubtfull) I suppose would not be unwillinge to sende for me by a messinger to the Councell table to gratify the burgecs of Leedes. But yf any such matter should be, I pray you, or any frende of yours, to undertake for me that yf this course cannot preuent theyre desygne, I will not be refactorie and yf you should attempt to see theyre certificate in the priuy seale office, I suppose you could cease your labour, for how can there be any certificate, considering the blankes are not yet returned?

And I am of opinion yf they were to be publiquely chardged with any partialitie, they will [on] the insdent haue blankes to be suddenly sent to the parties to excuse themselues, yf you thinke not of some course to preuent them in that poynte. Yf you lyke not deliuer my letter to the Chancellor in person, which one frende and cuntryman may do for another in common curtesie and neighbourhood, then lett ytt be sent unto Mr Cowper, my Lord Keeper's man, to deliuer ytt in my name and as you shall dyrect him. Soe as nowe enough of this matter for your full informacon till I can heare from you restinge, Your affectionate and asseured frend, H. Savile. Metheley the first of May, 1626.

I haue sent you a coppie of the Lords' letters for our dischardge of collectinge and another sent from Leedes of the ioy there conceyued by the Burgecs in congratulation of Mr Harryson, maior *in futuro*, soe I shall shortly be in as good grace there as you. Anthon: Foxcroft hath a priuy seale for x$^{li}$, his father none, some say Fr. Stringer hath one they say of x$^{li}$. To my honorable good frend

Sir Thomas Wentworth Baronet at his lodging in Fetter Lane London.

**290.** *Sir Henry Savile to the Chancellor of the Exchequer* (*SC*, xx/259) [*Copy*].

May yt please your honor. Myselfe togeither with Sir Henry Goodricke, my brother in lawe, wear by letters from my lords of the counsell of the third of Marche nomynated and appointed Collectors of the privie seales within the West Ridinge of Yorkshire and wee then receuied 300 privie seales by the messenger, whereof by consent of my fellowe collector I dispersed withall care and expediton 200 and odde and he the reste. Upon these privie seales wee had receaued the sume of fifteene hundred pounds ready to be paid into the Exchequer in the beginninge of Maye. Nowe in the midste of our colleccon, when all men in effecte weere readye to paye, soe as I doubted nott to haue paide into the Receipte by the latter ende of this moneth att least 3000$^{li}$ and within a moneth after 1000$^{li}$ more, are newe letters from theire Lordships of the xiiiith of Aprill procured by Sir John Sauile, upon pretence of desiringe an abatement, supposinge a surcharge of the cuntrey, nott onely to require us to forbeare the further execucon of our offices, but alsoe to paye back such monies as wee shall haue receiued and to returne unto my Lord Privie Seale the whole number of privie seales receaued and wholye dispersed by us; which in regarde of the greate extent of our barren cuntrey hath and must cost our seruants neare a thousand myles ryding for the delyuerie and recollecting them backe againe. To the pointe of surcharge I maye nott to muche agrauate any thinge against a cuntrey where I and my posteritye intende to lyue; on the other side I maye not be silente in regard I had a principall hand for the partes neare unto me as a deputie lieutennant in the certyfycate of the names of the lenders, whose estates I knowe as much (and use them lesse) then Sir John Sauile dothe. And thus much I well knowe that if Sir John Sauile had not interposed betwixt the kinge and the cuntrey, his Maiestie's coffers had been supplyed with 2500$^{li}$ more money then nowe they are like to be and in soe readye a course of payment as that 1800$^{li}$ he hath undertaken to bring in, instead of 4 or 5 thousand; neither is his good seruice to his Maiestie ended heare, but haueing obteined fauour of the lords to interrupte the proceedings of the former privie seales, well settled for the greater advantage of his maiestie's affaires, the necessetie whereof was the cause I thought my cuntreymen weere iustlye bounde att this tyme to streche theire purse strings and yett without sinking under the burthen. I being bounde aswell to the loue of my neighbours as to serue his Maiestie and in this affaire, the rather because his Maiestie is neuer truely serued by his subordinate instruments where pressures are imposed to extinguishe loue of subiects. The said gentleman, allowing noething for good but what he dothe himselfe, hath soe farre and powerfully prevailed with theire Lordshipps as he hath nott onely procured this greate abatement to make him popular in the cuntrey to the disseruice of his Maiestie, but theire Lordshipps haue, upon his requeste, displaced us of our collectorshipps to put in three persons of his owne choyce and who altogeither are nott able to make the worser of us (yett perchance sufficient for the payment of $1800^{li}$). But I suppose his intent in that was principally, if not onely, to affront us, whoe, if wee weere fytt to be collectors for 4 or 5 thousand, could nott be unfitt for $1800^{li}$, though abatement weere to [be] yeilded unto. Theire Lordshipps haue further giuen waye to recall in all the former privie seales and lefte the imposeinge and assessinge of the newe in effect, if nott altogeither, to himselfe whoe hath soe partially dealte in the distribution thereof betwixt his freinds and such as he doth nott affect, as I forbeare to mencon; and for myselfe in pertyculer, to requite my seruice already done in this busines, hath sente me one of the largest syze which I conceaue is to litle to do the seruice I owe unto his Maiestie, but onely in regarde of the greate troble I haue already susteined and am still like to doe by the doeing and undoeing of ytt and that ytt is done unto us nott without shewe of indignitye, as though wee weare nott worthie to be still trusted with the king's money aswell as such as are farre our inferiours.

I shall be a troublesome suter unto your honor, of whose fauour I cannott but a little presume, to lett his Maiestie or my lord Threasorer understand howe this busines hath beene carryed to his preiudice in pointe of profett and to the disreputacon of such as are ever readiest to serue him in theire countries. For howsoeuer my Lord President might be misguyded with the citizens att Yorke, yett I hope there weare noe such mistakeings or pressures where wee dealte. And if I exceded the presidents of former tymes, which was the greatest motiue to abatement, I am the rather to be excused, because no rules weere giuen me to followe and if my zeale to doe his Maiestie seruice be accounted an error, I presume yt deserues rather pardon then punishment by sending me a newe privie seale, for discharge whereof I esteeme nott the burthen to be soe heauie that I would once moue your honor to speake a word either to your owne power, or to any other man lyueing for me. But to putt by

an affronte uniustly putt upon me by one that professeth himselfe a
kinsman and of my name, I cannott but humblye entreate your
honorable assistance in a good cause to right me, soe farre forth as
to your honor's wisedome shall be thought fitting, craueing pardon
for my boldenes, I being thereunto encouraged by your former
honorable respects towards me. Soe reste, Your honor's humblie to
be comaunded, H.S. Metheley the first of Maye 1626. I durst haue
undertooke to haue supplied all mistakes in the former privie seales
of 4 or 5 thousand pounds value with a matter of 300$^{li}$, but in all
these letters from my Lords I doe nott obserue once your honor's
penne to any of them.

**291.** *To C. Radcliffe. Wentworth Woodhouse* (*SC*, xxi/36) [*Copy*]

W.W. 19° Julii 1626. Mr Radcliffe, before the receipte of your letter
I hard from aboue that Sir John Savile hath for himself gott the
custoship. And for my owne interest I doe nott envye him hauing
itt att a dearer rate then I trust in God I shall, or any of myne, ever
enioye anythinge. Butt for your interest I am right sorye, yett itt is
not fitt for mee to strive in your behalf where I see well I can doe
you noe good, which, if there were hope of, I assure you I would not
be negligent in your behalf. For the meanes you may of your self
make to this old dogge, I leaue itt wholie to your self, nott louing
you so little as to wish you nott to use all you have with iudgment
and ground, butt I am fully perswaded you will never wynne uppon
him the least tincture of any favour. I have delivered unto your
sonne my opinion barelie, as an advise to a frend that desires itt,
butt nott in any wise byndinglie unto you, for I shalbee truely glad
of any satisfaccon you may geue yourself in any other waye and soe
leaue itt to your owne free libertie and choyce. We see daily things
to happen beyond expectacon, this I must confesse beyond my beleef
and that as I thought uppon some reason. Now doubtles the old
fellow thinks itt is my night, yett hauing a little knowne the vicisitude
which raignes here amongst mortall men, I doe with all pacience
and modestie expect better tymes and in the meane space have
within my self as cherefull a light as maybee. For I nether am conscious of any fault from hence, nor yett guiltie of any vertue in him
that might iustlie occasion this remove and, seeinge I haue soe
much pacience my self, I may well wish you my frend some part of
ytt. For in truth I think I can spare you some and leave ynough for
my self that in other things itt may bee want of ytt sufficientlie.
With this neverthelesse that as wee fall together, soe when itt shall
please God to think a better chance more fitt for us, wee will likewise

rise together, which that I may remember the better, I pray you lett mee haue a coppie of this letter when wee meet next and itt shallbee well seene I will nott forgett. Farewell to you hartilie and soe I rest, your euer assured affecconate frend, Th. Wentworthe.

**292.** *Wentworth's speech at receiving the writ putting him out of the Custos-ship (Knowler, i, p. 36; SC, xl/50), July 1626.*

**293.** *Wentworth to Sir Richard Weston, July 1626 (Knowler, i, pp. 35–36, SC, xl/50); asks him to testify to the esteem which King James had for Wentworth, who is not conscious of any guilt requiring him to be put out of all commissions and humbly asks that his faults should be explained to him.*

**294.** *Wentworth to Sir Richard Weston, July 1626 (Knowler, i, pp. 34–35; SC, xl/50). He has been privy to his dealings with Buckingham during the parliament at Oxford and their reconciliation last Easter term, despite which Wentworth has been dismissed from his place as Custos Rotulorum.*

**295.** *To Sir Edward Stanhope. Wentworth Woodhouse. 10 Oct. 1626 (SC, xxi/41).*

Sir, I thanke you for the letter you sent me, which I had formerly hearde of, but not seen; a plainer flatter peece of stuffe, I haue not reade; the pen a man may without profanation say was none of the curiouse cutt ones, butt itt is like all the rest. I send itt you hearinclosed. You will excuse me I writt not unto you by your seruantt; it was afternoone and to say truthe I was ague-idle. Ther shallbe noe distresse taken or leuye made upon any your landes you maybe sure, soe long as I am sheriffe. I pray you presse your undersheriffe to gett you a dischardge, for he is a slippery colt, I knowe him well. I must confesse I haue a kalender of Sir John's proceedings att Wakefeild, butt not of that which past from him att Leedes. If by your meanes I could gett the particulares of that too in writing with the wittnesses' names, I would lay itt up with the other, till they might be in season and in the meane time take my self much beholden unto you for them. My wife remembers her best respects to yourself and lady, my seruice to you both and soe I rest, Your euer affectionate cosin and asseured frend, Th. Wentworth. W.W. this 10th of October 1626.

**296.** *To Sir Edward Stanhope. Gawthorpe. 23 April 1627 (SC, xxi/42).*

Sir, Ther came of late a letter from his Maiestie's Priuye Counsell directed to the deputie lieutenants and justices of the county of

Yorke, requiring them, all excuses sett apartte (which had been formerly made by the deputie lieutenantts), to leauye upon the cuntrey the thirde partt of the setting forth of three shipps for his Maiestie's seruice forth of the portt of Hull. Which letters being soe pressing and urging of this dutye and the time hastening us either to the work or to a present answeare, the deputie lieutenants wear forced to appointe a present day for meeting of us all togeither att Yorke, the 26th of this presentt moneth; and we togeither (with notice of the time and place) to send the letter away to thos of the other Ridings. Itt falls then to my lott to giue you notice therof and in the name of us all to desire you ther to assiste us with your presence and counsell, being as we conceaue itt a matter of very great consequence and generally importing the whole county. I desire my wife's and mine best respects may be remembred to your noble self and lady, and soe in sum haste I remaine, your most asseured, affectionate frend and cosin, Th. Wentworth. Gawthorpe, 23th of Aprill 1627.

**297.** *Lord Clifford to Wentworth, 30 April 1627 (Knowler, i, pp. 36–37; SC, xvi/169). As the stream runs strongly against refusers of the loan, who are being imprisoned, he urges Wentworth to answer in person to the Privy Council.*

**298.** *Lord Baltimore to Wentworth, 1 May 1627 (Knowler, i, p. 37; SC, xii/5). He urges him either to pay the loan to the Commissioners or reserve his answer for the Privy Council.*

**299.** *Lord Clifford to Wentworth, 2 May 1627 (Knowler, i, p. 38; SC, xvi/171). He urges him to pay the loan to the Commissioners; only friends of Sir John Savile want him to come before the Privy Council; the king vows perpetual remembrance against refusers.*

**300.** *From Sir Henry Savile. York. May 1626 (SC, xxi/43).*

Sir, your agues will proue lyke my goute, *supersedeas* to all ill busynes. There mett this morninge att the Castle some fewe number more then the last tyme, in all under a score and dyuers that were present the last tymes to sympathize with you came not. The first thinge put to the question amongst us was whether to doe any thinge in the busynes in regard of noe greater apperances. The greater nomber were of opinion to proceed; my reason in particuler was that I thought this a fayre tyme to withstand an inouacon of soe ill consequence. After many debates I was entreated to make a draught of the letter enclosed, which receyued some little alteracons in wordes, but little or nothinge in matter, saue that I denyed further that euer there was any precident of a generall levye upon the countie in generall, which was confessed to be true *de facto* by all, but ytt was not thought fitt to mencon any matter of precident att all. To be short, *opus huius diei* that kepes me heare 2 nightes and your footemen one *patet in quadam Schedula huic annex'*, with the copie of our letter to the Lordes with such handes as were present.

This morninge Sir William Ellis of the Counsell came to my lodginge and ytt was to acquaint me with the letters from the lords of the Counsell to call all you non-payers of the Loane within the Westryding before certayne of us and for not payinge to bynde you ouer to the Boarde. I sende you a copie of the liste, beinge some 17 in nomber, great and little. Sir William Ellis yt seemes beinge att good leysure had drawen formall letters readie to be sygned, which dyuers of us sygned accordingly. The letters I haue in chardge to conuey unto the collectors to distribute to euery seuerall person which hath not payd within the diuision where the collectors dwell respectiuely. The day appointed to come in ys the 29th of this monthe att Yorke. There ys one to be sent to you by Vescie or Spencer and yet are you a comissioner appoynted by the Lords' letters to take both your owne and other menne's answeres; yf you will haue a copie of the Lordes' letters for this affayre, upon your desyre knowen, I will sende ytt you by the Messinger. Soe you see I giue you lawfull warninge and reste euer your assured frende, H. Savile. Yorke, this Thursday night.

Yorke and Hull had certifyed a senight agoe absolutely that they were not able to undergoe theyr chardge and what could our thirde do where 2-thirdes fayled but fall to the grounde for companye? To my honorable good frend Sir Thomas Wentworthe att his house Gawthorpe. [*Endorsed*] 9 of May 1627.

**301.** *Lord Haughton to Wentworth, 19 May 1627 (Knowler,* i, pp. 37–38; *SC,* xxii/60), *giving news about refusers of the loan, Buckingham's tardiness in sailing and a projected toleration in Ireland.*

**302.** *Lord Baltimore to Wentworth, 21 May 1627 (Knowler,* i, p. 39; *SC,* xii/6). *He is about to leave for Newfoundland and urges Wentworth to pay the loan in the country.*

**303.** *To Manchester. WentworthWoodhouse. 3 June 1627 (SC, xxi/44).*

May it please your lordship. By letter of the 27th of the last month
I promised his Maiestie's Commissioners (as I take it) for the last
loane to appeare before my lords of the counsell. This I shall most
readily performe as soone as possibly I maie, but truly a violent fitt
of the stone this last weeke hath soe indisposed mee as I write euen
these lynes in greate paine and doubte I shall not bee able to endure
soe long a journey thes seauen or eight daies, till I bee a little better
confirmed in my health. Therfore least a stay thus condiconed might
seeme neglect of my duty and undertaking, I haue made bold hereby
humbly to beseech your lordship to impart thus much to the rest of
my honorable good lords, if there bee occasion, and that both they
and your lordship out of your accustomed goodnes will vouchsafe
to dispense with mee for a few daies, seing I will by God's grace
without faile, or causelesse delay, waite their good pleasures as in
all humblenes and obedience I ought. My Lord, I will presume noe
farther to trouble you, more then to write myselfe, your lordship's
most humbly to be commanded, Th. Wentworth. Wentworth
Woodhouse, this 3ᵈ of June 1627. To the right honorable the Earle
of Manchester, lord president of his Majesty's most honourable
priuie counsell.

**304.** *Wandesford to Wentworth, 14 July 1627 (Knowler, i, pp 39–40; SC,*
*xvi/263); asks for a copy of his answers before the Privy Council.*

**305.** *From Sir Arthur Ingram. 16 July 1627 (SC, xii/7).*

Nobell Sir, wee hear in the cuntry thatt you ar now a prissoner in
the Marshallse, the which I know by you itt was expected long
sines thatt the yssew would bee as now is fallen outt; in regard how
you stod in your opinion ryssing from a good hartt and outt of a
good consiens and therfor I make no doutt thatt itt is anny trobell
to you att all. For your freinds to say the ar sorry for itt, suerly for
my self thatt professeth my self to bee one and such an one as doth
truly and faithfully loue you, I cannott, nor shall nott in the lest
kind bee soo. Imprissonmentt to such as dow fowell and bass
offencis must neads trobell both the party committed and all his
freinds thatt loue him, butt to bee committed in a causs of this nattur
doth so much redown to your honor and to the honor of your
posteryty thatt your freinds [should] rather bee glad of itt then other
wiss, with all itt is [*page torn*] to your freinds to hear how braue —
— — discreetly you carryed your self — and in thatt you ar much —
to my Lord Presidentt who repor — — therof. The greatest trobell

thatt — friends in this causs is thatt th — — good compani and the best good the — — presentt can dow for you is to pray — God for the contineewing of your helth. Butt yf in any of your occasions hear in the cuntry your sarvantts and such as you putt in trust shall wantt my help in any thing, yf you pless so much to fauor me as to directt them to me, I shall most willingly, ether by riding, or gowing, dow any thing thatt shall ly in my power. And so, praying you to remember my seruis to your nobell Lady, my Lord Clar and his nobell compani, nott forgetting honest Mr Rattclyff, I rest, your faythfull and most asuered freind to the uttmost of my power, Ar. Ingram. This 16th of July 1627. Yf you pless to return any answer to Mr Wansford and me you may d[eliver] them to this messenger safly.

**306.** *From Sir Richard Hutton junior. Thornhill. 21 July 1621 (SC, xii/7+1).*

Sir, give me leaue to salute you with the newes of my wife's safe deliuerye of a daughter, not doubting but that a neece is wellcome to you, though may be not soe wished for as a nephew. But fearing that if it had come now itt would haue lacked a godfather, I hope 'tis but defferred, if we be thankfull for this, which, ioyned with her health and good recouery, I shall euer account of as a great blessing. I thinke it will be called Anne, a name 'tis thought you well approue of; I need not tell you who it is like, the weomen neuer vary in that poynt, though the time might question itt. I haue nothing else to acquant you with, theyrfore I am the larger in this and the freer because I am confident that you will ioy in itt. I desire you to present my humble seruice to your Ladie, praying for her safe deliuery which I hope you will returne us eyr longe, ioying us with that we shall be all heere glade to heare of. My wife remembers her seruice to you both and I desire you to remember me to my Cousen Ratcliff and wife. I wish I could stand you in any stead in this your restrant, but I knowe your owne resolution giues libertie to itt, soe God giue you health, which I shall allwayes pray for and euer rest most reedie to serue you in anything wherin you are pleased to command mee, Your affectionate brother and seruant, Ri. Hutton. Thornhill, July the 21 [1627].

**307.** [*Endorsed*] Mr Chancelour of the Dutchy and my answear, 25 July 1627 (*SC*, xxi/45).

Sir, I knowe not what destiny infatuates men of understanding of late times that they neither take nor understand any thing in the right order, but hauing to doe with authority they procure ther owne harme, working contrary to ther owne good and ther owne ends and by a strandge fate dayly hurting the publique which they pretende soe much to uphold. If you thinke me able to giue you safe aduise and willing to doe it faithfully, be you none of thos ninnies that refuse to goe to the places whear they are confined, nor send noe such excuses as want of money and horses, which must be interpreted rather scornes then answeares that haue either truthe or duty in them. If you haue care of any beside yourself, conuey this aduise to them for yourself, since you will not be wise, yet I am lothe you should be madde. Returne me this letter by this bearer and if I doe not see you before you goe, take this with you that you are in as fond and as foolishe a way for the publique, for your priuate as euer wise man was. H. M[ay].

Sir, my eyes were not my owne this morning, else should I haue returned your letter by the bearer, but in good faith I mistooke it in that point uppon the first reading which I will rectifie presently uppon the secound. Sir, I giue you humble thanks for your care of me, which I esteeme as an acte of a noble frend and shall soe endeuour to deserue it. I am none of those which will refuse confinement. I will not dispute but obay, allbeit I must undergoe this cours with as much inconueniencye (itt may be) as any. I was euer of that minde from the first, as one naturally more delighting, more comforted to serue my soueraigne his owne way then my owne; and when I doe otherwise seemingly, I shall allways iudge it my misfortune, nay my greatest misfortune. Onely your Clerk of the Councell which now waites useth me not well; for he will still committ mee, warne me to prepare and confine me too by an other man's name, not my owne. For if he looke upon my appearanse, he will finde me appeare as knight and Barronet and not knight which other men ar styled by and not I. Neither will he mend it for any thing I can say. Such warrants as theis I must indeede stick upon, least I might seeme voluntary to embrace that which of all other I would auoyde, to be thus made a stranger to my owne countrie and estate. But itt befitts not the clay to question the fashon, but to take such figure yeeldingly as is pressed upon him; and I trust soe in the conclusion, according to the Italian prouerbe, he that bends himself shall fitt himself. Sir, I will waite of you befor my departure, Godwilling, and shall allwaies rest, Your honour's humbly to be comanded, Th. W.

**308.** *From Lord Darcy. Aston. 31 July 1627 (SC, xii/8).*

My good cosen, as a frend and kynseman I cannot but greve for your restraynt and the rather because I feare the same may endanger your health, to prevent which mischefe I praye, as you are wyse and iudiciouse, that you will imploy boath for your owne good and use such meanes as that with spede you may gayne your freedome, which obtayned will not only be comfortable to all those that love you, but to me more particularly, who shall never fayle to wish unto you all prosperetye, neither to manefeste to yourselfe and the world that I am, Your assured frend and cosen, Jo. Darcye. Aston this last of July [1627]. I pray you present my service to your right noble and vertuouse Ladye, for whose saftye in parting with her great bellye I shall pray.

**309.** *Denzil Holles to Wentworth, 9 August 1627 (Knowler, i, pp. 40–41; SC, xxii/61). He tells of economic distress caused by the war and lack of prizes; more refusers have been sent for.*

**310.** *From Sir Richard Hutton junior. Thornhill. 10 Aug 1627 (SC, xxii/5).*

Sir, I can returne you nothing for the passages you were pleased to write to me, but my thankes accompanied with my ioy of your health and my best wishes for the longe continuance of itt. Thes parts afford noe nouelties, but what they first receyue from you and truly that is soe well ordered that it growes mightily. The inch in the isleland being a large elle in the continent by this and soe confident we are of the great Duke's atcheivements that the ileland is but the moldhill, tis the mountaine the kingdome that we looke for, such an enemie is much expectation to performance that it makes great actions seame nothing. All heere, thankes be to God, are well; my wife growes stronge remembring her seruice to your selfe and your Ladie, to whom I desire to haue my owne presented and euer to be commanded as Your most affectionate brother and seruant, Ri. Hutton. Thornhill August the 10th [1627].

**311.** *From Francis Burdett. Birthwaite. 14 Aug 1627 (SC, xii/9).*

Worthy Sir, albeit it is my regreet not to fynde you there where I wish, yett my obligacon incites me to tender you my best remembrance there where I would not have you. I cann doe no more then heartily pray for your good health in this your restraynte; we say you must be for Wiltshire or else transplanted into Devonshire. God be your keeper where ever you goe. The bayliff [? George Radcliffe] writt me he was like to become Kentish; it is not good he should tarye there long lest he be inriched with a tayle, yet the theefe will have a gowne to hyde it.

We heare our men are landed on the iland, but with losse of divers our commanders. What if you be taken for one to supply a roome there? I knowe you are borne for your king and country, yett all babyes are not of like in dareing. And I wish you a mease of ladds (by that good mother) before you become a knight militant. There is talke of a parliament; consider whether your present estate and the strict letter of the statute will not disable you for being one of that company. If not and that you take a mynde to stand for your country, lett your freinds know in tyme. For though you be now under the wheele, yett I am perswaded you will fynd some that love you. Sir, lett me not be troublesome to you; in good earnest (might it so seeme good to his Maiestie) none shall be gladder to see you soone resident agayne att old Wentworth Woodhowse then he who is and always will be unfaynedly yours, Franc: Burdet. Birthwayd, August 14th 1627.

**312.** *From Wandesford. Sept. 1627 (SC, xvi/262).*

Sir, yours dated 17 of August together with your prittye booke giues us the first hope that the fort may be taken, though for my part I beleve, as you doe, that pert of the tayle is but weakely grounded and for any thing you have sayde I am yet a Richmundshyre man slowly beleeuing of thoss lardge promises from that iland. You have had the sceane your turne in the South, nowe we turne to the North for news and a whyle I shall intertayne you with our enterprises here. I suppose you have heard before this tyme of an advertisement from Scotland that 16 Spanish ships were landed nere Catness in the Northern perts of that kingdome, had wasted the iland of Zetland and destroyed men, woemen and children there. You may imagine howe this startled poore Barwicke, moved Northumberland to crave assistance of there levetennant, who with the spede he could poasted from Snape (where this intelligence found him) towards his chardge, his duble sumpter Peter Middleton and my self battring after as fast as we could. We found Newcastle standing where itt was wont to doe and all the trayned men of that towne marching, to mete my lord Clifford I meane. But before we had remayned 24 houres in that cuntry amonst them, the worst enemye I sawe was Mr Maior's greate peces of beife and the profuse intertainment we had from the gentlemen in thoss parts which indaingered our healths more then the Spaniards did our coastes; for the harme which was done in Zetland was committed by certayne Turkish pirates, the Spaniards never offring to land att all, but, chased about Ireland with that pursute which the duke mayde after them in his going to Fraunce, were forced this way to Dunkerke and by the way interrupted something the Holland's fishing in the nothern perts and did them and one or two of thoss men of warr which were there to defend them some harme. But the Admirall of Scotland, putting to sea upon this alaram, hath mett with them I hope by tyme and if they escaped him I knowe not howe they could pass by certayne Holland men of warr who are watching there returne upon our coastes.

But thinke you I had nothing to doe but quarell with Mr Maior's meate att Newcastle, I had the happiness to se the six men of war belonging to Sir John and for the proicet ittself I cannot say much, but I shall ever commend the discretion of the captaynes that made choyce to lye in so safe a harbor as is that of Newcastle and neare to so good a towne, whear they are feasted and courted in expectation. And can you blayme there providence when they solemly intreated my lord Clifford to intercede for them to the towne that they would lend them some powder (there owne shot serving them but for five howres fight) for which they would deposite so much mony in pawne? His answer was his commission was for land service and not for the sea. The sixpence a chaulder is nowe dewly payde and wilbe; they being subiect to that admiration of Recorder Fletewoode— when I se your welth, I admire your witt; when I se your witt, I admire your welth. The man whom I suspected to you before for a ringleader hath absolutely left the towne and the power he had among them. There is a kinsman of myne more guiltye then any other of whatsoever the towne doth good or bad, Sir Thomas Ryddall, there recorder. Yet itt is observable that divers going out of the harbor layden with coales and refusing to pay were threatened that some of there men should be taken immediately for the king's service, whereuppon they yelded, which I was sorry to heare that a good business should be spoyled in the handling. And as doth this imposition here (though by the way in the king's letter to Newcastle itt is stiled nether imposition nor composition) so doth the composition att Yorke go on smothly, the recusants having a nother saint for ther calender and rather then thear shall want rome for the temporall they will putt him in the place of the spirituall Jesuite Ignatius. Men of 800$^{ll}$ per annum have compounded for 34$^{ll}$, some that payde twenty pound monthly shall be abated. The worst is the commissioners cannot agre among them selves. Sir Artheur Ingram, having crossed a proposition mayde by the greate Oneale for a quicke dispatch of the business, was tolde in a scornefull manner (if he can doe any thing soe) that he came in his gowne and was nere his owne fyre and did eate his owne meate. But in fath I was not behynd with him, for I presently quitt the place and satt not agayne untill Sir Thomas came to intreate me. Nether were things so smoth betwixt my Lord Scrope and Sir Thomas; he had the witt to tell my lord he was a commissioner as well as he and his voyce was equall to his. In a word they were all in ielosyes, for Sir John hateth my lord and Sir Arther for combyning together to overthrowe the king's service. My lord sitts but a few dayes, leaves them to themselves, poastes away, as we thinke here, to London to informe aganst him, which we beleue the rather, because Sir Thomas Savile is gone up likewise, the truth of both which is better knowen to you by this tyme. The commissioners have adiurned ther meting untill the tenth (I take itt) of this month. They say att thess low raytes they have all ryddy compounded for 3000$^l$ per annum rent.

Your letter came in good tyme and in a good place to my hands yesterday to Scriven, a house of Sir Henry Slingsbyes nere Knaresbarrow (where Sir Arthur Ingram lyes for the sparre waters) to reforme our errors of a present parliment which so strongly had possessed him that he tould me, if I would not stand for the shyre (which he thought was fitt) he would himself; for certaynly Sir John had lost many by his harsh carradge of things in the cuntrye. But I tolde him what I beleve yet to be truth, if he hath lost one protestant, he hath gayned ten recussantts, but your letters came in the niche to stay his stomacke; but while we speake of this subiect, though I thinke itt will be like the buying a summer sute in the mid of winter, only to lye by a man 4 or 5 months, direct me howe far I shall name you to him for standing, or indeavor to stop the current of his owne conceit for himself, because we shall conclude here of the Parlimentt att least a month before you att London. I am glad to heare of your mirth by Robin Trapps and indede to fynd itt concocted in your letters. He tells me you have some hope to be downe about Michelmas for a while; if itt be so, give me lawfull warning that I may mete you any where. And if you stay there but lenten and long dayes (God willing) I will se you and once a yeare as long we live so far asunder. We lern here Sir William Cunstable should be cumed downe; if itt be so, I pray you let me knowe upon whatt tearmes, for itt is but a rumur lately cumed into thess perts. I hope you will be tyred before you reatch thus far. I pray God bless you and my ladye with health and then with a son. Remember me to Geordge and his good wife [*early September 1627*].

**313.** *From Clare. Bugden. 9 Sept. 1627 (SC, xxii/52).*

Sun Wentworth, when you and I wear hear last togeather at Bugden,

my lord of Lincolne[1] lent me a book of many Parliament notes and
precedents and among those sum of Sir Walter Rawleis, which book
yow then desyred to borrow of me and which as yet yow haue not
returned. Now my lord of Lincolne demanded it of me and I haue
promised to bring it with me at my return this way in the terme.
Whearfor I pray yow without fayle send it me downe by your seruant
Richard Morrice, or sum other safe messenger, and that as speedily
as yow cann that I may haue sum tym allso to look into it. God
graunt you and my daughter healthe and bless you bothe with his
best cumfort. Amen. Bugden this 9 7br 1627. Your very louing father,
Clare.

**314.** *From Wandesford. 9 Sept. 1627 (SC, xvi/261).*

Sir, as I was setting pen to this paper to continewe our wekely discourse, I am saluted with yours of the 23 of the last month; they cum
so slowly, so uncertaynly to us that I doubt we must interfeare
sometyms one letter of another and a litle more tyme may be allowed
for your remove further from us. I thanke you for the good news of
your accommodation att Dartford. I hope you are well placed ther by
the state for your better education. They thinke you to be (I beleve)
in your nonnadge, not fitt to governe your owne estate. Confynement,
the heler of the tyme, may perhaps work a reformation in your to
absolute and peremptorye perseverance in your owne interist and
when they se that conditionns of that bastard chylde, libertye (for itt
is begott and borne of the people) perverse and croked, are chandged
into the obedience and dewtye of a naturall subiect, you shall be
inlardged to your owne house; and therefor you doe well to begin
with that lesson first of humilitye and knowedge of your self, or
rather to repeate itt again and nowe comment upon that which you
writt before, as that which will advance you most in both thoss scoles
of religion and vertue. I shall in this envye you, though if I could
make the like use I have the same opportunitye almost that you have
to improve and studye my self. For, according to your advice for
absence, I have the contrary way absented my self from all other
places but some private pert of my owne house, knowen only to
4 or 5 of my servants. But you will say what answere to them, where
were you, when our messinger or letters came to your house? I know
not what tyme they came. I heard nothing. I was att home that very
tyme you mention, but your servants denyd you. There answere is:
though my master commanded us not to conceale anybody, yet our
mistris did (my master not being well and not fitt to be troubled)

[1] Bishop Williams.

forbid us to tell any of his being att hoame and I must blame my wife for taking so much upon her. So she must beare all and this is another poore shift of myne and please your worship, I would itt might serve there lordships as well.

But in eardnest the best I have att this tyme, my business not suffring me to remove from home, but I hope you will in good tyme release me agayne by some happy direcion, for you know my mynd. I am not one jott nerer a safe harbor then I was before, for I will ether lanch into a noble port, or abyde the storme and sea, unless itt be so rough that itt be not in the labor of the marriners or direction of the pilate to save me from shipwracke, but howe to direct me betwixt this olde rocks, Scilla and Carybdis, you are my only landemerke. Therefore I hope I shall not have a letter from you without a lyht burning to guide my passadge. But in the meane tyme for this 3 daye's sake I will forsweare the fath of anchorite while I live. I must nedes thanke you for your kind offer to afford me a bed, when in good fath I doubdt you are hardly worth above [a shilling] in all the sotherne pert of the worlde. You say a iourney to London will be the worst; itt is not so with me. I doe not thinke itt fitt for me to desyre to give my answere att the table, or if I should, could I obtayne itt, but I must deny here and then no tyme to talke of the Exchequor after. For I thinke if I prove a foole, I shall continewe so, no turning backe after we once put on motley, that must be wornee as long as the playe last.

Your newes of Denmarke seconding here what we heare from all hands is an affliction to every honest spiritt, an argument in my opinion of God's grete iudgment upon us; as though we should be cleare syghted to discerne thess false colors of our flattering promises from Fraunce and dimsyghted to not [be] able to beholde the trewe obiect of our honor and safety consisting in the welfayre of Denmarke and Germanye. And for a parliment I am never two dayes in one mynde, wauering betwixt the two argumentts in your letter, and blayme me not, for in good fath I thinke they are so themselves, even as there uncertayne iuncture and disiuncture of things (as your olde freind the duchye sath) leade them. But I cannot make that use of this smoking proclamation you doe, had itt bene a contrarye remedy they woulde have sett this gloss upon some ritcher worke; I rather compayre itt to the begining and subtily creping in of carragies which like a frutefull serpent hath had so numerus, so poysonus a progenye. All we can doe that are lokers on is to implore the almighty to direct his Maiesty['s] heart and hands aright in thess greate and important necessityes. For my pert if the howse doe mete, I pray God send them the discrete mixture of patience and and curradge to apply the proper cure to thess bleedings wounds. The fewer Corritonns and

Katesbyes the better, itt is no tyme nowe to playe at sharpe with the Crowne. For the subsedyes I will tyme itt out till Michelmas and expect what there councells will then bring forth. But I doubt I shall not haue patience to forbeare any longer from discovering my self whether a Bullinbrukian or Cowcichyan. You will remember my wife's service and myne to your red fish and that dish please not your pallett, I wish you were bound to drinke nothing but vinegar all your life.

Your Ant Dandby since she sent to you is better then she was, but Marther Britten thinkes she was taken with a palsy, her right hand and foot being benumnd so that she cannot stir them and att the first her tung a litle taken from her, but she tells me itt is the grief, howsoever (God be thanked) she is very harty and plesant and shall want no trewe comfort or service I can doe her.

Tell Geordge [Radcliffe] I thinke he is much like Will Herbert, never writes to one in debt; but if itt be so with me, itt is more then he knowes, for I have sent the 100[1] to Mr Grenewoode upon Saturday last, September 9 1627.

**315.** *From Sir Thomas Vavasour. Haslewood. 10 Sept. 1627* (*SC,* xii/11).[1]

Worthy Sir, I am glad of this opertunitye to present my seruice unto you, hopeing to heare you are ether upon absolute inlargment, or els confined toe some place which wyll afforde full conueniencye for your recreation soe as your health wyll not bee preiudesed by restraynte, ther you wante this countrye pleasures. For the occurrents of thes parts you haue many freinds more able to relate, yet being it doeth trench upon my freehold I wyll presume to name Sir John Sauyle his comition and the traile thereof which was fayre and equall to all sutors in generall during the last cession, thoe some particuler parsons had heauye burthens layed upon them. I supose it wyll rayse a great some, for most men resolue to compounde, thoe at first some dyslyked that course. My father and my selfe haue presented our selues before the bentch, humbly laying our great scrole at theire feete; wee haue a large rayte sett upon us 70[1] by yeare, I hope it is the worst, yet cannot promis my selfe any abatement. He is begun to sitt agayne this daye. I here of many sutors, but know nothing of his course. Sir, if you please to remember wee haue had speach concerning the parsonage of Thorneskowe and one Dickinson whoe pretends some interest therin, which is not soe fully determyned that I can treate with an other and not preiudyce what I profes to you. There-

---

[1] Partly printed in *Catholic Record Society,* lii (1961), p. 372.

fore I desire you wyll returne by this bearer such an absolute resolution as may inioyne Mr Dickinson ether to compounde for the next presentment or els to renounce all further clame, least his pretended tytle deterr others from dealing therwith. Sir, I am unmanerly to presse this hasty resolution from you, but the incumbent's age and my selfe being to goe out of the countrye before the sixt of October is my apologye and hasts mee to leaue things heare at quyett, which I hope you will admit for my excuse and concur with my desire herein. So, haueing noe further to troble you, but my best wyshes for a merry meeting I rest, your affectionate cosen and professed seruante Tho: Vauasour. Haslewood this 10th of September 1627.

**316.** *From Charles Greenwood. 7 Oct. 1627 (SC, xxii/4).*

Sir, I haue receaved your letter, for the which I humbly thank you and shall (by God's grace) doe my best to giue you satisfaction. I have not seene Richard Marris since his retorne from London, but I heare he wil bee att Thornehill within 2 dayes. I wish my head and feet were answerable to my hart, then I am sure that neither iudgment nor execution should be awantinge to performe that service I so truly owe; your goodnes will pardon what I cannot, what I can is and shall ever be ready. I feare Sir Iohn S[avile] hath by his tendernes towards the Recusants stowlen their harts in taking their moneys, yett hath he giuen them noe other assurance for the halfe receavd, but att the next payment they shall have the seale, a powerfull marcarie [?]. He tould a frend of myn he is sorie your confinement should deprive the countrie of your many excellent parts, but I am perswaded the countrie is more sory then hee. Yett we rest under hope, you give us a great deale of comfort in saying you intend to see Yorkshire about Martinmas, if God make us soe happy. Your servant Anthony Foxcroft is disigned for a Captayne *brutum fulmen* to be sent to the king of Denmark, but hath taken noe presse-money. Sir, I beseech present my humble service to your honorable Lady, whom I pray God make a ioyfull mother and send yow both many happie dayes, your ever dutyfell and obedient servant, Ch. Grenewoode. Oct: 7 [1627].

**317.** *From Wandesford. 12 Oct. 1627 (SC, xvi/222).*

Sir, the opportunitye of this messinger (who will bring myne and deliver yours) invites me more then any business of importance since my last by Sir Arther. Unless you would converse with us in oecuminicall affayres, then should you se me att this instant stepping into a troubled and vexatious life, burthened with all thoss waspish and angry trifles that ley before hevye upon sometymes a most fathfull and diligent servant; but acquaintance with the title of Mr Steward and the confidence of a bettered fortune, I meane of his owne private, hath so shewen me the harshness and clownish shurlishness of my man Hunton that we are now after ten yeares acquaintance turning one another toe grass. You will say one of us is verye skittish in the meane tyme, but if you make no other use, yet I pray you let me be excused from G:[eorge] R:[adcliffe's] hard and rash iudgment of unfreindly and uncharitable. If I come not presently to se you I shall be so far from that nowe that I shall heardly have leasure to pray for you as I did before and this is in requitall of your chayres and stoules you were so busyed about the last weake. I hope by this tyme you thinke all your labor well bestowed and I long for your next letter to pertake with you in the blessings and comforts itt shall please the almighty out of his goodness and grace to bestowe upon you and your house. For treuly I thinke if you live to deserve so many severall transmygrationns and remoues (as I am afray[d] you will); my ladye will make you a newe father in halfe the shyres in Ingland and therefor give G. R. fayre warning that he may start with you and begett a Kentish man as you meane to doe, then take the rest in order.

Your Ant Dandby is much better since she sent her man to London for a empericke surgeon to helpe her for the gout, wherwith I suppose you are alryddye acquainted. Your perticular for Swinton will be ryddy before we mete att Kirtlington. I beleve Kent will be the rendivous and yet that place is so neare the fiery furnace, the purgatorye of the Councell table, that I dar not byde itt. Methinks we live in a good moderate temper here. I thanke God I am well yet and lookes every day for some certaynty ether way, for for my owne pert I am but where I was this tyme twelue month, uncertayne what familye to adhere to, that of Bullingbruke or Cowicke and if any figureflinger could assigne me but a daye for determination of this question *et il[le] mihi magnus Apollo.* Yours and yours ever and ever, C. Wandesforde. October 12 1627. To my most honored kinsman and freind Sir Thom. Wentworth att Dertford. Leave this letter with Willim Wandesforde att the syne of the King's Heade Mr Haigh's shopp in Paul's church yeard to be sent according to the supersription.

**318.** *From Clare. 17 Oct. 1627 (SC, xxii/63).*

Sun Wentworthe, I hope ear this God hath giuen yow the cumfort of an other playfelloe for Will and I would be most glad to hear it so with the mother's saftie and good healthe, God grant it so, which is my dayli prair. I haue receaued the book from your seruant Edmunds and purpose to restore it at my cuming up which, God willing, shalbe within this fortnitt, if a paltri pacht building I haue hear will giue me leaue, nether will I stay the finishing of it, but to leaue the house shut and safe, which now by the means thearof lyes open. This place affords no news nor other but market tales, whose subiect is corn and cattell, which ar both very cheap, as those traders say, otherwys I know nothing, for I nether buy nor sell any of those commoditeis. The lord of heauen graunt yow and my daughter healthe and bless yow both with the mutual comfort on of the other. Amen. Your very louing father, Clare. This St Luke's euen [17 October] 1627.

**319.** *From Thomas Bancroft. Grey Friars. 23 Oct. 1627 (SC,* xii/13).

Sir, I receyved yours of the 10th of this instant upon Satterday last, as alsoe one inclosed therein which yesterday, beinge Monday, I delyuered to Mr Chancellour, whoe commaunded me to attend him some weeke hence when I shall have an answere. I have acquaynted Mr Gibbons, his secretarye, with the particlers of your busynes and your desyre, whoe hath faythfully promised me not only to put his master in mynde thereof but to give yow his best assistance therein. Newes I can write noe certentye more then a confydent affirmacon by them that wisshed for theire owen endes and I could wish it weare soe to, although otherwise. And soe for this present, beinge to goe to see the funeralls of the noble gentleman Sir John Burroughes, I committ yow to the protection of the most heighest and shall ever remayne, your most faythfull servant, Tho: Bancroft. Grey Fryers this 23th of October 1627.

**320.** *From Sir Richard Hutton jnr. Thornhill. 24 Oct. 1627 (SC,* xii/13(1)).

Sir, I thanke you for your many littles, which put together make much, and the least of them much more then I, though I roue abroade, can intertane you with from hence. Our great counsellor is more power-full by land then by sea, for ships to the great preiudice of the mer-chants are dayly taken, but in the cittie he conquers all, better know-ing how to execute a commission then to manage a fleet furder then to receyue 6$^d$ a chaulder. His commission ended the last weeke and in his comeing home upon Satturday, as itt is reported, he fell danger-ously ill, how he contineus I know not; if he recouer, 'tis though[t] he is for London, not comeing with his finger in his mouth, but bringing his wellcome with him. His sonn, Sir Thomas, doth now lord itt att

Pumfrett keepeing the dignitie of a high Steward att the hight and doth patrizare in commissions concerning coppyholds; haukeing and hunting are pleasures royall and permitted to some of spetiall grace, but not to such as Mr Tyndall within the honor; you maybe better informed of this by the bearer. I am wonderous glad to hear of the increase of your comforts by your ladie's safe deliuerance, to whom I desire thes lines may haue the fauour to present my seruice with my best wishes for her good recouery, which accompaned with your inlargement shall be most wellcome newes too Your most affectionate brother and servuant, Ri: Hutton. Thor[nhill] Oc[tober] the 24 [1627].

**321.** *From Sir Arthur Ingram. 30 Oct. 1627 (SC, xii/15).*

Nobell Sir, I haue r[eceived] your letter and the drauft of your petyshion, the which I will haue fair writt with a littell addyshion which shall bee nothing butt this, to express thatt you [have] som bussines this term besids and nott leaue itt to thatt perticculer only. Uppon thatt I hard from you when I was last with you I did nott intend to dow any thing till this month wear outt in which Mr Mewtys doth waight. Butt I did sines I see you speak with Mr Trumboll, who doth waight the next mont for Mr Dickenson, who I fynd to respectt you very much and will bee most glad, as hee sayth, to dow you any seruis. I will, God willing, speak with my Lord of Dorssett; the Lords sitt on Fryday next and thatt day, God willing, itt shall bee d[elivered]. For our ould great master I am nott idell and thatt he will fynd, when hee cometh up, I beleeue he will fynd many Sir Mylles Fleetwoods to deall withall.

Hear is Mr Goyffin and Mr Burlamachi's brother come from the Ill of Reass and bring word thatt the fortt will bee tacken forth with and withall say thatt the town of Rochell hath releued my Lord very much with vittalls. The say likwiss that the duk Rouhan is up with 8000 men and thatt ther is lick to bee greatt trubells in Fraunce. This day att the side bar of the King's Bench was a petyshion d[elivered] in the name of dyuers gentellmen thatt stand committed abought the loans, wherin the complained the had a mocion to make befor them and could get no counsell. The iudges dessiered to know whatt counsell the would haue; the were tould Mr Sergientt Headly and Mr Sergientt Bramston. To morrow the will moue, butt itt is thought itt will cum to nothing and so praying to bee remembred to your nobell Lady and to honest Mr Rattcliffe I rest, your most assuered to loue you, Ar. Ingram. This 30th of October 1627.

**322.** *From Sir Arthur Ingram. 4 Nov. 1627 (SC, xii/16).*

Worthi Sir, I pray you excuss me thatt you haue nott heard from me
in all this tym. On Fryday last your petyshion was read att the
Tabell and all the Lords thought itt very ressonabell, but as I wrott
you the could dow nothing in itt till the accquantted the king
therwith. The which was donn this day and I will assuer you so donn
by some of the Lords thatt was much to your aduantadg. The king
was plessed to giue way to itt and named the tym him self which is
shortter then I could haue wyshed, butt we must bear thatt with
paciens. Butt though the tym bee shortt, the manner plessed me well,
the particculer wherof I will accquantt you with all att lardg att our
metting, which I dessier may bee this nytt, being Monday. For your
lodging you shall haue a chamber reddy for you wher I lye, to which
place I pray you com thatt I may inioy your compani the tym you
tarry hear and so I rest, yours euer most faythfully to loue you, Ar.
Ingram. This iiiith of November 1627, Sonday nitt.

**323.** *To Richard Marris. Dartford. 4 Nov. 1626 (SC, xxi/46).*

Richard Marris, I haue deferred my writing to you thes seauen or
eight dayes till I might haue dun itt more fully in sum things att
London, but leauing partt till I am ther, especially concerning the
accompt of moneys (which you shall haue particularly from me soe
soon as I am ther, or speak with Peter Man) I will by this conuence
write att lardge of all the rest. I doubte very much wee shall be
troubled with Ouerton, for he that should haue bought itt finds itt
soe ingaged that he will not meddle with itt soe as I can giue noe
hope but that wee must prouide for payment of Mr Fotherley. The
man that should haue bought itt is one Cooke, to haue estated itt att
the rate of 300[li] by yeare upon charitable uses, being therwith trusted
to that end by the late bishope of Winchester and, soe that itt might
hold the rent, rather chose to giue twenty yeares purchase att 300,
then fifteen att 400[li] by yeare. Hearupon I haue a conceite cums inn
my head that makes me desirouse to be in London that I may speake
with this Cooke, hauing allready sum acquaintance with the man. I
will see if I can putt of unto him Thornton, Sharphill and Stratforth
att the rate of 350[l] by yeare and twenty yeares purchase, taking a
lease of them back for 3 liues and forty yeares after, which if I effect
(and me thinks itt is feasable, God giuing a blessing unto itt) I shall
purchase Ouerton and afterwards putt itt of to my brother William
and with the price therof and the rest dischardge and free myself of
my debts. This makes me sitt on thornes till I be about itt; neuertheless

goe you on with Mr Croslande; with whom wee may either proceed or fairly breake of, as wee see cause, for this would be an in-
comparable good bargaine.

As concerning Potte and Swinton, I will write to my cosin Wandesforde and presently get him putt an information aganst us in the
Courtte of Wardes, whear wee may examine the whole matter and
soe lett it rest att after in peace, only it will require sum aduise first
how itt maybe dun. I approue well of letting Thorpartche at 50$^{li}$ by
yeare and Harwood Parke and the Holme att the old rentts. For the
farme att Wicke, I am not aganst Thomas Wiltons [*or* Willons]
hauing itt, allways prouided that I haue such a rent for itt as may in
sum sortt answeare the chardges itt hath stood me inn, both in the
purchaise and likewise in the husbandry bestowed upon the grownds,
espetially the South Intacke, being seauen and thirty acers, which by
this meanes I shall leaue exceeding ritche and well fenced, besides the
howses hath cost me a great deale in reparing, all which must be
considered. Besides I must reserue all the beast gates belonging to
that farme in Wicke Banke and in Wicke Oxclose, you know out of
what reason, as allsoe the fence be made beetwixt South and East
Intacke by him. Yet I say Thomas Willon shall haue itt under such a
rent and other conditions, as upon my cumming into the cuntry shall
be founde indifferent betwixt lord and tenant. For what I shall
bestowe upon him upon his good seruice and deserrt, he is not to
expect any partte of itt out of this, but out of my purse as I shall see
cause, whearin I will asseure him he shall not finde himselfe or
paines unrewarded, if he be not awanting on his partte, I will not be
awanting on mine.

Mr Greenwood writes me worde that for Skipton Scoole lands att
Wicke the writings must be drawen hear att London by my directions
and sealed in the cuntry, which willbe harde for me to doe, but I will
aduise with George Radcliffe and doe as well as I can. The rest
togeither with the nams of the parcells, the dayes of payment and the
rentts reserued you must make up in the cuntry. I doubte not but
Mr Justice Hutton will peruse the booke, if ther be cause and helpe to
sett you streight; I desire, if itt maybe, itt might be dun before
Candlemas terme. For Robert Baines we shall haue time enoughe
hearafter, if anything be to be dun. I like well that you giue ouer your
earth workes both at Woodhowse and Gawthorpe for this winter. I
am glade you haue founde soe good a quarry att Woodhouse and the
springe att Gawthorpe, for now we shall make use of the one as a
frende and prouide aganst the other, God willing, as an ennimy;
and hear by the way in the letting Harwood Park, the ponds must be
reserued and the great ells killed if it be possible, [or] they will deuour

all else. If I cum downe before Christmas, as I may if I will, you shall haue time enoughe for taking up horses.

I writt unto you for owne of the howse bookes as allsoe wheather Ben. Wade had his bucke, as concerning the restrainte att Brierley and touching Samuel Wilkinson, but I heare nothing att all of any of them; forget them not in your next. The phesants and partridge you sent by Peter Man and up with Mr Snauden were passing good, thos sinc not soe. The last that came by the carrier cam but heather on Satterday last. You must take such order that the carier may be directed to deliuer them presently att London and that soe they may be sent away; I would haue you send no more capons, they are passing old and leane and not worth the sending and for the rest send them rather in baggs then boxes, as little hay with them as maybe, soe will the cariadge and chardge be lighter. If the phesants be either sore brused with the peece or any thing old, itt is better baking of them and soe send them; your phesant pies wear passing good ones. Robin Adney tells me you desire sum vines and woodbines, for the latter itt is but speaking to Jhon Wood to lay downe sum of the branches of thos att Woodhowse under grownde this winter and ther willbe enoughe both for you and me this next Michelmas. For vines I will get you sum and send them you downe. I pray you follow your course to gett as much as of the euidence of Pott and Swinton as you can, for M. Hugginson tells me that my Antte hath them all. I will end hear for the present, you shall hear againe from me before itt be long. God of his goodnesse guide us all. Soe rests Your master and freinde, Th. Wentworth. Dartford this 4th of Nouember 1627.

You writt unto me for directions what to doe for the weekly releefe of the poore att Gawthorpe and Woodhowse, as allsoe for cotes for the poore. I haue thought of itt; I would be loathe the poore should faire the worse for my absence, yet at this time itt is fitt they should finde a wante of me and complaine of ther misre and therfore I would haue you giue ouer the weekly allowance and prouide no cotes for them. Itt may be said I am a prisoner myself and soe noe reason for them to expect I should doe as when I was att libertye. Yet neuerthelesse by God's grace hearafter upon my absolute inlardgment I will at once giue amongst them soe much as they shallbe noe loosers by the forbearance which will carry with itt a more wellcum, after soe long a discontinuance, and shew them too they are the better for my being amongst them. To my trusty seruant Rich. Marris att Wentworth Woodhowse.

**324.** *Denzil Holles to Wentworth, 19 November 1627 (Knowler, i, pp. 41–42; SC, xxii/62). He hopes to visit him shortly and describes Buckingham's misconduct of affairs at Rhé.*

**325.** *From Wandesford. Nov. 1627 (SC, xvi/242).*

Sir, I have mayde a greater breach upon your wekely kalender then you expected, I can still excuse itt upon the constant relation we receved here from thoss that mett with you att London of your cuming into the cuntrye before Christenmas, which I have given ouer so much as the hope ittself, ever since I understoode howe the iudges determined for there *Habeas Corpus*, not crediting in the least iot that fayre gloss the nobleman that lefte his coach to salute you made upon this tast of prerogatiue. For I knowe this privilidge will be mayde use of and no tyme can ever be chosen more for the king's advantadge then this, whether we looke upon the action preceding (which induced this question) or that which will followe perhaps governed by this; for we are mayde beleve here many thousands privye seales are showring upon us, some for thowsand pounds, the least for hundreds and so far hath thess former proceedings wrought upon us and mayde us so malleable that in Richmondshyre we yet goe no further then for our *quota pars*; every man praing that the safe shelter of collector-ship may cover and protect him. And for my pert I should be glad of the seruice, for I had rather travell up and downe in my owne cuntry where I knowe the wayes then hyre a guide perhaps to Constantinople, for I looke for a bolt [?] of the Controwler's offic, unless you can play that Magnus Apollo and abate the edge there before itt come downe so sharpe upon us. For to speake truth the king's demands this way, especially to thoss that have not payde, are less resestable. For my pert I must profess when the privy seale cums, I thinke itt will be the proportion only that shall trouble me, for the king's wants must be supplyed and since he declines the ordinarye way, what can be more warrantable for the subiect then this? If this fayle, what doe we knowe but the same prerogative may be extended hereafter to the laitye, which nowe the clergy conceaues is exercised upon them, who now are dayly paying upon warrants from the ordinarye the subsedyes granted by the Convocation at Oxford; upon this pretence (as they beleve) because the king by the act of Parlia-ment hath the same power which the pope had and he severall tymes had subsedyes, or other aydes of that nature, granted by the bishops only, without confirmation of the laytye, which were payde by the Cleargye. And they say the same power may reatch us who were often forced by the popes to pay towards the holy warrs and otherwise upon his commandement. But all my beleue of thess things I suspend untill I gayne your confirmation.

We have here also (God knowes) the fatell newes of the loss of the Sound and the greate distresse of that king: I cannot say the king-dome, because they are sayde to inclyne there neckes to the Emperor's yoake.

To returne home I shall tell you for a domesticke as harsh a thing as can be. This last weake I presented your cosin Danby according to my covenant (which indede is a proviso upon forfeyture) unto the Councell at Yorke to be examined of his religion and manners and among other questions of religion this was one he could not answear, how many articles is there of your Crede? And yet he receved the Communion severall tymes att Cambridge and was placed under a strict Puritane who toulde me he had mayde him acquainted with religion. And you may iudge what olde Sir William Ellis woulde thinke of us bothe. I am nowe out of hope to see you till I come to Dartford and treuly I nowe begin (as you knowe my manner is after things be past) to apologise for my self, for I long to se you, but my wife drawes near her tyme and I dar not leave her. Remember both our services to your good lady.

I forgott to tell you, whatsoever your freind Mr Wandesforde reports of your health and cherefulnes, thoss that come from you say that you wear never more healthfull and merry [? *November 1627*].

To the right wor[ll] Sir Thomas Wentworth at his house in Dartford giue these. Deliver this letter to William Wandesford dwelling att the syne of the King's Head in Paul's church yeard at Mr Hough's shop, a draper, to be sent according to the directions aboue.

**326.** *From Wandesford. 26 Nov. 1627* (*SC*, xx/262).

Sir, the latter end of your last letter, leaving my ladye in her extrem-ityes, begetts in me more then an ordinarye desyre to heare the happy and welcome tydings of her safe deliverance which I hope a fewe dayes will bring unto me, expecting also from your active perts some more certayne resolutions then hitherto we haue had. For me thinks thess necessityes wherewith we are surrounded on everye syde should prepare these councells and ripen thoss things which lye yet under consultation and unfolde thoss misteryes of darkenes, wherein we haue bene so long inwrapped. And onless our state have the use of that invisible ring, we (that iudge all things by outward acts) must nedes thinke the benifitt of thess surprisalls (for I knowe [no] fitter name) to be greater and more valuable towards the chardge of this war then we have heard; otherwise how could they subsist untill the recept of a parlementarye supply, though never so certayne to obtayne itt? For I beleve all other extraordinarye courses shalbe waved untill the event of the other be knowne, as more agreable to his Maiesty's justice, most to his honor, both which are preferred when necessitye (which giues lawe to all things) putts him upon itt. Though for my owne part I imagine the howse wilbe fownd much more moderate and inclinable to his ends then formerly. The miseryes, or iniuryes (call them as you please) fallen upon perticular persons will not possess them so totally as to make them neglect the prosecution of the whole; save the ship first and then punish the neglect of thoss mariners that brought her into hazard. For I cannot with you beleue us to be in better case then apparent dainger, if the making and provocation of enemyes before we be ryddy to defend our selves, or offend them, be to litle; the contemptous violation of freinds, even thoss too besydes whom we have not to relye our selues, will certaynely serue the turne.

Nowe to looke a litle nerer home, my cosen Mallory promiseth a visitt att Dartford, therefor I take the opportunitye to prepayre you for his discourse concerning the knight for the shyre, wherein I touched him the other day. I tould him Savile I thought would stand; he beleved none could oppose him in your absence. I replyed if the cuntry understoode themselues (what allowance you would make of itt, itt were no matter) they could doe no less then make choyce of you, though absent; he agreed and that, H: Belassis ioyning with you, the feild was yours, unless precedence hyndred the business. I thought that could be nothing, for you never expected that, but when itt was your right, in this case itt was not, unless Mr Bellassis were pleased to resyne itt. And so the dialogue concluded with a mutuall promise to send one to the other, upon the first notice of a summonce. Therefor if any thing pass betwixt you of this subiect, let me knowe; the most wilbe from you, I suppose, an inclination to ioyne with him before another. For the less you speake of itt the better, more then to discover the worke, as itt were like to be terible if he shall attempt itt, especially to this man whom you knowe to be fethered of another wing. The truth is, if you stand, that must be the partye and though he be strongest you can make choyce of, yet will the worke be difficult enough, so litle doe we esteme our libertyes and so lowe a valewe do we sett upon thoss that are borne to defend them; there being no man I mete with more sensible of the ryght we have then my neybor was when he only inquired for the *Quota pars* of Richmondshyre. But least I holde your sterrop and goe a foote, when I haue done, laye wayte with Corryton, Francis Semer and thoss tribunitiall orators of the west for a place for your servant, if you desyre me to kepe your syde warme by the bar agayne. For I suspect my neybors of Richmond will serve me like themselues and then you culd sweare I haue to long served a heard master. But all this you thinke is att rovers. In the meane tyme the other arrowe flyes yet in the ayre betwixt the bowe and the merke. For I cannot thinke my self secure from the wind of itt, if itt fall upon me, but yet I heare nothing (I thanke God) that tends towards me, letter, message, or whatsoever else, only it seames to me the strandgest accident that befell me these many years when I consyder howe differently this disease handles you and me that are so neare att this tyme of a temper; a fever almost pestilentiall upon you and I fynd no more then a grudging in my self. Howe the poett applyed this verse I cannot tell, to them in his fable, but me thinks itt suets our condition well: *Causa fuit meritis melior tua, tempore nostra.* And so with a pece of Lattin to bed, now I bid you farwell, I pray God bless you and yours, remember me to gentle Mr Geordge and good Mr — Novemb: 26 [1627].

I pray you in your next letter forgett not to direct your gardener att Wodhouse to giue me some tulips' roots acording to your promise and if you can fynd in your heart to furnish a yong beginer with any thing ells, but I pray you remember me that I may have them this season. [*no signature*]. To my most honored kinsman and frend Sir Thomas Wentworth at Dartford.

**327.** *From William Wentworth. 26 Nov. 1627 (SC, xxii/3).*

Sir, if it please God I entend to morrow beeinge Tuesday to goe to Oxforde to take my part of the griefe or ioy wich the almighty pleaseth to send and to doe the uttermost seruice of a brother. Mr Cokeson is but newly come to towne and cannot possible goe. My lorde Clare is well and will bee shortly at Dartforde; hee sayth your petition is not answered, the counsel is soe wholy taken up wyth the businesse of the *habeas corpus*. Yet my lorde of Dorset sayes if your petition receiue any stoppe, hee will speake to the kinge himselfe, which if hee doe Mr Chancellor of the Exchequer will second it and, as I take it, my lorde Clare sayth hee hath spoken wyth Sir Arthur Ingram to deliuer it to my lorde of Dorset and to attende him. To morrow by instance from the kinge the Iudges giue iudgment uppon the the *habeas corpus*. Thus I rest, You[r] most respectiue and affectionate brother and seruant, W. Wentworth. London. 26 [? November 1627]. I pray remember my humble seruice to my lady Clare, my lady Eleanor, my lady Arbella.

WP—T

**328.** (*SC*, xxiv–xxv, 8). To the King's most excellent Maiestie.

The humble peticon of Sir Thomas Wentworth Baronett:

Humbly sheweth unto your Maiestie that whereas the peticoner by your Maiestie's grace and the fauor of the honourable Board had licence to repaire to London and Westminster and continue there sixe dayes to dispach some buysines of importanc, duringe which tyme he understands of much preiudice which he hath sustained in his affaires, boeth at London and especially in the countrye by reason of his fower moneths' restrainte and the farre distanc between his owne howse and the place of his confinement, to which he is nowe returned againe and inforced to leaue the greatest parte of his buysines for want of tyme undispached.

Therefore his humble suite unto your royall Maiestie is that in accomplishment of your former goodnesse he may haue leaue to come againe to London to make an end of his buysines there and afterwards to goe unto his howse in Yorkesheire and there to remaine one moneth to dispose of his countrie occasions, which without his presenc cannot bee done, but to his extreame inconvenienc.

And the peticoner shall daly praye for your Maiestie [? *late November 1627*].

**329.** *From Sir Gervase Clifton. 30 Nov. 1627* (*SC*, xii/19).

Sir, to hear well and often of you hath allwayes ministred matter of much comfort to mee, placing you amonst my frends in one of the cheefest roomes of my dilection, but nowe to receaue the pleasing testimony of your too long doubted wellfare, when I am bereft of my supremest worldly happines by the loss of your noble sister in lawe (whom none but your owne saincted lady of all the sex could match) must needs sollace mee in farr greater measure, setting my rest to honour the alliance and familiars I gained by that match, aboue all the frends and acquayntance I haue by the like or any other meanes besids. For the iustnes and worth I found to be in hir, theyr frend and kinswoman, whose prayers, christian and charitable actions stood in the gapp and restrayned many plagues which ere nowe would else haue fallen on this pore familye. But shee hath left so many impressions of hir vertue and piety, both in life and death, behind hir as nowe she is gone to receaue the gayne of them hirself. I hope my self folowing them and whilest I liue teaching them to my children, wee shalbe all the better in the end and to the end for them. I confess I shall neuer be ashamed to learne for my parte of such a woman, to whom the strongest men in comparison were but nouices in practise of religion. What a desolation in human respects is com'd upon me, your iudgment will easily tell yow when you please to consider the eldest of my fiue children by hir scarcely able to discerne they haue lost a mother and the three youngest unable to knowe theyr right hand from theyr left. But my case shall be speedily and constantly bent to prouide competently for them and my ioy is that they are of one side, the children of the child of God, who neuer suffred the righteous to be forsaken, nor theyr seed to beg theyr bread. More I will not trouble you with at this tyme, but present my prayers to God for his blessing to be perpetuated upon yourself, noble lady and issue, my seruice to you both and my suyte to honor your deceased frends memory with voatchsafing to weare thes blacks, brought you by my seruant som few dayes; my lord Clifford diswading the cost of a funerall, as more aptly conuerted in my case to the orphans' benefitt. I humbly thanke you for your larg and well putt together discours and rest, Your faythfull and most affectionat brother and seruant, Gervas Clifton. 30 Nouember 1627.

**330.** *From Sir Arthur Ingram. 1 Dec. 1627 (SC, xii/20).*

Nobell Sir, I know you may thinck much thatt in all this tym you haue nott heard from me conserning your petyshion; the causs whereof hath byn thatt howerly I haue had expectingse of the dyspach therof and would haue byn glad to haue sentt in either word to you, but thatt itt had byn donn. Butt nott being donn as yett, I haue thought fytt by thes few lynes to giue you an accountt of my proseading therin. Mr Trumbull, your good frind and myn, d[elivered] the petyshion att the Tabell and when hee had d[elivered] itt brought me outt word thatt itt must bee made unto the king and then itt should bee dyspached. Upon this I was much trobelled whatt to dow and of my self durst dow nothing therin, butt resorted to my Lord Clare, to Mr Chansellor of the Excheker and to Phillip Manering and the all thought fitt itt should bee donn, upon which I made itt new, the coppi wherof I send you hear inclossed; and when I had donn, I delivered the same to my lord of Dorsett who immediattly wentt into the king and staying som littell whill brought me outt word thatt itt should bee dyspached. Butt I attending him often sines for the dyspach therof haue r[eceived] no other answer butt sartaynly itt will bee donn, desiring me to haue a littel paciens. And this [? thus] for the presentt itt stands. And of this I thought good to giue you knolledg and dow dessier thatt I may haue tow lynes from you, assuering you thatt yf I haue erred in any thing, it hath byn outt of my loue and car unto you. And so I rest, your faythfull louing frind,

Ar. Ingram. This first of Dessember 1627. I send you hearwith a
letter which Jn° Taylor gaue me.

**331.** *Lord Haughton to Wentworth, 7 December 1627, from the Hague*
(*Knowler*, i, pp. 42–43; *SC*, xxii/64). *He sends and asks for news.*

**332.** *From Clare. Bugden. 25 Dec. 1627* (*SC*, xxii/65).

Sun Wentworthe, when I was in the towne I was twyce or thryce to
haue visited Mr Chancelor of the Duchi, but he was not within.
Besyds the visit I had this busines with him: the Duchy tennants in
my bayliweeke pay not thear rents which [they] should half yearly
bring to the court leets of the liberte, so as to my charge and trouble
I am forced to send twice or thryce about theme ear I canne haue
theme. Other baylies, namely Sir Rafe Hansbe, haue warrants to
distrayne for the rent and charges and it is iust I haue, so that the
king may haue the rents duly paid which ar not now. And thearfor
I pray you speake to Mr Chancelor for suche a warrant for gathering
the King's rents within the libertie of Bersetlaw and send it me downe
by sum safe messenger. For this belongs no fee, being the king's
service and nothing my particular; for my self I will pay, but not for
the king.

   Bycaus I would not ryde Christmas day, I obey my lord of Lincoln's importunite, but tomorroe, God willing, I am gone and hope
the night after to be at Haughton and yet the days ar short, the
iornie long and ways superlatiuely foule. Fare well, good sun, the
Lord of heauen bless you and all yours. Bugden this Christmas day
1627, Your very louing father, Clare.

**333.** *From Sir Humphrey May. 27 Dec. 1627* (*SC*, xxii/20 + 1).

Sir, Yesternight out of more grace and fauour then all you refractary
fooles can deserve, his Mayesty gave order for a generall releasement
out of your seuerall confinements. I call you fooles, aswell for the
damage you have donne to yourselves, as for the interest of our
posterities that may suffer by your ill example. Do not construe this
course as an argument of a parliament at hand, for I protest faithfully it is very far from it. I send you this notice that you may
presently aduise to dispose of youre selfe; within a day or ii the
shreeue will receive warrant for your discharge, but in the meane
time you may take your liberty, if you haue a minde to it, for the
king hath already expressed his pleasure, your frend and servant,
H. May. This Thursday morning [? *27 December 1627*]. To my

honorable frend Sir Thomas Wentworth knight and Baronett at his howse at Dartford or very nere it.

**334.** *From the earl of Dorset. 27 Dec. 1627 (SC, xxii/2).*

Noble Sir, I presume itt will nott displease you to know thatt the king hath perioded his indignacon touard all those gentlemen hee hath stiled refractoryes. Last night by advice of the whole board itt was resolued to take of the restraynts and within a day or two the shreefe shall haue descharges of thee former commands. I am glad in contemplation of the generall, butt more particularly thatt you are att liberty, where by to inioy your home and preuent othere preiudice in your private fortune, which so long an absence and so great a distance must needs expose your estate to suffer under; God send you a better and reacher New Yeare. I rest yours to doo you seruice, E. Dorset [? *27 December 1627*].

**335.** *From Wandesford. Jan 1628 (SC, xvi/246).*

Sir, the benifitt of this messinger will save us both a labor. For all thoss things concerning the commission at Yorke (the principall fountayne of my intelligence) he will more perticularly informe you, for the other touching Newcastle all the care that can be is allryddye taken, there is an honest and discrete eye over that business. That for the election (if such a harbor be to be discovered in this dangerous passadge) will be likewise fitt for your owne agitation; you will nowe fynde the height of our hopes here something abated with the universal dependence Sir John Savile hath from the Catholickes, become so Catholicke nowe that not only in this action on foote alrydye, but in all others concerning there future peace and quiett they will implicitly beleve in him; besydes the advantadge he will have from the basness of thoss power and lowe spiritts that devotes themselves to a servile adoration of any temperary greatness. And whether we live in such an adge or not, that abounds with that increase, our former actions will declare sufficiently. If I had any more from hence I would not omitt, but you for your pert, have given me iust occasion to distrust the councell you gaue Hotham and thoss that came without warrant, grounded in my opinion upon a mistaken conclusyon that they can be no worse then before, yet they shall be so much worse that twelve monthes' imprisonment perhaps shall not acquitt them for this iust contempt when thoss upon the mayne are released with the first hiring of the tyme.

That part of your letter for your cuming doune I apprehend best, but with this caveat that you kepe itt to yourself till you have leave, least your freinds here be sorry and your adversary be glad you be desapointed of your expectation, as nowe itt befalls with Radcliffe, unless he come downe very lately, for every man talkes of itt and no man knowing the reason a worse interpretation may be putt upon itt then his freinds wish, Yours, C. Wandesford. [? *January 1628*].

**336.** *From Sir Gervase Clifton. 11 Jan. 1628 (SC, xii/21).*

Sir, I was putt in very fayer hope (contrary to my expectation when I sent last to you upon the sad occasion you too well remember) that I should haue had the happiness to see you at the meeting of frends by mee drawen together as witnesses in some parte of the worth of the noble deceased allye, being told of your coming downe with Sir Arthur Ingram neare to that tyme in your coach, but it proued not to fall out so fortunatlye, eyther for hir honor or my contentment, by his trauaylling home without you. I that office performed, it pleased my Lord Clifford most nobly to command my attendanc on his lordship backe to Londsborough, wher I remayned till the morowe after Twelfdaye and then taking my share of a bounteous entertainment with him at Yorke I wayted on him so farr as Tadcaster towards Crauen; he going then to his pleasures and curious newe structures, I the direct waye to my rendeuous of sorrowes and ruynes; in which time of my Christmas aboade with him his lordship pleased to acquaint mee with a letter of yours by your owne desire, full of the times best fruytes and of your antient noble respects towards my poore self which, following your other, brought mee from Woodhowse by one of your owne seruants, so choyse a piece as only time not want of care must weare out, made mee charge my self with too much slownes to take notice therof to yow. I beseech you therfor, Sir, to excuse the same, to conceaue I depended of an opportunity promised and fayled to me in that place and to accept of my humble thankes for your multiplied fauors to mee, nowe in the season that my glory is putt out till I may double them by visitts and voyse, as I purpose to doe shortly. For weary of my station about Shrouetide I mean to make a remoue to London and there (for a yeare or two) with three seruants and my self spend my freehold if I can. I haue giuen yow an accoumpt of the time past and to come and nowe will troble you no further, but presenting my humble seruice to your noble lady, wyshing with my best deuotions the happynes of you and your hopefull sweet children, I rest, Your faythfull brother and humble seruant, Geruas Clifton. 11 of January 1627[8].

**337.** *From Wandesford. 16 and 20 Jan. 1628 (SC, xvi/245).*

Sir, Your last letter hath the tune of a merrye larke singing and mounting after she hath escaped the hunter's ginn; be not too wanton, the next day may prove a larkin daye agayne and who knowes your fortune then. Perhaps some that beleve Sir Thomas Wentworth to be of Sir Thomas Cheke's mynd rather may procure his death upon the depe wound of a privye seale of a thousand pounds then suffer him to languish with this small stroake of five subsedyes. But the height [of] Wandsford's providence is to feare and itt is a maxim concluded of both by your greater wisdome and eke Mr Radclife's prudence that Wansford is naturally iealous and fearefull. Be itt so, I am not ashamed of this charactere, only I would not excuse the iudgment of an obstinate man that calls that naturall which a better inspection might (with more semblance of reason) call a habitt bredd and nourished by the accidents and contingencyes of the tyme; shall I beleve in a fellowe that spends his tyme in dissembling and iudling with the same constancy and resolution that I doe in an ordinarye artesan who works in an orderly and direct way for his living? When they deale constantly I will beleve stedfastly. In the meane tyme what a magnaminitye, what a vertue is this in Sir Thomas Wentworth that hath so fitted his vessell for every season; if the stormes blowe and the waves goe hye, he casts out the steddye ankor of resolution and patience thereby to preserve himself from shipwrack; if a calme come he hath the discretion to take the first safe harbor he metes with. When we went in itt is no matter, we will save 1000$^{li}$ per annum by this tricke and that was the lord['s] will. When we cum out, honor and success doth torment us, but fooles only iudge by the event. And nowe we smell so strong of this prison spiritt that cuntrye burgesses (who are not obdurate and hardned by a wilfull backe slydinge) will play the fooles forsooth, if out of misapprehensyon of the pretended doinges they giue there mony to ryddyly. Nay they are fooles that prepayre the way to a parliment by thess hobgoblings and skarcrowes; treuly if I were to give direction for after adges howe poeple should carry themselues to there king, they shold be animated and mannadged (after the performance of there reasonable dewtyes) to maintayne that heriditary and naturall interest which God and nature hath giuen them in there libertye (because princes should be mayde sensible howe equallye the daingers respects them and there people) but now by your leave our gayme is to far gone to make a blott if we can helpe itt. For if we doe, itt shall be hit by a third person, a by-stander, an adversarye, who will take the benefitt of our oversights and howe shall any of us shewe the nobleness of an Englishman, if we have not England left us as a fayre staege to act our severall perts upon? Thearfor (as I conceaue) the case was mistaken; they are not bugbeares we hear of inuented only to skar us; pull of the more hydeous and danting vesards wherewith thess monsters are disguised and yet may a discrete and regulated iudgment apprehend cause enough of feare from the naked aspect and trewe proportion of the things themselues. Whether we looke upon the daingers from abroade (the sworde hanging but by a thred over this kingdome), or upon the distractionns at home, the hands of our allyes and fellows are ether altogether cut of, or so manackled they cannot helpe us, stand we mor nede then of an united strength att home to defend our selues. And unless there be such a fatallitye upon us that the goodly tre which hath borne the blessed fruit of tranquillitye and peace in this kingdome some hundreds of yeares (sometyme more sometyme less frutefull) shall nowe be cutt downe and the roote therof bound about with iron that itt may never growe agayne. Why should there be this litigation, this darknese [?] proceding betwixt prince and poeple? I speake but my opinion the tymes of Ed. 3 and H. 7 (the greatest examples of wisdome and spirit) would better have induced this sterilitye, this defection in the poeple. I will say no more, if there be a dislocation betwixt one member and another, much more betwixt the heade and the member; the weaker must be drawen up to the stronger, or else they will never be ioyned and confirmed together. Thus many degres is my Richmondshyre dyall set belowe yours in Kent, which in my opinion is a litle to much elevated and let this paper witness betwixt us hereafter wheather you will be forced, ether to allowe of this opinion, or at the least with a distinction to defend your owne. And thus much by way of fooling for the publicke.

For your private my last letter you must remember (for I looke to be putt to defend my opinion) was before your release was knowne to us. That perticular concerning Tom Dandby's going to Leydon nedes trouble us no further, for he cannot be perswaded to excede the *quatuor maria* and in this (howsoever in others I agre with you) I may not force him. For my cuming to se you I have receved a duble supersedeas, your owne cuming downe so shortly and your fayre construcion if I had cumed. Present our services to your noble ladye; my wife is still as she was every day expecting. Remember me to my cosen sir Radcliff and for Mr George tell him his intellegence out of Yorkeshyre is ryddye and well warranted. I will not appollogise for my self. I thinke what I have sayde in this business might have bene a warning to the father, if he had any witt and what I have done may be an example to his sonne, if he were wiser then his father, to take out such good lessons; nether will I use any recrimination, only thus I fynd written in olde jesstes:

> Ho where so busy a man as he there was
> and yet he seamed busyer then he was

But fooles only iudge by the event. I have sent the inclosed to Pott and delivered the other here that I hope will worke a good effect; this is taken patiently; I perceaue so much by his countenance for not a worde he discovers to me what you writt. Thoss letters savored more of a Yorkeshyre spiritt I will no more of a Kentish. Send me, I pray you, the coppy of them if you can; your Ant continewes as she was, rather better (God be thanked) then worse. January 16 [*1627/8*].

Being at Yorke the report here is so fresh of a parliment that Sir Ferdinando Farefax (who disdaynes much the olde fellowe should carrye the place) offred a treatye with me for your ioyning with Henrye Belassis and the busines is so agreed betwixt us that, waving al others whatsoever to stand with you, he will if he can ingadge Henrye, and giue me notice, when I promise to undertake for your pert, if I se cause. So that by this meanes I hope you shall come fayre of from Sir Arther Ingram and Sir William Constable, from the former by his absence, from the other by the undertaking of his freind. I tell Sir Ferdinando (and he himself is sensible of itt) you must ioyne with a man gratious with the papists, which only Henrye is. 20 Januerye [*1627/8*].

To my most honored kinsman and freind Sir Thomas Wentworth att his house in Dartforde.

**338.** *Viscount Mansfield to Wentworth, 24 January 1627/8 (SC, xii/23). He is glad to hear of his liberty and is complaining to Buckingham about Sir John Savile.*

**339.** *From the Earl of Clare. Houghton. 25 Jan. 1628 (SC, xxii/10).*

Sun Wentworth, God be thanked your string is lengthened at the last. For I cann not term you, nor my self, a freeman, when law hath no protection for us; this diseased boddi our councellors haue left us and the disease still strengthneth uppon us. Nether do the lawyers, the phisitions for this subiect, hele us any whit, for *meum* or *tuum* betwene comen persons they croe in euery corner, but when the question transcends between the hed and the boddi, they are crest-falne and haue nothing to say and if accedentalli sumthing *of them be heard*[1] and shew them self in the lawne, they only beray the place and

---

[1] The words in italics have been obscured by a blot.

leaue the matter wurrs then they fownd itt; witnes the late *Habeas Corpus*. But as Gundemar used to say *Patear y callar*. I may well put upon yow that Frenche saying *celui n'est pas eschappe qui traine son bien*. For the voice in the cuntrie is that priui seals must cum after the non lenders which sewerly must be very great, els will they do the king litell good and wighti burdens oueriornted hakneis cann not bear. But I hope better and yet I beleeue litell in a Parliament that ether it wilbe, or being, will doe the kingdom any good; I leaue the reasons to your owne iudgment. And as our condition is we cann feche no cordial from former tyms and the royal power knows well enoughe; thearfor *in rebus integris* it is best to be a curtier;[1] I say not so in the present occasion, for that part is half played. With such strays as thes am I drawen to fill this paper, wanting the ordinary stuffings of letters, busines or news, and yet the bunche of fleshe in the beast's forhead may be termed a horne and thearfor the Italian instructs us well *Il tacer non fu mai scritto*, but yow ar not euery boddi. The Lord of Heauen bless yow, my daughter, Will and Mari. Haughton this 25 Janua. 1627[8]. Within a day or 2 of Candelmas tide or ouer I purpose, God willing, to see yow. Your very louing father, Clare.

**340.** *Sir John Jackson to Wentworth, 5 February 1627/8 (Knowler, 1, p. 34, wrongly dated 1625; SC, xx/265). He has decided to stand for Pontefract, joining with Sir Francis Foljambe and will support Wentworth for the shire, but hopes Wentworth will find a worthier partner.*

**341.** *Lord Haughton to Wentworth, 16 February 1627/8 (Knowler, i, pp. 44–45; SC, xxii/66), about his cousin, Lieutenant Wentworth's negotiations to purchase a company in Morgan's regiment.*

**342.** *From Lord Clifford. Londsborough. 22 Feb. 1628 (SC, xvi/179).*

My deare brother, I hope you have slepte in youre owne house at Wudhowse before this cum to you, soe as Mr Greene goeinge this daye to Kirkebye I was glad of the oportunety to wellcome you home and to giue you this shorte accounte of youre owne busines. I sent yesterdaye againe into Crauen to my Cosen Lowther and haue deuided the busines soe (as beeinge nowe in partes) particuler men

---

[1] A possible reading is cunter.

will with more ease and to more purpose sollicitt the apparence at
Yorke. Sir John Hotham was with me when youre letters came by
my footeman and he went yesterdaye to Sir Mathew Bointon and
Sir Henry Griffith and soe alonge towardes Sir Richard Cholme-
leyes. George Butler came but hither the laste nighte and soe youre
letter came not to him before, but this daye he is gon to Mr
Stapilton. Let me entreate you cum hither soe soone as you have
visited youre neerest bloode, for I longe with all my harte to be-
houlde youre fayre face; Mr Greene is gon to horse and I must
seale up. Present my seruice, I praye you, to youre sisters at Thornehill, youre most affectionate brother and seruant H. Clifforde.
Londesbr. 22 of Feb: [*1627/8*]. I moued my father for his assent as
you wished me and he has freely granted it.

**343.** *Sir Henry Savile to Wentworth, 12 March 1627/8* (*Knowler,*
i, pp. 44–45; *SC,* xii/24). *He congratulates him on his victory in
the shire election and hears that York is petitioning against Sir
Thomas Savile's election.*

**344.** *From Sir Thomas Fairfax of Walton. York. 26 March 1628*
(*SC,* xii/25).

Noble Sir, I haue this day receiued a proteccon from Mr Francis
Nevile to inlarge out of prison one Luke Whiteham committed to my
custodie in the Gaole of York Castle upon a *capias utlegatum* after
iudgment in execucon for xxiiii<sup>li</sup> and lykewise upon a commission of
rebellyon for his contempt in not answering an informacon at the
sute of his Maiesty before the Lord President and Counsell of these
partes for forgerie supposed to be committed by him, and one John
Whiteham. He was brought into the gaole the third of this moneth,
where he hath contynued euer synce. And this day one Clayton (a
man to me unknowne), yet (by reporte) of no good demeanor, did
shewe me the proteccon, which is dated the third of March, which was
the verie day Whiteham was deliuered into prison. And seing he hath
bene in prison so long and neuer shewed nor spoke of proteccon
before this day, it makes me something suspitious that Mr Nevile
hath bene abused therein and the proteccon surreptitiously procured. I haue written to Mr Nevile desireing him to signify his
pleasure therein unto me and if the proteccon were duely obtayned,
I will willingly inlarge the partie and in the meane tyme beare his
charges myself from the tyme of the proteccon shewed. Now if yow
heare me questioned for this busynes I pray yow do me the favour

yow lawfully may for my excuse herein. For I would be loath any
should conceiue me so unworthie to endeavour to violate or infringe
the libertyes of that honorable howse, whereunto I owe all duety and
respect (myself having dyuers tymes bene a member thereof), so on
the other syde I would not willingly incurre any daunger that may
iustly be layd on me. Secondly I intreat your lawfull favour in the
behalf of the Attorneyes at York, concerning the Patent sett a foote
agayne by Sir Thomas Mounson, so oft condempned by Parlement
in Lepton's tyme and the orders of that howse so oft confirmed by
the Lords of his Maiesty's privie counsell who concurred in opynyon
with the Parlement. Thus with my loue remembred I rest, Your
assured loving frende and cosin, Tho. Fairfax. York, 26 Martii
1628.

**345.** *To Sir Edward Stanhope. 6 April 1628 (SC, xxi/47).*

Sir, I shall dischardge my promise allbeitt shortly, yet not omitt the
principall stages of our proceeding in Parliament heathertoo. The
howse hath in the first place past solemny by the question the here-
ditary right that wee haue in our goods and that they cannot be
taken from us, but with our owne consentts in Parliament. Secondly
that our persons ought not to be imprisoned, but the cause must be
shewen and, if his Maiestie or his Counsell doth otherways committ,
they are to be inlardged upon ther *habeas Corpus.* Wee shall haue a
lawe to declaire and confirme this right with a greeuouse penalty
upon the infringers. The grande committee hath voted for fiue
subsedies, but are not as yet to be reported to the howse, nor will
not I thinke, att least by my consent, till wee be in sumthing a better
readinesse for the security of the subiects in thos fundamentall
liberties before rehearsed. For itt is resoled by the howse that thes
tow, for the king, for the people, shall goe hand in hande as one
ioynte and continued actte. His Maiesty is wondrouse well pleased,
hath sent us a gratiouse messadge, aseuring us he will conferme our
liberties and giue a gratiouse answeare to our Petition of Religion.
This latter I doe not soe much stande upon. yet I loue itt as well as
another, bycause I know that if the state be onc sett on the right
foote againe, this will necessarily follow in pointe of state, which for
the most partte binds strongliest with princes. Soe as if wee gett the
former, wee haue both this and all the rest. In truthe I hope wee shall
haue a very happy parliament, if God giue us the grace to make
use of the occasion as wise men should.

Sir, in exceeding hast, I rest your most affectionate asseured cosin
and frend, Th. Wentworth. 6 of Aprill 1628.

**346.** *Sir Henry Wotton to Wentworth, 8 April 1628 (Knowler, i, p. 45; SC, xii/27), sending him Dubravius' book* De Pisciniis.

**347.** *Lord Haughton to Wentworth, 9 April 1628 (Knowler, i, p. 46; SC, xxii/68). He sends a cast of hawks from Gelderland and news of Germany, Switzerland and Amsterdam.*

**348.** *From George Calvert, Lord Baltimore. Cloghammen. 17 April 1628 (SC, xii/28).*

Sir, I haue left in England many acquaintances and few fast freinds; of these I haue yow are *prima classis* and good cause haue yow given me to esteeme yow so. For since Fortune and those that are her idolaters frowned upon me, I have yet fownd your countenance always the same, loving and cherefull, an undoubted argument both of your constancy to me and of the noblenesse of your disposition. In confidence of both I have presumed to make yow a kynd of executor of a will that I hope shall be performed in my life tyme and I have joyned Sir Francis Cottington with yow and yow neede not feare that it shall putt yow either into danger or any great trouble. It is concerning my sonne Cecill, whom I leave behind me, and being desirous to settle him and to prefer him in my absence to some such marriage as my poore fortune may seeme to deserve, I have to that purpose estated upon him on certaine conditions the land I have in England in possession with 2 parts of my silke farme and the land in Ireland after my decease, provided he marry within a yeare and that with the good liking and consent of your self and Sir Francis Cottington, or one of you, and to also pay me a certaine summe of money expressed in a deede indented betwixt yourself and Sir Francis Cottington as feoffees in trust on the one part and my self on the other. I am assured yow will neuer give your consent, but to such a one as your judgement shall tell yow is a wife fitt for him and to prescribe yow any other rule I cannot mor, being [?] where I know I have so much affection. My thoughts are so busyed now about my preparations for my Newfoundland voyage as I leave yow sooner then I would, being as lothe to part in a letter as wee had wont to be in a chamber. God sending me safe into Newfoundland, I shal write at more length; in the meane tyme commending humble service, I pray you to your noble lady and to my lord of Clare and remember me in all hearty affection to Mr Wandsford, not forgetting the promises yow made to visitt me in Newfoundland, though yow neuer meane to performe it. God send us a happy meeting in heaven and in earth yf it please him. Cloghammen, 17 Aprill 1628. Your faithfull frend and servant, Geo. Baltimore.

**349.** *From the earl of Sunderland. Lindsforth. 17 April 1628 (SC, xii/29).*

Noble freinde, for other I assure my selfe I shall neuer haue cause to esteeme of you, the like confidence maye you assuredly haue of me. Thankes for your kinde remembrance and your well wishes; I will bee free to you, I protest itt is nott much shorte of my siknes the greife I conceiue of beinge att this time debarred from the happinese of enioyinge the companye of so manye of my true and worthy freends as are now togeather of you. I haue taken phisike seauen tymes in nine dayes, which I haue found to bee noe iestinge matter for mee. As for the mouths of malitious people, the kinge himselfe canne nott free himselfe from them, therfore poore subiects must bee content. I haue this daye reaceiued a letter from my seruante that tells mee I am nott forgotten in your house, though absent. For I am to bee giuen up for a non-communicate. I will nott finde faulte with proceedings, yett this maye I bouldlye affirme I neuer yett harde a man condemned befoer he wase harde what he could answere for himselfe, nor iff they hade, durst I haue made anye without the leaue of our house. Yett to your selfe in whose secresye I doe confide in, I dare saye that when the informers haue done theare worst, they shall neither in this particulare, nor anye other, be able to touch mee. And I shall bee able to abide the hammer whensoeuer I shall come to my triall, which I know will nott displease you, tell which oure and euer, I rest your faithfull freende, E. Sunderland. Lindsforth this xviith of Aprill, 1628.

**350.** A Speach spoken by Sir Thomas Wentworth in the Commons house, 1 May 1628, Mr Littleton being then in the chare, in a Committee of the whole howse in consultation about the bill to be drawen for securing the subiect in the fundamentall libertye of ther persons and propriety of ther goods (*SC*, xxi/48; *Wentworth's hand*).[1]

Mr Littleton, the subiect is weighty, your present resolution, if I mistake not myself, criticall. Be pleased therfor patiently to admitt my humble aduise and, if I incline to farre either to the one hande or to the other, voutchsafe gently to leade me into a streighter, a directer way by the light of clearer reason; soe shall I conforme

---

[1] The manuscript is faint, heavily corrected and at times almost illegible.

myselfe with thankfullnesse, you performe an acte of charity, of supreame charitye, sinc errors to the minde are as diseases to the body.

Wee are hear assembled togeither thoroughe the goodnesse of his Maiesty to close up the hurtt of the daughter of our people; our worke to establish unto the subiect liberty of person, propriety of goods and estate. All our hopes, all our desires are mette in this bill, which well setled, men must rest contented with our indeauours, left unsecured, wee loose our labours, treade the oliue, not annointe with the oile; be soe farre from satisying others that wee shall not be able to satisfye ourselues. It imports us therfore to looke well aboute us and, as in all things els, soe principally in this to carry ourselues euen betwixt prince and people that soe the streames of soueraingty and subiection may run still and smothe togeither in the worne and wonted channells without sincking or raising the bancks on either side.

First, I agree that the foure resolutions of this house which relate to the person are according to lawe that wee may not, nay that wee cannot, reseade a title from them, that ther can be no other foundation laid then that which is allready laid, to witt noe man ought to be imprisoned without a cause shewen. But the single question now only is wheather itt necessarily conduceth to our end that all thes resolutions be inacted in this law *terminio terminientibus*.

All our discourse as yet hathe been only applied to the first, to witt wheather a cause shall be insisted upon to be expressed upon the originall committmentt, or only upon suing forth the *habeas corpus*. Let us call now to minde, equally consider, weighe the reasons of both sides and then iudge on which hande the ballance is like to falll.

1: those that argue for the firste protest that shewing of cause will preuent committmentts this remedye under ta[ken] cums not home to the greefs, in regarde ther may as easily be a false cause pretended, or an insufficient cause alleged with as *much facility*[1] as to committ without any cause att all declared.

2: if noe cause be shewen upon the originall committmentt, the partie's papers may be searched before he can gett his *habeas corpus*, and soe be chardged with a springing crime, neuer thought of at the time of his first restrainte. This carries with itt rather the shew then the weight of an obiection, for who doubts but that, albeitt the cause wear expressed upon committment, yet still the papers might be searched and if by that any matter discouered the party can be charged with treason as well as if ther had originally been noe cause at all expressed.

[1] These words were crossed out, but the words replacing them are illegible.

3: if noe such cause shewen, a man might be committed and lie ther all a vacation before he could be sett at libert[y]; soe he might, allbeitt the cause be showen, for if he be committed for example after Trinity terme, then he must lie till Michaelmas terme, for out of terme the party can haue no grant or returne of his *habeas corpus.*

4: if noe such cause shewen then a prisoner might be remoued in such sortt from prison to prison as that his *habeas corpus* should neuer finde him, nay allbeit the *habeas corpus* brought him to the King's Benche barre [and] he ther deliuered, yet might he be instantly recommitted againe by a new warrant and thus may *ad infinitum before his bailement;*[1] thes would appear by your leaus, acts and streanes of a distempered licencouse power, which I trust falls into contemplation *only that* wee neuer *shall*[2] liue to see them practised upon freeborne, louing, faithfull people such as are the Englishe. But could there be times soe ill conditioned, would shewing cause in the warrant to [commit] preuent one of these violations, nay might not thes oppressions trample under feet, as well with cause shewen, as unshewen? surly they might, soe as still this medecin reatches not the diseases for which itt is prescribed, to which it is applied.

5: if it be not now fully cleared [and] determined that cause ought by the laws to be shewen upon the first commitment, wee quit the right of the subiect, leaue him in worse condition then wee found him, wee lessen, wee weaken Magna Carta. Allbeit wee doe not expresse it, yet doe wee not therfor grant that the cause cums sun enoughe upon the *habeas corpus*? Nay, wee haue declared for law solemnly by the question in our owne howse that the cause ought to be shewen upon the originall committment which setts us euen in this circumstance so well onwards of our iurney. As for Magna Carta and the other 7 statutes wee hear inserte them into this law *totidem verbis.* How then can that lessen that recites *verbatim*, how can that weaken that declaires, that establisheth, that inacteth? But if it doe, shew us whearin, for in good fathe under fauour I haue not hearde it as yet.

From that other single argument grounded upon the statute *de frangentibus prisonum* it proues the truth of the assertion that the cause ought to be shewen originally which is at peace and by me granted, subscribed unto; [it] applies itself to the benefit of the iaylor who is not answearable for an escape whear the cause is not set forthe in his warrant, rather then conuinceth a necessity of hear expressing it one way or other. For wee know many things may be

---

[1] These three words are partly struck through.
[2] Words in italics struck out.

legall which are not in all dyscretion [?] to be upon euery occasion att all tims pressed, inforced, either upon councell or state.

In the next place let us consider the reasons which perswade us not now to presse for an inacting in expresse termes that the cause shall be shewen upon the originall committment by necessary authority.

1. Itt is agreed by that honorable gentleman Sir Edward Cooke that this pointe [?] is declaired to be law by thes statutes which hear wee recite; whie then should wee indanger our act by explaining that partt internly [?] to our owne enslauing bi [?] rot inclusiuely? a consession all ready, or whilest we gather this fruicte of substance, of matter, what need wee care who take the leaues of forme, of manner? much rather take it then as granted and maintaine our right.

2. The words of the former lawes which are without exception and cannot be denied us are more exclusiue to the Counsell borde then thes we couet. For the statutes of 25 and 45 Ed[ward] 3 explaine *legem terrae* of Magna Carta to be writt originall at the Common law, the *Iuditium Parium* of Magna Carta to be presentment or indictment, declare that noe freeman shall otherwayes be imprisoned and that of 36 Edward 3 taketh away all other committment, though by the especiall commaunde of the king himself. Soe as it seems to me if we had euer our owne desire, yet wee left the subiect worse then wee found him. For as the law is now itt is expressly, strongly negatiue: none shall be committed at all but by the laws of the land and this law which in deed is the knub of the question, expounded as aforesaid, to be neither order of the Counsell bord nor yet the king's commaunde. But grant our owne resolution that the lords of the Counsell shall not committ without lawfull cause shewen in ther warrant and it imples that then they may committ upon a iust cause expressed, which upon considered reading will I thinke neather be founde the language nor the intention of thos wise lawgiuers and which, allbeitt I will not dispute hear wheather they can or not, yet shall I lybralle lysence them to move [?] for[1] what they might, till I see them use that power better, more equally, more moderately for the good and benefitt of the subiectts then of late they haue dun.

But since in cures itt is a prime, an important skill to applie the remedies right, let us consider whear and how this desease holds us.[2]

---

[1] This word may have been struck through.

[2] Nicholas's notes on the debate show that Wentworth was answering points raised by Robert Mason, who spoke immediately before, P.R.O., SP. 16/97, pp. 51–52. The fullest report of the speech is in the *True Relation*: 'Wee are here mett to close up the hurt and danger of his Majestie's people, all our desires are bent to this bill and this left unsecured makes us loose all our labour, we shall tread the olife and loose all the oyle. I agree the resolucons are according to lawe and that wee cannot recede a title; wee can lay noe other foundacon then

WP—U

**351.** *Corporation of Pontefract to Wentworth* (*SC*, xii/31).

Honored Sir, albeit that our pore maligned Corporacon hath of late suffered some preiudice in haveing our franchises and priviledges, graunted by his Maiestie's most noble progenitors, lately called in question upon a *Quo Warranto* and some other things urged against us by some not well affected to us, nor to our corporacon (though without iust cause), yet wee are not altogither dismayde in regarde wee hope that God hath raised up some freinds to stand with us in our true iuste and honest cause, amongest which number wee presume to assure ourselves that your worshipp wilbee one of the cheifest pillars for our good, and the rather in respecte of your clemencie and favor, both of late and from tyme to tyme, so lovingly offered and manifested to us (though by us altogither undeserved). Upon which growndes wee are bolde at this tyme to requeste your worshipp's helpe and assistance on the behalf of us and our towe brethren, the bearers hereof, Mr Hitchinge and Mr More, whome wee have requested and prepared to attend your worshipp and our Burgesses for the renuinge of our charter and obtayning of such thinges to be inserted into the same as they will imparte unto yow and them, not doubting but by your good meanes and paynes (which wee humblie crave at your handes) his Maiestie wilbee graciously pleased not only to suffer so auncient a corporacon as ours is (though opposed with potent adversaries) to enioy all the liberties and jurisdiccons to the same graunted by his Maiestie's most noble progenitors without questioning herafter, but also will add thereunto such new graunts

---

what is already layd. All the argument is on the first and some haue objected and said a new cause may bee searched out after his imprisonment, but this is of shew and noe waight; there may bee this search, before the comittment, as well as after. Others say the cause shewing preuents the committment, but may the committment bee upon another cause and hee that will commit for one cause may show a wronge cause. But here lett us see how this miserye comes on us: First by too speedy committments at Whitehall and by too slow baylement at Westminster hall, then there is noe hope but neither is it to bee neglected. Let us make what Lawe wee can, there must, nay there will bee, a trust left in the crowne, for this the lawes already prouides; wee haue assureance of His Maiestie's promises and wee may sure with condicons and urged necessities. But for that that concerns Westminster Hall, that that concerns the the *Habeas Corpus*, let us so secure itt that the Iudges in Westminster Hall dare not deny us and soe wee shall secure ourselues from the greatest punishment; take now all the lawes declared *a posteriori* wee are secured to bee bailed and if wee haue goods shew mee if euer any law since Edward 3 was of greater consequence' (Bodley MS. Eng. Hist. c. 202, fos. 304ᵛ–05ʳ). Nicholas's notes give a different ending: '. . . such a lawe will exceede all the lawes that we haue had for the good of the subiect and if it be soe then he desires to know whether our cuntry will not blame us, if we refuse it; he is to be charged by letter wryten that he see it.'

as may tend to the good thereof and hurt of none, whereby wee may be the better enabled to doe his Maiestie that true and faithfull service which wee desire to performe in all loyalty to his highnes. In which doing your worshipp shall not onely bynde us, but also our posterities in a perpetuall bond to your worshipp and all yours and to pray for your prosperitie and increase of honor here and euer lasting happines hereafter. And so wee most humblie take leave, desiring to rest, att your worshipp's service euer (to our powers) to be comaunded; Richard Clementt, Maior; Jo: Skipton; Willm. Talam; Leonard Warde; William Wilkinson; Stephen Cowper; William Cotes; Peter Skipton; Maximilian Adams; Edward Busbie. Pontefract 6 Maii 1628.

**352.** *Speech, 24 May 1628, on the Lords' proposed addition to the Petition of Right (SC, xxi/210)[1] [Wentworth's hand].*

Cosin Radcliffe, you desire a copy of what I spake yesterday; hear I will doe itt, as near the words as I can remember, but sure I am the same and no other in substance.

Mr S[e]r[jeant] Hawkins [Hoskyns] before you go to the question in this second, I shall speak a word to the third point, referred by the howse to the consideration of this grande Committee, to the entent ther maybe noe further expense of time then needs must.

Wee haue laid aside a bill hear debated for the securing unto the subiects of ther iust, fundamentall, vitall liberties. Wee are now fallen to a petition of right, lower then which wee cannot goe, with honoure to the howse, with faithfullnesse to thos trusts for which wee are accomptable.

Now unlesse the Lords cooperate with us hearin, the sinew is cut in peeces that giues motion, the stampe taken of that must imprint valew upon this action. Ioyne with them, the benefit communicates itself to posterity, becums a recorde; seperate from them, our laboures are as the grasse upon the howse toppe, of small continuance. With a declaration of both howses in pointe of right, a moderate answer is considerable, without that, none desirable.

It befitts us then to intend the union of them to us, who indeed are as the soule to the body of this Petition, giuing therunto life, being and season.

Ther are therfore tow expedients in this businesse, the one not to

---

[1] The addition expressed '. . . due Regard to leave entire that Sovereign Power wherewith Your Majesty is trusted for the Protection, Safety and Happiness of your People.' The speech was part of a debate following the conference between the Houses on 23 May, *Lord's Journals*, iii, pp. 801, 813–20.

recede from our petition, noe not in a title, either inn the whole or in the partts; the other, to winn the coniuncture and concurrance of both howses therin, for if wee faile in either of thes, we destroy our owne worke.

Our minds, our intentions are mett, we desire noe new thing for the subiect, wee intend not to diminishe the iust prerogatiue of the Crowne, we lessen noe power of his Maiestie to punish a criminall, wee only desire to preserue, to secure the innocent. Are the children cum to the birthe and is ther not strengthe to bring forth? Surely the wisdum of both howses is able to expresse ther ioynt meanings in wordes, in manner without disaduantadge, either to king or people. Els shall I thinke God is angry and that for our sinns he hath taken our understandings from us that we may fall into all the ill consequences, into all the mischeefes which our unhappy parting might seem to threaten us withall, but I hope for better things then thes.

Farre bee itt from me to propound anything in soe weighty a businesse, I am not able to maister soe great a difficulty. Only giue me leaue humbly to moue yow that we may close up this Conference mannerly, as towards their lordships, and to auoide in sum measure ther present voting of any thing till wee be upon nearer termes of agreement.

Therfore my humble petition is that, as we haue in all our debates in this howse, our former Conferences with ther lordships by our Speaker to his Maiestie and, which is more then all thes, in our owne harttes, soe we nowe againe professe our equall cares with ther lordships to preserue the sacred rights of the Crowne without the least diminution and that therfore allbeitt wee may not admitt of this adition, or any other of like nature, being in truthe in termes destructiue to our whole petition. Yet if ther lordships be pleased to propound any other thing that may giue themselues contentment, euer preseruing and not in a title abating from the substance of our petition, either in the whole or in any of the partts, we shallbe gladd to heare and consider of itt.

Hear you haue itt. And lett me now say I desire any equall mind, when he hath considered itt, to shew me whear the obliquity of itt is; for I ingenuously confesse I should [do] the same ouer againe [to deliuer for] the like occasion.[1]

---

[1] The 'True Relation' reports the speech: 'Wee are now fallen from a Statute and a new lawe to a peticon of Right and unlesse the Lords cooperate with us, the stamp is cutt of that giues a vallue to the action; if they ioyne with us it is a record to posterity, if wee seuer from them noe longe continuance and therfore lett us labour to gett the Lords to ioyne with us. To this there were two things considerable; first not to recede in this peticon, either in part or in whole from our resolucons, secondly that the Lords ioyne with us or els all is lost; wee haue

**353.** *Speaker Sir John Finch to Wentworth, 28 May 1628 (Knowler, i, p. 46; SC, xii/32). He sends copies of the speeches for which he wrote and wishes him success for the great business tomorrow.*

**354.** *From Wandesford. 30 July 1628 (SC, xvi/247).*

Sir, your honorable letter of the 20th (for there is neuer a lyne that wants the name of some greate Lord or Councellor) hath sett the olde Cavillier a cocke horse, but I hope the thing you note of will dismountt him with a pouder before Christenmas, or else you remember the story; we will putt him out and putt you knowe whome in his place. To reflect a litle upon Richmondshyre, the perticulers you mention to be receued from Mr Man I heare not of, but I wish I had them, for if we dar venter, there will be matter to worke upon in the mannor of Middleham (for that I haue most searched into) worthy our labor and freinds. I fynde the towne itt self of Midlam and two or 3 more (amonting in all to aboutt 60$^{li}$ rent) to be worth twentye for one att the olde rent, besydes the commoditye of a chayse in Couerdayle, not far from Midlam, which will fall within thes bargain, because there are fewe or no deare in itt nowe (not aboue 30), being no perticular place alloted for the deare but an ancyent forrest and chayse ouer which the king's deare haue fre liberty of feding and being without interruption after the manner of the rest of Massamshyre without the parke, a place which for hills and woods is well fitted for hunting, especially if the orders of the chayse be observed to which the inhabitants being all the king's tenants are sworne; that is to permitt the deare to feede quiett without interruption so much as by a dog, aboue succh and such a sise. But the want of care in the keepers hath nere destroyed the deare. There are likewise some small woodes in this same Couerdayle (within which the 3 townes I spoake of doe lie) but not to make any benefitt for sayle

---

protested wee desire noe new thing, wee leaue all power to his Maiestie to punish malefactors. Let us cleare ourselues to his Maiestie that wee thus intend. It is far from mee to presume to propound anything, I dare not trust my owne iudgment onely to preuent a present voting with the Lords. Lett [us] againe address ourselues to the Lords that wee are constant in our grounds that wee desire noe new thing, nor to inuade upon his Maiestie's prerogatiue. Butt lett us add, though wee may not admitt of this addicon, yet if theire Lordshipps can find out any way to keepe untouched this peticon, wee will consider of it and joine with them' (Bodley MS. Eng. Hist. c. 202, fo. 421'). Nicholas did not record this speech. British Museum, Stowe MS. 366, fo. 189$^r$, gives a briefer version, ending 'But I would add allbeeyt wee may not admitt of these wordes, yet if there Lordships can finde out any thinge which way to cause an agreement, lett them express it and wee shall condiscend.'

worth the mention. Together I must tell you the condition of thess
peple is not to yealde from there ancyent clames of Custumary
withowt much difficultye, though that Custome whearupon they
builde is ouerthrowen by taking other leases and not for the like
tearme that formerly they had; so in lawe they can haue no reliefe,
nor I thinke in any Court of Equitye, but howe far thear clamor and
a manne's owne concience will bynd him I knowe not. Certaynly
a man may gayne well ether by selling itt presently, or wearing out
thear tearme; if that other defficulty which occurrs next to our
consyderation doe not deter us, that is the feare of resumption,
which me thinks should not worke upon a valuable consyderation,
nether if this course holde a whyle will ther be any such feare, the
generalitye of the purchasers, like that case of Abbyes, securing the
purchasers. Nowe whether we should enter into tearmes of bargain
with the cittye thus early breaking the we[y] to others now, before we
have a little consydered of itt, or only make meanes to them by my
Lord Treasurer that they will be pleased to reserue the towne of
Middlam and 3 or 4 townes more, nere adioyning upon itt for a
freind of his (neuer naming any) untill Michelmas tearme, I refer to
your iudgment. But the many perplexetyes weighed in this business,
the latter I thinke will be the safer, unless you perceaue some to be
busy about them thear, for truth I can suspect none so hardy as to
meddle with them. Howsoeuer, if circumstances bende you to bergain
by all meanes let a third person's name be used in the purchase. But
whatsoeuer reasons may deter us from meddling with the rest, I
should be glad to haue the command of the deare passed to me
together with the woods growing upon itt (not for profitt, but being
underwoods for the deare) together with two or 3 closes called the
deare closes, ancyently the lodge for the keper and is worth a matter
of 12$^{li}$ per annum; all which are reckned of no valeue to them in the
purchase, these closes being but at a noble rent, nor can benefit them
in the sayle, but would be a convenyentcy to me, though itt lye 14
myles from me, hauing no other place for deare. This deare close, as
all the rest of the lordship, is in lease for 25 yeares or there about.
You may, if you please, let my lord moue them for the whole manner,
but the names of thoss 3 townes are Casselton, Horse house, Gowes-
ton, or Garrerstang. This is all I can say of Middlam, that of Richmond cartaynly is a very good penniworth to, if it wear looked into
as I purpose to doe; howsoeuer it be for the profit, I am sure for the
royaltyes and command exceding the other. And whether you will
thinke fit (beinge we may haue both in our choyce) that my lord
moue them for to haue ether of them in his freind's choyce, I refer
to your self. But we nede not feare ther customholde more then

clamor which our owne good dealing may qualifye; howsoeuer att the worst the comons, the quit rents and all other perteculars of the royaltyes will be secured to us.

One thing more I must trouble you with for my self that you will nowe deale effectually for the stewardship of Rippon for me and send to Sir Thomas Hoby and acquaint him plainly you heare the bishop will dispose itt to some others, desyring him to put the bishop to itt whether he will continew him or not. And if he refuse that, you may cause Philip Manwaring or Mr Pernham to learne of the Bishop whether he shall kepe it or not, but treuly I hear Sir Thomas shall not haue itt of all men, but that Sir William Hungate, or William Mallorye; shall, but I feare Grymes most, itt lying nere Horton. I pray you deale plainly with Sir Thomas and if there be any waye Mr Kirkham will doe itt hansomly with my lord, not [?] by my sute (though I would not loose itt for that) but that he may doe well to conferr itt upon me, as one that by my neyborhoode to Ryppon may doe him some good service. Howsoeuer one way or other (I meane alwaye honestly towards Sir Thomas and all men) I would haue itt. For I see this is like to be a mad world; euery man snatcheth what he can for himself.

For your cosen Dandby least I fall into whole volumes, I will say nothing till we mete. Your Ant is much after the olde mannar, sath you shall be a vicount she hears, but seames to be well enough pleased with itt; and so doth no bodye else in the cuntry, the comon opinion passing you nowe under Sir John Sauile's character and that there is a Thomas as well as a John for the king. Well we shall nowe heare shortly from you; the next fart I heare of you I beleue will be a lordly on and the next letter you may subscribe as our cuntry neybor did after his newe smithe [?] your frind my lord such a one. Remember my seruice and my wife's to your good ladye and all with you. I pray God bless you both and all yours and send us happy meting, Your most obliged kinsman and freind, C. Wandesforde.

I hope to heare once more from you before I see you. You se I trouble you with this business, but in good fath toe deale plainly with you now after, your lordship I thinke will doe as you doe with your owne business, neuer mynde itt. For I knewe you neuer dispach any thing seriously, but in your bed in the morning and what you doe there I knowe not. July 30 [1628].

**355.** *From Wandesford. Kirklington. 30 July 1628* (*SC*, xvi/223).

Sir, this day by other messingers I writt more att lardge to you concerning other business att this tyme only to desyre your further paynes concerning that personadge att Caselforth bridge whereof I spoake to you the day we parted. The case stands thus: I thinke I shall upon reasonable tearmes compound with the incumbent, only the difficultye will be to deale safely for the oath. I am advised to procure the next advowsyon from the king, who is the patron, and then the incumbent acknowledging his owne insufficyency before the ordinarye (as he is ryddy and not without cawse being mad att certayne tymes) my brother is to be his substitute for his life, paying somewhat we can agre of yearely, so then he shall have itt upon reasonable tearmes for the present and hereafter for nothing. This only course will avoyde simonye, for he must neuer be sworne therefor, if this course will stand good (I meane that the king cannot revocke his grant of the advowsyon). I desyre you hartily to indeavor it and perfect itt before you come awaye and what cannot be done, leaue to my brother Osborne, or my brother Michaell himself (who in this case may be acquainted with any thing that is to be done) to finish. I pray God we come not to leyte for Sir Thomas Bland I am afrayde and olde Sauile hath preuented us, but of that you will be pleased to be informed whether there be not a grant passed of the advowsyon or presentation alryddye, I pray you lay downe the mony for the passadge and I shall pay itt agayne with thanks. Thus, with my harty prayers for all your healths and my seruice to you all, I rest your most obliged kinsman and frind, C. Wandesford. I am ashamed I have forgott the person's name. Kirtlington, July 30, 1628. To my most honored kinsman and freind Sir Thomas Wentworth att Clerkingwell in London or ells where with spede. Leaue this letter with Willim Wandesforde att the syne of the King's Head in Paul's Church yeard, Mr Hough's shop, a draper, to be deliuered according to the direction above.

**356.** *Sir Richard Hutton junior to Wentworth, 12 Aug. 1628 (Knowler,* i, p. 47; *SC*, xii/34). *He announces the birth of a son and congratulates him on his recent honour.*

**357.** *From Sir Gervase Clifton. Skipton, 15 Aug. 1628 (SC, xii/35).*

Right Honorable, I heard but euen nowe of my lord Clifford's messinger's coming with whom I must present my seruise and seuerall ioyes of your late honor and arriuall into the cuntrye, both which congratulating with as much truth and cheerfullnes, as I use to doe the good of my frendes wherin I dare compare with the best of men and hope you will not feare mee to fall shorte in your lordship's case, for I assure yow I neuer yet found it in myself. But I conceaue these two thinges I haue mentioned will participate of the nature of other felicityes, be very shorte if the latter proue so and that your lordship is for your libertye in thes partes as I am, rather itinerant then stayd and certayne at Woodhowse to be visited, I desire to heare and will putt off my otherwayse not to be diuerted obseruanc till we both become resident agayne. Your other I shall easily pardon, if it be only as I guess transitory and as a rise to an higher pitch. Mean while I am hartely glad the drye herbe tyme affords any iuyce where it is so aptly conferred. I doe not understand your Ladie to be comed downe with you; therfor I beseech your lordship doe mee the fauour to lett me knowe howe you left hir and my sweet cosens and to be assured of my being euer, my lord, your lordship's faythfull brother in lawe and humble seruant, Geruas Clifton. Skipton 15 of August 1628. To the rt. honorable lorde my lo. Wentworth at Woodhowse present these.

**358.** *From Sir Edward Osborne. London. 24 Aug. 1628* (*SC*, xii/36).

My Lorde, with noe less sorrow in your behalfe then ioy for the state, giue me leaue to lett you know thatt yesternight late ther came 2 seuerall posts from Portesmouth, bringinge newes that the Duke of Buckingham was slaine by one Liewtenant Felton, who was as it seemes cashered and demaunded his pay soe peremptorily (with his hatt on) of the Duke, as he kickt him, wheruppon he stabde him in the back, leauinge him butt soe much time as to say 'villaine thou hast slaine me' and soe died. A iust rewarde for killing a poor marriner the day before with his owne hands, for a little sawcines, as it is saide, in askinge his pay as the Lieutenant did who was presentlye apprehended. The kinge was saide to be sicke before, but now much perplexed more. This may be false, butt very unlike, it is soe generall a reporte, none contradicting it.

Aboutt 2 dayes sinc and before his death I had 2 chronograms giuen me with 2 verses after them, in my opinion very strange ones: *Jacobus Stuardus Magnae Britanniae Rex*, the numerall letters whereof makes iust this present year of our lord 1628; the other is *Georgius Buckingamiae Dux* the numerall letters whereof likewise makes iust the same year and the verses were these:

As both these Stiles with this yeare doe agree
So thou to it or it to thee shall fatall bee.

What change this will worke God knowes, butt I would to God you were here to play your owne cardes, I would nott doubt, butt your game would be fairer nowe then euer, for I feare he was

not soe reall as he seemed. Good my Lord, pardon my bould op-
pinion it proceeds from an hart as zealously desirous of your Lordship's honour and aduancement as any man's and with that assurance be pleased to esteeme me in the number of, Your Lordship's
faithfullest freindes and seruants, Ed: Osborne. Lo[ndon] the
24th August 1628. Be pleased (good my Lord) to present mine and
my wiue's humble seruice to your noble Lady.

**359.** *From Sir Ralph Hansbie. Tickhill Castle. 31 Aug. 1628 (SC,*
xii/37).

Very muche honoured Lord, yours to my selfe with the inclosed to
my Lord Treasurer I haue receiued for which I retourne you humble
thanks with assuraunce that I will not fall shorte to obeie your
commaundes, either in the deliuerie thereof, or in pressing of an
accompte to bee giuen att a full Boarde, the king presente, and my
lord Savile and Fanshawe commaunded to attende to render theire
reasons for theire soe slender prouesion made either for kinge or
people; and whatt the fruites of my labours in this dothe produce, I
will att my retourne waite upon you and giue full satesfaction therein,
till when and euer, my suite is to bee continewed in your good open-
ion. And soe I kisse your hands and rest, Your lordship's humble
and faithfull seruante, R. Ansbie. Tickhill Castle, this 31 of Auguste
1628.

**360.** *Lord Treasurer Weston to Wentworth, 8 September 1628
(Knowler, i, p. 47; SC, xii/38). He has received two letters from
him, hopes affairs may be settled in the ancient way without
raking into the ashes of the dead, or seeking new quarrels against
the living and relies on no man's counsel more.*

**361.** *From the earl of Clare to Wentworth. Houghton. 20 Sept. 1628
(SC, xxii/69).*

Sun, my daughter your wyf is cum to yow and as the case standeth
with her muche against myn and her mother's will; nether can you be
altogether ignorant thearof, her midwyf being sent for and my lady
Sauil, your sister, lately hear, so as when your seruant came this
morning I rather expected your care of staying her hear (till her condicon had bene sumwhat better assured) then of feching her howsoever away. And to tell yow the matter how it was: though she had
prepared herself for the iorne, yet not being well and her hedd aking,
I presumed uppon the tytell a father hath for her good to stay her,

her husband not hauing then interposed; but, your seruant cum, my interest gaue place to a greater and so yow have her with yow. God bless yow both and graunt this iorne cause no discumfort. Amen. Your very louing father, Clare. Haughton, this 20. 7ᵇʳ 1628.

**362.** *From Sir Edward Graye. Morpeth Castle. 24 Sept. 1628.* (*SC*, xii, 40).

Right honorable and my honorable good lord, I must intreate pardon of your lordship for beinge bolde to become sutor to yow in the behalfe of this bearer, my kinsman, who haith a suite now dependinge att Yorke and to be hard the second of October next that is for the greatest part of his poore estate; and albeit I make nott the least doubt of the goodnes of his cause, yett fearinge his adversarie will make better meanes to obteine fauoure att the Counselle's handes then he is able to doe, beinge but a stranger there, makes me assume soe much boldenes as humblye to entreate your lordship to be pleased for my sake to affoorde him that noble fauoure, as to write or send, which your lordship shall best lyke, to any of the learned Counsell of Yorke that they would take notice of his cause and afford him there lawfull fauoure; which your lordship's extraordinarie fauoure and respect amongst many I haue tasted of from your bountie, I shall euer be readye to deserue with all fayhthfull seruice. And soe, craueinge pardon for my boldnes and remembringe my humble seruice to your lordship, I humblye tak leaue and rests, Your lordship's humble seruant euer to be comanded, Edward Graye. Morpeth Castle, 24th Septembris 1628.

**363.** *From Lady Grace Darcy. Sutton. 3 Nov. 1628* (*SC*, xxii/70).

May it please your Lordship. The many fauours and late greate kindnesses which I haue receaued from you, doe binde mee in all humble thankfulnes to acknowledge the same and they may justly silence mee and stoppe mee from makeinge any new mocons, or other requests unto you. Neuertheles upon your former courtesies presuminge, I am embouldned and encouraged to bee an humble and earnest suitor unto you for one fauor on the behalfe of my sonne, which is that you would bee pleased to doe your endeuor to procure him to bee a member of the lower house of Parliament this next sittinge in the place of a Burges of some part of your country, or ells where, if it lye in your Lordship's power to effect it. In which greate request, if your lordship can pleasure mee, I shall euer acknowledge it as a great fauor. For my desire is to giue him as good breedinge

and educacon as I cann, yett by reason of the dangerousnes of the
times I cannot send him forth to trauaile, howsoeuer by this meanes
hee might see the ordering of matters here att home which may in
some respects bee as avayleable for him. And soe for this time I
cease any further to trouble your Lordship and rest, Your Lordship's
true freinde, Grace Darcy. Sutton, this 3º of Nov. 1628.

**364.** *From Wandesford to Wentworth. 13 Nov. 1628 (SC, xvi/224).*

My lord, in the first place I cannot thinke of your paynes taken in
your last letter, dated the 28 of October, without many thankes and
least you thinke us idle here in the cuntrye I will giue you an account
what concernes your cosen Dandbye's affayres; that his dubble
treatye with Faucolnbridge for himself and for Armitadge of
Kirkleyes for his sister, and the latter though last in proposition takes
up all our tyme, all our cunning. Yet I nede not use that word, he hath
met with so malliable a subiect of the yong man that the work nedes
not mutch hammering. This treatye is so far advanced that olde
Armetadge (as my cosen tells me) demands a 2000$^l$ portion, but
seames but to stand upon 1000$^l$ and if his sonne get nothing with
his wife itt will be worse for him, he will be worse able to liue hereafter. His sonne for his pert courts the yong ladye (and trewly he may
perhaps spede there, he is so like our first love John Walker), waytes
upon my yong brother in lawe, speaks of nothing but howe hyly
a neybor and a freind is to be valewed. On the other syde my coosen
sollicitts his freinds to make good this demand (for itt were unfitt
though it were in our power to put her off with nothing) perticularly
my wif, by a letter from Mr Richards insinuating this match was
fownd out by himself in pursuance of a motion of my own to
T. Dand[by] that itt weare fitt his sister weare marryed and howe
commodious itt may be for the yong gentlewoeman, howe much
to be desyred by her freinds, finally desyring my countenance and
helping hand, profers his service to negotiate this expedition (for so
he calls itt) by my directionns. My lord Darcye (I thinke) alreddy
consulted withall in this point and I beleue your olde Ant mayde
acquainted with itt this day by my cosen who carryed the yong
gentlleman from hence to Pott, from whence they are gone to
Newbrugh to acquaint him with his newe kindred. Howe you will
beleue I was not a litle doubtfull of my answere, but looking more
at the future to prevent the inconvenences that may fall out upon a
breatch rather then upon the hopes of accomplishing the mach in
present I mayde this ansere that, though my dawghter's yeares and
his consydered, this motion might come seasonably enough two

yeares hence, yet in answere to this demand mayde by Mr Richards
I could not doe less then express my meaning in this business whereupon the other so much depended, therefore I would be ryddy if my
cosen and I could agre upon tearmes of mariadge (whereupon all
expectation from me was grownded) to lye downe that 600$^l$ to this
gentleman presently, which by my couenants to your lordship I am
to pay a yeare after full adge, or if all pertyes were so pleased, a
greater pert of the 1600$^l$; that I would ether maintayne my cosen
Dandbye, his wife and children for 3 or 4 yeares in my house till his
owne could be mayde fit for him (which I would annually bestowe
some cost upon) or release his wardship to him and his estate presently upon reasonable tearmes.

Tom Dandbye's answere to this was full of dryness and (I thinke)
dissimulation; his sister he wished well and if this occasyon fayled
he would labor to prefer her aswell hereafter, but he would not
marry yet; when he did my daughter might be as nere him in affection as any other; and the same night is posted to Henbrugh, contrary to his profession when he tooke horse. But till I better explayne
my selfe, you will say I was to blayme in my answere. Treuly, my
lord, I am not, for this I conceaue tends indifferently to the one of
thoss two ends of marrying presently with me or Fawcolnbridge,
nether of which shall displease me. For if I [or? it] be accepted,
I shall most willingly venture upon your kinsman, as one whom
good usadge and better experience may tymely fre from all thess
misunderstandings betwixt us. If not, yet may itt call on the other
with Fawcolnbridge who cannot giue less satisfaction to his freinds
then I [or any] other besydes that hereafter whensoever I shall be
questioned (which his hott spiritt underhand much heatneth) this
lardge offer will iustefye me much in the eye of iustice and equitye.
All this I wryte at lardge that your lordship may not be ignorant
what to answere in this perticuler, if you be sollicited in itt before we
mete. And treuly were I but a bystander yet would I wish Faul-
conbridge were rather treated withall nowe, when thess offers may
out balance him and the intercession of freinds drawe greater con-
detions from him, then when his drye and sly dealing shall have
nothing to counterpoyse against itt, but the affection of the yong
gentleman and that much corrupted too and by that tyme more and
more disabled to discerne. But if I weare to blame in this, itt was
only in this circumstance of tyme that I deliuered this answere my
self nowe and not by your motion, according to your Lordship's
agrement and myne nowe that could not be prevented for the sol-
licitation of the messenger and the nature of the business itt self
quickned my answere.

Now the end of all this I knowe not, but I may easyly imagine by yong Armitadge his caradge and procliueness too me [how] the game will goe. I beleue my cosen Dandbye's word for 1000[1] or perhaps less will serve his turne. And this I thinke will be enough for one matter, perhaps you will say for a letter. I pray you forgit not to give notice of your coming to Gawthrope, if itt be befor Christenmas. I long to heare what becomes on you; I am verye confydent, if you be not to confydent that is if you depart something from your rigid resolution of not medling, the business will be doone, but no fishing in thoss streames with empty baytes.

I pray God returne you in health into the cuntry and that shortly too, for the longer you stay the worse I think for your business, all things must be done att spring tydes. In the meane tyme giue me leaue to salute you with the harty prayers and unfeyned respects of your Lordship's most obliged kinsman and freind to serve you, C. Wandesforde. Nouember 13 1628.

I writt two or 3 words which G. Rad[cliffe] will tell you for Ryppon. I loke you should chyde and tell G. R. I protest to God Wansford is an ass for suffring T. D. to ryde up and downe and spend his tyme in this manner idling in the cuntry, but his cosen nowe in playne tearmes will nott be perswaded by me. For I sent him to Cambridge with his quateradge 25[1] before hand, he posts to Henbrugh and up and downe, pretends nowe this match of his sister deteynes him in the cuntrye.

**365.** *From Clare. Haughton. 15 Nov. 1628 (SC, xxii/87).*

Sun Wentworthe, I receaued your letter dated the 8, the 4th of this present, for which I thanke you, but by it I fynd my last is not yet cum to you; thear I writ that I doubted of my cuming up this term, Christmas being so near and the Parlament imediately after it, when though ways and wether may be the same or peradventuer wurs, yet the days wilbe longer and wee shal haue more light to strugle with the durt of Stangate hole.

I am very sorri Sir William Harbert hath so rooted his freind Sauil in that looce earth of Pembrok and Montgomre that he dare yet berd truth with his impostuer, which is an instruction to my lords, the Tresorer and Arundel, to strengthen themselfs as sone as they can at that bord, rather with waight then number, for both thear habiliteis be such as they need nether fear nor enuy able men, according to the imperfection of former tyms under Salisburi and others. But I hope in the close of the day's wurk you shal lay his infidelite so open, his corruptions and the betraying his trust, as at the last you will turn the *morosum senem* to his Hooley to expiat by a better contemplation the error of his actions. For me thinkes in an empti Exchequer 20,000[1] should fynd credit; howeuer if you truss him not within a Parl[iament], that bord, yourself and all honest men will still be trobled with him and therfor, sun, make account to be up agayn at that court's sitting.

Your news of Rochell to be so owld and no further flet [?] me thinkes be uncertain; Walsingham would have had an intelligencer in the French king's armi, but our Secretareis, ouershadowed by fauorits, haue lost that dewti. If it be lost, I wonder not; wee gaue theme by our eight shipps in taking the sea from them the deadly bloe and euer since interteyned them with weak and seeming remedeis, nether seasonable, nor strong enough, nor applyed by good artists; so as our latter error was wurs then the former, for what wee did aganst them was cordial and so it succeeded. Yow giue a trew iudgment of the consequence, Fraunce is therby entyr, thir freehowld being purchased owt, which the great men of that nation will sone repent thear retrat being taken away and, peradventure, wee ear long. For Throgmorton can fynd thym no more work at home which was the usuall diuertion this state used. Lybells are suntomes of ill gouernment, that things be amis and none to complayne unto, and if any by interest or impatience will neuertheles fynd fault [and] such be punished, which lerning others a more warei sylence, sum vent themselfs thus in the dark, as yow style it rightly by a chargeable wit, witnes Tacitus unde Tiberius, Nero and the other few Caesars, yet that Minister's punishment proportions not with Mannering's, though Mannering's misdeamenor in the ey of Iustice cann not be exceeded. I say not this to extenuate the one, but I wishe to bothe thear dew measuers and aboue all this fearfull Court sum limits, for seuerly this 3000[1] fyn is not *saluo continemento*,[1] though his parsonage wear as good as the Bishoprik of London. But let these pass. My daughter, your wyf, Will and Nan ar God be praysed all well. God bless them with yow and yow with them, Amen. Haughton, this 15 9[br] 1628, your very louing father, Clare.

**366.** *From the Earl of Bedford. Bedford House. 20 Nov. 1628 (SC, xx/266).*

My Lord, I was this day pressed by one that hath a barrony or vicuntship, as I think, in his power toe gett to know of me whether

---

[1] This probably refers to the fine on 6 November on Alexander Gill for words spoken in the beer cellar of Trinity College, Oxford, against Charles and Buckingham and for drinking Felton's health, though the fine was £2000; D. Masson, *The Life of John Milton*, i (London, 1875), pp. 150–52.

I had any frend that would tuch with appetiet that way. So that I, knowing your Lordship hath a Nephew of yours, whose estat and worth will well keep it, I thought I was in my obligationse to your Lordship to tender it unto your Lordship. Resting your Lordship's seruant and frend, Fra. Bedford. Bed: house, this 20 of November 1628. To the right hon. my very good frend the Lo: Wentworth.

**367.** *Sunderland to Wentworth, 15 December 1628 (Knowler, i, p.* 48; *SC*, xii/71), *thanking him for giving the next attorney's place in reversion at York to his secretary, James Howell.*

**368.** *Sir Henry Savile to Wentworth, 23 December 1628 (Knowler, i, pp.* 48–49; *SC*, xii/43). *He promises to attend him when he makes his entry at York. He may be induced by his friends to stand for the shire for parliament, but is as yet uncertain.*

**369.** *Henry, Lord Clifford, to Wentworth, 25 December 1628 (Knowler, i, p.* 49; *SC*, xii/72). *He congratulates him on his return and asks for news from Court.*

**370.** *From Philip Hodson. York. 26 Dec. 1628 (SC,* xii/45).

It may please your Honour, I no sooner heard that you were so eminently fixt in this our northerne spheere, but I was carefull to lay hold of the first opportunity to congratulate your honour and our happines that shall liue under your gouernment and, if when those letters come to your hands which missed you on the way, but I suppose will shortly be sent to you by Sir John Gibson, your honour shallbe pleased to pardon that liberty which my thoughts and pen tooke to expresse my selfe to your Lordship; I shall no more offend in that kind. All I haue to add is my humble and hearty thankes for your early remembrance of me, whereby I esteeme my selfe repayred and recouered from that contempt, wherin by my lord of Sunderland's obstinate power, I had so long laid. And since your honour hath bene pleased so far to manifest your opinion and affection to me, I shall hold my selfe unworthy of your respect, if euer I be wanting to doo you any seruice that shall fall within my reach. And so, being loath to stumble againe upon the same stone, I leaue your Lordship to God's grace, Your Honour's most ready to be commaunded, Ph. Hodson. York, this 26 of December 1628.

**371.** *Wandesford to Wentworth, 29 December 1628. (Knowler, i, pp. 49–50; SC, xvi/226). The Papists already fear his coming; he wishes to know whether the day holds for the parliament. If it does, he will spend three or four days with him on his way thither.*

**372.** *From William Raylton. London. 31 Dec. 1628 (SC, xii/47).*

May it please your Lordship. The present occasion offered by Sir Arthur Ingram invited me to acquaint your Lordship by way of addicon unto your other occurrences from this place with a passage now in acting for Doctor Sibthorpe and Mr Cousins, men soe well knowen, the one for his prayer booke and the other for a sermon preached in Northamptonshire, as I shall need to doe noe more but name them; and now I must tell your lordship that after all their paines taken, they are to come to sue for his Maiestie's pardon by way of a coronacon pardon and it is now in passing the seales severally, every man his pardon.

I hope your lordship will excuse the fault in not sending downe the Comission of Oyer and Terminer with the other Comissions for the Peace, for the clerks in the Crowne office tould me that they did never use to make them forth untill the Justices of Assize doe goe the Circuite, neither did they know of the gaole delivery at Yorke which now shortly approacheth.

To trouble your lordship with the relation of Mr Porter's returne from Spaine and the unkind usage he mett withall and his company also here upon our owne coast, I thinke were needles, because I am perswaded yow haue it from better hands then can be delivered by me who am, Your lordship's in all humility, W. Raylton. London 31 December 1628.

**373.** *Sir Henry Wotton to Wentworth, November or December 1628 (Knowler, i, p. 48; SC, xix/130), presenting a cane to him.*

**374.** *From Sir Henry Savile. Methley. 5 Jan. 1629 (SC, xii/49).*

May ytt please your Lordshipp. The Dutch menne's new workes in Dychmarsh doe not more drownde the uplande cuntrie then the inondation of the vaste and ambitious fooleries of my neighbour Corporation of Leedes trouble theire newe gouernment in obtrudinge theyre newe deuyses to the oppression of such as are under theyr base subiection. I thinke they conceyue that that lawe under which all the whole kingdome subsistes ys not sufficyent to gouerne them, but must haue the clothiers within theyr libertie (which dryves not a 4th

WP—X

parte of the trade of our cuntrye) to be gouerned by newe lawes, not parlementarie, but some sage constitutions of theyre owne making and accordinge to theyre highe capacities, seekinge to reduce theyre clothiers, as they haue theyre taylors, shoemakers and other mechaniques (some of them already beginning to mutyne) into companies in imytacon of London and other great citties. These bearers, very honest sufficient men attende your Lordshipp concerninge that busynes, who can informe your lordshipp of the particulers and pray your Lordshipp's honorable protection, accordinge to the justice of theyre cause; your Lordshipp well understandinge of what importance yt ys to upholde and mayneteyne this trade, which ys of the essence and indeede the very subsistence of our neighbourhood.

I purpose, Godwillinge, to present my seruice to your Lordshipp in person att Woodhouse before I be many dayes elder in regarde of your Lordshipp's short staye in these partes. Touchinge your Lordshipp's engagement for the election, though ytt were but for your little neighbour (who of himselfe ys able to doe soe little) yet *satis est dixisse.* I could neuer be drawen to oppose any designe of your Lordshipp's, when you were in our ranke, and that out of my loue, much less may I be seene to oppose a knowne designe of your Lordshipp's and that the first after the entrye to your gouernment, for that might nowe argue both want of loue, duetie and discrecon in me and I would be loath to be arraigned upon any of them towards your good Lordshipp, *satis est probasse* will I hope be my sufficient discharge in that behalfe. With my humble service I rest alwayes, your Lordshipp's to be comaunded, H. Savile. Metheley, 5 Januarye 1628[9]. Yf I wayte not upon your Lordshipp in the compasse of a weeke you may conclude I am layde upp of the goute.

**375.** *To Sir Edward Stanhope. Wentworth Woodhouse. 11 Jan. 1629*
    *(SC,* xxi/51).

Sir, I understood by my cosin your brother, your kind intendment of visiting this place whear your cosin would haue bid you wellcum. You shall allwayes doe us a fauoure when wee may see you and yet soe as may stande both with your health and conueniency. I shall be for London, God willing, on Tuesday and soe hauing much businesse yow will excuse my shortt and ill writing. My wife thankes you for your kind letter, desires me to write her excus that her Grandfather's picture she couetts, prayes you will cause itt to be copied for her and she will see the picture drawer satesfied for his paines. For your seruant Cripling, I should haue been willing to haue gratified him for your sake, but that I was before ingaged to an other, soe as I must intreate he will rest satesfied, for if I had knowen in time I should haue giuen an other answeare. I wishe you much good health and soe in much haste must write myself, Your very affectionat cosin and freinde, Wentworth. W.W. 11th of Janu. 1628[9]. My wife and I desire to be remembred to your good ladye.

**376.** *From Sir Henry Savile. Methley. 31 Jan. 1629* (*SC*, xii/53).

My honorable good Lorde, I haue bene able to wryte noe letters with my owne hande since my last to your Lordshipp, otherwyse I had not suffered soe longe happly under your Lordshipp's censure of goinge to Yorke to the election, as nowe I feare I doe, consyderinge my voluntarie promise to the contrarie unrequired by your Lordshipp, who I perceyue had engaged yourselfe as a priuate frende, but not as a Lord president. Wherein I thinke your Lordshipp hath done honor to yourselfe and right to your place, for a heade ought to be a gouernor and moderator, but of noe faction. The truth of my caryage in this busynes was thus: upon a generall dislyke of your little neighbour in all our parts, sauing where he had made his peace by extreme labour, and upon some discontents of the whole bodie of the clothiers about us and some pretence of affection to myselfe and name, they gathered together in companies and sent messingers unto me that I must needes stand for the cuntrie. I made answere my present healthe was doubtfull, not being able to take any longe iourney, neyther could I promise them to be att Yorke, yff I should entertayne theyr offer. This serued not the turne, for they vowed whether I were able to goe in person or noe, they would and must goe for me. Herein I tolde them they would undertake a rashe peece of worke out of theyre too much confidence and not performinge what they undertooke, I should come off with a foyle, soe instead of honouringe they would disgrace me. They would not admit of any denyall, some of the malcontents murmuringe secretly and taxinge more openly that I had noe harte nor will to serue my cuntrye. Some sayde I loved my thrift too well to enter upon any publique seruice that would bring with ytt chardge and expense. In conclusion out of their importunities I was enforced to entertayne the busynes when in all lykelyhood ytt was to late, *vzt.* when my concurrent had laboured all the cuntrye and had engaged a great number, many of our neighbour gentrie and particularly my nearest kindred, as Sir Richard Beaumont and Sir John Ramsden, who make ytt a punctillio of creditt to come of, neyther shall I desyer them. My nephew Jackson sayth he hath promised, but ytt was with a tacitt reseruacon to his uncle always forefrased.

Soe, my Lorde, you see howe I was drawen truely into this busy-
ness, neyther out of desyer, or seekyng of my owne, till att length I
was forced to giue way to theyre importunities. Then, my good Lord,
I confesse I thought not fitt to relye solely on such as had been formerly deccyued out of theyr too much ouerweeninge. But some 15
days before the countye day I worked to strengthen these mutinous
bands by such frendes as were yet unmade to the contrarie and soe
put the matter to a great deale of hazard and disadvantadge. Howe
wysely I cannot saye, because all undertakinges of this nature are of
a doubtfull euent, but nowe ytt ys lyke to be putt as farre as ytt can
well goe. One obiection I must answer, fallinge heare in the cuntrie
from one of your seruants that sayd he thought I was sett upp by my
Lord Sauile, your Lordshipp hauinge some hand in the contrary
party, upon my saluation I haue nothinge to doe with them, or they
with me in this affayre. They neyther sende me a voyce, nor did I begge
any of them; ytt may be trewe that many of my neighboures and
wellwillers are of the olde bande of reyters. Soe haue I troubled your
Lordshipp too longe, addinge this concː ısion that I must alwayes
put myselfe rather in your Lordshipp's mercie then upon your
rigorous censure, yf I haue tresspassed towards your Lordshipp, soe
rest, your Lordshipp's alwayes most humbly to be commanded, H.
Savile. Methley, *ult*° Ja[nuary] 1628[9].

**377.** *To Sir Edward Stanhope. Westminster. 8 Feb. 1629* (*SC*, xxi/53).

Sir, you shall receaue hearwith a letter to Sir Henry Goodricke,
which is nothing but by way of supplement, in case by reason of the
goute you should not be able to sitt, in which straite you will send
him the letter that soe the sutors upon this next sitting may not be
disappointed. But if your healthe serue you, as I trust itt shall, then
you may keep itt by you, for ther is nothing in itt but verbatim as the
other to you, which names you my vicepresidentt. That letter to the
Counsell you will deliuer, being noe more but only that they shall
in all things obserue you as to them appertaines. I will this next
weeke send downe my secretary, who shall attend you, and by him I
shall write unto you more at lardge then for the presentt my leisure
will giue me leaue. Mr Atturney Generall for being too free in a
confession before the Commons, touching a pardon procured by
Cosins, stands commaunded by his Maiesty to his chamber, but this
day itt is thought he shall haue his liberty. The Bishop of Winchester
hath been chardged before the commons for saying sum words to
one Dr Moore who is sent for to iustifie them, what willbe the issue
wee shall with in a few dayes see. The Parliament goes on slowly;

by the end of the weeke wee shallbe able to iudge much of the successe, which I trust (and God soe grantt) willbe good. The weather is cold, my occasions hasten and soe I heare rest, Your very affectionate cosin and freinde, Wentworth. Westminster, this 8th of Februa. 1628[9].

**378.** *To Sir Edward Stanhope. Westminster. 19 Feb. 1629 (SC, xxi/54.)*

Sir, I haue hear sent my secretary to attende you and to acquainte you with sum particulares concerning as well mee as himself. You willbe pleased therfore to hear him and to take that care for me which I promise myself att your handes. As for your self I desire that you would in all things hold up the dignity of your place and cause the learned Counsel to performe towards you such outward respects as that place hath had formerly from them, whearin you shall be sure to be seconded. I doe desire you likewise in a quiet calme manner to tell Sir William Ellis from me that I sent to him to vew the copper and other things in question, weather they weare the King's or my lord of Sunderland's, which I perceaue he did not, that I could not beleeue he had thought himself too good to doe his maister seruice, for it was not mine but his Maiestie's interest that called him unto itt. Which is more I heare (which yet I will not beleeue till I haue more grounds) he made himself merry at my letter and with me, relating how smoothly he treated with my seruantt that broughte itt. But tell him, if I finde itt to be true, I will teache him better manners then to make himself sportt either with me or with my letters. The Parliament proceeds very slowly and for myself I wishe they would speedily fall to sum resolution, least they bee cutt of before they cum to what they aime att. Other occurrentts heare very small, soe as I will hear conclude with my paper and rest, Your affectionate asseured cosin and frende, Wentworth. Westm: this 19th of Febr: 1628[9].

**379.** *To Marris. 20 Feb. 1629 (SC, xxi/55).*

Richard Marris, for Weddensday night fast let the Counsell say what they will, as I found itt soe will I leaue itt, espetially hauing allready continued most partt of my lord Mograue's time and all my lord of Sunderland's and therfore be sure you hold them too itt. I am gladde you haue settled the Clerkes of the Signet and soe let them rest. For the goods you buy at Yorke you will make up a perfectt inuentory of them and as for bruing Aprill will be soon enough, but the principall thing is casks, without which all will be cast away and therfore you must be carefull to get itt good and sweet in the beginning and then it willbe an easy thing to keep it soe. Neither would that beare which you bought of my lord of Sunderlande be keept longer then itt is good, but put of, and new brued in steade therof. My lord of Kingstone is not hear but in the cuntry, soe as you must take sum time to goe to him and take the grounds of him for the copper and other things in the bruhouse; if soe it be that Exeter bought them, Moulgraue of him and Sunderland of Mulgraue, then I would haue you pay the thirty poundes they are rated at, otherwayes suspende till you may receaue further directions from me. For whiting, painting and mending the roofs at the Mannour they are of necessity to be dun and therfore the sooner you begin them, the better, els will they not be ready in time for my use. But you must be sure carefully to keep bills of all the money you issue in that matter, bycause you know I must haue itt allowed me backe by his Maiesty. For the Porter, if he wronge informed, the more knaue he and I pray you let the Atturney know that I desire only he may haue such dues as formerly hath been accustomed and noe otherwayes. I am sorry that anything should be stollen out of the storehouse; you shal doe well to discipline those that had the chardge therof as you haue dun in setting on new lockes. The commission you desire to haue renewed is dun, Thomas Edmunds hath itt and will, when the signet is putt, deliuer itt you.

I haue hear sent you the indenture of saile for Stratford to Mr Robinson, togeither with a letter of atturney. I haue hear likewise sent you a recognisance, allbeitt a most unreasonable security and therfore I would haue him you send with thes things to Robinson to stand upon itt to haue a note under his hand that in case he be not troubled within the space of seauen yeares he shall then redeliuer me my recognisance to be vacated and seem as, if he sticke at this, to breake the bargaine, but rather then make any more laboure, if needs must, deliuer itt him and receaue your money. I haue gotten my $250^{li}$ for Christmas quarter and I would now haue you to giue warning to the receauoure that I will receaue my pention halfe yearly according to my instructions and soe that he will make fiue hundreth poundes therof redy for me aganst Lady Day, to the receat wherof you will looke. For the thirty pounds which Richard Burnurs had upon bonde my cosin Rockley, if he be spoken too, will repay itt againe; for the other particulares disbursed they are partt of thos we forsaw, soe as thos moneys all cumming in, sauing Sir George Reresbie's, I doubt not but ther willbe to serue our turne. For the hundreth pounds to be laid doune for yourself, itt shall be ready if your brother cum to me for itt. Sauile is recouering his health apace, allbeitt he confessed to a neare freind of mine that he neuer had sicknesse all this while, only the hartte greef he had taken in my being thus advanced before him, which confession was not without contrition; for when he spake itt, he sobbed and wept like a scoole boy with his bretches about his heeles. If I had dun such a thing and they could haue knowen itt, how poore a spiritt should I haue been in ther mouthes att euery ale benche, whear ther emissaries had been presentt. As for me I despise them and will in silence let twenty such things as thes passe without spending aire upon them.

As for the deodand at Eastkeswicke which you mention in your letter to Edmundes, all I can say for the present is this, that I haue within Harwood by charter the same liberties which are att Richmonde, which I take to be very lardge, and therfore I would haue you lett the Coroner know that I haue comaunded you not to deliuer the goods, but that I will iustifie the keeping of them by my charter, which you cannot cum too, being locked up in my study amongst my euidence, whear noe body can cum before my returne into the cuntry, when I shallbe ready to giue them satesfaction. In the meane time I will keep my possession and I pray you doe soe take the goods and remoue them if cause require to Woodhouse; for I am sumthing confidentt my charter will carry itt and tell both the Coroner and Amner that they shall not meddle with them. For the businesse of vicepresident, I had taken order before the receate of your letter in such sort as I hope shallbe requisite. And soe I rest your Lord and Master, Wentworth. February 20th 1628[9]. Robinson's bond you will receaue from Peter Man, wee hauing performed on my partt as much as was desired.

**380.** *From Clare. Westminster, 6 Aug. 1629 (SC, xxii/58).*

Sun Wentworthe, I am and euer shalbe most glad to hear of yours, my daughter's and my 3 grandchildren's good healthe, the lord of heauen continew it to all our cumforts. Hear, God be praysed, ar wee partakers of the same benefits, euen Den though still a close prisoner and not to be sene by wyf or parents, but at a grate, through which spectacle I haue not yet looked. His condition keeps me hear from the cuntri and those ocations whear though I cann not help him, yet may my near being to him be [mor] to his content then further of and sumthing is it to our freinds and to our owne satisfaction, when we do what we cann, though not what we would, or what is behooffull to them. I am sorry my daughter's payne in hir backe still continews, it is an ill inhabitant and shews natuer weak and needing sum strengthening comfortiues to haue helped hir to haue dislodged such a gest ear now. For till which tym the tree get faste roote, he may be

SIR THOMAS WENTWORTH'S PAPERS

remoued and this is an ill concomitant for a chyld bearing woman, that hath most need of strengthe in that parte. The lord of heauen bless the means which you and she ar to use thearfor and suerly if meanes be not neclected, youth will wurk owt a greater inconuenience then that.

My cours of liuing hear affords litell knoledge of things worth the looking after. I am no courtier nor haunt that conuersation[1]; with what walkes the streets I meet now and then and that changes with the fashion euery other day, so as I embrace it not. Thearfore of the seidg of Bolduke [Bois-le Duc] and Vanderberg's doings, or intertanment in Holland, or wheather as yet thear or no in person with the grosse of his strengthe, I can say nothing. All this is coyned with the stamp of our affections hear, no free trade but of lying, not as yet monopolized by any, ether Hollandlyke or Spanishlyke affected. Sir Thomas Edmunds I hear is not yet admitted to that king, the last night's post saith bycause the Cardinal is in Itali and absent throughe siknes, but it is conceaued they are angri for sooth bycause we intend a peace with Spayn allso. The fortune of those that beg peace at any man's hand and be deuided among themselfs and as things doubtfull admitt sundri coniectures; sum allso say this councelor was forward in discarding the Frenche and that ryds yet upon thear stomakes what so it be; he is a man well understood in Fr. and might, for ought I knowe if in the latter he bore a part, haue bene spared at this tym, unles our barrenes be such as no other is to be found, espetially upon such easi termes and though the king's image will make any siluer currant, yet if it be too muche alloyed wee shall haue less commodite for it, but *ne sutor ultra crepidam*.

I thank Mr Ratcliff for his begining with Walker, but he must proceed and neuer belieue what he sayth, for he is a very fals felloe and thearfor, sun, now hauing roused him he must follow him and whatsoeuer he disburses in this poursuit I will (God willing) return it. The king is in progres, yet flutters hearabouts, the queen, not lyking well her Tunbridge waters, is hear at Somerset House, to morrow she mets the king at Otelands. This is all I haue for this syd of the paper, concluding with my praiers to the Allmighte for yours, my daughter's and my grandchildren healthes. Amen. Westminster, this 6 of August 1629. Your very louing father, Clare.

---

[1] In 1628 Clare had shown less detachment and was eager to exchange news and rumours from court (25 Nov. *SC*, xxi/86); he thought '. . . the waters be at a still, yet sum expectation thear is which way the flood will goe . . .' at a report of Weston, the new Lord Treasurer's, '. . . coniunction with my lord Savage and b(isho)p Lard . . .'

# APPENDIX

*Extracts from Sir George Radcliffe's draughts for his life of Strafford* (*SC*, xxxiv, not numbered).

Thomas Wentworthe, Erle of Strafforde, was borne in Chancery Lane London at the house of Mr Robert Atkinson, his grandfather by the mother, the 13th day of April 1593.

He went to schoole at Well under the government of Deane Higgins, where learnd together Henry lord Clifford, the last Erle of Comberland, Sir Thomas Wharton, father to the now Lord Wharton, Christopher Wandesford of Kirklinge and diverse others.

After some tyme spent at Cambridge in St John's Colledge under the tutelage of [Richard Senhouse] afterwards Bishop of Carlile and then at the Inner Temple London; he was married to the lady Margaret, eldest daughter to Francis, Erle of Comberland, he beinge then 18 yeares olde and shortly after he was knighted by king James. And imediately his father sent him into France in 9ber 1611 under the government of Mr Charles Grenewood, then fellow of University Colledge in Oxford. He stayed a while at Paris and afterwards at Orleans, then went down the Loir and so by Tholouse and Marseilles to Lions, the tower of France. He came back into England about the end of January 1612.

He served in the Parlament 1614, 12° R Jacobi.

His father dyed about 7ber 1614 and then he came into his estate, free from all encombrance except 110$^l$ a piece to his three youngest brothers and 1500$^l$ a piece to two younger sisters, with an addition of 500$^l$ a piece to them after they should be married with the consent of some friendes nominated to that purpose.[1]

[1] Sir William's will made 29 June 1614 left his daughters £1500 each; if either married before she was seventeen, she was to have £500 at seventeen, £500 at eighteen and £500 at nineteen; if either married at eighteen to have £500 then and £1000 at nineteen; if either married before nineteen to have £1500 at nineteen. These payments were in addition to £500 each assured by deed 9 December 1611. Each was to have £40 a year while under fifteen and £50 a year from fifteen till nineteen, if unmarried till then; in addition they were to have diet and lodging. The poor round Wentworth and Harewood were to have £20 in lieu of all such 'doule as is used to be giuen at the Church'. His five younger sons received £3-6-8 each. The governing and bringing up of his younger sons was left to Wentworth and his wife, '. . . charging them both for the loue that I beare unto them and the trust that I repose in them upon my blessing and befor God (to whose judgement I referre the punishment of thire abuse of my trust, if they shall be faulty in performance thereof) that they will be carefull for all my said children's good bringinge upp in God's feare and seruice and in good maners and

He was tall and of a middle habit of body, neither leane nor fat, a very white and tender skin. His dyet was temperate, he eat little, was never drunke, loved fruit. Cholericke exceedingly which he studyed much to bridle; a stronge wit and of an eloquent expression, both by his tongue and pen. Well read in story and in the English lawes, so farre as concerned the office of a Justice of Peace. He had studdyed the controversies of religion then agitated betweene the Churches of England and Rome. He was bred up in Calvin's opinions, wherein he was afterwards more moderate, preferringe piety before contention. Labouringe to be well grounded in fundamentall truths rather then to trouble himselfe with disputes, and he chose rather to be devout then to make shew of it. Yet his externall carriage in thinges relatinge to God's service was very reverend. He never put on his hat in a church for many of his last yeares; in his devotions he used Gerard's meditations and *exercitium quotidianum*, besides the English Leiturgie.

His recreations were in his younger yeares Persius and Spencer's Poems; afterwards he delighted much in Ovid's *Metamorphoses*, which he carried comonly about him. He played very well at Primero and Maw, but used neither very much. His cheife delighte was haukinge, which his much busines in his later tyme did seldom give him leysure to follow. His family was great, but very orderly; prayers twice a day read by his chaplaine, an able divine, usinge the leiturgie. A constant plentifull table never diminished in his absence, though he was much abroad. The accompts of his revenue and expence duely kept and examined by himselfe. He had a counsell of 2 or 3 of his trusty freinds and 2 cheife servants to met quarterly and considered with him of all things belonginge to his estate, expenses, improvements, purchases, buildinges, suits, etc, setting down his resolutions for the future and taking accompt of what done therein from tyme to tyme.[1]

... But now that I speake of his suits I may not forget the trouble he underwent on the behalfe of his nephew, Sir George Savile baronet. Sir George Savile knight and baronet, the grandfather, allowed Sir George Savile knight, his sonne, certain manners in Yorkshire called the nine townes for his maintenance. These consisted much in segnioryes, little in demaine, being in all scarce worth 300$^{li}$ per annum. Upon the death of Sir George the sonne

learninge to the best of their power and iustly and truely account for and pay unto them all such somes of money and other dueties, as of right, equitie, or of good conscience they ought to account for and pay . . .' Proved 25 October 1614. Borthwick Institute, York Probate Registry, vol. 33, fo. 330.

[2] Compare Knowler, ii, pp. 430, 433, 434, 435.

(which happened in August 1614, not many weekes before the death of Sir William Wentworth) Sir George, the grandfather, havinge diverse children by a second wife (who was not favourable to her sonne in law), claimed these townes to revert to him and so the lady Savile, Sir Thomas Wentworth's sister, and her two sonnes, George and William, were leaft with out any meanes at all, but onely the charity of Sir Th. Wentworth. An inquisition was then taken upon a writ out of the Chancery, as the manner is, to enquire of what lands Sir George, the sonne, dyed seised and thereby it was found that he was seised of these nine townes and dyed seised thereof, that they were descended unto George Savile his son, an infant of 3 yeares and odde moneths, and beinge holden of the kinge in knight service, the childe was thereby his maiestie's ward. Hearupon Sir Thomas got possession of these lands for the use of his nephew. Ould Sir George, the grandfather, was much stirred at this, alledging that Sir George, his sonne, had onely a terme for yeares in these landes determinable by his death. And hereupon arrose 3 great suits, one in the Chancery and another in the Star chamber wherein Sir Tho. Wentworth was defendant[1] with others and the third was in the Courte of Wardes to force ould Sir George, the grandfather, to produce such evidences of these landes, as might shew what estate Sir George, his sonne, had in them.

Old Sir George had married to his first wife the lady Mary, daughter to George, Erle of Shrewsbury, by whom he had issue this Sir George his sonne; and it was believed that the erle, who was a very provident man, had made provision for the maintenance of the issue by his daughter and that presumption was increased by the old Sir George, the grandfather's, backwardnes to produce his evidence which he did contrary to severall orders of the Court of Wardes, for which contempt he was committed to the Fleet and lay there a great while.[2] But I shall not need to mention the particulars of these suits which cannot be done without the bookes and papers which are in the possession of Sir George Savile's friends who now hold the estate, beinge sonne to Sir Wlliam Savile, younger brother of Sir George, the grandchilde, who dyed without issue at Oxford of the small pox about the 16th yeare of his age, leavinge Sir William his brother and heir. These suits between old Sir George, the grandfather,

---

[1] P.R.O., St. Ch. 8/261/9, 31. Sir George's complaint is dated 22 June 1618. Depositions were still being taken two years later.
[2] *Ibid.*, 26 and 5. Sir George Savile and his wife were in the Fleet between 2 December 1617 and 1 January 1618. Their petition to Parliament shows they were committed to the Fleet 24 May 1617; H. C. Foxcroft, *Life and Letters of Sir George Savile, First Marquess of Halifax* (London, 1898), i, pp. 15–16.

and his daughter-in-law and her sonnes ended not until the death of old Sir George after they had held about 8 yeares as I remember.[1] For 7 of which yeares Sir Thomas Wentworth never missed terme from goeinge to London about them. Wherein he shewed great tenderness to his sister, tender care of his nephewes, but especially a rare example of friendship to his most deare brother-in-law Sir George Savile, whose memory was the principall motive to make him most chearfully undergoe and constantly goe throwgh with all the troubles and inconveniences of these suits to the neglect or layinge aside of his owne occasions.[2]

These suits occasioned my beinge knowne to Sir Thomas Wentworth. Sir George Savile, the 2d, was my godfather and when I spent my tyme, beinge about 11 yeares of age, for want of a schoole maister he made me come to him twice a day for many months together and read Latin to me, causinge me to repeat my Latin grammar to him and to make exercises in Latin as he enjoyned mee. Afterwards Mr Charles Greenwood, who was my cosin german[3] and tutor at Oxford, havinge a great obligation to this Sir George Savile for his passionate affection and great expressions of kindenes to him. This Mr Greenewood was the cause of my takinge upon me the profession of the law, his intent beinge to make me serviceable to Sir George Savile, my godfather, as I had great reason to be, both for that my father had had his dependence on old Sir George, his father, and in gratitude for his care of my education and other kindnesses showed towards me. Mr Greenwood afterwardes, havinge alwayes a great respect showed towards him by Sir Thomas Wentworth, brought me to him the Christmas after that I was called to the barre, which was in August 1618, there beinge then a comission to be executed at Rotherham betwene the Lady Savile and her father in law which being dispatched I went home with them to Wentworth Woodhouse. Where Sir Thomas Wentworth was pleased so to looke upon me as there grew a most intimate familiarity betwixt us, dayly increasing and never interrupted as long as wee lived. I was after-

[1] Wentworth exhibited his information in the Court of Wards in Michaelmas term 1615. Eight orders were made in January and February 1622; P.R.O., Wards 9/538/703, 707, 721, 727, 750, 783, 789, 841. The order book for March 1622 to March 1623 is missing. Old Sir George died 12 November 1622, according to his inquisition *post mortem*, as cited in Wards 9/95/53.

[2] P.R.O., St. Ch. 8/261/9, 26. In his answer Wentworth said Sir George 'on his death bedd did earnestly entreat this defendant to have a faithfull and louinge care' of his wife and sons 'and of their educacon, maintenance and rightes . . .'

[3] His father (Nicholas Radcliffe)'s sister, Cecilia, was Greenwood's mother; T. D. Whitaker, *The Life and Original Correspondence of Sir George Radcliffe* (London, 1810), p. 7.

ward of councell both with my lady Savile and Sir Thomas Wentworth in all their law businesse and indeed in all other affaires, savinge that in the suits betwene Sir George Savile her father in law and her I had never any hand, nor was I ever of counsell against him or his interest. Some other little suits Sir Thomas Wentworth had of his owne wherein I doe not remember any thinges very remarkeable and the passages of them doe fully appeare in the writinges leaft in his study concerninge them.

His first wife, the lady Margaret, dyed in July or August 1622, he beinge then scarsely recovered of the great sicknes which he had in London at the Austin Friars that summer. He continued a widow till the later end of the year 1624. In which time he was a suitor first to the yonger daughter of Sir William Craven, some tyme lord mayor of London; she was afterwards married to the now lord Coventry and brought him nere 30,000$^{li}$ portion.[1] That motion not succeedinge he was next a suitor to the lady Diana Cecil, one of the daughters and coheires of [William] Erle of Execeter who was afterwards married to the Erle of Oxford and now to [Thomas] Erle of Elgin in Scotland. Before the death of the lady Margaret, he, having bene longe without children, thought of preferinge his next brother William in a marriage answerable rather to the possibility of his inheritinge the whole estate then to his present appenage and there he proposed him to the lady Craven, as a suitor to her elder daughter[2] who was afterwards married to Sir Percy Herbert, the lord Powis's eldest sonne. To make this proposition more acceptable, he undertooke to settle 2000$^{li}$ per annum (as I now remember the somme) for their present maintenance and 5000$^{li}$ per annum after his decease. I asked him what moved him to make so large an offer, especially seinge he might yet have children of his owne. He tould me that his brother was an honest man and in case Sir Thomas should have children, he might both raise a good fortune to himselfe out of his wife's estate and also reestate the land againe upon the right heire of his house which Sir Thomas said he hoped that Will would doe, trustinge his worth and gratitude for this great kindenesse whereby he came to obtaine so great an advancement. I tould him that it was an unusual thinge to put so great confidence in a brother, but if the lady Craven did belieue that the land would be reestated on his children, in case Sir Thomas should have any, though there was no security for it either in writing or promise betwene the brethren, yet that expectation would make her refuse to match her daughter to

[1] For other evidence showing that the portion must have been over £20,000, see *Economic History Review*, 2nd series, xi (1958), p. 230, n. 1.
[2] This was in 1619, see above, p. 120.

WP—T

William. And I was not satisfyed that this secret trust betweene his brother and him, beinge reserved from the lady Crauen, was not just dealinge with them. Others who were also consulted with were of another opinion and the proposition was made, but rejected by the lady Craven.

This I ghesse was the event of it that when Sir Thomas Wentworth came to be a suitor to the younger sister for himselfe, they remembred what he had ofered for his brother which gave them occasion to conjecture that he knew some imperfection in himselfe which putte him by the hope of havinge any children and this I take to be the reason why he was refused to be accepted of as a husband to the younger gentlewoman, for other wise there was no visible cause for it and the yonge gentlewoman entertained his company with kindnes enough. Perhaps also he failed in his desires concerning the lady Diana upon the like ground, for there was a generall whisperinge of his insufficiency and disability to get children. Though some to pretende to understand him well indeavoured to persuade the contrary.

There was also a motion concerninge the Countess Dowager of Dorset, afterwards married to Philip, Erle of Pembrooke and Mountgomery. She was daughter and heir to George Erle of Cumberland, whose armes instead of the armes of Francis, his brother, Sir Thomas his father in law, were (I know not by what chance) set upon a chimney piece in the best lodginge chamber at Wentworth Woodhouse. This lady was cosen germain to his first wife and of that age which did not give any great hope of childrene.[1] There was little done in it and most of the particulers are gone out of my memory.

Att last he fell to be a suitor to the Lady Arbella, secund daughter to John, Erle of Clare, a lady of great beauty and comelines, but the indowments of her minde were farre more lovely then the shape and proportions of her body. He grew passionately in love with her after his first acquaintance, insomuch that for 3 or 4 moneths before they were married, he missed not 3 dayes from beinge most part of the afternoones in her company. She was but 16 yeares ould when she was married, which was the 24th of Februarii 1624, privately in my lord her father's hous, the then Deane of Canterbury officiatinge and the Lord Keeper of the Great Seale, the bishop of Lincolne, with a few private friends onely present. Sir Thomas Wentworth was much afflicted that day with a fit of the stone and bloody urine, which he bore out without any notice taken of it by anybody, but Mr Christopher Wandesford and me; at night it leaft him. Within a day or two in a morninge I came into the roome where my lady was dressinge herselfe, her haire hanginge loose about the stoole

[1] Lady Anne Clifford was born in 1590; Dorset died on 28 March 1624.

whereon she sate covered her like a vaile. Her eyes were so large as that an eye cuppe I used to wash myne eyes withall would not come on her eyes, which were so set as gave a great advantage to all other features in her face. Her countenance was always cherefull free, but extreamely bashfull and apt to blushe upon all occasions, which always added a new bewty to her. When she laughed she had always a dimple in her cheekes, as some of her children also have. I ones caused her to measure her wast with another lady whom I thought very well shaped. My lady Arbella, beinge then with childe, was slenderer in the wast by more then an inch and yet was more then an inch broader in the shoulders, but I need not say more of her bodily shape where in I am confident there was not a blemish. Her legges and feet I never saw, but I have reason to believe that they were extraordinarily well shappen.

   She spoke French as English, phrase and accent not discernable from one that had bene borne in Paris; she understood Italian and Spanish perfectly. Her behaviour was full of freedome and modestie, never out of countenance in any company. When multitudes of neighbours of severall sorts came to visit her, she never wanted presence of spirit, nor civility, for them all, not one could escape her with beinge taken notice of with such respect and signification of favour, as ever sent them every one away with contentment and satisfaction. She had not a servant in the house that she did not some particuler kindnesse too to oblige them, nor a person in all her neighbourhood that was poore or sicke that she did not particularly take care on, dayly sendinge to their supplyes and herselfe at fit opportunityes visitinge them. She was bountifull with great large-nesse of heart and discretion, as farre from ostentation as basenes.

   Digressions to be incerted in fit places.
   Of the education of a gentleman: First let him learne French of his nurse: that language is easily learned and pronounced by a childe, hardly by a growne man. 21y. learne Latin by company and imitation and translating good authors out of Latine into English againe. Learne eloquence by imitation of those that are excellent in that faculty. A few rules well understood and practised are better then so many as trouble the memory and distract rather then direct. My lord's great rule was to speake or write of an arguement whereof some great master had treated and then to compare both together to see his own defects and his author's excellencies.
   It is necessary for a gentleman to learne Latine and French per-fectly, some Greeke, logiqe and rhetoriq and philosophy, at least the elements of it and especially morall and politique. Some of Cicero's

Orations and poets Latine and English are recreations rather then study. But aboue all historye and thearin the moderne storyes are farr more usefull then the ancient, though these have more show of scholarship. It is fitt for every man to know the lawes of his own country, especially that part which concernes criminall iustices. And for a man that is to haue any part in the publiqe governement thear wilbe great use of the elements of the Civil and Canon Lawes. For a solderr the mathematiqs are necessary. But it is a great error to propose more then can probably be attained unto. Ther is a temperance to be used in the studye of knowledge and it is a great fault to be over bookish. Geographie, heraldrie and genealogie are great ornaments and easily attained for so much as is absolutely usefull. A good study of bookes is a delight and a helpe, but the best assistance is the company of an able scholler. It is great discretion to make choice of a very few good books and reade them very diligently: for the rest it is enough to know what they intreat of and how to turne them upon occasion. Good institutions, or elementall treatises, are very usefull, but rare. And next those that handle usefull points in any learninge fully, which are easier to be met with all.

I learned from a great scholer that it was losse of tyme to read without a pen in my hand to note something for helpe of memory, which notinge is either briefer to make a table to the book I read or larger to abridge the booke and write out the choise sentences, which though it seeme to require some paines yet it caryes his recompense alonge with it.

# INDEX

Figures in italics refer to the numbers of the documents, those in roman to page numbers.

Letters to and from individuals (save in the case of Sir Thomas Wentworth) have been indexed under their names.

Middleton, Robert, 68
Mompesson, Sir Giles, 153, 155
Montague, Henry, Viscount Mande-
    ville (1620), earl of Manchester
    (1626), Lord Treasurer (1620-1),
    69, 149-50; to, *155, 303*
Montpellier, 49
Moore, Dr, 314
More, Sir George, 66
More, Sir Thomas, 65, 81
Morehouse, Edward, 48 n. 1
Mounson, Sir Thomas, 290
Mountain, Mountayne, George, bp.
    of Lincoln, to, *96*
Mulgrave, earl of, *see* Sheffield
Muscovy Company, 6
Musters, 228, 249 and n. 1, 263
Mynne, Robert, 191, 210

Neile, Richard, bp. of Winchester, 314
Nevile, Francis, 289
Newby, John, of Wakefield, 48
Newcastle, 263-4, 283
Newfoundland, *302*, 291
Nicholas, Sir Edward, parliamentary
    diary, 296 n. 2
Nimes, 49
Nine towns, *see* Halifax
Noblemen, 11-12
Norcliff, Stephen, widow of, 196, 199
North, Council of, 182, 196, 249-50,
    277, 289-90, 305, 314-16
North, Lord President of, 11, 179,
    188, 254, 259, 289; sale of, 250;
    pension of, 316; *see also* Cecil,
    Thomas; Hastings, Henry;
    Sheffield, Edmund; Scrope, Em-
    manuel
North, vicepresident of, 314
Northumberland, earl of, *see* Percy

Ogle, Mr, 147, 181
— Catherine lady, 147-8
Oglethorpe of Thorner, ?Michael, 248
Orgrave Moor, 44, 45
Orleans, 50, 51
Osborne, Sir Edward, 302; to, *80,
    225, 235*; from, *358*
— Lady, 214
Overton, 273
Owen, Sir Robert, 67-8
Oxenshawe, 106

Oxford, University, 319, 322

Palmes, Sir Guy, of Lindley, message
    to, *122*; 240, 246; to, *123*
Papists, 18, 60, 61, 63, *227*, 233-4,
    248-9, 264, 283, 287, 292, 311
Paris, 50, 172
Parker, Edward, lord Morley, 95-6
— William, lord Morley, 223
— Henry, 223
— Frances, *see* Danby, Christopher,
    widow of,
Parker, John, defaulting bailiff, 133
Parliament, (1610), 67 68
    (1614), opening, 63-4; attorney-
    general, 64-6; impositions, 66-
    72, report on, 73-6; French
    Company, 70-2; Cambridgeshire
    election, 73; undertakers, 63, 76;
    supply, 80, 82; 152
    (1621), elections, 141-6, proceed-
    ings, *152*; bill against informers,
    154-5; free speech and Sandys,
    *162*; end of session, *163*; dis-
    solution, *164*
    (1624), elections, 202-3
    (1625), elections, 230-2, 234; supply,
    *267*
    (1626), elections, 243, *283-4*; 248
    (1628), 290; and recusants, 292; bill
    of rights, *350*; *353*; petition of
    right, *352*; 2nd session, *360*, 308,
    311, 314-15; seat for, *363*
    book of precedents, 266
Parry, Sir Thomas, 77 and n. 2
Peasely, Mr, 210; to, *192*
Pembroke, earl of, *see* Herbert,
    William
Percy, Henry, earl of Northumberland,
    196, 232
Perient, Sir Thomas, 233
Petition of Right, 298 n. 1, *352*
Peyton, Sir Samuel, 233
Phelips, Sir Robert, 240
Philip III of Spain, 128
Pickering, Thomas, 122
Pierrepoint, Robert, to, *76*
Plowden, William, 61
Pontefract, 138; seat at, 8 n. 2, *151*, 202,
    *258-9, 266, 340*; Corporation of,
    from *351*
— honour of, copyholders, 212,

INDEX

verses by, 2; *Account of providences*, 25-35, marries, 29; his inheritance, 29-30; buys Harewood, 30-1, 33-5; sells Burton Leonard, 34; epitaph on wife, 35; illness 53, 79; and the earl of Shrewsbury, 5-7; Sheriff of Yorks., 37-8, 41, 47; provides horsemen, 40; instructions for his children, 54-5; will 319 n. 1; from, 52 n. 1; to, 6(*a*)-(*i*), *8-17, 19-22, 25*
— his wife Anne (Atkinson), portion, 29; 35, 51
Wentworth, Sir William, younger sons of:
— John, 49, 54, 56, 57, 73; to, *105*
— George, 55
— Mathew, 55
— Michael, 54-5, in France 161; from, *265*; to, *167, 209*
— Philip, 55
— Robert, 54; to, *159*, 172
— William, 49, 54, 57, 147, 273; from, *20, 21, 327*; marriage proposed, 120-1, 323-4
Wentworth Woodhouse, 2, 9, 29, 39, 40, 41, 102, 274; poor at, 275, 284, 303, 312, 322, 324
West country, 70, 71, 278-9
Weston, Sir Richard, 240, 251, 271, 279, 281; Lord Treasurer, 300, 308, 318 n. 1; from, *360*; to, *290, 293, 294*
Wharton, Sir Michael, 88-9
— Sir Thomas, to, *87*, 319
Whiteham, Francis, 289
— Luke, 289
Whitelock, James, 67
Whitley, Thomas, 251
Whitson, John 69
Whittingham, Sir Timothy, 58
Wicke, 274
Wilbore, Mr, 233
Wildsmith, Richard, felon, 92

Wilkinson, Samuel, 275
— William, 297
Williams, John, bp. of Lincoln, 8; Lord Keeper, 204, 240; 266, 282, 324
Wilton, Thomas, 54, 274
Winchester, bp. of, *see* Andrewes, Neile
Wingfield, Winfeild, South, Derby, 98
Wingfield, Sir Robert, 233
Winwood, Sir Ralph, 64
Witham, Henry, to, *66*
Wodroue, Woodrow, Richard, 199
Wood, John, 275
Wool, sales of, 126-7
Worcester, bp. of, *see* Thornborough
Worcester, earl of, *see* Somerset
Wormhall, John, undersheriff 1601, 37, 41
Wotton, Edward lord, 58, to, *53, 93, 109*, 62 n.1
— Hester his wife, to, *77*
— Sir Henry, from, *346, 373*
Wynne, Sir Richard, *151*
— Sir Thomas, 235 and n. 1

Yelverton, Sir Henry, solicitor-general, 60
Yonge, Younge, William, to, *94*
York, archbishop of, *see* Mathew
York, 31, 53, 58, *124*, 142, *137*, 181, 183, 189, 231, 254, 257, 258, 284, 289, 313, 315
York Castle, 92, 241, 257, 289
York, King's Manor, 88, 316
Yorkshire, shire elections, 4, 5; (1597), 37 and n. 1; (1604), 47-8 and n. 1; (1614), 73; (1620), 141-6; (1624), 202-3; (1625), 230-2, 234; (1626), *283*; (1628), 278, 287, *340, 342*; by-election 1629, *368, 374, 376*
Yorkshire, receivership of, *165*, 174; value of, *175-6*, 185, *188*, 189, 194-5

Zetland, 263

KING ALFRED'S COLLEGE
LIBRARY